BLACK LIVES IN ALASKA

Black Lives in Alaska

A History of African Americans in the Far Northwest

IAN C. HARTMAN AND DAVID REAMER

FOREWORD BY
CALVIN E. WILLIAMS

UNIVERSITY OF WASHINGTON PRESS
Seattle

A V Ethel Willis White Book
Black Lives in Alaska was made possible in part by a grant from the V Ethel Willis White Endowment, which supports the publication of books on African American history and culture.

Copyright © 2022 by the University of Washington Press

Composed in Minion Pro, typeface designed by Robert Slimbach

All rights reserved. No part of this publication may be reproduced or transmitted in any form or by any means, electronic or mechanical, including photocopy, recording, or any information storage or retrieval system, without permission in writing from the publisher.

UNIVERSITY OF WASHINGTON PRESS
uwapress.uw.edu

LIBRARY OF CONGRESS CATALOGING-IN-PUBLICATION DATA
Names: Hartman, Ian C., author. | Reamer, David, author.
Title: Black lives in Alaska : a history of African Americans in the far Northwest /
    Ian C. Hartman and David Reamer ; foreword by Calvin E. Williams.
Other titles: Black history in the last frontier.
Description: Seattle : University of Washington Press, [2022] | Includes bibliographical
    references and index.
Identifiers: LCCN 2022015082 (print) | LCCN 2022015083 (ebook) | ISBN 9780295750927
    (hardcover) | ISBN 9780295750934 (paperback) | ISBN 9780295750941 (ebook)
Subjects: LCSH: African Americans—Alaska—History. | Alaska—History. | Alaska—
    Race relations.
Classification: LCC E185.93.A4 H37 2022 (print) | LCC e185.93.a4 (ebook) |
    DDC 979.8/00496073—dc23/eng/20220331
LC record available at https://lccn.loc.gov/2022015082
LC ebook record available at https://lccn.loc.gov/2022015083

∞ This paper meets the requirements of ANSI/NISO Z39.48-1992 (Permanence of Paper).

CONTENTS

Acknowledgments vii

Foreword: Go North! by Calvin E. Williams xiii

Introduction: Black History in Unlikely Places xvii

CHAPTER ONE. Black Exploration, Labor, and Travel in the Icy Northwest 1

CHAPTER TWO. Black in the Gold Rush Era 21

CHAPTER THREE. The World War Era and a New Alaska 44

CHAPTER FOUR. Discrimination, Opportunity, and Community in Postwar Alaska 73

CHAPTER FIVE. Civil Rights under the Northern Lights 99

CHAPTER SIX. Black Alaska during the Oil Boom 118

CHAPTER SEVEN. Criminal Justice, Law Enforcement, and Race in Urban Alaska 140

CHAPTER EIGHT. Resentment, Resilience, and Cultural Rejuvenation at Century's End 164

Conclusion: The Black Past Meets Contemporary Alaska 179

Notes 193
Bibliography 239
Index 255

ACKNOWLEDGMENTS

THIS BOOK BEARS THREE NAMES ON THE COVER, BUT MANY MORE shaped the project. Most fundamentally, we build on the findings of Everett Louis Overstreet's 1994 study, *Black on a Background of White: A Chronicle of Afro-Americans' Involvement in America's Last Frontier, Alaska*, and George Harper's "Blacks in Alaska" collection at the Archives and Special Collections at the University of Alaska Anchorage / Alaska Pacific University (UAA/APU) Consortium Library. Overstreet and Harper, both of whom had successful careers outside of academe, took to history as enthusiastic hobbyists and masterfully chronicled African Americans in Alaska for a general audience. Bruce Melzer, a reporter for the *Anchorage Daily News* and KSKA, Anchorage's public radio station, also collected the stories of African Americans in Southcentral Alaska. Melzer's oral history interviews are housed in the Consortium Library and were also central to our research. The HistoryMakers digital archive documents the lives of several Black Alaskans and references others who have spent time in the forty-ninth state. These records left a rich tapestry from which to build this narrative, and we owe all of those who have collected records, sat for oral history interviews, or were simply gracious enough to share with us their stories a debt of gratitude.

We especially thank Eleanor Andrews, Ed Wesley, and Cal Williams for their encouragement and counsel. Without the keen insights of these three, this book would be missing many key details and influential people. Andrews, Wesley, and Williams are longtime residents and have dedicated their lives to advance greater levels of equity; they have shared their perspectives and enriched our understanding and appreciation of Black history in Alaska. Williams's knowledge of Alaska is deep and broad, and without his feedback, this book would be incomplete. We are honored that he agreed to write a foreword to this book and know that his voice makes it an immeasurably stronger contribution. But even with the inclusion of such valuable perspectives and what we believe is an impressive base of primary source material, *Black Lives in Alaska: A History of African Americans in the Far Northwest* is far from comprehensive and should be viewed as an invitation for additional research rather than a final word on the topic. We have not told every story that deserves to be heard, nor have we included everyone who has contributed to Alaska's Black past and present. In that spirit we expect the reader will find this study informative, but more importantly, we hope others might find inspiration to research and write the next volume of Alaska's Black history.

Research for this book has received generous funding from the National Park Service (NPS) and the University of Alaska. In fact, the book you now read is a much expanded and thoroughly revised version of an earlier released monograph, *Black History in the Last Frontier* (2020). That volume was printed with support from the NPS and the University of Alaska Anchorage. Historian Janet Clemens and anthropologist Rachel Mason, both with the NPS, provided regular feedback. The research from that book was helpful in the development of the exhibit *Black Lives in Alaska: Journey, Justice, and Joy*, which was on display at the Anchorage Museum from April 2021 through February 2022. The exhibit would not have been possible without the support and diligence of several people at the museum, including Julie Decker, Francesca DuBrock, Monica Shah, and Julie Varee. Their efforts ensured that this topic received a wide public audience in and around Anchorage.

Furthermore, we are grateful for the support from the Selkregg family and the Center for Community Engagement and Learning (CCEL) at the University of Alaska Anchorage. This project is rooted in collaboration and should be viewed as a chronicle of community in Alaska as much as it is an academic history. We received assistance from students at the University of Alaska Anchorage and thank Erika Coker, Hannah Dorough, Danielle Holness, Zakiya McCummings, Olivia Petroccia, and Michael Squartsoff for their efforts. Kaylene Johnson-Sullivan edited an earlier draft of this text with care and precision. Mike Baccam at the University of Washington Press expressed early interest in the book and has worked with us closely through the revision process. We're grateful for his patience. We are also indebted to the anonymous reviewers who read earlier drafts of the book and furnished incisive commentary. We believe the final product is much stronger because of their feedback.

At risk of forgetting anyone, we would like to express our deepest gratitude to the many others who have shaped this book and our thinking on the topic. We have discussed the book's progress and shared with our friends, colleagues, and families the details of the many characters and events. Nonetheless, Ian would like to thank Jenell Hartman for her partnership and insight. She has taken an interest in the topic and has given valuable feedback; she's been an enduring source of inspiration. Ian is also thankful for his two feline companions, Poe and Cole. David thanks his lovely wife, Donna Aguiniga, for her constant love and support. Without the positive reinforcement from our loved ones, we could not have completed this book.

Finally, we wish to acknowledge that the land on which we have researched and written much of this book, and the land on which we reside, is that of the Dena'ina people, the Alaska Natives of Dgheyay Kaq' (Anchorage). As white settlers on Dena'inaełnena (Dena'ina land), we recognize the place of privilege from which we have completed this study. We also recognize the complex ways in which a colonial project continues to shape Alaska and profoundly impacts the world we live in. We are humbled in the presence of those who have come before and stewarded the land and water around us. Though we have learned much, our access to knowledge and the history in this book is inevitably partial and incomplete. We further acknowledge the communities and people with whom we have engaged and learned from as settlers on this land. Without the assistance of many individuals, this book would not be possible. While we have been fortunate to have received valuable insights from numerous people, any errors are our own.

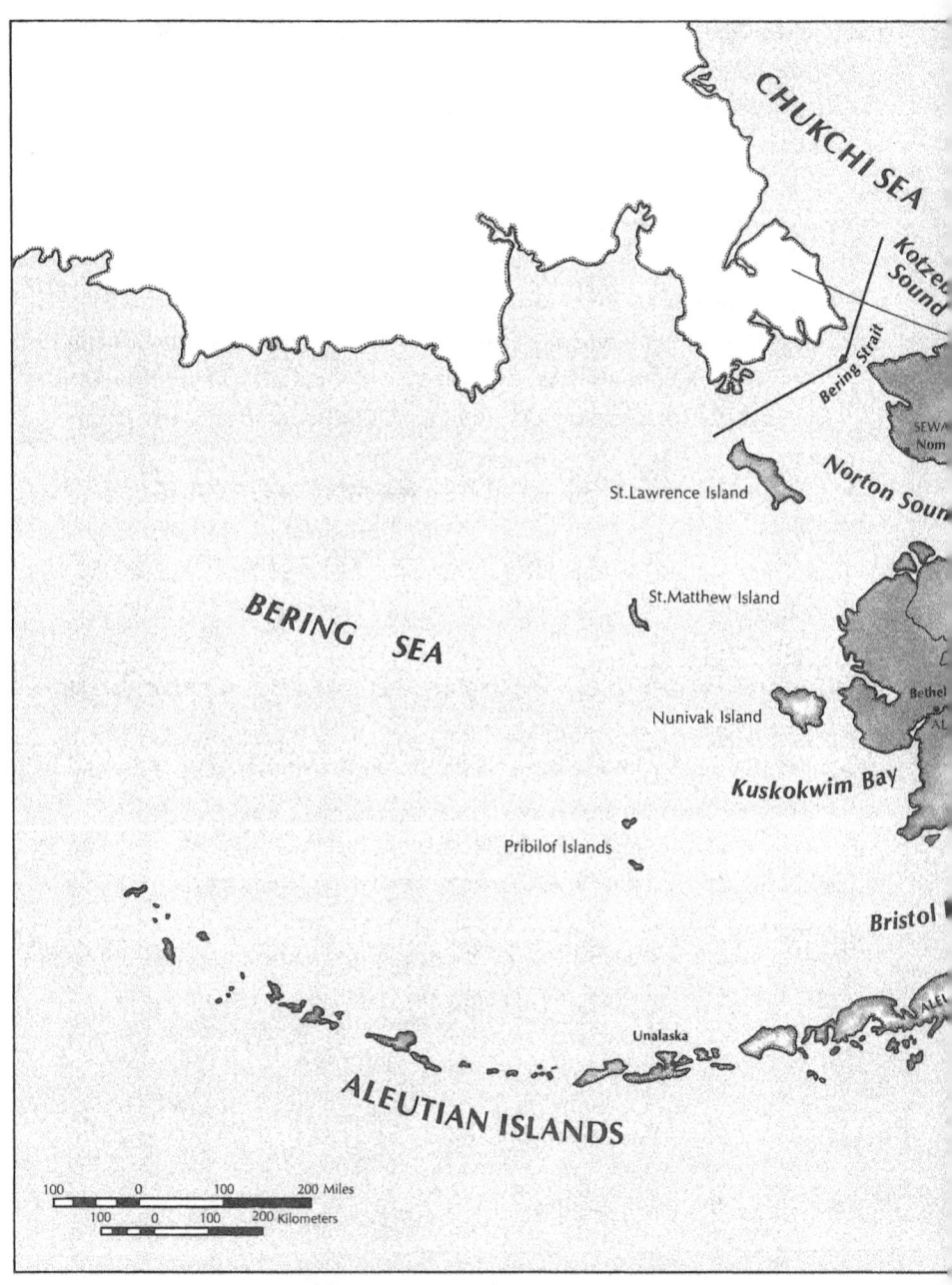

Map of Alaska. Reprinted from Antonson and Hanable, *Alaska's Heritage*, 586–87. Courtesy of the Alaska Historical Commission.

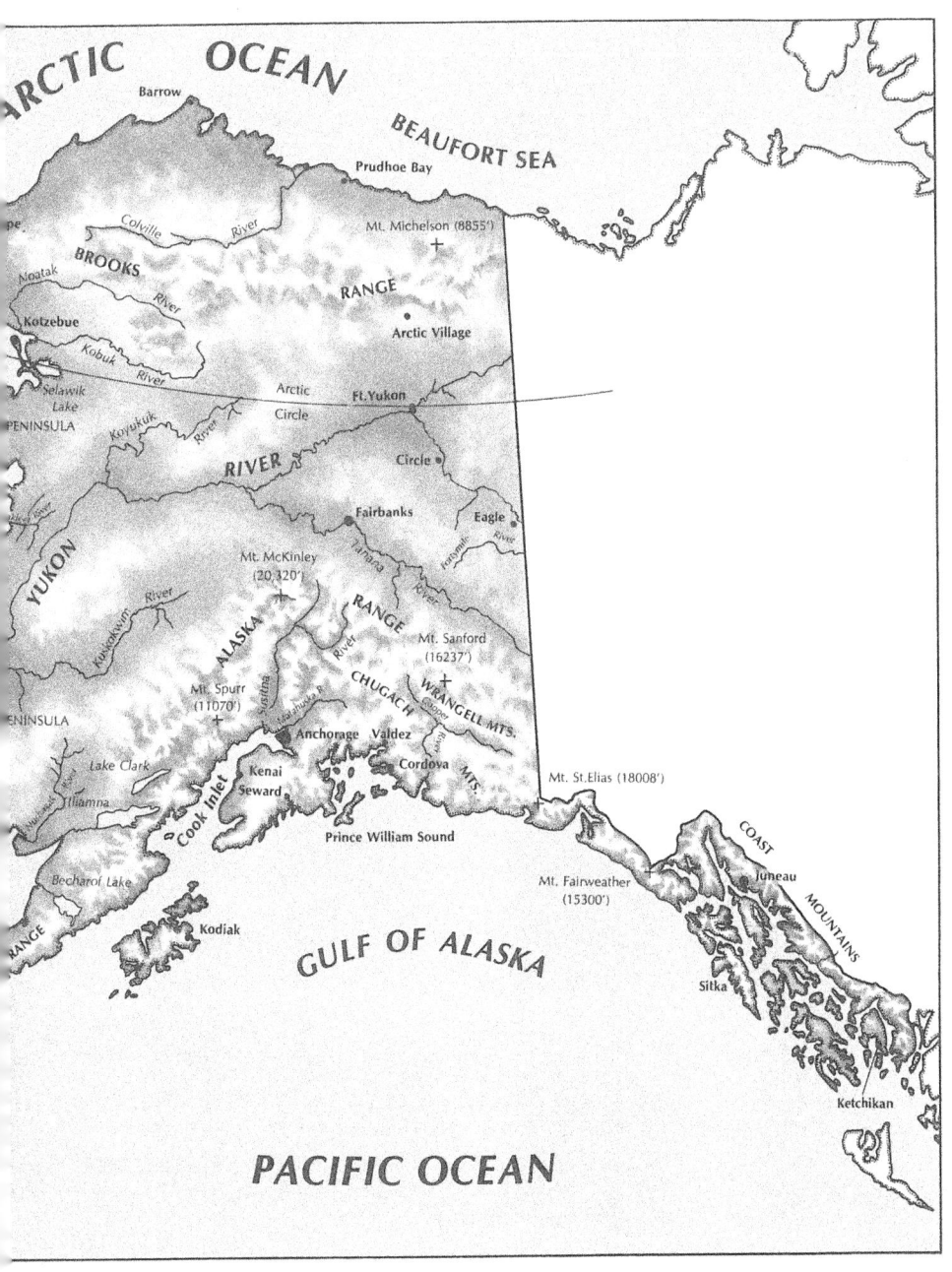

FOREWORD

GO NORTH!

CALVIN E. WILLIAMS

SINCE THE LATE NINETEENTH CENTURY, AFRICAN AMERICANS have come to Alaska to start fresh and make a home for themselves. Many who came north have since left. It's a challenge to live here, and it's not for everyone. But some have stayed for generations and put down roots. I've made Anchorage my home for over fifty years. I've worked with others to organize Alaskans from all backgrounds to vote and participate in the political process. We've lobbied to invest in public transportation, bring electricity to low-income communities, and build affordable housing. And I served as the president of the Anchorage chapter of the NAACP, an organization with which I'm still involved.

To understand my Alaska story, though, we'll need to go back to where it all began: Monroe, Louisiana, deep in the Jim Crow South. That's where I was born, a week before the Japanese attacked Pearl Harbor. My mother worked in a factory, and my father joined the army and fought in the Pacific. I was mostly raised by my paternal grandmother, Lillor Culpepper. She owned a three-bedroom home in Monroe, which was tall stepping for a "colored lady" in the 1940s. She saw after kids in the area and wanted me to have the best education available, so I was enrolled at the school across the street run by the Franciscans, the Little Flower Academy. My grandmother appreciated the school's academic rigor, and she also liked that she could stand on the back porch to keep an eye on those "Holy Penguins," as she called the nuns.

The Little Flower Academy emphasized what we'd call "service learning" today. We served the less fortunate, fed the hungry, and helped those in need. Little Flower had such an impact on me that I even became Catholic. But I attended church elsewhere too. On Sunday nights, I was Baptist at the Riverside Missionary Baptist Church, singing along with the chorus. After high school, I attended Grambling State University to pursue theater and performing arts. Like my father, however, I decided to enlist in the military. Once I completed my service, I returned home to care for my father, who'd been suffering with post-traumatic stress since he came back from war nearly two decades earlier.

By then it was the early 1960s, and the civil rights movement had arrived in Louisiana. I had to get involved, so I joined CORE, the Congress of Racial Equality. In addition to voter registration, we integrated what was then known as Northeast Louisiana State College. But the racist violence in the South gave me pause, and I long considered a life beyond Monroe. So, in 1965, I left Louisiana. Close friends of mine, John and Charles LeViege, moved to Alaska and encouraged me to join them. Jobs were plenty, and Black folks had more opportunities than down South. North to Alaska I went.

Just because I left the South didn't mean that I abandoned my commitment to civil rights, though. In fact, it was a good time to be an activist in Alaska. The population was small, and one could make a difference. I met others who were committed to equal rights and social justice, folks we'd call "allies" today. It was a critical era for Alaska's Indigenous population. Alaska Natives settled their land claims and were determined to preserve their culture amid the onslaught of newcomers.

Alaska was impressively diverse, even in those days. Alaska Natives, Asian Americans, African Americans, and whites lived in relatively close proximity in Anchorage. Not everyone got along, but it was unlike Louisiana, where segregation defined the social order. I, like the thousands of others who had recently moved, viewed Alaska as a place to start over. I quickly found a job at the local hospital and earned decent money. By day I worked, and by night I was active in my adopted community, making friends and getting involved.

But as much as I took to Alaska, I always dreamed of being in the movies and decided to relocate to Hollywood in the 1970s. This was the era of Blaxploitation films. Athletes and celebrities sometimes found work, but trained Black actors like me were overlooked. In addition, I didn't care for the depiction of

Black folks, and ultimately, I missed Alaska. The people and the opportunities the state provided brought me back, and this time for good.

It didn't take long to reestablish my life up north. I worked in television as a production manager for KTUU, the Anchorage NBC affiliate. I also produced and hosted the talk show *Cross Cultural* on the public television station, KAKM. The program highlighted Alaska's underserved populations and presented lively discussion about the burning topics of the day. We talked about violence, racism, bigotry, and all the ugly stuff that marred most urban communities. We also emphasized Alaskans who worked together to overcome the past and build a better future. During that time, I interviewed several national civil rights luminaries, including Julian Bond, Benjamin Hooks, and Dick Gregory. What a thrill!

Meanwhile, I participated in anti–domestic violence campaigns, community councils, and efforts to address institutional racism in the criminal justice system. My faith guided these activities. Throughout I remained a dedicated parishioner at St. Anthony's Catholic Church in Anchorage. The church afforded me the chance to engage my love of music as the director of the Filipino Gospel Choir. St. Anthony's is a multiracial, progressive church that represents the best of Alaska. Through its outreach program, I've held Bible studies with incarcerated men and performed regularly for the patients at Providence Hospital and our senior care center, the Pioneer Home. My greatest achievement came in 2017, when I received the St. Francis Stewardship Award from the Archdiocese of Anchorage. Saint Francis was the patron saint of the Little Flower Academy. This honor represented my having come full circle from my youth in Louisiana to my time in Alaska.

Beyond these pursuits, history has been a lifelong passion, especially the history of African Americans in Alaska. I believe in the emancipatory role of education and propose that knowing our history is an empowering tool to achieve greater freedom, higher levels of citizen participation, and a functioning democracy. As a historian of Anchorage's Black community and someone who's lived a good chunk of it, I was particularly excited to assist Ian Hartman and David Reamer with this book and ensure that we get it right.

We've long needed greater documentation of our community's history, and this book is one part of that effort. The Anchorage Museum's recent "Black Lives in Alaska" exhibit also showcased the state's little-known Black history. Indeed, there is great interest in the topic, and I'm encouraged to see it. Alaska is one of the nation's most diverse states, and for too long, we've ignored the history of most of its peoples. That's beginning to change, but more must be done. After all, we must know our history and our struggles, and it's up to each generation to pass on this knowledge. Reckoning with our shared past and documenting our struggles provide a way forward. Collective struggle, activism, and connectivity are central themes of this book. Like much of Black history, the story here is one of movements, migrations, and people who've come together to create a more just society.

Alaska seems a world away from Louisiana, Hollywood, or most anywhere else for that matter. A whole other country separates us from the rest of the United States. Yet we have more in common than you might think. We've fought for justice, made history, and created a space of our own. It hasn't always been easy, but I'll continue to do my part to make the future brighter for my daughter, Marsha, my grandchildren, Leslie and Precious, and my great-grandchildren, Tony Keshaun, Kaleb Deshaun, Toni Keyunna, and Cing.

Alaskans pride themselves on doing things differently than how they're done in the Lower 48, and sometimes we do. This book, however, presents what we have in common as well as what makes Alaska exceptional. It doesn't tell us everything. No single book does. We have lots of history to make and additional stories to tell. There are unsung heroes who've achieved much and deserve recognition. This book shines a light on a few of these individuals and strikes a cautiously optimistic tone. True, we have more to do, but if we learn from our history, Alaska might become a more accepting place for all.

INTRODUCTION

BLACK HISTORY IN UNLIKELY PLACES

FROM JOHN MUIR'S LATE-NINETEENTH-CENTURY DESCRIPTIONS OF pristine wilderness through today's ubiquitous reality television programs, Alaska has long fascinated the American public.[1] Presented in popular culture, Alaskans often fall into a few predictable stereotypes: the rough-and-tumble fortune seeker, a gold miner, or perhaps the maladjusted loner looking for refuge in the isolation of Alaska's unbounded wilds. Another is the crude, racially charged image of the "Eskimo," a one-dimensional representation of Alaska Natives frozen in time and subsisting amid the world's harshest conditions. Yet these portrayals of Alaska and its people ignore the complex history as well as the diverse population of the nation's forty-ninth state. In just over a century, the state's largest settler city, Anchorage, has become Alaska's cultural and economic center as it transformed from a World War–era railroad hub into a modern metropolitan region and home to some of the nation's most multicultural communities and schools. Other areas of Alaska—from its rural Indigenous villages accessible only by air to smaller towns on the limited road system—have undergone equal levels of change.

However, fitting neither the stereotype of a white settler–turned–sourdough nor an Alaska Native whose culture has been connected to the land and sea for generations, the state's Black population has been largely ignored by scholars and casual observers. Decades before statehood and earlier even than the Klondike Gold Rush of the 1890s, Black individuals participated in Alaska's politics, economic development, and culture. They hunted whales, patrolled the seas, built roads, served in the military, opened businesses, fought injustice, won political office, and developed community. This book presents their stories and documents a seemingly improbable topic: the history of Black settlement and life in Alaska.² From vital participation in the gold rush to the military and defense buildups through civil rights advocacy, Alaska's Black population, though small, has had an outsize impact on the culture and civic life of the region.

Black Lives in Alaska joins a list of correctives to historian Walter Prescott Webb's oft-repeated though specious claim that the West, excepting California and Texas, lacked "water, timber, cities, industry, labor, and Negroes."³ Indeed, scholars have compiled vibrant studies of Black history in Seattle, Portland, Silicon Valley, Spokane, Phoenix, and the Great Plains, among other western cities and regions.⁴ But they have yet to explore the topic in one of the most remote, western places in North America: Alaska. Even comprehensive volumes on Blacks in the West, such as Douglas Flamming's impressive survey *African Americans in the West* and the more recent *Freedom's Racial Frontier*, edited by Herbert G. Ruffin II and Dwayne A. Mack, do not include analysis of the so-called last frontier.⁵ We position Alaska at the center of this scholarship and propose that this study sheds new light on Black history in the West even as it reinforces many of the conclusions of scholars who have explored the topic. For instance, historians of Blacks in the West have found that the region possessed unrepentant pockets of hostility and deep currents of white supremacy, and many migrants faced hardships and encountered harsh discrimination. But Black westerners resisted, persevered, and just as often seized upon freedoms unimaginable in the places they left behind. Alaska was no different.⁶

Black history in Alaska is a topic worthy of scholarly attention and one yet to be fully written.⁷ Most texts that narrate Alaska's history fail to recognize the contributions of African Americans or the complexity of Alaska's racial landscape. Arguably, the most notable and enduring of these books, Claus-M. Naske and Herman E. Slotkin's *Alaska: A History*, does not muster a single reference to Black contributions in the territory or state.⁸ Other standard academic treatments of Alaska's history fare no better.⁹ But as this book relates, the history of African-descended peoples in the region is extensive and spans generations. It begins during the era of Pacific whaling in the mid-nineteenth century and extends into the present, touching on such pivotal events as the gold rushes, world wars, and the civil rights movement. Alaska's Black history dovetails with contemporary issues of mass incarceration, police violence, and multiracial movements for social justice. *Black Lives in Alaska* presents this expansive story and emphasizes the process of community formation in Alaska; it locates the Black past as a central through line in the state's broader history and bolsters our understanding of the diversity of Alaska and the American West.

Furthermore, we heed historian Quintard Taylor's call to move beyond the "recognition school" of simply acknowledging the presence of Blacks in the West and position African Americans as key contributors to the history of the nation's most vast and geographically distinct state.[10] To do so, the book employs a variety of heretofore unexplored archival sources and oral histories, enabling Black Alaskans to tell the story of discrimination, resistance, and self-activity in a place not normally associated with their presence. The book also relies on secondhand accounts and pieces together the lives of Black men and women based on fragmented evidence and incomplete documentation, leaving much of the interpretation to the historian. But taken in sum, there exists copious evidence to demonstrate the impact that Black women and men have had upon Alaska, both individually and collectively. While *Black Lives in Alaska* conveys the history of African Americans throughout Alaska, much of the study—particularly the latter chapters—emphasizes its urbanized areas. Anchorage and its surroundings, with nearly 70 percent of Alaska's population, receive significant attention. Nonetheless, we believe that this book demonstrates that despite its distant location, Alaska was not excluded from major trends that shaped Black history over the past century and a half. Rather, the defining themes of Black history—migration, racial discrimination, community formation and resiliency, and civic activism, to name a few—are present and compose a dynamic story that until now has never been told.

Although Alaska's Black history intersects with broader themes of the African American experience in the United States, this case study is sui generis in at least a few ways. For one, Alaska's reliance on federal spending and its lack of a large industrial working class separates Anchorage and Fairbanks, as well as the more isolated towns and villages, from the larger northern and western cities where millions of Black families settled during the Great Migration. Black migration to Alaska—particularly during the early and middle decades of the twentieth century—more likely resulted from enlistment into military service or from an opportunity that accompanied the defense buildup than it did the pull of industrial wage labor.[11] Relatedly, Alaska's Black population has generally lacked a radical tradition that one finds in such western locales as the Bay Area, Southern California, or the Puget Sound.[12] The best explanation for this could again be the disproportionately large role compared to other states that the military has played in Alaska. Another reason may be the relative ease with which money could be made in Alaska, either through mining or the oil boom later in the century.[13]

The comparatively modest levels of Black working-class formation, or "proletarianization," as historian Joe Trotter usefully described it, has had political and cultural implications that also separate Alaska from the more heavily industrialized cities and regions of the Lower 48.[14] In addition, Alaska's highly itinerant and mobile population has historically been more likely to relocate than engage in sustained social movements. More commonly, Black Alaskans have held a range of occupations and are found across the income distribution. This has led to a fairly high level of class-based diversity among the state's Black population, particularly by the 1960s and 1970s. As such, this book spotlights an array of figures, some of whom may be considered poor or working class and others who represent a professional class of state and federal employees, entrepreneurs, lawyers, and educators. But to be clear, while it may lack a consistent and well-defined strain of working-class radicalism visible elsewhere, Alaska's Black population has engaged in activism on behalf of a variety of causes and participated in politics for as long as men and women of African descent have been counted in the census.

Alaska's demographics present yet another difference in how Black history has transpired here in comparison to elsewhere. For one, the largest ethnic minority in Alaska has long been its Indigenous people. Alaska Natives, an exceedingly variegated and diverse population, have collectively been Alaska's most marginalized population throughout the last century; the white population first narrowly exceeded the Native population during the gold rush era. And to this day, Alaska has the largest percentage of Native peoples among any state.[15] The modern history of Alaska is thus partly a history of settler colonialism and the expropriation and exploitation of Native lands. A predominantly white population, backed by governmental and corporate entities, has claimed legal title to Indigenous land and exerted ownership over the resources above and below it. Indeed, one might propose that this is the history of the United States writ large. Yet these forces remain far more visible in contemporary Alaska than in states and regions with a longer, more extensive history of white settlement as well as smaller Indigenous populations. Alaska

Native activism has then typically prioritized tribal sovereignty, the reclamation and maintenance of land, and the stewardship of natural resources. Much of this activism continues to occur as Alaska Natives also struggle to ensure cultural survival and resist further colonial encroachment.[16]

Furthermore, Alaska has long been a site of Asian migration, largely because of the commercial fishing and salmon canning industries as well as the territory's sprawling location across the North Pacific. Asian labor has proven central to those industries and has served as a pull factor for individuals and families from China, Japan, the Philippines, and more recently, the Pacific Islands of Polynesia. Over the last several generations, people of Asian descent have settled throughout coastal Alaska and compose over 30 percent of residents in Kodiak and Unalaska. In Anchorage and Juneau, and in the state overall, Asian Americans are the largest ethnic population after whites and Alaska Natives.[17] Literary scholar and historian Juliana Hu Pegues has proposed that Alaska's Asian and Indigenous populations are "entangled," whereby Native peoples are viewed as "never modern," and Asian Americans are "forever foreign." She continues: "Once associated through an imperial discourse of racialization, Asian and Native peoples in the territory were narratively separated under settler colonial machinations, even as they lived and labored in close proximity."[18] Although Hu Pegues's analysis does not emphasize Alaska's Black population, her insights are germane to this study.

Blacks in Alaska have therefore assumed a different geopolitical station than they have in other parts of the country where they constitute the largest, most visible minority population. While Alaskans of African descent have been targets of racialization from the white majority, the Black presence in Alaska must be considered amid the wider context of settler colonialism and extractive capitalism. As a result, the incorporation of Asian labor has complicated Alaska's class-based hierarchy and bears a specific racial imprint to the nation's history of western expansion, notably in the Pacific. Anti-Native racism in Alaska is thus constitutive to the machinations of the nation's settler empire; so, too, are the attendant economic and cultural dislocations that the Native population have endured. And to mobilize Hu Pegues's insight, anti-Black and anti-Asian racism might both be viewed as entangled in the same colonial project, even as both populations, Black and Asian Alaskans, have at times seized upon specific opportunities that the state has presented.

One should not then assume that the movement for Native sovereignty in Alaska corresponds to or runs exactly parallel with the freedom struggles of Black men and women in Alaska or elsewhere.[19] Not surprisingly, while Alaska's disparate populations have encountered discrimination, Native, Asian, and Black activists have not always unified in common purpose to fight oppression and injustice. The struggle of Alaska's Indigenous people has not typically been taken up en masse by other communities of color, let alone whites. The Black freedom struggle in Alaska, meanwhile, has mostly remained the province of people of African descent; however, allies of color have played an increasing role in the recent history of anti-racist activism. Anti-racist and anticolonial coalitions that reflect Alaska's population have emerged, but inter- and multiracial activism has been more the exception than the rule. This suggests the complexity of racial identity, the limits of civil rights mobilization, and the logistical challenges of building and sustaining movements dedicated to social justice in a state as large and multifaceted as Alaska. Nonetheless, African Americans, Alaska Natives, Asian Americans, Pacific Islanders, and whites have all, at various times, initiated collective action to address the state's systemic inequities. Our current moment presents a fertile environment for multiracial organizing, a topic we address later in the book.[20]

While multiracial coalitions have formed inconsistently, readers will note the impressive documentation of African American women who have not only found success in Alaska but have had a steady and substantial impact upon its politics and culture. True, Alaska's demographics have historically skewed male, regardless of race. Typical of other western states with boom-and-bust economies, Alaska has drawn greater numbers of men than women to labor in the various extraction industries: fishing, mining, timber, and oil and gas, to name those most foundational to the economy.[21] The military, of course, is also an overwhelmingly male institution.[22] A local joke has long circulated among women who have entered Alaska's dating pool: "The odds are good, but the goods are odd," a reference to the gender imbalance as well as an enduring perception that Alaskan men are a bit offbeat. Although men have historically outnumbered women, women have taken on active roles across industries and government. Alaska affirms what historians Shirley Ann Wilson Moore and Quintard Taylor noted in their edited volume on Black women in the West: "Whether individually or collectively, they [women of African descent] turned to their work of building communities, caring of families, founding and maintaining institutions, and attaining social and economic justice with a profound conviction in their own abilities to move beyond the limitations racism and sexism placed on them."[23]

Moore and Taylor not only paved the way for scholars to locate Black men as instrumental to the history of the American West, but they also highlighted the myriad ways African American women initiated social change. Black women who settled in Alaska reinforce this scholarship and challenge the conception of the territory and then state as a space dominated by the sturdy, indomitable male pioneer; indeed, some of the wealthiest and most successful Alaskans of the last hundred years have been Black women. Aside from starting businesses, participating in the gold rush, and fighting for civil rights, the Black women featured in this narrative served as pillars of their respective communities, and they blazed trails in fields as divergent as real estate, law, politics, education, and entertainment. In every era of Alaska's modern development, Black women have been at the forefront of its political economy and civic life.[24]

Taken as a whole, *Black Lives in Alaska* maps the trials and challenges African Americans faced in America's northwesternmost territory and then state. Black individuals participated in the creation of Alaska's civic institutions and contributed to its political life, even as they endured racism and fought injustice. Alaska's history of race relations and civil rights also reminds the reader that the currents of discrimination and its responses—self-activity, activism, and perseverance—are American stories that might be explored in the unlikeliest of places. And while Alaska's Black history displays much continuity with the larger, nationwide Black freedom struggle, the forty-ninth state's demographic and spatial complexities at times belie that narrative. In the end, however, these complexities enrich the history of people of African descent in North America, be they in Florida, California, or Alaska. The last of these states, it turns out, offers a far more compelling piece of the story than many may have imagined. As the history presented in this book meanders between adherence and disruption to the larger themes of African American and western history, we believe that it augments our understanding of both.

The first chapter, "Black Exploration, Labor, and Travel in the Icy Northwest," takes a broad, introductory view by recounting the history of Black participation in Alaska, as well as the North Pacific and the Arctic, from the middle of the nineteenth century through the early twentieth. This era straddles the Treaty of Cession between the United States and Russia, through which the 663,000 square miles land and water known as Alaska came under nominal American control in 1867. The first documented presence of Black men in Alaska's waters and perhaps on land occurred as early as the 1840s, as whalers set out from New Bedford, Massachusetts, and other New England ports to ply their craft in the icy waters of the Pacific and the Arctic oceans. A few crews established temporary settlements in Point Hope and Point Barrow, north of the Arctic Circle. Evidence suggests these men arrived as free people of color in the North; other documentation suggests some had been enslaved and fled to freedom. Black whalers believed a life at sea was preferable to a life in bondage or the day-to-day discrimination they experienced in their home or adopted communities on land.

Though scant documentation remains of these men and their activities, more evidence exists from the gold rush of the late 1890s and early 1900s, as described in chapter 2, "Black in the Gold Rush Era." This chapter showcases the first well-documented period of American control of the territory. During these years Black men and women came by the hundreds—some through the military, others to prospect or set up businesses in support of mining activity. In any case, by the first decade of the twentieth century, a permanent and growing Black population called Alaska home. Blacks who arrived after the Treaty of Cession are among the most understudied population in Alaska, yet they contributed mightily to Alaska's culture and economy in ways that historians have yet to fully record.

As a result of federally restrictive legislation, world wars, and the nation's worst economic depression, immigration from abroad slowed from 1916 through the early 1960s. However, those years correspond to what historians have called the "Great Migration"—the mass movement of Americans from the South to the North and West, including millions of African Americans. Alaska did not attract Black men and women on the scale of Illinois, Michigan, New York, or California; still, thousands arrived through the armed forces and on their own accord. The world wars shaped and redefined Alaska unlike any other events, and the military's enduring presence in the Far Northwest and Arctic continues to impact the region's culture and economy.

Chapter 3, "The World War Era and a New Alaska," thus highlights the war and interwar years to demonstrate the numerous ways that global conflict at once issued new opportunities for Alaska's Black population and limited them from pursuing others. Black soldiers built the most treacherous stretches of the Alaska Highway, served in the Aleutian Islands campaign, and were stationed across the territory. These men landed on Attu and helped retake the island from the Japanese in what was the deadliest fighting in North America throughout the war; several went to Adak Island, and still others served at the US Army Air Corps bases at Cold Bay and on Umnak Island. Despite these contributions, African Americans faced discrimination, notably from the military commander of Alaska Territory, Lt. Gen. Simon Bolivar Buckner Jr. In the face of racist mistreatment, Black men served valiantly and with distinction. Consequently, the US military would never be the same, and neither would Alaska. The wartime achievements of Black troops in the territory presaged and facilitated the integration of the US armed forces and helped launch one of the nation's great social movements. Chapter 3 therefore recasts World War II–era Alaska as not only a critical staging ground to the global conflict but also an early battleground for civil rights, anticipating rather than following the social movements that would emerge in force during the postwar decades.

Chapter 4, "Discrimination, Opportunity, and Community in Postwar Alaska," details the years between the end of World War II and the early 1960s. Alaska's Southcentral region emerged as the economic and population center of the territory and eventually the state in the 1950s and 1960s; Fairbanks and Alaska's interior experienced significant growth during these years as well. The onset of the Cold War and the geopolitical significance of the circumpolar North and Pacific ensured Alaska would receive copious levels of federal appropriations, much of which went to defend the territory. This rapid expansion of Anchorage—and to a lesser extent, Fairbanks—in the postwar decades offered the possibility of establishing a life anew in ways not possible in the older cities of the Lower 48. But like their counterparts elsewhere, Black Alaskans continued to experience racism on personal and structural levels. As Alaska grew, its white residents at times restricted prospective Black homeowners from purchasing property; this was particularly true in urban Alaska. These discriminatory policies effectively froze African Americans as well as other minority families out of much of the housing market. As a result, Native, Black, and Asian families settled on the edges of town or outside Anchorage's official boundaries, often in poorly built homes on marginal land. Discrimination and neglect from the city's political leadership fed a spirit of collective action and spurred a wave of civil rights mobilization.[25]

Chapter 5, "Civil Rights under the Northern Lights," delves further into discrimination in urban Alaska as well as the opportunities that Black men and women cultivated through the 1960s and 1970s. And though Alaska is not usually considered a focal point for the civil rights movement, activism rooted in a vibrant and collective sense of identity took hold. As in the rest of the United States, Black Alaskans took to the streets to assert their rights and call out the various forms of injustice they encountered. While Alaska certainly experienced racial conflict before the 1960s, this decade marked a series of hard-fought victories for communities of color generally. Alaska Natives built the framework for the Alaska Native Claims Settlement Act (ANCSA), passed into federal law in 1971. That landmark legislation ensured that Alaska Native people receive a place at the table alongside multinational oil corporations that flocked to the forty-ninth state to extract natural resources.[26] While Native activism understandably centered upon land claims and securing a cut of the pending oil wealth under Indigenous land, Black activists in urban Alaska more typically took up causes associated with the civil rights movement in the Lower 48. Issues related to job security and employment discrimination, access to housing, and inclusion in politics and business predominated.[27]

Although Black and Native activism did not typically intersect in these years, African Americans and Alaska Natives had success in the courts, the legislature, and on the streets. Both populations opened new jobs and accessed better housing; Alaska's business community and its state politics grew more reflective of its demographics. Alaska Native activism and the land claims settlement that culminated in ANCSA reshaped state politics and the economy in fundamental ways. While that topic lies beyond the scope of this book, the reader should note the era's disparate forms of activism and the significant achievements of Alaska's diverse population. The actions taken by men and women of color, alongside their white allies, in the 1960s and early 1970s fostered a more open and inclusive state. Yet patterns of discrimination remained stubbornly persistent.

The sixth chapter, "Black Alaska during the Oil Boom," documents race relations and Alaska's Black history from the 1970s through the 1980s. Over a decade after the 1968 discovery of oil on Alaska's North Slope, thousands of new arrivals adopted the state as their home. The population influx included many white men and women from the American South; they tended to be more religious than the previous generation of migrants and more conservative too. Some clung to the days of segregation and resented the advances of the civil rights movement. Black Alaskans reported increases in both opportunity as well as animosity in these years. A new wave of activism among Blacks and allies emerged to confront the resurgent currents of racism that remained after the height of civil rights. Alaska may have gone from one of the nation's poorest states to one of its richest, but access to the newly created oil wealth was never equal.

Chapter 7, "Criminal Justice, Law Enforcement, and Race in Urban Alaska," emphasizes the tense relationship that developed between Anchorage's Black residents and the police department, particularly amid the economic downturn of the 1980s that resulted from a price collapse in the global oil market. The chapter explores fraying social bonds and locates Black history in Alaska within a broader discussion of urban history, federal and state disinvestment from communities of color, and growing levels of inequality that defined American life in the Reagan era.[28] High-profile police shootings put a bright spotlight on the tensions that plagued Anchorage during these years. However, due largely to the resource wealth that flooded the forty-ninth state throughout the 1970s and early 1980s, Alaska's largest city presents a rather different case study from major cities in the Lower 48 that experienced decline. In short, from the middle of the 1970s through the present, Alaska's economy has become inextricably linked to the price of oil. Likewise, the state's social tensions have played out against the backdrop of a boom-and-bust cycle that is a hallmark of resource dependency. These final chapters grapple with how Alaska's Black history and race relations have intersected with the state's economic precarity.

Our final chapter, "Resentment, Resilience, and Cultural Rejuvenation at Century's End," investigates race and migration in Alaska during the final two decades of the twentieth century and first years of the twenty-first, with an emphasis again on the Southcentral region. To the surprise of many national observers, the 2010 United States Census revealed three Anchorage neighborhoods ranked as the most diverse census tracks in the nation, surpassing many of the largest metropolitan centers and traditional destinations for immigrants in the Lower 48 and Hawai'i. Local and state politicians, as well as civic boosters, praised Anchorage as a center of multiculturalism and tolerance. Despite positive sound bites, though, the men, women, and young people of color who grew up in Anchorage in the late 1980s and 1990s reported a rise in racial antagonism and white supremacy. Documented hate crimes reached new highs. The combination of a sluggish economy with dwindling hope for workers and an increasingly diverse population resulted in an environment rife with tensions. However, Black Alaskans, as well as other Alaskans of color, refused to live in fear. Alaskan youth created a vibrant culture that reflected the state's emerging multiculturalism and presented a vision divergent from that of a dwindling white majority. Alaskans of color who came of age at the turn of the century celebrated the state's rich Indigenous heritage and its increasingly global population. Like the earlier chapters, the discussion in the final one is inseparable from the context of Alaska's ever-changing demographics and economic fortunes.

The conclusion reflects on the last twenty years and buttresses our argument that Black history in Alaska has paralleled yet at times deviated from Black history in the Lower 48. Alaska's Black population has built vibrant civic institutions that have endured into the present. The vitality of these institutions is even more impressive given the comparatively small number of people who have created them. *Black Lives in Alaska* should thus be viewed as an interpretation rooted in community and expressive of perseverance and agency. It would be impossible to convey this history without candidly addressing the presence of white supremacy, racial hatred, violence, and individual as well as systemic inequities. But those are only part of the story. We have therefore provided equal measures of triumph and Black excellence and have sought to go beyond narratives of victimhood or powerlessness. Our conclusion also locates a measure of optimism in the multiracial organizing that has become more prevalent in the era of Black Lives Matter. As we prepare this book for publication, frank discussion on the topics of racism and colonialism are ongoing here in Alaska, as they are nationwide. And like this latest rise in national activism, Alaskans of color have broadly stood in solidarity with one another.

BLACK LIVES IN ALASKA

CHAPTER ONE

Black Exploration, Labor, and Travel in the Icy Northwest

BY THE 1880S WILLIAM T. SHOREY HAD BEGUN TO ASCEND THE ranks of whaling crews and eventually worked his way up to captain by 1900. He led voyages on whaling barks, such as the *Emma F. Herriman, Andrew Hicks,* and *John & Winthrop,* which traversed the Pacific Ocean.[1] The *John & Winthrop* was particularly notable as one of the few whaling ships with an entirely Black crew. Shorey's status as one of the era's most skilled whalers was as unlikely as it was remarkable. His parents had been enslaved on a sugar plantation in Barbados. Shorey, however, seized upon greater opportunities as he left Barbados for New England in his teen years. Finding work as a whaler, Shorey took his maiden voyage in 1876. On one early expedition, a sperm whale nearly capsized the boat, endangering the lives of the crew. A crewmate threw a makeshift bomb at the whale, saving the ship and the men from almost certain death. Shorey, undeterred, stuck with the industry and withstood its often brutal working conditions, becoming a boat steerer and eventually a captain.[2]

As the industry shifted from the North Atlantic to the Pacific in the latter decades of the nineteenth century, Shorey found himself whaling ever farther from his adopted home in Boston, Massachusetts. The *Herriman* crossed the Atlantic to the Cape of Good Hope, off the coast of southern Africa, and reached the waters of the Indian and the South Pacific Oceans. The men aboard kept watch for the bountiful whale populations, prized for their blubber and oil. The *Herriman* wound its way north to the Gulf of Alaska and the Arctic before heading back south to San Francisco. These icy waters would be a focus of the whaling industry from the 1880s through its decline in the first decades of the twentieth century.[3]

Meanwhile, Shorey had come a long way from his childhood in the Caribbean—touching down in Australia, the islands of the South Pacific, and the waters of the Bering and Okhotsk Seas. He viewed the Arctic Ocean from Alaska and just beyond the shores of eastern Russia. By then the *Herriman*'s port of call was San Francisco, and Shorey was promoted to first officer. By 1886 Shorey had become first in command and was among the most skilled whalers in the Pacific. Captain Shorey continued to sail until 1908, and by then he and wife, Julia Ann Shelton Shorey, had become members of San Francisco's high society. Undoubtedly, whaling led to Shorey's success. In the captain's time, he witnessed the industry diversify its labor force as many native-born white men looked elsewhere for employment and viewed its unsafe working conditions and declining prospects as better left to others. Such assumptions were true, as Herman Melville famously related in his classic novel *Moby-Dick*. But beyond the heyday of whaling in the middle of the nineteenth century, the ships of the West Coast continued to employ men of color, economic castaways from the Far East, Europe, and Africa, many of whom were drawn to a job with a level of meritocratic advancement in an era otherwise rife with discrimination. Shorey's life provided evidence of these limited opportunities.[4]

Historians referred to the last quarter of the nineteenth century and the early twentieth as a nadir in race relations, a time when Reconstruction came to a violent end and the policies of Jim Crow dominated the US South. Rampant discrimination also occurred throughout the North and West; exclusionary laws often prohibited people of Asian and African descent, as well as Indigenous people, from gainful employment and decent housing. In this context, whaling became a refuge for Black men. It was one of the few jobs to offer decent pay and a chance to move up in rank. Still, the turnover was high and the conditions exceedingly dangerous.[5]

William Shorey was not the first African American to sail through the Gulf of Alaska and the Bering Sea, but his story reveals how and why a Black man reared in the Caribbean, a region thoroughly defined by racial slavery, ended up in the world's northern latitudes. Early Black history in Alaska began at sea, as some men escaped slavery and, later, the punishing brutality of segregation in the American South. Others, like Shorey, a free man of color, believed the open seas supplied the best chance to advance and were determined to leverage the industry to their maximum advantage. Shorey ultimately captained whaling ships until 1908, a thirty-two-year career at sea during which he garnered wealth for his family and secured a life that was almost certainly better than what was available on land.[6] This chapter details some of the first African Americans to arrive in Alaska and its waters. Though a mass migration into the region never occurred, hundreds of African Americans and Afro-Caribbeans sailed north. Most of these arrivals remained at sea, but some came ashore and settled, at least for a brief time. A small number stayed in Alaska and made it their home. The men who arrived in Alaska during these years primarily did so with the whaling industry, especially if they came before the 1890s. But smaller numbers of African Americans traveled north with the military or worked as prospectors or businesspeople looking for a place to start fresh.

Fugitives from Slavery and Free Blacks in the Civil War Era

Well before Shorey sailed through Alaska waters, the whaling industry had been a haven for enslaved men who had escaped their bondage and free Blacks in the North who sought more lucrative employment. Many fugitives from slavery risked the trek to cities such as Philadelphia, New York, and Boston and smaller towns like Nantucket and New Bedford, Massachusetts. The latter two coastal New England towns had suitable ports and, by the 1820s, became the center of the nation's whaling industry. Both had also become known for their relatively sizable population of free Blacks and vibrant strains of Black entrepreneurialism. In 1820 Capt. Absalom Boston, a man of African and Wampanoag descent, left Nantucket with a Black crew aboard the whale ship *Industry*. Financed entirely by Black families in the region, the *Industry* returned a half-year later with a full hull of whale oil.[7] For certain, Captain Boston was not the first Black man to participate in the emerging industry, but he and his crew exemplify the refuge and success that could be found on the high seas.

Nantucket, a town confined on an island with a relatively shallow port, had limited prospects to develop as the largest center for whaling. New Bedford, on the other hand, situated on mainland Massachusetts, possessed a deeper port, a more rapidly growing population, and greater commercial connectivity to the nation's East Coast. Twenty thousand people called New Bedford home by 1850, and, by some estimates, it was the nation's wealthiest

William Shorey and his wife, Julia Ann Shelton Shorey, and daughters, Zenobia Pearl and Victoria, ca. 1890s. National Park Service (NPS SAFR P00.2178x).

city per capita for several years after the War of 1812. Fueled by the whaling industry, New Bedford drew women and men from across the young nation. Others migrated from Western Europe, the Azores, and Cape Verde off the Atlantic coast of West Africa. Some came from as far away as the islands of the South Pacific.

New Bedford was home to several notable African Americans, including some of the era's most distinguished abolitionists and businessmen. Paul Cuffe, who at the time of his death in 1817 was one of the wealthiest men in the nation, hailed from New Bedford. Cuffe built his fortune in the shipping and whaling industries and later led efforts to settle those who had escaped slavery and free people of color in Sierra Leone, on the western coast of Africa.[8] American revolutionary Crispus Attucks lived briefly in New Bedford, as did abolitionist Frederick Douglass. Many lesser-known yet successful African Americans made their lives in New Bedford as well. In the years leading up to the Civil War, wealthy Black men such as Bela C. Perry, William Berry, and James Vassal wielded significant local influence.[9] At the same time, New Bedford also hosted out-of-work whalemen and others who flocked to the city in search of employment. The whaling industry was notoriously boom and bust, and many of those who arrived in New Bedford looking for work endured bouts of homelessness and destitution between jobs. Black whalers were among the last hired and first fired when the industry entered recession.[10]

Still, thousands of whalers claimed residency in New Bedford through the 1840s and 1850s. Historian Kathryn Grover estimated that in these years 18 percent of the New Bedford whalers arrived from slaveholding states, many, if not most, as fugitives. As many as seven hundred fugitives from slavery, men and women, lived in New Bedford, a greater proportion of the population than could be found in any other North American city.[11] Other Blacks arrived from Portugal and its colonies in the Azores and Cape Verde. These men were the backbone for the whaling industry as it shifted focus from the Atlantic and the nearly extinct right and sperm whales to the North Pacific and Arctic Oceans. There whalers targeted the plentiful and oil-rich bowheads. Not only were these whalers the first African Americans to make their way to Alaska, but they may also have been the first men from the United States to see the vast territory.[12]

The number of the formerly enslaved men who escaped their bondage to whale in Alaska's waters is impossible to know. As there are no known diaries or other written records by these whalers, details of their experiences around

Alaska are similarly lost to time. But the New Bedford captain logs provide insight as they describe whaling ships bound for the North Pacific as early as the 1830s. These ships scoured the waters off the Pacific Northwest and British Columbia; some made their way as far as Kodiak Island and toward the Aleutians. However, these ships rarely, if ever, came to shore. To do so would have risked conflict with the Russian American Company, which was then in control of much of the southern and eastern coasts of Alaska.

At least a few American whalers bypassed their Russian counterparts. Capt. Thomas Roys and his crew aboard the bark *Superior* left Sag Harbor on Long Island, New York, and after months at sea, Roys navigated through the Bering Strait and into the Arctic during the summer of 1848.[13] An ardent student of the voyages of the navigators James Cook and Frederick William Beechey, Roys was determined to sail where no other English-speaking captain had gone before and locate waters stocked with enough whales to ensure a fortune. Historian John Bockstoce called Roys's voyage through the Bering Strait "not only the most important whaling discovery of the nineteenth century but . . . one of the most important events in the history of the Pacific."[14]

While the Roys's expedition initiated more than seven decades of commercial whaling in the Arctic, the Bering Strait, and the northernmost reaches of the Pacific, the industry's peak in the region lasted only a brief time. Due to rapidly depleted whale populations, Grover notes, the "real window of opportunity for the settlement of fugitive whalemen in Alaska is quite small, from roughly 1842 to 1859."[15] Still, hundreds of ships sailed to Alaska's waters; expeditions lasted between one and four years, with stopovers across the Pacific. To note one representative example, the whaling ship *Arctic* sailed from Fairhaven, Massachusetts, on December 9, 1850. It made its way to the port of Lahaina on the Hawaiian island of Maui, before heading north; by then it had been at sea over a year. True to its name, the *Arctic* sailed to the Arctic Ocean through the Bering Strait. The *Arctic* also sailed to the Sea of Okhotsk off the coast of Russia. Two Black crewmen entered their names in the *Arctic*'s logbook: Stephen Hascell and John Stillwell. Each man identified his skin tone and hair texture. Logbooks recorded Black men with the letter *D* for "darkskin" or a *B* for "brownskin," and they noted one's "woolly" hair, marked with a *W* in another column. Logbooks also recorded where the whalers had last resided, but for obvious reasons, it would not have been prudent for a man who escaped enslavement to document the town he fled.[16] Ships and barks bound for the waters of the Northwest and the Arctic sailed with crews of at least fifteen to twenty men, a significant number of whom were described as dark, brown, or woolly.[17]

Most whalers sailed back to their home port or simply abandoned their whaling crews in San Francisco or Hawai'i, two popular ports of call.[18] Some whalers, however, spent significant time in Alaska. One man of African descent, John Davis, signed up for the *Marengo*'s whaling crew, bound for Alaska in 1848, around the same time Roys's *Superior* left port. In contrast to the *Superior*, the *Marengo* sailed to the Northwest coast and then to the Gulf of Alaska and into the Prince William Sound. Davis listed his place of residence as Salem, New Jersey, at the home of Abigail Goodwin.[19] Goodwin, a known Quaker abolitionist, worked with nearby activists in Philadelphia to assist fugitives.[20] While one cannot be certain if he was the first, Davis was among the earliest Black men to see the shores of Alaska.

Then again, we might look to Reuben Winslow and Robert Eliot, who in 1843 joined the crews of the *Lagoda* and the *Cossack*, respectively, which were bound for the Northwest coast. As with Davis, there can be no absolute proof that Winslow or Eliot was the first Black or fugitive from slavery to reach Alaska. Nonetheless, both men show up later in the logbooks as "no proofs."[21] This category indicated they were not white and probably arrived in northern port cities under ambiguous circumstances, likely as fugitives from slavery or fleeing their circumstances for one reason or another. Reports demonstrate whaling crews had a desertion rate as high as 30 percent. Still other whalers—many of whom were men of color or fugitives from slavery—arrived in New Bedford or other ports, set sail, and reached San Francisco, Hawai'i, or the islands of the South Pacific before deserting. Their whereabouts and final destinations may never be known. Following the discovery of gold in California in 1848, desertion rates spiked further. San Francisco emerged as a boomtown popular with fortune seekers and land speculators but also deserters and fugitives from slavery. Undoubtedly, the hope of a gold strike enticed several whalers. Desertion in San Francisco developed into such a problem that whaling captains bypassed the nascent city altogether by the early 1850s and wintered in Hawai'i or elsewhere in the South Pacific.[22]

In any case, Black men reached Alaska's southeastern panhandle via whaling ships by the early 1840s and sailed through the Bering Strait and into the Arctic by the late 1840s and early 1850s. The names of the barks and ships include the *Arctic, Bartholomew Gosnold, Cambria, Caroline, Cherokee, Copia,*

Hercules, Janus, Magnolia, Minerva, Roman 2d, Samuel Robertson, and *William Hamilton*, among others. The crews of these vessels included men with so-called woolly hair and dark skin. More than a quarter of the men on some of the voyages identified as Black or dark skinned. According to Grover, 74 percent of the Black crewmen claimed to have come from a free state.[23] It is likely that a noteworthy portion of those who claimed to have come from free states were fugitives from slavery who dissembled to avoid detection by those seeking to catch them. As soon as President Millard Fillmore signed legislation making it legal to pursue fugitives from slavery across state and territorial lines, as part of the Compromise of 1850, slave raiding ramped up in the North, particularly in the border states of Maryland and Delaware. Not surprisingly, the activity of the Underground Railroad and the movement of Black men into shipping, whaling, and other maritime professions increased during that pivotal decade.[24]

Before the Civil War, several African Americans arrived in Alaska and its waters, well before the United States purchased the territory from Russia and a century before it entered the union as the forty-ninth state.[25] Though Alaska was certainly not a stop on the Underground Railroad, whaling in the Pacific gave an untold number of men—certainly in the hundreds and possibly the thousands—one avenue to find work after escaping bondage in the American South. Other free Blacks sought employment in the whaling industry because of its reputation for practicing less discrimination than most land-based industries. And yet others may have been impressed into service on whaling ships under the fear or threat that they would be caught and returned to the South. A life at sea, while exceedingly harsh and perilous, ensured refuge from the slave catchers who, by the 1850s, increasingly roamed the nation's northern cities and towns. As historian W. Jeffrey Bolster has concluded, antebellum-era whaling was "dirty, dangerous, and notoriously exploitative ... [But] with limited options for employment, free blacks manned them in disproportionately large numbers. Slaves on the lam regarded whalers as a refuge, preferring to risk the vengeance of furious whales to that of slavemasters."[26]

Black Settlement and Whaling in Alaska after the Treaty of Cession

Hundreds of Black men who joined the whaling crews found an alternative to life in bondage in the South or the daily discrimination visited upon them in northern cities. These men risked much to advance in a climate and conditions radically different from anything they had previously known. In another sense, that has been the story of Black life in Alaska writ large. For certain, successive migrations in the latter decades of the nineteenth and twentieth centuries had nothing to do with escaping chattel slavery. The whalers who arrived and plied their trade in the frigid waters of the North Pacific and Arctic Oceans nonetheless revealed the aspirations of a people who believed the Far North provided a stronger chance to improve their lot in life. Sometimes they were right but not always.

A freedman and veteran, Isaiah King was one of the earliest post–Civil War figures to reach Arctic Alaska. Representative of a broader postwar movement of African Americans, King took to the sea for a brief stint as a whaler. Born into slavery in Washington, DC, in 1848, King escaped bondage thanks in large part to the efforts of his mother. The family fled to New Bedford and joined the ranks of the city's escaped slaves, free people of color, and motley crews of whalers and day laborers. Once the war broke out, King enlisted in Company D of the Massachusetts Fifth Cavalry. King took part in the siege of Petersburg and encountered gunfire but noted: "No. I never was wounded, for which I count myself very lucky." His service in the Union army took him to Texas, where he received an honorable discharge in October 1865. Soon after, he returned to New Bedford and took a job on the bark *Hercules* under the authority of Captain Howland. The *Hercules* left New Bedford at some point between 1866 and the spring of 1867. Bound for the Arctic, King found the life of a whaler "much too cold." Unfortunately, the crew timed the voyage poorly and were stranded in Alaska, where King and his fellow whalers spent "a year with the eskimos." Once rescued, he was enthusiastic to finally leave and head toward "the Orient." After reaching ports in China and Japan, the crew arrived back in New Bedford in 1871.[27]

Nearly fifty years after King's unplanned Alaska sojourn, anthropologist Livingston Jones documented the confused Tlingit, a southeastern Alaska Native people, response toward Blacks. Wrote Jones: "The first Negro that appeared in their country was a great puzzle to them. They held all kinds of theories as to what made him Black. Some maintained that he had lived where there was too much smoke."[28] Herbert Frisby, a war correspondent for the *Baltimore Afro-American*, reported much the same experience when visiting a remote Alaska village in 1944.[29] While King never elaborated on his interactions with Alaska Natives, his reception was likely similar. But in any case, King's experience captures the fleeting and itinerant nature of Black settlement and exploration in mid- to late-nineteenth-century Alaska. It also reveals the steady flow of Black men who participated in the whaling industry before and just after the 1867 Treaty of Cession. During these years the federal government never tabulated the precise number of settlers—let alone runaway slaves— in Alaska. Therefore, if King's presence in Alaska was limited to several months or a year in 1867 into 1868 or 1869, no census records would have reliably documented his stay.

The demographic picture becomes clearer once the United States exerted control over its newly acquired territory in the decade after 1867. In fact, by the 1870s American census takers counted 391 non-Native civilians living in Sitka; they did not yet reach the Arctic. Six modest army posts dotted the territory; each one was hastily constructed to house servicemen and lent the United States the impression of permanence in Alaska, especially in the panhandle of Alaska's Southeast. These early census records document six Black individuals. James Walker, Tom Steward, and Albert Richter, from the Caribbean and Central America, worked as cooks or bakers in Sitka. Walker married a Black woman named Maria. In addition to these four, Thomas and Martha Groves were listed as a "Colored couple, freshly married." Another Black woman, Mary Fitzgerald, arrived as a servant with an army family in 1874. Under the guardianship of Jenkins Fitzgerald, an army physician, Mary allegedly contracted a venereal infection, was fired, and returned to Portland. Little else is known about the circumstances that brought these men and women to Alaska or what their fate may have been.[30]

By the 1880s Charles Hallock, a white journalist, naturalist, and champion of the Treaty of Cession, made his way to Alaska's southeastern panhandle and confirmed the wisdom of the US purchase of the territory in his publication, *Our New Alaska*. A small population of Black men living alongside the Indigenous Tlingit in Juneau was one of the many surprises Hallock encountered: "Baths there are hot and cold, and shaving-parlors with veritable Black men behind the chairs, quite comfortable and luxurious to observe and enjoy."[31] According to Hallock, two of the Black Alaskans "under stress of local pressure, have instituted a very creditable barber shop."[32] He concluded: "There were no less than five negroes in Juneau last year . . . The African is as widely scattered as the Israelite!"[33]

In 1900 the census offered a more comprehensive portrait of Alaska's population than the anecdotal observations and written accounts of men such as Hallock or the unreliable clumsiness of Alaska's first official census records. The 1900 census counted over 63,000 people in Alaska and for the first time considered the reaches of the territory's capacious interior and intricate coastline. Indigenous people formed a majority, though the white population boomed because of the gold rushes. Notably, these records include 168 Black settlers who lived in the territory: 151 men and 17 women. Of the total Black population, 98 lived in Skagway. Most Blacks who arrived in the 1890s did so with the United States military and kept order as prospectors and gold miners passed through on their way to Dawson. The census counted no Black children.[34]

Once the Klondike Gold Rush entered its fourth and fifth years (1900–1901), 484 non-Native men resided on Alaska's western coast, and several hundred more settled along the southeastern portion of the territory. Most of these settlers simply passed through to the goldfields of Canada's Yukon Territory. Four whaling stations remained along the northwestern coast and marked the location where whalers settled for the season. According to the 1890 census, most were white, but ninety-seven were "all other [races] . . . negroes, mulattoes, Hawaiians, Malays, and Portuguese mulattoes from the Cape Verde Islands." The census justified its lack of precision by asserting the effort to count everyone was "inadvisable, partly on account of their small number, but chiefly because they all belong to the class of temporary and transient residents of Alaska, being nearly all engaged in the whaling industry."[35]

While these newcomers had little interest in permanently settling in coastal Alaska, there were exceptions. Within that population of ninety-seven, nonwhite whalers spread across the western coast, at least seven identified as Black. Thomas C. George remains the best documented of this group and an example of a man who stayed in the territory for several years. George, born in 1864 in St. Thomas, Virgin Islands, made his way north to the United States as a boatsteerer, or harpooner, on whaling vessels. According to Jim Allen, one of his shipmates, George "arrived at Point Hope only a week before I did, but he found himself a place to live."[36] By the early 1900s George had organized his own whaling crew and married an Iñupiat woman named Owngachuck. The couple raised three children. George settled in Point Hope, north of the Arctic Circle, and developed a relationship with the Alaska Natives who lived in the area.

Thomas George's cordial relations with Alaska Natives he encountered along the coast contrasted with a whaling industry that had long been at odds with the area's Indigenous people. Commercial whaling devastated the local bowhead population and later the walrus population, both of which were vital to the subsistence of the Iñupiat and Yup'ik of coastal Alaska.[37] For this reason the Iñupiat seldom welcomed the whaling crews. Conflict sometimes broke out between Indigenous whalers and their commercial rivals. As John Bockstoce reported, captains complained about Alaska's Native people and viewed them as stubborn, believing they should be dealt with coercively. One whaler, John W. Kelly, referred to the Iñupiat as "a band of hypocrites and shylocks, possessing a large share of brazen effrontery."[38] Such perceptions sometimes led to violence. In July 1877 the brig *William H. Allen* sailed from Honolulu through the Bering Strait between the Diomede Islands and Cape Prince of Wales. Capt. George Gilley described a fight that broke out as a trading deal fell through between his crew and the Iñupiat who lived in a coastal village on the cape. Gilley claimed that treachery and drunkenness on the part of the Native men led to a deadly gunfight. Gilley and his crew of Hawaiians, African Americans, and Cape Verdeans killed thirteen Alaska Natives; one of Gilley's crew died in the scuffle. The episode reverberated for years, and trust between the whalers and the Native population around Cape Prince of Wales never recovered.[39]

Similar stories reverberated stateside as firsthand accounts made their way across the continent. Walter Noble Burns, the famous novelist and writer of western fiction, recounted his year as a whaler aboard a ship captained by William Shorey. Aptly titled *A Year with a Whaler*, Burns recalled making landfall in Alaska along the Bering Sea coast in Port Clarence. He found the "Eskimos were as primitive in their life and mental processes as people who had stepped into the present out of the world ten thousand years ago."[40] Burns continued that although there was "little crime among them . . . they sometimes steal from white men—the sailors on the brig were warned that they would steal anything not tied down."[41] Though Burns repeated racist assumptions, his views echoed a majority of the whalers—be they white, Black, or Pacific Islander. The very prospect of commercially whaling for bowheads was bound to ensure tension with Alaska's Indigenous people. The disruption caused by the introduction of a commercial economy into the subsistence culture of coastal-based Alaska Natives that began in earnest with the whaling industry would of course continue unabated in the generations to follow.

In the North Pacific and Arctic Oceans, the contours of race thus played out quite differently than they would have elsewhere in the United States. Multiracial crews of whalers found themselves in the uncharacteristic position of wielding power over a disempowered population of Indigenous people who sought to defend their way of life. In this limited context, the exigencies of an industrial market economy cast men of African descent—among others—as aggressors in a foreign land.

In the final decades of the nineteenth century and into the twentieth, whalers pushed farther into the Arctic and very nearly exhausted the bowhead population. All the while, the crews retained their multicultural characteristics, representing men from around the world. But in 1924 the last whaling ship set sail from New Bedford. By then whaling was no longer central to the economy. Petroleum, coal, and electricity powered the nation. Still, it was a landmark moment. While commercial whaling continued in a limited capacity in the United States through the early 1970s—subsistence whaling still occurs in Alaska—the multiracial crews of drifters, runaway slaves, freedmen, and immigrant laborers from around the world were no longer prevalent.[42]

Whaling brought more Blacks into contact with Alaska and the Pacific Northwest than any other industry during the latter half of the nineteenth and early twentieth centuries. Most of these men had experiences not wholly dissimilar from Isaiah King or William Shorey. These men never intended their stay in Alaska or the Arctic more generally to last beyond a couple of months. A small number found the experience meaningful enough to stay and put down roots. At the same time, the United States exerted more influence in Alaska's waters and on land because of two events: first, the end of the Civil War, followed by the Treaty of Cession and the conquest of the American West, renewed the nation's commitment to more thoroughly police its waters and western lands. Second, gold strikes in the Canadian Yukon and Alaska interior brought thousands of additional people north and west. Beginning in 1896 and lasting over fifteen years, the gold rush era demonstrated Alaska's potential for the extraction of mineral resources. Together, the military and the extraction industry have continued to present a base of employment in Alaska as well as being pillars of its economy. Then, as today, Black men and women have arrived through one or both sectors, including one of the most skilled captains and seamen in the nation's maritime history: Michael Healy.

Black whalers posing for a photo at Point Barrow, ca. 1900s. Alaska and Polar Regions Collections and Archives, University of Alaska Fairbanks (66-10-136n).

Michael Healy and the US Revenue Cutter Service

After the Treaty of Cession, the US Revenue Cutter Service—the forerunner to the US Coast Guard—patrolled Alaska waters and maintained a presence along the coast; it was among the first federal institutions to do so. No captain assumed as large a role in the region than Michael Healy, a man of mixed African and Irish descent. After the Civil War, Healy developed a reputation as a skilled navigator and demanding captain. Born in Georgia in 1839, Healy was the son of an Irish-born slaveholder and a Black woman enslaved on the plantation. Many white slave owners fathered children with Black women they held as property, but it was unusual for enslaved and free people of color to receive an education and travel about the country as Michael Healy did in his youth.[43]

After the Civil War, however, Healy faced limits to his advancement, and it remained nearly impossible for a light-skinned, mixed-race man to become anyone other than a second-class citizen in the South. But Healy's skin tone and education allowed to him to pass as white, an identity he apparently embraced. Like other Black men, Healy looked to the United States armed forces for employment. But unlike the Freedmen's Bureau, where thousands of Black men served in the years after the Civil War, the US Revenue Cutter Service prohibited African Americans from enlisting. Therefore, Healy kept his status as a man of African descent hidden as he sought a commission at sea. In 1865 he received one when none other than Abraham Lincoln signed Healy's commission, making him a third lieutenant.[44] Over the next forty years, he ascended the ranks of maritime law enforcement in the Pacific. He claimed the identity of a white Irishman and received access to better jobs and housing than he would have as an African American.

As soon as Secretary of State William H. Seward finalized the terms of the 1867 Treaty of Cession with his Russian counterparts, the Revenue Cutter Service provided the bulwark of American defense and ensured the nation's standing along twenty thousand miles of Pacific coastline from California to Alaska. In addition to patrolling choppy waters, Healy and others in the service aided ships, whalers, and commercial fishermen in distress and maintained law and order on the high and tumultuous seas of the North Pacific.[45] He always maintained a white identity and distanced himself from his African ancestry. As he and his crew patrolled the North Pacific and waters of Alaska, Healy commonly remarked that he encountered only "white men and natives," counting himself among the former.[46]

In 1883 Healy became a captain and solidified his standing as one of the most skilled navigators of the North Pacific's notoriously treacherous waters. He captained several cutters, including the *Rush*, the *Bear*, the *Corwin*, and the *McCulloch*. Healy and his crew had proven themselves to be the most reliable—and sometimes only—federal presence in the more than three thousand nautical miles from San Francisco to Barrow, on Alaska's North Slope. The whalers who operated off Alaska's coast viewed Healy as an adept seaman and a potential lifeline. In one instance, Healy and his crew aboard the *Bear* persevered in the face of gale force Arctic winds off the coast of Point Barrow to save 160 men stranded amid the icy sea.[47] The same year, aboard the *Corwin*, Healy and Lt. George Stoney mapped the Kobuk River. While the Iñupiat people had used the river for generations to fish and travel through Alaska's interior, Healy and Stoney were most likely the first non-Native men to set their sights on the Kobuk Valley and the western edge of the Brooks Range. Today it is a national park.[48]

Healy also developed relations with Alaska Natives who lived along the Bering and Chukchi Seas. These communities relied on marine mammals for subsistence, which led them into conflict with commercial whalers. As whalers arrived in greater numbers after Roys's 1848 trip through the Bering Strait, Healy served as an arbiter between outsiders who hunted the bowheads for profit and Indigenous people who relied on them for food. In Healy's travels he noted that Indigenous men and women on the Russian side of the sea in Siberia supplemented their diets with reindeer, or domesticated caribou. They herded the animals on the tundra and used their hides for shelter and clothing and their meat as a source of protein. Though Alaska's Indigenous people had long hunted caribou in the wild, reindeer herding held potential as an alternative means of subsistence. Healy teamed up with missionaries, most notably Sheldon Jackson, to introduce reindeer herding to the region. The two led crews aboard the *Bear* between the two continents, shuttling over twenty caribou each trip. By the 1890s the Iñupiat and Yup'ik on Alaska's western coast and the Seward Peninsula came to regard reindeer as one source of food and took to herding in a limited capacity.[49] According to historian James M. O'Toole, reindeer herding never proliferated in Alaska as it did in Siberia, "but their [Healy and Jackson] efforts showed a genuine concern for Alaska and its people at a time when that was rare for representatives of the United States."[50]

Given his position, Healy was a rare, official representative of American power and agent for American interests in late-nineteenth-century Alaska.

Though he developed a working relationship with the Iñupiat and Yupik along the coast of the Seward Peninsula, Healy dealt harshly with Indigenous people elsewhere in Alaska. In fact, he played an instrumental role in the infamous, deadly bombardment of Angoon, a Tlingit village on Admiralty Island in Southeast Alaska. The episode took place in October 1882, after a series of escalations and eventual communications breakdowns between federal authorities and Tlingit elders. Federal authorities accused the Tlingit people of Angoon of taking hostages; the Tlingit accused the United States of failing to follow through with compensation for the earlier death of a shaman who was highly regarded in the town of Angoon. After the Tlingit failed to return a requested number of blankets to federal agents, US naval commander Edgar Merriman ordered his forces to fire on the village and its people. Merriman and Healy, along with his crew aboard the *Corwin*, shelled the Tlingit with Gatling guns, a howitzer, and cannon fire. Once the smoke settled, six Tlingit children had been killed and several others injured. After the bombardment, Healy, Merriman, and the men under their command stole blankets and other key supplies that the Tlingit relied upon to subsist through the winter, causing more men, women, and children to die from exposure in the months to follow.[51]

Tlingit scholar Rosita Worl and anthropologist Philip Drucker have suggested that more sinister motives lay behind the massacre: the military had located a rich seam of coal and required the land upon which the Tlingit had long lived to access it and bring it to market. In any case, the bombardment of Angoon was the third military assault on a Native village by the United States; American forces had attacked Wrangell and Kake, also in Southeast Alaska, in 1869.[52] Capt. Michael Healy, passing as a white man, earnestly participated in the expansionist project of developing an American empire at the dawn of the twentieth century. In Alaska fashioning that empire required the systematic subjugation of Indigenous people, just as it had elsewhere in the American West in the preceding decades.[53]

Beyond Healy's fraught relationship with Alaska's Indigenous population, not everyone stateside appreciated his skills at sea or the lifestyle of the men he commanded. The Woman's Christian Temperance Union (WCTU) viewed masculine seafaring culture as rife with the excesses of drink and debauchery. Healy, in particular, offended the sensibilities of temperance leaders and many others. The WCTU described Healy as a man who succumbed to his addictions, namely "demon rum." The temperance union demanded that the young men who left their homes for work in the whaling industry, protecting the coast, or laboring in other dangerous jobs in the North Pacific have "a temperate and humane man" as a boss. Healy, they believed, was neither temperate nor humane.[54]

Corroborating the allegations of the WCTU, Captain Healy handled his crew with harsh discipline fueled by alcohol-induced rage that bordered on abuse. He twice appeared in court under charges of drunkenness, recklessness, and failure to meet the protocols of the Revenue Cutter Service. In one instance he was alleged to have verbally assaulted a woman on board; other allegations included spitting on crew, physical assault, and at least one bout of suicidal rage.[55] Though he was never found guilty of the various transgressions, his reputation suffered. That he was never stripped of his rank, according to maritime historians Dennis Noble and Truman Strobidge, demonstrated his value to the service and adeptness at sea. His nickname, "Hell Roaring" Mike Healy, suggested a man with a short temper. Few, however, disputed his skills as a captain or his ability to brave harsh conditions.[56]

At the peak of his career, Healy knew Alaska's icy waters better than any other single individual. As evidence of his reputation as a sailor, Healy led several men, including John Muir, the naturalist and cofounder of the Sierra Club, up the Alaska coast in the 1880s and 1890s into what is today's Glacier Bay National Park. Though the 1899 Harriman Expedition is sometimes credited with delivering greater awareness of Alaska's natural beauty and its geologic features to a popular audience, Healy's work with John Muir set the stage.[57] Despite increasing evidence of an escalating drinking habit and what crew members aboard the *McCulloch* described as a psychotic episode in 1900 somewhere between the Aleutians and Seattle, Healy captained ships until 1903. He succumbed to heart failure a year later.[58]

Closer to the topic of this book, Healy crossed paths with William Shorey several years before he led the Harriman Expedition. In 1892 Shorey and his crew ran into trouble outside St. Paul. In the raucous waters of the Bering Sea, the shipwrecked men lurched for assistance. When another ship came through, they believed they would get back to port in Dutch Harbor in the Aleutians. However, the ship that was supposed to assist them left during the cover of night, and Shorey's men were all but abandoned. Over a week later, Captain Healy and his crew came through the sea and assisted the shipwreck; dozens were on the brink of starvation. Word spread back to the states of the incident, and Healy's reputation grew as a result. The circumstances under

Capt. Michael A. Healy on the deck of the US Revenue Cutter *Rush* with passengers, ca. 1900s. John Taylor White Photography Collection, University of Alaska Fairbanks Archives.

which the two men met could be viewed as nothing short of harrowing. But that a man born enslaved in Georgia and another born one generation out of enslavement in Barbados would have such a chance encounter in the Bering Sea reveals the extent to which the Black diaspora continued to shape the world as it touched down in nearly all corners, including Alaska.[59]

From Sailing the Sea to Settling the Land

Healy and the thousands of others who sought distant land and sea, be it in the goldfields of the Klondike or the icy waters of the North Pacific, shaped Jack London's perception of Alaska and the Yukon in the late nineteenth century. London's 1904 novel, *The Sea-Wolf*, conveyed the drama and intrigue of life in the circumpolar North; it portrayed the men at sea as a particularly hardy, steadfast bunch.[60] Healy relentlessly navigated the waters of the North Pacific and mastered them as much as possible given the limits of his era. In 1999, ninety-five years after his death, the Revenue Cutter Service's successor, the US Coast Guard, named an icebreaker after him, the USCG *Healy*.

The story of Michael Healy—from his achievements at sea to his encounters with Alaska Natives to his many detractors and his inclination to excessive and abusive behavior—must, of course, be understood in context. As a man who fled the South and passed as white, no one at the time interpreted Healy's rise in the US Revenue Cutter Service through the lens of Black advancement; his African ancestry remained hidden and seldom noted publicly. Still, it is imperative to note the long journey Healy made as the son of an enslaved woman in Georgia to become a captain who commanded crews on the Pacific's turbulent waters. Indeed, most Black men and women could not pass as white, let alone find work with a nascent federal agency like the revenue cutters. But that did not stop African Americans from coming to Alaska. Some arrived because they believed whaling might provide a decent life. Others, like Healy, served their nation as it expanded into the Pacific. In either case, Black history in Alaska began at sea. But it did not stay there. At century's end Blacks resided in Cape Smyth, Point Barrow, Point Belcher, Port Clarence, and likely elsewhere; these were settlements that ringed Alaska's Arctic and Bering Sea coasts. Not long after, Black men served as military law enforcement in the stopover towns en route to the goldfields after the famous strike along Bonanza Creek in Canada's Yukon. Black women started businesses and participated in the gold rush too. The next chapter captures their stories.

CHAPTER TWO

Black in the Gold Rush Era

LIKE MICHAEL HEALY, MELVIN DEMPSEY WAS BORN ENSLAVED. THE son of a North Carolina Cherokee plantation owner and an African American slave, Dempsey escaped the bloody collapse of the Republican-led Reconstruction government in his home state and the violence associated with Jim Crow rule in the late nineteenth century. Dempsey caught gold fever and came north to prospect. He was among the many thousands who flooded Alaska and Canada's Yukon in search of gold. Displaced by the industrial upheaval of the period and the intensity of white supremacy throughout the nation, Black men like Dempsey assumed great risk to prosper and attain a quality of life far beyond that which they knew in their youth.[1]

In contrast to the popular conception of a grizzled, white miner with pickax in hand and sourdough starter tucked in close to his chest, Dempsey was among a small but notable group of African Americans who traveled north to settle in Alaska during the gold rush. Dempsey first arrived in Valdez via Alaska's Prince William Sound, aboard the ship *Alliance* in February 1898, more than a year into the Klondike Gold Rush. A veteran of the previous gold and silver booms along the Front Range of Colorado's Rocky Mountains, Dempsey had exhausted his claims there and moved on. When he finally settled in Alaska, Dempsey was a relatively old forty years of age; with over two decades of experience swinging an axe, his strength had waned. Miners and prospectors worked their bodies relentlessly and struggled to maintain such a brutal pace for more than ten or fifteen years.[2]

Recognizing his physical limitations, Dempsey had little interest in working the goldfields along the Yukon River and Bonanza Creek. He knew the life of a prospector well enough to understand its grueling conditions and the luck it took to walk away a rich man. He had grown weary of the life of a full-time miner. Rather, Dempsey knew other ways to earn a living. Miners required basic services and entertainment. In response, Dempsey opened a restaurant and inn in Valdez, the fledgling town with an ice-free port, rivers, and mountain passes that provided access to the Alaska Interior and the Yukon. Always a miner at heart, he also intermittently worked a few small claims along the Chisna and Chistochina Rivers, north of town. Dempsey also established a Christian Endeavor Society, a nondenominational organization that promoted a "Christian life among its members."[3] The society also housed a small reading room and provided a gathering space.

Within months of his arrival in Alaska, he was appointed a town trustee in Valdez and later elected as a marshal. Unlike many who came to Alaska during the 1890s and early 1900s, Dempsey never viewed it solely as a place to make money and then leave; indeed, by all accounts he loved the land and the lifestyle.[4] Despite his age and local prominence, Dempsey's experience was not wholly divergent from that of many other fortune seekers in Alaska, regardless of race. Yet Dempsey, like Healy, may have passed and presented himself as someone he was not. After his 1915 death, the *Valdez Daily Prospector*, his hometown newspaper, described him as "full blooded Cherokee," likely a reflection of Dempsey's attempt to emphasize his Indigenous ancestry and elide his African ancestry.[5] To be identified as Black presented a potential liability for Dempsey and a risk he may not have been willing to take. In any case, his success in Alaska hinged upon the steady influx of miners who would pass through to seek their fortune. Resource exploitation—from the era of Russian colonialism to the American whaling industry—had long been a pillar of Alaska's economy, and the gold rush was simply a continuation of this history.

African Americans, men and women, in notable numbers, were a part of this rush; they included miners, entertainers, politicians, and soldiers. Some, like Robert Creecy and Lena Walton, worked claims. Walton would emerge as one of the wealthiest women in America. Others operated cafés, boardinghouses, and brothels. In the coastal towns of Skagway and Dyea in southern Alaska, buffalo soldiers imposed law and order as thousands arrived on their way to the goldfields deep in the interior of Alaska and Canada's Yukon. These soldiers built infrastructure and ensured a modicum of safety and security at a time when the United States had a rather limited presence otherwise. Indeed, Black migration to the northern reaches of the continent cannot be disentangled from the broader history of Alaska and the Yukon during the 1890s and into the early twentieth century. This chapter explores the vital contributions of the Black individuals who settled in Alaska after having been drawn to what turned out to be the nation's last great gold rush.

A Gold Rush in the North

In 1896 George Carmack and Skookum Jim Mason struck gold along Bonanza Creek, a tributary of the Klondike River in Canada's Yukon, about a hundred miles east of the Alaska border. A rush into Alaska and the Yukon ensued. The story is familiar to those who know the history of Alaska, the Yukon, and the American West. Like other gold rushes in North America, tens of thousands of young men—and some women too—arrived from around the world. Most of them left within a year or two and did so poorer than when they arrived. Only a few struck it rich. At the peak of the Klondike Gold Rush, in 1898, the town of Dawson, in the Yukon, swelled to nearly forty thousand residents. Other towns that hosted prospectors, argonauts, swindlers, and those who sought a payday also experienced rapid growth. Seattle developed as the key transport point in the Pacific Northwest en route to the northern goldfields. Thousands of others eventually made their way to Skagway and Dyea.[6]

Seattle was better equipped than the two Alaska towns to handle the people who arrived in advance of their expedition north. Skagway and Dyea had neither the infrastructure nor the accommodations to support thousands of miners. Both towns lacked law enforcement, and the young men who came through often clashed with the local Indigenous population and showed little respect for the surrounding environment. Making matters more complicated, the Northwest Mounted Police—now the Royal Canadian Mounted Police—required all who crossed the border into the Yukon to do so provisioned with at least one year's worth of food and supplies. As a result, gold rushers needed to haul roughly one ton of goods up the steep and unforgiving Chilkoot Trail or the less steep but equally treacherous White Pass.[7]

The Klondike Gold Rush thus facilitated the theretofore largest migration of settlers into Alaska since the United States signed the Treaty of Cession with Russia. For the thousands of fortune-seeking men and women, the setting became increasingly more dangerous and lawless the farther north they traveled. The federal government soon sent troops to patrol Skagway,

Dyea, and for a brief time, Wrangell (sometimes posted as Wrangel), a small settlement farther south on the Alaska panhandle; barracks already existed in the vast territory in such places as Fort Saint Michael, Fort Gibbon, Fort Egbert, Fort Davis, and Fort Liscum, with detachments in Rampart and Circle. Reports of crime and violence increased as prospectors arrived with thousands of pounds of personal belongings and valuables. One patrolman from the Northwest Mounted Police declared, "Skagway was little better than hell on earth, about the roughest place on earth."[8] To address the apparent social dysfunction, four companies of the Fourteenth Infantry deployed to Alaska in February 1898. Companies B and H arrived in Dyea; Skagway hosted Companies A and G. An additional Hospital Corps briefly served in Dyea. The arrival of the soldiers quelled moderate unrest at the camps, but by the end of April, most of the stampeders moved on to the goldfields in preparation for the long days of summer. Companies H and B of the Fourteenth Infantry remained in Alaska through the spring of 1899, at which point the Twenty-Fourth Infantry relieved them.[9]

The Twenty-Fourth Infantry: Alaska's Buffalo Soldiers

The Twenty-Fourth Infantry Regiment was a segregated unit composed of Black men, known colloquially as "buffalo soldiers." Plains Indians allegedly bestowed the moniker upon the troops after having encountered them during the Indian Wars that embroiled much of the American West in the post–Civil War era. Indeed, Black troops had fought in every major American conflict. Yet they encountered more rigid segregation as the nineteenth century evolved. In 1820 the US Congress barred Black men from serving as regulars in the army. However, thousands of Black soldiers nonetheless flocked to the Union lines during the Civil War and were subsequently organized into segregated regiments known as the United States Colored Troops. These troops fought valiantly throughout the Civil War; namely, the Fifty-Fourth and Fifty-Fifth Regiments of Massachusetts saw action and faced unspeakable hardship. Still, the Black troops deserted at a consistently lower rate than their white counterparts, likely the result of having fewer chances to advance in civilian life and the deeply held conviction that they were fighting for their freedom.[10]

In 1866 Congress recognized the valor of the soldiers and formally established six Black divisions that would become widely recognized as the buffalo soldiers. These included four infantry regiments and two cavalry regiments. Three years later, Congress reorganized the Black regiments, this time consolidating the four infantry regiments into two: the Twenty-Fourth and Twenty-Fifth. The Twenty-Fourth Infantry Regiment was primarily composed of Black troops who served in the Thirty-Eighth US Colored Infantry Regiment and the Forty-First US Colored Infantry Regiment. The Thirty-Eighth and Forty-First Colored Infantry included Black soldiers who saw action in the Civil War and would participate in the Reconstruction efforts in the postwar South. But in the main, these regiments would serve primarily in the American West and participate in one of the most formative eras of American expansion.[11]

Many of the men born into enslavement fought for their freedom in such places as Texas and Virginia during the war. Other soldiers originally hailed from the North and Midwest but served for similar reasons. Indeed, even those who had never experienced enslavement nevertheless knew well the sting of discrimination and race hatred. Both the formerly enslaved and the free Black soldiers viewed military service as a way to lay claim to equal citizenship and showcase their value to a nation that had too often devalued them. Black soldiers received ten dollars per month, from which they had to pay back three dollars for their clothing and uniform allowance. White soldiers received thirteen dollars in monthly compensation, with no deduction for clothing. But despite the inequitable compensation and substandard conditions, many Black men viewed life in the army as one the few employment options that afforded regular pay, food, and shelter as well as the dignity that came with wearing the uniform of the nation's military.[12]

Upon being reorganized into the Twenty-Fourth Infantry, most of the 655 Black enlisted men first garrisoned at Fort McKavett, Texas, a remote outpost 180 miles west of San Antonio. A small contingent of others took up positions at Forts Davis, Concho, and Stockton, presenting a 250-mile front along the Texas-Mexico borderlands. From these posts, the infantry served as agents of the nation's imperial expansion in the West. The Twenty-Fourth Infantry, like other Black regiments, provided logistical support as the US military conquered the expansive Great Plains, Rockies, and Pacific Coast from the regions' Indigenous inhabitants. Beyond Texas, the Twenty-Fourth also spent time in Oklahoma's Indian Country, where the soldiers serviced the reservation land to which the Apache, Arapaho, Cheyenne, and Comanche Indians had been forcefully relocated during the last quarter of the nineteenth century.[13]

Before arriving in Alaska, the Twenty-Fourth Infantry also served in New Mexico and Arizona during the late 1880s and 1890s; the regiment performed many of the duties in the Far West as it had in Texas and Oklahoma. By the time Company L arrived in Alaska, the men had extensive experience building roads and forts, locating and securing scarce water, and protecting the supply trains along the trade routes and trails that led settlers deeper into the North American interior. They had proven themselves in various roles, from support to combat; several had gained recognition for their service. Twenty-three Black soldiers who served with the Twenty-Fourth received Medals of Honor, and the regiment had gained the accolades of the white officers who led them. In one incident, Sgt. Benjamin Brown and Cpl. Isaiah Mays thwarted a robbery as they escorted the army's paymaster, Maj. Gen. Joseph W. Wham, from Fort Grant to Fort Thomas in Arizona. Wham noted, "I served in the infantry during the entire Civil War . . . in sixteen major battles, but I never witnessed better fighting than shown by these colored soldiers." Indeed, the buffalo soldiers had proven indispensable to the broader effort to gain control of the vast interior and borderlands of the American West.[14]

The Twenty-Fourth Infantry also deployed beyond the continental United States. They participated in the famed charge up San Juan Hill in Cuba during the Spanish-American War. Just two years after the Supreme Court delivered its decision in *Plessy v. Ferguson*, upholding the legality of the "separate but equal" doctrine, Black soldiers came under heavy fire but prevailed on July 1, 1898. For certain, some men recognized the contradictions of fighting for a country that did not permit them the freedom of their fellow white soldiers. The *Plessy* decision solidified the status of African Americans as second-class citizens and ensured that the government would not recognize their humanity. As historian Willard Gatewood has observed: "The black soldier appeared vacillating and uncertain in his observation regarding America's imperialist ventures. To an extraordinary degree he became the victim of conflicting emotions and attitude spawned by his unique position in these ventures."[15] The nation's expansion into the West, the Caribbean, and Pacific were in fact predicated upon the doctrine of "manifest destiny"—the projection of white superiority and belief that the world's lighter people were inherently fit to govern the darker people.[16]

Still, the soldiers dutifully took up arms, secured the Spanish Blockhouse, and set up guard to protect the strategically vital city of Santiago. That the soldiers were sent to Cuba in the first place revealed racist assumptions of the military at the turn of the century. The buffalo soldiers composed the "immune regiments" of Black men who white officers believed possessed race-based immunity to tropical diseases and were, as a result, uniquely suited to endure battlefield conditions in Cuba. The *New York Times* noted that these men "have not passed through a yellow-fever epidemic" but were nonetheless "thoroughly acclimated to a hot climate and are accustomed to outdoor life."[17] However, in contrast to the predictions of military leaders who believed that Black soldiers possessed immunity to tropical illnesses, the Twenty-Fourth Infantry Regiment suffered a higher death rate from disease than they did from combat. Lt. Isaac C. Jenks, a white officer in command of the Twenty-Fourth, recalled that "no pen can depict the suffering endured by the officers and men in this regiment during the time it was in Cuba, and those who endured the agony of the ordeal decline to speak of it except in confidence."[18] Racist and unfounded justifications for the use of Black soldiers in some circumstances and not in others would continue well into the twentieth century.

Despite the fatal toll that illness and fighting took on the infantry, the Twenty-Fourth heroically completed their mission and left Cuba by the end of the summer of 1898. They sailed to New York before once again heading out West to Fort Douglas, Utah, where additional soldiers joined the garrison.[19] In March 1899 the Twenty-Fourth added two new companies to accommodate the increased size of the regiment, Company L and Company M. Company L would head north to Alaska, and Company M remained elsewhere in the West and eventually deployed to the Philippines. Amid the rise of Jim Crow segregation, coupled with the nation's rapid imperial expansion, Black soldiers then proved time and again their centrality to a country that grew ever more stratified by race.[20] These men held out hope that service to one's country would ensure full inclusion in it. Their actions largely reinforced the words of abolitionist Frederick Douglass, who proclaimed, "Once let the Black men get upon his person the brass letters *US*, let him get an eagle on his button, and a musket on his shoulder, and bullets in his pocket, and there is no power on Earth or under Earth which can deny that he has earned the right of citizenship in the United States."[21]

Company L in Alaska

Two months after being established, the men of Company L left Utah for brief stopovers at the Presidio in San Francisco and then the Vancouver Barracks in Washington, not far from Portland, Oregon. After a stay of nine days in the barracks, in May the soldiers traveled to Seattle, where they boarded the SS *Humboldt*, destination Alaska. Just about a week later, forty-six soldiers disembarked at Fort Wrangel under the command of Lieutenant Jenks. However, most of the men with Company L were bound for Dyea under the command of Capt. Henry Hovey, where over one hundred men arrived between May and July 1899. The largest contingent came ashore at Dyea on May 20 just as the white soldiers with the Fourteenth Infantry prepared to leave the area. The *Seattle Post-Intelligencer* reported, "Colored Troops to Relieve Soldiers at Wrangell [sic] and Dyea."[22]

Dyea and Wrangell (Fort Wrangel) were to serve as primary entry points to the Yukon and Alaska's interior. But after an avalanche damaged Dyea in the spring of 1898 and the construction of the Yukon White Pass Railroad bypassed it, the town was gradually abandoned. A fire further expedited the death of the Dyea townsite in the summer of 1899. Skagway thus emerged as the more important and populated of Alaska's coastal gold rush settlements. The area around Fort Wrangel, just over 250 miles south of Skagway and Dyea along Alaska's inside passage, also briefly hosted miners on their way to the Yukon's gold mining districts. However, the southerly location of Wrangell on the peninsula rendered it a less desirable port of entry for those bound for Dawson. These three communities (Dyea, Skagway, and Wrangell) had long been home to the Indigenous Tlingit people, who had for generations lived, subsisted, and traded along much of Alaska's panhandle. Not new to settlers, the Tlingit had sustained contact with European traders during the era of Russian exploration and colonization from the 1730s through the 1860s.[23]

When Company L arrived in Alaska, the territory retained its reputation for lawlessness and was still very much in throes of the Klondike Gold Rush. As the previous soldiers imposed a semblance of peace and order, tensions persisted between Alaska Natives and the settlers who treated them with disrespect and, in some cases, violent contempt. Gambling, prostitution, drunken revelry, and brawling remained common pursuits in the makeshift settlements.[24] Just before Company L arrived in Skagway, one notorious outlaw, Jefferson Randolph "Soapy" Smith, fixed card games, extorted greenhorns, and terrorized those who ran afoul with him and his gang. Smith's shady ways caught up with him, and he wound up on the wrong side of a gun during an infamous shootout on Juneau wharf. The death of Soapy Smith in the summer of 1898 marked a turning point and represented the peak of

Skagway's frontier days. Still, Company L found a settler and prospector population woefully unprepared to live and prosper in the North.[25]

Under the command of Capt. Henry Walter Hovey, Company L continued the law enforcement efforts of the Fourteenth Infantry Regiment. As they had elsewhere, the soldiers in the company also provided food and built permanent structures to shelter the men who came through Alaska on their way to goldfields around Dawson City. The more than one hundred soldiers constructed roads and bridges to connect the town with outlying settlements. The company remained in Alaska until May 1902.[26] Of the men who arrived in 1899 with Company L, at least ten came from Kentucky. The Bluegrass State sent more Black men than anywhere else to serve in Alaska.[27] Massachusetts, Pennsylvania, Tennessee, and Virginia also sent numerous men to Alaska to serve with Company L. The 1900 census provided the most in-depth look at Alaska's population growth and illustrates the impact that the gold rush had upon the state's demographics. The regiment's first sergeant, Robert O'Connor, brought his wife, Sussie, from Louisville. She was one of the few women in the makeshift town. Yet with meager salaries, the ennui of camp life, and gold fever, desertion among the men in Company L was relatively high, particularly among the Black soldiers, who had earlier had a reputation for low desertion rates and high rates of reenlistment—trends that dated back to the Civil War.[28]

The men faced discrimination from white prospectors, settlers, and others who called Skagway home. Tensions at times boiled over into open conflict. In one instance, in April 1901, a white madam known as Marie Melgrim refused to admit a Black soldier, Pvt. Robert Grant, entrance into a local saloon and brothel on Seventh Avenue, a central spot for nightlife in town. Angered by the indignity of being turned away because of his race, Grant threw a rock through the front window of the establishment. Grant later confessed to the deputy marshal what he had done and was in turn arrested and soon after sentenced to three months confinement in Sitka. Grant deserted after being returned to Skagway. At no point did the deputy or military leadership confront the racist and exclusionary policies that had led to the confrontation in the first place.[29]

Skagway, with a few exceptions, generally adhered to a loose form of Jim Crow. Though Private Grant was denied entry into the white brothel, a few establishments catered to the town's Black soldiers. One of them, run by Rose Arnold and Ruth Brown, opened in 1900 in response to the arrival of Company L.[30] Black soldiers were not accepted in other social clubs either. During

Company L, Twenty-Fourth Infantry, Skagway, July 4, 1899. Paul Sincic Photo Collection, Alaska State Library (P75-144).

the summer of 1900, the YMCA established its first Alaska location at Skagway and enrolled over three hundred men in a matter of days, including many of the soldiers. The YMCA cultivated a reputation for racial inclusivity and was proud of its egalitarian mission to serve all men. This came as a surprise for some white members, who quickly dropped out in protest after the association accommodated the Black soldiers. One white man discussed the matter with the *Daily Alaskan*: "I withdrew because I do not like to associate with colored peoples." The YMCA remained steadfast: "The Young Men's Christian Association knows no color line. It stands for young men regardless of nationality the world over."[31] However, discontented locals established other social clubs, and the Skagway YMCA closed within two years of opening, likely a repercussion of the anti-integration protests and the town's declining population as the gold rush waned.[32]

From Skagway to the Interior

Once the men of Company L completed their service, some settled in Canada or the interior of Alaska. As one example, Cpl. Benjamin Green received his discharge from the army after his service in Skagway. But Green's time in Alaska had just begun. He remained in the territory for another four decades, until he died of a stroke in Fairbanks in 1940 at the age of sixty-four. It is not clear whether Green ever struck gold, but at one point he shined shoes by day and became best known as a performance singer by night. Green traveled with a "Negro minstrel troupe" and graced his audiences with his thundering bass voice.[33] Eugene Swanson, another veteran of Company L, traveled through Alaska and the Yukon in the hopes of claiming his fortune. Known disparagingly among other miners and settlers as "Nigger Swanson," Eugene Swanson endured the racist epithets and settled in the Yukon River town of Rampart. A veteran of the Spanish-American War and the charge up San Juan Hill, Swanson arrived in Skagway with the Twenty-Fourth and served as a corporal; his superiors noted his "excellence" in the infantry and discharged him honorably in 1902. After Skagway he traveled to Dawson for "a couple of years, then went to Nome and finally in 1904, settled in Rampart," he reported to the *Fairbanks News-Miner*. Swanson worked claims on Hess Creek, a tributary of the Yukon River, not too far from Rampart, for thirty-five years and apparently did so effectively enough to earn a living and hire workers to assist his efforts. He supplemented his income as a teamster and married twice before he passed in Fairbanks in December 1942. Swanson had undoubtedly come a long way from his hometown of Rockford, Alabama.[34]

Not all African Americans who came to Alaska during the gold rush did so through the military. Peter Brown also traveled to Alaska from Kentucky. Brown, "a well-known colored miner," first settled in Skagway in 1898 but soon relocated to the small mining town of Porcupine to open a saloon and work some claims.[35] More notably, St. John Atherton and William T. Ewing were among the most successful of any of the prospectors. Atherton, born enslaved on a plantation near Atlanta, Georgia, cashed in over $30,000 (roughly $750,000 adjusted for inflation in 2019 dollars, according to the US Bureau of Labor Statistics) in gold after a few months' labor in 1897, an impressive fortune at the time. Atherton left after just a few months, despite plans for a longer stay. In 1900 Ewing staked a lucrative claim in the Tanana Valley, not far from Fairbanks. He mined for six years before leaving with enough money to then purchase a ranch in California and live out his days in comfort. He died in 1923, having amassed a fortune of nearly $150,000 (over $2 million in 2019 dollars) in addition to real estate holdings in the Bay Area. Ewing left most of his fortune to Booker T. Washington's Tuskegee Institute (later Tuskegee University) in Alabama.[36]

Though they were exceptions, the accomplishments of Atherton and Ewing were not total aberrations in the history of gold mining or even of Blacks in the West. Instead, the two men fit in a broader context of notable Black miners, prospectors, and businesspeople who traveled across the continent. African Americans participated in the California Gold Rush, and a few made modest fortunes. Black men and women could be found in mining booms elsewhere too—from Colorado to Montana to Idaho. Closer to Alaska, fifty Black men traveled to British Columbia in early 1873 to mine in the Cassiar region. Most notably, Henry McDame, a Black prospector and veteran of the California Gold Rush, struck gold on the Dease River, sparking still another small stampede. The camp became known as "McDame." A few years later, in 1880, prospectors struck gold in Juneau. Two Black men reportedly made their way to the perimeters of the gold camp and set up shop as barbers. The prospectors related their satisfaction with the services the barbers provided, but little else is known about their identities. This was common during the gold rush. Men and some women came and went, often with little trace or even a partial accounting of their day-to-day whereabouts or itinerary.[37]

The allure of isolation enticed some Black men to Alaska, and it could not have been a more radically different setting than the congested cities of the North or the rural and agricultural South. An erstwhile Mississippi sharecropper named George Flowers showed up in Alaska around 1910 emaciated and in need of assistance from the Native Ahtna, who resided in the village of Mentasta. Flowers, a Black man who fled the Jim Crow South for the goldfields of the West, hopped a freight train and made it to Seattle. There, he claimed, he was denied entry on a steamboat to Alaska because of his race. Undeterred, Flowers allegedly walked from Washington State through Canada and into Alaska, before finally reaching the Native community north of the Wrangell Mountains. By then the Yukon gold rush had waned, and Flowers traveled on in isolation in search of work. The primary employer in the region was the mining company in Kennecott. Flowers described that they turned him away, again on account of his race. Journalist and historian Tom Kizzia concluded that Flowers worked briefly at a few gold placer mines and then gathered a grubstake to settle alone near Long Lake, not too far from Kennecott and the small town of McCarthy. According to Kizzia, "He learned to live off the land, hunting and trapping furbearers in winter, and gardening and fishing in the summer, when bright spawn-red salmon swam up the Copper and Chitina and into his net." He developed a reputation as talented guitar player and something of a loner. Once the Kennecott mine shuttered and the workers and managers left, Flowers rejoiced in the peacefulness of Long Lake and busied himself fishing, berry picking, and tending to his garden.[38]

Roshier H. Creecy, born in Campbell County, Virginia, in 1867, made his way to Alaska after giving up on the South and postbellum urban life. He served in the Ninth Cavalry as a buffalo soldier in the Plains Indian Wars, and upon completion of his service, Creecy returned to Virginia just long enough to get married. Chafing under the apparent constraints of domestic life, Creecy once again fled the South, this time to participate in the Klondike Gold Rush in 1898. He spent three years in the Klondike but came up short as a miner. Instead, he opened a roadhouse that was eventually billeted by Canada's North West Mounted Police. Creecy then took off, using a team of dogs to haul his possessions, with his sights on Alaska's interior, where he remained the rest of his life. He passed through Fairbanks and by the early 1900s staked claims in the Koyukuk mining district of the Endicott Mountains in the Brooks range.[39]

Creecy was not afraid to express his beliefs, shy away from a confrontation, or pull off a prank from time to time. The *Fairbanks Daily News-Miner* reported that he was "arrested for seditious utterances—accused of making statements against President Wilson and criticized government actions in carrying out the war" in November 1917—a particularly volatile year in the nation's history, as federal officials issued a domestic crackdown on wartime dissent.[40] Authorities took Creecy's son, Nathaniel, into custody around the same time for failing to register for military service. It is not clear how committed Creecy was to the antiwar movement, and no evidence suggests that he had a history of political activism. Yet Creecy's experience in the Jim Crow South and his service in the cavalry may well have hardened his views on a nation that failed to defend the rights of its Black citizens.

Aside from his opposition to the Great War, Creecy's offbeat sense of humor landed him in hot water on at least one other occasion. In late December 1927 or early January 1928, Creecy placed a distress note that read, "My days are short and I am looking for a place to die," along a fairly well-traveled trail on the Wild River. Someone soon came upon the note and sent it to the district's commissioner in Wiseman.[41] Area men from around Koyukuk assembled as a search party and scoured over two hundred miles, only to find Creecy in high spirits, good health, and decidedly not in distress. After the men sternly questioned him, Creecy claimed he had left the note as a joke. The *Anchorage Daily Times* reported that search effort occurred "at an expense of several hundred dollars to the territory."[42] His sister, Lettie Trent, reported his death in 1949; he would have been eighty-two years old.[43]

Creecy welcomed a life beyond the urban center of Washington, DC, and relished the solitude of the remote mining camps. Flowers, too, found a life alone among the extreme conditions of Wrangell Mountains delivered a level of satisfaction. But loneliness and desolation took a toll on other men. Many met their fate as they toiled alone or in remote areas with little or no access to health care or emergency services. Dave Colgate, a Black man who arrived from the South, mined gold, operated a roadhouse, and ran a dog team to transport goods between his homestead along Dorothy Creek and Nome in Banner Station. Nome was removed enough from society as to present a rather precarious existence in the event of an emergency or mental health crisis. In December 1947 Colgate, then seventy-nine years old, evidently committed suicide while running his dogs back to Nome. An area commissioner who found Colgate reported: "A gun lay alongside his body . . . His four dogs remained beside the body, standing lone vigil without food from 10–12 days."[44]

Other Black miners—much like their white counterparts—suffered similar fates. Ronald Griffin appeared to have died while taking a bath; it may have been suicide or an accident. A fellow prospector found him frozen to the floor, perhaps weeks after he died. Mrs. M. E. Cooper, a woman who ran a restaurant that served southern favorites, died alone as she attempted to perform an abortion on herself.[45] Walter Preston, a prospector who roamed between Dawson City, Yukon, and Paxon, Alaska, fell on hard times and experienced legal troubles. At one point in the early 1900s, he was convicted of stealing a dog from another area prospector and served ten days in prison. Preston reemerged in the newspapers throughout the interior, but by the late 1930s, he had disappeared, never to be heard from again.[46] Another Black prospector named Willie Hooper was "brutally assaulted by some person whose identity is not yet fully established," according to the *Fairbanks Evening News*. Authorities eventually made an arrest, but the outcome of the case is not known.[47]

Violence and quick tempers also prevailed and cost the lives of more than a few miners. In one instance, Benjamin Starkie and Minnie Jones, both of whom were Black, traveled to Alaska from the Deep South in 1898.

The two lived just miles from the home of the local judge. A white man named Tim Callagan demanded entrance into Starkie's cabin for an unknown reason. Starkie refused, and a fight broke out. As Callagan forced entry, Starkie struck him in the face with an axe. The judge declined to file charges against Starkie, ruling that he was protecting his home.[48] While it was notable that a Black man did not receive a punishment for defending himself against a white aggressor, color-blind justice did not always prevail in the mining camps and towns of the Far Northwest. In any case, reading the detailed reports from the fly-by-night newspapers that sprung up in Alaska's interior during the gold rush suggest the tenuousness of life and vulnerability that many experienced, either due to the elements or from their neighbors. Life in and around the mining camps could be at once lonely and dangerous. And as these sources indicate, most did not stay in one place for too long.

In 1898 a group of "disappointed gold seekers" ran afoul with "red minions" and "snake legs"—derogatory names given to the North West Mounted Police.[49] The gold seekers then crossed into Alaska's interior to establish an independent town. This group included "three colored people among our population," one of whom was a woman referred to as "Black Becky White."[50] White made her money as a laundress. "As far as was known," one report proclaimed, she owned "the only outside washtubs in the Klondike."[51] These men and women wanted to locate their new town close to Circle and Rampart, two small Alaska settlements farther north along the river. But one evening, so the story went, the goldfield castaways came upon a scenic bend in the Yukon River and a high bluff; they pitched a tent, then spotted an eagle soaring above. After convening a brief council, they decided to stay and call their new town "Eagle City" (most today know it as Eagle). However, the three Black settlers did not stay long. According to one account, the town grew "too hot for them."[52] The exact nature of their departure, whether from racial tensions, personality clashes, or an amicable decision to leave, remains unknown.

These stories remind us of the hardship and isolation faced by the men and women who came north in search of fortune or simply a better, more peaceful life. Violence and tragedy did not discriminate by race or nationality, and men and women of all colors, faiths, and persuasions faced indescribable hardship in Alaska's harsh environment. Nonetheless, racially motivated violence persisted in Alaska and in Canada's Yukon even as the levers of justice appeared more evenhanded, if never fully balanced.

CHAPTER TWO

Women, Entertainers, and the Service Economy of the Gold Rush Era

As tens of thousands of men looked northward for fortune, women also realized that opportunities might be found in Alaska. One Black woman, Lena Walton, gained nationwide recognition as a most unlikely prospector. Walton left her home in New Jersey and slowly made her way west. She first settled around Washington's Puget Sound and worked as a seamstress and dressmaker. But upon learning of the gold rush and likely seeing thousands of men take off to Alaska, she decided to join the fray. She arrived in Nome in 1899, after brief stints elsewhere in western Alaska, including Kotzebue. Once in Nome, she quickly struck it rich, much to the astonishment of the townspeople.[53] The *Philadelphia Inquirer* went so far as to suggest that her fortune from the gold strikes outpaced that of Hetty Green, the infamous "witch of Wall Street," then thought to be among the wealthiest women in the United States. Such a claim was never confirmed, but Walton prospered by any stretch of the imagination.[54] Said Walton, "When we see the great multitude of white men and women leaving Alaska yearly with fortunes of enormous proportion we can readily appreciate the importance of having our people share in the riches of the country."[55]

May B. Mason also made a fortune in the North. She migrated to Seattle in the mid-1890s with the intention of traveling to Alaska. In early 1897 she left Seattle and briefly staked a claim at Hunter Creek, not far from the settlement of Knik in southern Alaska. She also claimed to have been the first Black woman to reach Dawson City. She returned to Seattle in August 1898 with over $5,000 in gold dust (a sum of well over $150,000 in 2019).[56] However, Walton's and Mason's path to wealth was atypical of the gold rush women. Most had far better success "mining the miners"—providing a variety of high-demand services for the prospecting men in the gold camps and along the various routes in and out of the Yukon, Nome, and Alaska's interior.

In 1896, as the gold rush was just beginning, Bessie Couture opened her Black and White Restaurant in Skagway. Couture was perhaps more representative than Walton or Mason in her path to economic success in the Far Northwest. These women provided the foundation for an informal service economy that developed in response to the mining activity. Couture's modest restaurant was the first known Black-owned business in Alaska. Another Black woman, Mrs. G. B. Verden, never worked a claim or stuck gold but still

Bessie Couture, ca. 1900. Bessie Kendall Couture Collection, Anchorage Museum (B1987.2.44e).

prospered during those years. Verden operated a hotel just outside of Nome, at Gold Run. Prospectors rented rooms for $109 a month, a large sum for the early twentieth century. After a decade in Alaska, she returned to her hometown of Des Moines, Iowa, in 1908, "fashionably clad with jewels and gold nuggets galore." She relocated her parents, who had been born into slavery, into a new mansion.[57]

Charles and Lucile Hunter traveled from the American South to Fort Wrangell, Alaska. They rode the rails, hitched a ride on a steamship along the inside passage, and eventually floated along the Stikine River, reaching their destination in 1897, well over a year into the gold rush. Lucile Hunter was nineteen years old and nine months pregnant by the time the two arrived in Alaska. She named her child Teslin after the lake next to where she gave birth.[58] While Lucile gave birth with no complications, her husband, Charles, died months later of unknown causes. Lucile Hunter decided to stay in the North and brave the conditions as a single mother. She relocated from Fort Wrangell to the Canadian side of the border, in Yukon. There Hunter ran a business outside of Dawson and worked a silver claim in Mayo. Hunter's Cozy Lunch Room served bread, sandwiches, and desserts to hungry miners and passersby. Another Black woman, Sarah Robinson, operated a chicken ranch and laundry in Eagle; she arrived soon after Becky White and the two other Black settlers had departed the nascent town.[59] At the same time, Madame Jones opened the first known beauty salon in Fairbanks in 1905. Her business competed with that of another African American, John Taylor, who cut hair just down the road, though they seemed to have cultivated separate clienteles. There is no disputing the entrepreneurial spirit these women displayed. They may not have mined gold—though some, like Mason and Hunter, did—yet they contributed to their respective communities and led productive lives providing various services that new arrivals urgently needed or desired.[60]

Success stories such as those of Verden, Mason, and Hunter mask the danger and vulnerability that women faced in the male-dominated world of Alaska's gold rush era. This was especially true for women of color, who made their way through towns and remote mining camps with little to no reliable law enforcement. One woman, known as Mrs. Mattie Silks—a white brothel owner who made a fortune during the Colorado gold rushes—left Denver for Skagway in 1898 to set up a brothel in the Klondike and grow her already impressive fortune. She stayed in the Occidental Hotel, not far from the deputy marshal's post in Skagway. During her brief stay, Silks claimed to have overheard the notorious Soapy Smith and his associates hurling racial slurs and confessing to the robbery and murder of a Black prostitute named Ella Wilson. Assuming that she, too, would be targeted by the gang, Silks left Skagway as soon as possible. She sold the story of Wilson's murder to reporters, but Soapy Smith met his fate days later in a shootout. He faced neither charges nor questioning for the brutal crime that Silks claimed he and his gang committed.[61]

Silks's story recalls the crime and danger that typified life in Alaska during the gold rush. The men and women traveled great distances, expected lucrative payoff, and often stopped at nothing to secure it. This drive for fortune sometimes led to violence and ensured a market for vice; Soapy Smith's gang was only one example. Plenty of other men and women viewed the mining camps as fertile ground to make quick money; anyone could be a target of fraud or theft. Gambling, drinking, and prostitution proliferated throughout the mining camps and frontier settlements. Frontiersmen and women commonly resorted to shady deals and price gouging. Towns sprang up as quickly as someone struck gold and could be abandoned with alacrity. The characteristics of modern urban society—the rule of law, family units living together or in proximity to one another, a balance of genders and ages—were simply not present throughout much of Alaska during the gold rush era. With few exceptions, young men were free to fight, drink, steal, and generally wreak havoc upon one other. Still, more than a few women participated in the gold rush, and many displayed a keen savviness that led them to accumulate wealth. But the danger that both women and men faced was real and omnipresent.

Violence, for example, was not just an expected part of life in mining camps and boomtowns; it was part of the entertainment, especially boxing. One man, known as the Black Prince, was a widely feared and respected boxer who entertained hundreds with his fists in Dawson City. Other pugilists, such as Edward "Chicago Ed" Posey and even the era's most famous Black boxer, Peter Jackson, traveled to Dawson to fight and put on a show.[62] They challenged the Black Prince in what became must-see events in and around Dawson's mining camps. Posey also developed a reputation among the North West Mounted Police as a con man. He worked irregularly at Dawson's Fair View Inn but also sold household items, reportedly cased Dawson City homes, and sold the information to would-be robbers. Mounties arrested him for selling floor plans to a band of thieves. Posey received a sentence of six months' imprisonment with hard labor.[63]

While tales of charlatans, boxers, and miners conjure a frontier spirit often associated with the Wild West, so, too, does the world's oldest profession. Like most remote outposts where men vastly outnumbered women, prostitution flourished during the gold rush and beyond. And one of the most prosperous madams in Alaska was Mattie "Tootsie" Crosby, an African American woman who came to Alaska from the booming metropolis of Chicago in 1900. After a brief stay in Skagway, Crosby hiked the Chilkoot Trail to Dawson City. After a few years in Dawson City, in 1910 Crosby moved to the small settlement of Iditarod, where she lived for nearly fifteen years. There Crosby established a bootlegging operation. She served a six-month jail sentence in Fairbanks once the prohibition enforcement officers caught up with her in 1925.[64]

After her release, Crosby relocated to the Iditarod-adjacent Flat, where she catered to the area miners as a madam and bootlegger. Her customers recalled her outsized presence and "reputation for making the best whiskey in the whole area."⁶⁵ One of these men, John Miscovich, noted that once Crosby settled in Flat, she tried to avoid trouble despite the illicit nature of her businesses. She had mixed results. In 1947 an arsonist burned her home to the ground. According to Miscovich, "A pimp set it on fire with a smoking pipe or cigar that fell on the davenport that he slept on."⁶⁶ Only a minor setback, Tootsie Crosby rebuilt and opened what became affectionately known as "The Crosby." Throughout the 1940s and 1950s, Crosby advertised her business as the "finest bathhouse in Alaska." It provided massages and bath parlors as well as "medicated, mineral vapor, steam, tub, salt, and fresh water baths." Patrons could also receive "electric and faradic massage treatments by expert attendants. Lighted by a gas and heated system."⁶⁷ Miscovich estimated that as many as a dozen prostitutes and hundreds of men passed through The Crosby over the years. He believed Crosby and her "very decent prostitutes" kept the business out of view from area children and others who objected to the nature of the work. Crosby ran her business for decades before she moved to the Sitka Pioneer House, where she died in 1972 at the age of ninety.⁶⁸

Crosby did well enough to support herself as well as several others. In addition to sex work, Crosby provided basic services and shelter to the transient men who passed through—or in some cases got stuck—in Flat. Many of these men were down on their luck or had failed to earn the fortune they expected and had little means to escape or return to their homes and families. Even as Crosby's services remained in demand and her wealth increased considerably, she was never fully accepted among Alaska's polite society. Some of the men she took in offered protection and performed chores around the property. One of the men who mined in the area camps reported, "Tootsie was not ostracized like the prostitutes, but she was a loner."⁶⁹ The *Anchorage Daily Times* concluded years later, Crosby "was one of the first Black women in the Iditarod-Flat area, now the McKinley Mining District, and one of the early successful entrepreneurs."⁷⁰

Crosby may have been the most prominent Black woman to run a brothel in Alaska during the first half of the twentieth century, but others practiced the trade and gained local fame. These figures included women such as "Black Kitty" in Circle City, "Black Alice" in Nome, and "Snake Hips Lulu" in Dawson City. These women set up shop across the goldfields and mining districts of Alaska and the Yukon. Rarely did they dedicate themselves solely to prostitution. Black Alice, for example, established her business in proximity to the lucrative claims along Anvil Creek. She cooked and laundered clothes;

meals ran about five dollars, a handsome sum even for miners in far-flung Nome. In Seward, Elnora Jones gained a reputation first as a prostitute, then as a madam; she arrived in the late 1930s and was known as the town's only Black prostitute. According to Annaliese Jacobs Bateman, author of a National Park Service report on prostitution in Seward, Jones worked alternatively in the sex trades, as a laundress, and as a restaurant owner. The home where she worked as a prostitute doubled as a barbecue joint in the late 1940s and 1950s and had a dedicated following of diners. However, a restraining order shut down her business in 1954. Jones was arrested on two other occasions in the following three years. Bateman reports that Seward's vice squad arrested her and transported her to Anchorage in 1957. The documents fail to record her whereabouts thereafter.[71]

Enterprising women were among the wealthiest people in the gold camps and surrounding towns, and many of them never handled a pickax, shovel, or pan. Anecdotal evidence suggests these women managed their finances more effectively than their male counterparts. In addition, Black women who participated in the gold rush forged cross-cultural and biracial alliances of mutual convenience with area miners. At best, their lives could be only tenuously secure; at worst, dangers in the natural world or from neighbors posed daily threats. Nonetheless, these women believed that life amid the gold rush was a superior option to the alternatives available to women of color in early-twentieth-century America. And while the lives of these women reflect a combination of danger, purpose, and determination, ennui may best describe life on the frontier. Lillian Mabel Taylor joined her husband to prospect outside of Dawson. She recorded her experience as the only Black woman within the camp. She kept a diary and detailed the day-to-day events of life during the gold rush. She took naps, observed "drifting snow," played the violin, "made fancy cakes," and generally kept to herself. Taylor did all she could to stave off boredom in the remote setting of a mining camp. Perhaps more than any of the others mentioned thus far, Taylor most effectively conveyed the daily reality of the Klondike Gold Rush: a quotidian pursuit of meaning in a place with few amenities or creature comforts.[72]

Clifford C. Hancock's Alaska

What is known about many of the first Black residents of Alaska has been mediated through the recollection of others, newspaper accounts, or even law enforcement or court records. Finding a journal such as Lillian Mabel Taylor's is quite rare, and even then the entries are sporadic and provide at best a glimpse into daily life. But sometimes an unexpected voice provides a fresh and direct perspective. In 1899 Clifford C. Hancock traveled from Chicago to Fort Gibbon, Alaska. He lived at the confluence of the Tanana and Yukon Rivers and worked as a butler and family assistant to Capt. Charles W. Farnsworth, the commanding officer at the fort. Hancock penned an article for the August 1903 *Colored American Magazine*, the first African American culture periodical. Hancock's article, "Alaska: Unalaska and Other Points of Interest," stands as the earliest known firsthand account of the territory written by an African American, certainly the first to be published. He made his way from Chicago by rail and then traveled to the Aleutians by a steamship operated by the Alaska Commercial Company, reaching the interior via the Yukon River and viewing settlements as far as Eagle.

Reporting on his journey to Fort Gibbon, Hancock found Unalaska "a pleasant little town." He predicted the Aleutians would someday rival California and Oregon as a center for agriculture and cattle grazing. "The two great pioneers of civilization—the church and the school—were in full evidence" in Unalaska. Not all towns, however, shared Unalaska's level of advancement, according to Hancock.[73] "The dirtiest alley of civilization," wrote Hancock, "could not be compared to St. Michael." There he found grave sites with bodies not fully buried, a muddy landscape, and the days impossibly wet and dreary. He was happy to leave the settlement aboard a steamer bound for the Upper Yukon. There he found "Eskimos" and "Alaskan Indians" who at times allied with "the white race" and "acquired more readily the habits of the Anglo-Saxon." But in their love for a nomadic life, "they resemble[d] the American Indian." Both populations were "filthy and very hardy, living in tents as the temperature dropped to sixty or seventy below zero. They can endure more cold than the average animal in the United States."[74] As a Black writer, Hancock provided an unlikely voice to explain the relationship between Indigenous people and white settlers. His observations recall the words of white ethnologists and the era's notorious race theorists, the works of whom Hancock referenced. Curiously, Hancock never remarked upon his own subjectivity as a Black man. Indeed, the complexity of racial classifications and notions of biological advancement remained unaddressed topics throughout the article.

Instead, Hancock basked in the endless summer light and braved the darkness of the winter; he marveled at the size and scope of the land. He presented as poetic a description of the northern lights as one might ever read: "I find myself at a loss for words to express the grandeur of the electrical display as they begin each night to play tag with each individual star in the firmament, returning to their mysterious hiding places to come forth again with colors far more beautiful than those of the rainbow." He concluded, "The beauty of Alaskan scenery is so grand and varied that to call it the Norway of America would convey a faint idea of its magnificence." The reader gets a distinct impression that Hancock's experience in Alaska was transformative. His account is conversant with the naturalists of the day and at times conjures John Muir and others who found inspiration from the northern landscape.[75]

Whether it was Hancock's firsthand account or the secondhand accounts from soldiers, miners, trappers, sex workers, innkeepers, and pugilists, all conveyed the disparate ways in which Black men and women contributed to the social and cultural life of Alaska at the turn of the twentieth century. Collectively, these accounts complicate the traditional frontier narrative, demonstrating how Alaska was a more multiracial territory that many, if not most, would assume. The hallmarks of boomtown western outposts of the time—fortunes made and lost, violence and vice, loneliness and isolation punctuated by adventure and hardship—were present in Alaska. And as they made their mark in other western outposts, African Americans made their mark in Alaska.

CHAPTER THREE

The World War Era and a New Alaska

JOHN CONNA WAS BORN ENSLAVED IN TEXAS IN 1836, THE YEAR OF the Battle of the Alamo and the turning point in Texas's bid for independence from Mexico. During the Civil War, Conna found his way to the Union lines and fought for his freedom with a regiment of escaped slaves and freemen based out of Louisiana. After the war he relocated to the Pacific Northwest and led a small Black population to exert some influence in Tacoma politics in what was then the Territory of Washington, soon to be Washington State. Conna lost much of his influence and wealth in 1894 as a result of the nationwide economic depression that began with the Panic of 1893.[1] Six years later, perhaps desperate for money, the sixty-four-year-old Conna moved again, this time sailing north to Alaska. His destination was the small frontier town of Eagle, well into Alaska's interior along the Yukon River. Though they separated in Alaska, he was accompanied on the trip north by an old friend from Tacoma, James Wickersham, the newly appointed federal judge of Alaska's Third District.[2]

Like many others who came to Alaska at this time, Conna was lured by the gold rush and the hopes of fortune, or new fortune in his case. But as he advanced into his sixties, already having surpassed the average life expectancy of American men at the time, Conna was not in the physical shape to labor with pick and axe for hours a day in the goldfields. Still, he tried mining briefly in the Tanana Valley, near Fairbanks, before acknowledging his limitations. After failing to strike gold, Conna asked Wickersham for a job at the courthouse; the judge hired him as a custodian and to perform various jobs on the property. As a Black man, the best work he could initially find was menial labor. But with a steady employment record and some political connections, Conna also worked in real estate and put aside some money. Unlike many who had come in search of a quick fortune and never planned to stay, Conna lived out his days in Fairbanks and grew more involved in local and state politics.[3] In 1912 he ran for the territorial senate. He ran as a Socialist, after breaking with the Republican Party; the discrimination he faced provided a radical tinge to his politics even as he accumulated wealth from his property.[4]

At the time of his death, in 1921, Conna was eighty-five and had spent the final twenty-one years of his life in Alaska's interior. He owned six homes in and around Fairbanks and held a stake in some mining companies. His life bridged the gap from Alaska's gold rush era to the First World War. His status as a Civil War veteran was certainly not representative of most Alaskan settlers who arrived in the twentieth century. However, that he served in the military was quite typical of the men who arrived in Alaska between the 1920s and 1940s. At the time of his death, the territory had undergone major transformations, and it would continue to do so over the next twenty years.

This chapter explores the lives of Black men and women who, like Conna, arrived in the early to middle decades of the twentieth century. Like earlier Black arrivals, many did not stay long, but a growing population did, remaining in the territory through the tumult of two world wars and putting down roots. Few events have shaped Alaska like these conflicts, and perhaps no single institution has shaped Alaska as thoroughly as the military. An expanding economy, the result of Alaska's role in two world wars, led thousands of African Americans to work in the territory, open businesses there, and serve their country. The copious levels of federal investment and Alaska's emergence as a key strategic location in the nation's defense created ample jobs and opportunities for those willing to make the journey. The history of Black men and women in early-twentieth-century Alaska showcases perseverance and success balanced against the lived experiences of racism and discrimination. A few Black individuals arrived around the time of the First World War. Most, however, came to Alaska in the late 1930s and 1940s, amid the Second World War. These men constructed a mighty highway through the boreal forests and assisted in the retaking of the Aleutian Islands from the Japanese. But whether they arrived during the First World War or the Second, African Americans left an indelible imprint on Alaska's history during these years.

CHAPTER THREE

From the Great War to the Great Land

As John Conna carved out a space for himself in Alaska's interior, another Black man exerted his influence over the territory's newest town, Anchorage. Like many ambitious and adventurous young men, Thomas Stokes "Tom" Bevers had looked west. He came to Alaska following the completion of his service in the so-called Great War—World War I—and contributed mightily to early Anchorage. Most everything about life in the nation's northernmost territory looked rather different from what Bevers had experienced in his home state of Virginia. His father, William, farmed land on the Dan River in Pittsylvania County, a stretch of the American South defined by tobacco plantations and chattel slavery. William Bevers had developed a relationship with a white woman named Mary Ellen, and both lived under constant fear of intimidation, violence, or worse. It was against Virginia law for a Black man to marry or have a relationship with a white woman, let alone father racially mixed children. Nonetheless, Mary Ellen and William Bevers raised ten kids in violation of Jim Crow–era restrictions; Tom was the seventh.[5]

In 1917, at the age of twenty-eight or possibly twenty-nine, Bevers left Virginia to enlist in the war. Perhaps to leave the South, he joined the segregated army; however, it is not clear from the records whether he saw combat. Bevers completed his service and never returned to Virginia. Like millions of others, he participated in the Great Migration, seeking a better life elsewhere. Nearly three thousand miles from his birthplace, Bevers took up metallurgy in Seattle for a year before packing up for an even more remote destination, Alaska.[6] In 1921 he arrived in the fledgling town of Anchorage. There he made for himself a prosperous life that had eluded him in Virginia and Seattle. In those years the federally owned and operated Alaska Railroad held great sway over Anchorage's economy. Federal officials in Woodrow Wilson's administration had founded Anchorage just six years earlier as a hub for a new railroad. Wilson and his allies believed a government-owned railroad would safeguard Alaska's abundant natural resources from private ownership or reckless exploitation to benefit short-term business interests. In turn, the territory's strategic position in the North Pacific could be more effectively defended, and some of the blunders of development in other western territories and states could be avoided.[7]

Before the federal government set up the Anchorage townsite, the Dena'ina used the area as a fish camp and referred to the creek that hosted a seasonal salmon run as Dgheyaytnu. The non-Natives who arrived in 1915, most of whom were white Americans or European immigrants, settled on the land adjacent to the mouth of the creek, known as Dgheyay Kaq' by the Dena'ina. There the settlers began construction on a railroad to connect Alaska's southern coast to the interior of the territory.[8] No documents suggest a Black population present during the first years of settling Dgheyay Kaq', by then known as Anchorage. There was, however, a Black man who appeared in photographs of a recreational baseball team as early as the summer of 1915 and a report of the same man taking the field in 1916.[9] Known only as "Agee," likely a surname, the roster identified him as a "helper." Others on the team had such titles as "nozzle man," "water man," and "coupler"—allowing one to surmise that the team was composed of men from the fire department.[10] No additional evidence suggests where Agee came from, his role in the department, or how long he stayed.

The local newspapers do not mention a Black resident until 1918. The Alaska Bone Dry Act prohibiting the sale of alcohol took effect on January 1, 1918. Two weeks later a woman known as Anna West was arrested in Anchorage on charges of drunkenness and possession. The *Anchorage Daily Times* claimed she was the first person charged with violating Alaska's prohibition. She pleaded guilty and was sentenced to a year in prison. West likely served a lesser sentence if she ended up serving jail time at all. However, her name disappears from the historical record after the infraction, and little else is known about her.[11] Ten months later, for most of the month of November, Anchorage was under quarantine for the Spanish influenza. Notably, as news of the armistice ending World War I reached town, there were no celebrations other than the ringing of bells and blowing of train whistles because of the restrictions on public gatherings. At least twenty-six people in Anchorage died from the influenza. The first to die was the African American Ed Walker, on November 3, 1918. He was perhaps the first African American buried in the Anchorage cemetery. Like Anna West, much of Ed Walker's life remains unknown.[12]

Aside from Agee and West, Bevers was the most notable African American to call Anchorage home and likely the Black resident who left the most extensive record of his involvement in the territory during the 1920s and 1930s. Bevers spent most of his twenty-three years in Alaska making a name for himself in the fledgling town of Anchorage. But like Michael Healy, another light-skinned, biracial African American, Bevers lived his life in the American West passing as a white man, thus allowing him easier entrance into Anchorage's civic life and presumably paving his path to advancement in early-twentieth-century Alaska. He first worked as a blacksmith, and after several years of volunteering as a fireman and earning accolades and trust among his crew, Bevers served as the Anchorage Fire Department's first paid chief, from 1927 to 1940.[13]

Of at least equal significance, Bevers also took an interest in fur farming and land speculation. He, along with several other investors, purchased eight acres of land between Tenth and M Streets, now part of Anchorage's downtown. They established a fur farm and trading post that would soon become a key center for Southcentral Alaska's fur trade. Two decades later Bevers worked with Anchorage boosters and the chamber of commerce to formalize an annual fur trading exposition, an event Alaskans recognize today as Fur Rendezvous. Throughout the 1930s and early 1940s Bevers took an interest in local politics and in 1941 won a seat on the city council, where he served two terms with apparently broad and popular support from his constituents.[14]

Tom Bevers died tragically while on a hunting trip in 1944. By then he had worked his way to the top of Anchorage's social ladder and was a revered member of the community. The *Anchorage Daily Times* eulogized his death, writing, "Anchorage has lost one of its best friends and leaders."[15] It is hard to imagine a newspaper in Bevers's native Virginia publishing an obituary for him. Then again, we do not know if Bevers would have enjoyed such prestige in Anchorage if his friends and neighbors knew of his African ancestry. Evidence suggests Bevers never spoke openly about his upbringing in Virginia, and given the pervasive nature of racism in the United States during the 1920s and 1930s, he made a rational choice to conceal that part of his identity. After he died, his friends and associates were surprised to find out his family was Black. Only after his sister, who reportedly had darker skin, traveled to Alaska to settle his affairs and prepare his body to be returned to Virginia did Anchorage residents learn about his background. By then Thomas Bevers had accumulated the goodwill of his adopted hometown. Members of both the local Elks Lodge and the Masons lobbied to keep his remains in Anchorage and provide a proper burial, to which his sister agreed. The Masons read the burial rites and laid Bevers to rest at the Anchorage Memorial Park Cemetery, where one can find the headstone today.[16]

Thomas Bevers (fourth from the right), hand raised to chest, with others in the Anchorage Fire Department, ca. 1920s. Carl Lottsfeldt Collection, Anchorage Museum (B1978.111.25).

Bevers clearly understood how difficult it was to be Black in America. Anchorage shared much of the racial antipathy of other American cities. Whether one was Black, Asian, or Alaska Native, the white residents of Anchorage and its surrounding communities wavered between ambivalence, on the one hand, and violent hostility, on the other. If racism appeared lower on the list of social ills afflicting the newly established town, it was almost certainly because of its low minority population. The demographics of the young town—then usually referred to as the Ship Creek townsite by the prevailing population of white settlers—resulted from public policy decisions. One of the townsite's founding figures and head of the Alaskan Engineering Commission (AEC), Andrew Christensen, specifically excluded the Indigenous Dena'ina from residing alongside whites and working on the Alaska Railroad. Christensen and his colleague at the Forest Service, Arthur Ringland, also believed that Eastern European laborers, those whose ancestry included Russian, Slavic, Greek, and Italian, were "another class of trespassers" and needed to be excluded from the new town.[17] Referred to as "bohunks," the leadership at the AEC considered them inferior to what they proposed was the more desirable "Anglo-Saxon" worker.[18]

Though Anchorage town planners wanted to keep their nascent community lily-white, Alaska's coastal towns looked quite different, particularly those settlements built around the salmon canneries. The canneries depended on migrant labor, usually Chinese. However, immigration restriction reduced the number of Chinese workers and necessitated a multiracial workforce. Max Stern, a San Francisco–based journalist, wrote an exposé on Alaska's canneries and noted the presence of Black workers among the seasonal crews. In 1922 Blacks numbered just over 300 out of 27,482 cannery workers; whites and Alaska Natives constituted the largest percentages, according to Stern. Filipinx and Mexican laborers, among others, also migrated north to can salmon. Stern deployed racial stereotypes as he noted, "Guamese, Filipinos, South Americans, Mexicans, and Negroes—all thin blooded and used to warm and sunny climes near or south of the equator"—may have provided a pliant workforce but made poor Alaskans, ill suited for the cold climate.[19] And although Blacks represented a small percentage of the total workforce, their contributions remain among the least documented of the Alaska salmon canneries. Indeed, the canneries and their diverse workforce fueled much of coastal Alaska's economic development throughout the twentieth century.

Beyond the canneries, Black men also worked on the docks along the West Coast, including Alaska. Labor activist Frank Jenkins worked in Alaska periodically in the 1920s. Jenkins was the son of a Black Texan and a Filipina who met during the Philippine-American War in the early 1900s. The family eventually settled in Seattle in 1909, after stints in Hawai'i and California. Jenkins first traveled to Alaska in 1920 to work in a fertilizer plant; he subsequently accepted work with the Alaska Steamship Company, one of the few integrated shipping companies on the West Coast. Jenkins noted: "Alaska Steam [Alaska Steamship Company] had their own hiring hall where they hired their own people. They had blacks working down there, but Alaska Steam mixed them all together. It didn't make much difference to them." By the 1930s Jenkins had become radicalized following a series of waterfront strikes, most notably in 1934. He enthusiastically joined the International Longshoremen's Association (ILA) and its successor, the International Longshore and Warehouse Union (ILWU), a Left-led union at the forefront of the Congress of Industrial Organizations (CIO) in the 1930s and 1940s.[20] Jenkins spent most of his working life in Seattle and later participated in the struggle for civil rights. But throughout his life, he remained committed to industrial unionism and viewed Alaska as a crucial stopover in his broader political education.[21]

Alaska thus presented opportunities to a diverse workforce as migrants from the Pacific Rim joined those of Hispanic and African ancestry along the docks and in the canneries. Anchorage, for its part, was not representative of the rest of the territory in its leaders' desire to limit nonwhite settlement. The territorial economy, dependent as it was upon federal investment and extractive industries such as fishing and mining, hit significant headwinds during the Great Depression. Alaska encountered roughly two decades of economic stagnation as residents did what they could to find work; the territory's population declined between the 1910s and mid-1930s, only to rebound on the eve of World War II. For a short period of time, in the 1920s and early 1930s, Alaska Natives once again outnumbered whites in the territory. But throughout the interwar years, there were creative schemes to incentivize population and economic growth, the most famous of which was an idea hatched in the Franklin D. Roosevelt administration to relocate farmers who had fallen on hard times. The ideal candidates, the administration believed, hailed from the Upper Midwest. These men and women were "hardy Scandinavians," reflected Robert Sheldon, president of the Fairbanks Chamber of Commerce and postmaster of Alaska in the 1930s. As a result, white midwesterners were believed to be uniquely suited to the conditions of Alaska's Matanuska-Susitna Valley. Organized within the Department of the Interior by Secretary Harold Ickes, 203 families settled around the town of Palmer, creating the Matanuska Colony.[22]

Around the same time, a small group of Black activists calling themselves the "United Congo Improvement Association" (UCIA), proposed a similar scheme to relocate to Alaska four hundred Black families from the American South. Joseph "Joe" Thomas, a medical doctor largely responsible for planning the proposed relocation, envisioned a day when millions of Blacks would call Alaska home. Thomas believed the presence of Black farmers would at once provide a population and economic base for the floundering territory and contribute to its defense. Ernest Gruening, director of the Division of Territories and Island Possessions and later an Alaska governor and senator, quickly shot down the plan, suggesting that Blacks were inherently unsuited for colder climates. Thomas, undeterred, scaled back the scope of Black migration and requested that Black families be included among the white colonists who set out for Palmer. This idea, too, received no traction.[23] Gruening's later opposition towards efforts to shelter Jewish refugees in Alaska included similar language, suggesting little interest in disrupting what he believed was the optimal demographic of the territory: people from Northern Europe.[24]

Gruening's opinion regarding Blacks and cold weather was far from singular among American politicians and observers. During a 1930 congressional hearing on Alaska canneries, Ewin Davis, a representative from Tennessee, commented, "They [Blacks] are such warm-natured creatures that I could not imagine them wanting to stay in Alaska."[25] Conna's friend, James Wickersham, in attendance as Alaska's nonvoting representative to Congress, did not respond. During a 1935 congressional hearing on airmail service in Alaska, Anthony Dimond, Wickersham's successor, said, "On account of climatic conditions I doubt that a Negro settlement will be made there."[26]

Throughout the first decades of the twentieth century, Alaska possessed a white majority in and around the larger settlements of Anchorage and Fairbanks; Alaska Natives outnumbered whites across the hundreds of rural villages. The Black population grew in the interwar years but slowed just after the conclusion of the Second World War.[27] In this regard Bevers and Conna were more exceptional than representative figures in the territory. Beyond Fairbanks and Anchorage, there was a small yet distinct Black community in Juneau during the late 1910s and 1920s. One man, William Waddleton, surfaced in news reports of the era and claimed the title of Juneau's most visible and written about Black resident. Waddleton first arrived in Alaska in 1894, having left Washington, DC, to stake a claim in the Juneau mining district. In 1897 his hometown paper, the *Evening Times Sun*, reported that he had relocated to the Klondike to participate in the gold rush. In correspondence with his brother, who remained back in Washington, DC, Waddleton related the vast "mineral wealth" of Alaska and was determined to make a life for himself in the territory despite a climate that was "deleterious to the health of his race."[28] Waddleton did not stay in the Klondike long but instead cashed out at a profit and returned to Juneau, where he would live out the rest of his days.

By 1912 Waddleton landed in the news in his adopted hometown. In one story, Juneau's *Daily Alaska Dispatch* referred to him as a "colored barrister known as 'judge.'" But the paper reported that he "has never been admitted to the Alaska bar, although he has occasionally practiced in the commissioner's court."[29] Still, he fell on the wrong side of the law after allegedly "peddling liquor [to] an Indian maide [*sic*]." Waddleton pleaded not guilty to the charge of dealing liquor to Native women around Juneau.[30] The case was fraught with racialized and gendered anxieties at a time when the nation had become preoccupied with fears of so-called race degeneration and miscegenation.[31] The town was engrossed in the details of Waddleton's case, wanting to know more about a Black man who had invited Native women to drink whiskey in his cabin. The legal proceedings took place before a "packed courtroom" as Juneau's leading men and women expressed concern over the spread of alcohol among the town's Native inhabitants.[32]

While white purveyors of alcohol then received lesser or no public opprobrium, missionaries and teetotalers, led in large part by white Alaska women who had gained the right to vote in territorial and local elections in 1913, soon embarked on a campaign that concluded with the passage of the Alaska Bone Dry Act, which banned sales of alcohol in the territory effective January 1, 1918.[33] The 1910s Alaska temperance movement was marked with paternalistic overtones, given the lack of Alaska Native suffrage. While a literature has yet to develop on the introduction of alcohol to Alaska Natives, the population falls within the broader literature that notes alcohol misuse was uncommon to nonexistent among Indigenous Americans before the arrival of Europeans.[34] Alcohol misuse and addiction remains a critical concern among Alaska Natives to this day, one of many significant factors contributing to long-standing negative health disparities, including higher rates of diabetes and suicide.[35] To this day some primarily Alaska Native communities voluntarily restrict or ban alcohol sales.[36]

In any case, the jury convicted Waddleton on one of the two charges, and the judge sentenced him to six months in prison. Judge Folsom, presiding over the court, "argued that Waddleton's race made no difference in the case, and prayed the court exercise its own discretion in dealing out punishment." The judge and jury admonished Waddleton: "As long as you continue to associate with natives you will get into trouble."[37] And while Judge Folsom's words might be lauded for their racially neutral tone, the interest in the case and the level of passion it incited suggests that a liquor-induced liaison between a Black man and Native women represented a racial transgression that required a forceful response from Juneau's criminal justice system.

A few years later Waddleton found himself the target of another investigation, this one the result of his opposition to American involvement during the First World War. Like R. H. Creecy several hundred miles away, in Alaska's interior, Waddleton also expressed his belief that the United States should not enter the war. He, too, would face the consequences in an era of heightened nationalism and suppressed dissent. In fact, he was arrested and charged even before Creecy. The *Daily Alaska Dispatch* recorded that Waddleton was the "first arrest in the territory of Alaska during the present war." The paper described a "Colored resident of many years standing held on thousand dollar bonds for distributing socialist pamphlet said to contain anti-draft exhortations." Here again, the Juneau paper referred to Waddleton as an "unofficial lawyer."[38] Waddleton eventually posted bail at $250 and retained an attorney to fight the charges against him.[39] After the jury failed to reach a verdict, authorities demanded Waddleton face trial again; this time he was convicted of "circulating seditious literature," a violation of the territorial legislature's "act for the preservation of the public peace in time war."[40] The judge ordered Waddleton to pay a $75 fine for circulating Socialist literature and questioning American involvement in the war.[41]

The complete number of Alaskans charged with sedition is unknown. A review of Alaska newspapers between 1917 and 1918 revealed at least twenty-three cases of Alaskans charged with sedition, including the Creecys and Waddleton.[42] Of those twenty-three, only the Creecy men and Waddleton were racial minorities. As such, the Creecys and Waddleton do not especially stand out among the number of Alaskans charged with sedition, nor does Waddleton's punishment. Indeed, some Alaskans were more heavily penalized. In February 1918 a man from Douglas, a small settlement adjacent to Juneau, was fined two hundred dollars and sentenced to six months behind bars. After he could not afford the fine, the man received an additional three months to his prison sentence.[43] That August a Ketchikan man was fined a thousand dollars and sentenced to a year in jail.[44]

Waddleton landed in the news the next year as well. In 1918 he and other Juneau African Americans protested the showing of D. W. Griffith's *Birth of a Nation*, a film originally released in 1915 and notorious for its pro–Ku Klux Klan narrative. Juneau mayor Emery Valentine subsequently banned the film as it "tends to produce class hatred and is humiliating to many of our citizens."[45] Territorial governor Thomas Riggs also banned the film from being shown in Southcentral Alaska.[46] However, two months later, perhaps after the protest had lost its strength, the film was again advertised at the same Juneau theater.[47]

Though it is impossible to draw conclusions about the life in Juneau for African Americans based upon Waddleton's experience alone, his life in early-twentieth-century Alaska provides valuable clues. He encountered discrimination and harassment from law enforcement and townspeople even as he eked out a living as a miner. He took on the justice system not once but twice. And in both encounters with the law, Waddleton's race likely factored into his arrest and sentencing. But given the small African American population in Juneau—Waddleton was one of the few Black men and women who show up in the records—anti-Black racism did not register to the same extent as anti-Native racism. Widespread reports document the antagonism and discrimination directed at Juneau's Indigenous population; tensions between white settlers and the region's Tlingit and Haida communities would persist throughout the century.

That said, no evidence contravenes a more general assessment that Juneau's racial climate largely echoed the rest of the nation. In fact, reports from the Ku Klux Klan tabloid the *Fellowship* reported, "The boundaries of the Invisible Empire have been extended as far north as Juneau, Alaska." The article noted that the long nights were ideal to "stage their ceremonies."[48] That the KKK established a base of power or curried exceptional political influence in Juneau, or other Alaskan towns remains unconfirmed. However, one of the Klan's periodicals, the *Kourier Magazine*, based out of Atlanta, Georgia, claimed that eleven "charters" existed throughout the territory as late as 1931, some well north of Juneau.[49] The Klan sponsored at least one minstrel show in Kennecott, the copper mining settlement in Alaska's Wrangell Mountains. Fifteen performers donned blackface in a 1921 performance that was widely promoted; the KKK retained a presence in the small community during the early years of that decade.[50] Nativism, racial hostility, anti-immigrant sentiments, and a suppression of political dissent defined the years surrounding the First World War nationwide. So, too, did such a culture of white supremacy find expression in Alaska's capital as well as the small mining camps and settlements that dotted the expansive territory.[51]

Waddleton's 1938 death in Juneau corresponded with a transition from one era of the territory's history to the next. As Alaska's strategic location became clearer in advance of the Second World War, the demographics of the territory changed dramatically. Since the 1940s the Black population of Anchorage and Fairbanks has fluctuated between 4 and 10 percent; Juneau's never exceeded more than a percentage or two. These demographics are comparable to other cities in the Pacific Northwest such as Boise, Portland, Seattle, and Spokane; Tacoma, Washington, has historically had the largest Black community in the region, at between 10 and 12 percent of the population.[52] Yet even these relatively modest numbers belie the contribution of African Americans in Alaska during and after World War II. Their actions in the territory anticipated a broader civil rights movement in the years to follow.[53]

The Second World War Comes to Alaska

The Second World War reconfigured Alaska's history like no other event. The war once again showcased the territory's strategic significance to American policy makers and required an enormous logistical commitment to defend its shoreline, waters, and land. Alaska's sheer size and its remote location at once made it a target for the Japanese empire. At the same time, given its proximity to the Pacific theaters of war and the eastern half of the Soviet Union, the United States and Allied commanders recognized the usefulness that the development of an extensive military presence in the territory would have on the war effort. As a result, even before the attack on Pearl Harbor, the US military decided Alaska should serve as a location for new army and air bases. Once the nation entered the war, these plans grew more ambitious.[54]

During the 1930s the only permanent military presence in Alaska was the roughly three hundred soldiers at Fort Seward in Haines. Beginning in 1939, the military expanded in a flurry of activity through the early 1940s, including the construction of Fort Richardson and Elmendorf Field just northeast of downtown Anchorage; Fort Wainwright and Ladd Field in Fairbanks; Eielson Field, twenty-five miles southeast of Fairbanks; and other installations in Southeast Alaska, Kodiak, and the Aleutians. The military, of course, remained segregated. In fact, the head of the Alaska Defense Command, Lt. Gen. Simon Bolivar Buckner Jr., the son of a Confederate army general, was a staunch white supremacist and adamant segregationist. He forbade African Americans from residing in Alaska's towns and settlements. He believed the prevailing wages were too high and that job opportunities might entice Black men to travel north. If that happened, Buckner asserted, "the natural result would be that they would interbreed with the Indians and Eskimos and produce an astonishingly objectionable race of mongrels which would be a problem here from now on."[55]

While Buckner maintained military segregation in Alaska, forces in the Lower 48 were pressuring the White House and army toward the US military's eventual integration. Since 1933 President Franklin D. Roosevelt had consulted with his informally named "Black cabinet" on policy matters, including but not limited to racial issues. Members included Benjamin O. Davis, William O. Hastie, and Campbell C. Johnson, all of whom served in the War Department. Mary McLeod Bethune, a close friend of Eleanor Roosevelt, vociferously advocated for greater Black participation in the war effort as well. The Black cabinet requested the use of Black troops in both combat and noncombat roles; the plan became known as "segregation without discrimination." It called for 10 percent of every branch in the United States military to be staffed with African Americans. The selective service also mandated that 10 percent of inductees be Black. The plan received immediate pushback from top brass in the military, including the army chief of staff George Marshall, who opined that the war effort must not be viewed as a moment to advance Black soldiers or disrupt the conventions of Jim Crow.[56]

Outside the White House, Black leaders called for a "Double V" strategy—victory against fascism abroad and victory at home against racism and segregation. Perhaps most notably, the March on Washington movement, manifested in 1941 by a collective of grassroots activists, promoted civil rights and equality for African Americans as well as an end to segregation in the military. Movement leaders garnered an early victory when a planned march on New York was preempted by Roosevelt's Executive Order 8802, which prohibited racial and ethnic discrimination in the defense industry.[57]

Once the Japanese invaded the Aleutians in 1942, the urgency of the war effort necessitated Black involvement, regardless of the uneasiness of Buckner and his colleagues. Over the next three years, Black soldiers demonstrated valor on and off the battlefield, despite being targets of derision and bigotry. As with all enlisted troops, Black personnel took the army general classification test to measure their aptitude. But those who had little or no formal education, as did many Black enlistees, scored poorly and ended up in the bottom categories, classes IV and V. While white troops who scored in similarly low categories advanced into combat roles, Black troops were sent to the service units, usually the engineer general service regiments, to perform menial tasks. This system reinforced the assumption on the part of many white citizens that Black soldiers could not be trusted on the battlefield.[58]

The Japanese, meanwhile, continued their invasion of the Aleutians, even as they endured a major naval defeat at the Battle of Midway. The chain of roughly 150 islands stretching into the North Pacific constituted the sole North American theater of war. American military commanders long recognized the vulnerability of Alaska's fifteen thousand–plus miles of coast, and it came as little surprise when the Japanese occupied the islands of Attu and Kiska, two of the most remote islands in the Aleutians. Just a mere 650 miles from the Japanese base at Paramushiro, the capture of Attu provided Japan with a strategic, albeit temporary, victory. Japanese advances on the Aleutians intended to ease pressure on their supply lines farther to the south, pull American resources away from critical Japanese interests in the South Pacific and East Asia, and prevent oil from reaching Alaska by sea. The Japanese may have briefly achieved these objectives, but the Americans quickly regained the momentum in the Pacific.[59]

As has long been recognized, Alaska holds a significant strategic location between the Lower 48 and Russia and between the West Coast and Asia. As the Soviet Union developed as an ally during World War II, Alaska was the convenient, if underdefended, link. By 1942 American commanders used Alaska as an intermediary point in the lend-lease system to transfer weaponry and supplies to the Soviet Union as it engaged in conflict on Europe's eastern front. Despite its sudden military importance, Alaska was only accessible by sea or air and thus difficult to defend. As Gen. Billy Mitchell, an outspoken war hawk and advocate for an aggressive American posture in the Pacific, proclaimed, "For whoever holds Alaska will hold the world."[60] Only the construction of a land route to connect Alaska to the Lower 48 would turn Alaska's strategic liability into a strategic asset. Black troops would be pivotal in building it.

Black Soldiers and the Alaska Highway

In the winter of 1943, Froelich Rainey wrote an impressive twenty-five-page exposé on the Alaska Highway (also referred to as the Alaska-Canadian Highway or, simply, the Alcan) for *National Geographic Magazine*; he referred to it as an "engineering epic." Although it was the most comprehensive coverage of the highway yet received, Rainey nonetheless left out critical details of the story. While he noted cursorily, early in his essay, that both "Black and white" soldiers assisted in the construction, Rainey provided the Black engineers only three references and failed to detail their contributions. Not a single photo in the essay featured a Black soldier. One might be excused for assuming that only white soldiers toiled amid the frozen tundra and northern wilderness to complete the continent's largest wartime infrastructure project. Black regiments performed the most grueling work, and they did so in segregated units with inferior equipment and lodging. Rainey missed a central plotline in the story of the Alaska Highway, or maybe he simply left it out so as not to highlight the contributions of Black soldiers.[61]

Rainey was not the only author who ignored the contributions of Black soldiers in the construction of the Alaska Highway. A three-part series in the *Engineering News-Record* in 1942 to 1943 also did not mention Black engineers in the text, though three pictures among fifty-nine clearly depicted Black soldiers.[62] A 1944 *Collier's* feature, which suggested the road was a "dubious investment," did not note the presence of Black engineers.[63] African Americans during World War II received a more inclusive accounting of Blacks in Alaska from Herbert Frisby, a war correspondent for the *Baltimore Afro-American*. Frisby first visited Alaska in 1943 to report on the Alaska Highway and the accomplishments of "colored regiments." He was the first Black civilian to travel the road.[64] Frisby fell in love with Alaska and made numerous return trips during and after the war, including a tour of the Aleutians, where he was present during President Franklin Roosevelt's 1944 visit to the islands.[65]

A more exhaustive report would have started in 1940, when Black regiments assembled in the American South. Men such as Fred Spencer of the Ninety-Third Engineer Battalion gathered in the piney woods of Louisiana at the newly created Camp Livingston; the 388th Regiment reported to Camp Claiborne, also in Louisiana; and the Ninety-Fifth Regiment trained at Fort Bragg, North Carolina. Other Black troops trained in Camp Lee, Virginia. The officers of these battalions were white, men like Tim Timberlake, who hailed from a middle-class family and possessed a freshly minted degree in mechanical engineering from the University of Maryland. Timberlake was among the few white servicemen to lead thousands of Black troops through Canada and Alaska. Enlisted men, on the other hand, such as Willie Lavalais and Fred Spencer, were sons of sharecroppers and laborers who grew up in the rural South. At the time of their enlistment, these men did not know they would be shipping off to Alaska, and for most it was their first time away from home.[66]

Tim Timberlake wrote to his girlfriend that the Ninety-Third had boarded a train on April 12, 1942, on the Rock Island Railroad bound for an unknown destination. The train rambled northwestward through the high plains, traversed the mountain passes of the Rockies, and then entered Canada. The officers instructed the Black troops aboard the trains to keep the blinds drawn so the townspeople they passed along the way would not see them. But apparently word got out that thousands of African Americans had been transiting through the country. Curious Canadians greeted the train and caught what for many was their first sight of a Black person. The trains crossed back into the United States and left the troops off at Camp Murray, not far from Puget Sound in Washington. From there the men boarded well-provisioned ships and made their way to Skagway, Alaska.[67]

The idea to connect Alaska to the Lower 48 via Canada went back at least a decade. The Canadians had built a staging route for their military from Edmonton through British Columbia and terminating in Whitehorse, Yukon Territory. This route could presumably extend into Alaska, but it would take a significant effort to blaze a suitable path through the taiga and muskeg. The United States and Canada also desired a means by which to transport oil into Alaska via a pipeline. The result, the Canadian Oil pipeline (Canol, for short), moved light crude from Canada's Northwest Territories into Alaska. The road and pipeline were the largest North American infrastructure projects undertaken during the war and the most ambitious since the Panama Canal was built thirty years earlier.[68]

A herculean task, the construction of what was soon dubbed the Alaska-Canada, or Alcan, Highway involved ten thousand troops, four thousand of whom were Black. All labored intensively for nearly nine months in 1942 to blaze a passable road through fifteen hundred miles of boreal forest. The men lived in drafty pup tents and faced extreme temperatures and brutal working conditions. The Ninety-Third and Ninety-Fifth deployed to northern British Columbia and the Yukon, the Ninety-Seventh worked from Alaska, and the 388th received its orders in northern Alberta and the Northwest Territories. The white officers who commanded the Black troops expressed disdain for the men they led. Gen. William M. Hoge, for example, looked at his men in the Ninety-Seventh with contempt as he iterated racial slurs and questioned their work ethic. In one exchange Hoge recalled, "Those niggers just looked at all that snow—it was all white . . . I told them . . . the only way you're going to get home—back to Alabama or Georgia is to work down south. Head down south and keep working."[69] Hoge's bigotry belied the accomplishments of the troops who built key sections of the highway, including the most difficult stretch, a bridge that crossed the Sikanni Chief River. Located 160 miles from Dawson Creek, in Canada, the river raged three hundred feet across, icy rapids threatened the soldiers, and there was no way to reroute the road around the water.[70]

Making matters more challenging, many of the white commanding officers did not permit the Black troops to use heavy mechanical equipment. Racist logic dictated that Black men possessed brute strength and were biologically suited to muscular work, a trope rooted in the nation's history of enslavement. Instead, white officers provided Black men with hammers, saws, and axes. These men endured icy water and worked around the clock, singing work songs as if they were in a chain gang. Col. Heath Twichell Sr., a white commanding officer who bucked senior command, recognized the achievement of the men. He ordered his white soldiers to share space in the dining hall with their fellow Black soldiers.[71]

The Ninety-Seventh completed another important section of the road in the Yukon near Beaver Creek. One man, Corp. Refines Sims Jr., received permission to operate a bulldozer over a rough, twelve-mile stretch. There Corporal Sims met Pvt. Alfred Jalufka, a white man with the Eighteenth Engineers. The two men completed the final segment of the road and shook hands in a show of solidarity and a shared sense of accomplishment. The soldiers achieved what many thought impossible: the construction of an overland route from Alaska to the Lower 48.[72] Men such as Corporal Sims, Fred Spencer, Willie Lavalais, and thousands of others helped construct the largest wartime project in North America. By the time the road opened for military use, in 1943, thirty-three men, Black and white, had died in the effort to complete it. Temperatures reached ninety degrees Fahrenheit in the summer and plunged to seventy degrees below zero in winter. Black troops lived in segregated camps without the amenities of their white counterparts, and they worked mostly by hand while white troops constructed the road with mechanical tools. Despite the disparities, the Black troops pressed ahead, oftentimes exceeding both the pace of work of their white counterparts and the expectations of their white commanding officers.[73]

In 1944 Herbert Frisby returned to Alaska again and discovered that many Alaskans called the Alaska Highway the "Negro Road." And although one of the men Frisby interviewed claimed that "several colored persons live here," the correspondent located only three Blacks in Fairbanks. Therefore, it seemed that few Black men stayed in Fairbanks at the conclusion of the project. The high cost of living accounted for one reason few African Americans stayed in Fairbanks after the war. Frisby quipped, "There's nothing fair about Fairbanks but the name." To find a job, stay well fed, and keep a roof over one's head, Frisby calculated a cost of $2,500 to start, a large amount for someone to have on hand in the 1940s.[74] But as the years went by, the Black population of the Alaska Interior increased, especially after the integration of the military in the late 1940s. Since then, thousands of Black soldiers have

Soldiers pose during basic training in Louisiana before departing to work on the Alaska Highway. Lael Morgan Collection, Elmer E. Rasmuson Library, University of Alaska Fairbanks (UAF-2012-71-308).

served at Eielson Air Force Base (formerly known as Eielson Field during the war) and Fort Wainwright.

Secretary of War Henry Stimson lauded the so-called Negro Road and those who "pushed forward at the rate of eight miles a day, bridged 200 streams, laid a roadway 24 feet between ditches, [and] at the highest point, between Fort Nelson and Watson Lake, reached an altitude of 4,212 feet."[75] The Alaska Highway not only served the purposes of war; it opened to the public in 1948, and civilian travelers could drive on it through western Canada into Alaska. Motorists by the thousands continue to travel the highway each year. The Canol Project, on the other hand, fared significantly worse. It never viably transported oil to Alaska, and it became the focus of a Senate investigation led by Missouri senator Harry S. Truman. Truman burnished his credentials when he concluded the pipeline was a waste of money and a burden on the public treasury; the government soon decommissioned it. Truman's bolstered reputation led to his selection by Franklin Roosevelt to serve on the ticket as vice president in the 1944 election. Truman assumed the presidency upon the death of Roosevelt in April 1945.[76]

Meeting of bulldozers at Beaver Creek, Yukon, Canada, October 25, 1942. On the left, Corp. Refines Sims Jr., Ninety-Seventh Engineers; and to the right, Pvt. Alfred Jalufka, Eighteenth Engineers. US Army Corps of Engineers, Office of History.

In 1993 a remote Alcan bridge was renamed in honor of the Black Alcan engineers. In 2011 Alaska lieutenant governor Fran Ulmer declared: "If you've ever driven the Alaska Highway, you might remember a bridge just south of Delta on the way to Tok, that spans the Gerstle River. There's a sign on both ends displaying its name—the Black Veterans Memorial Bridge. It is a small gesture to name a bridge, but I hope that by doing so we will be reminded of the significance of the contributions of the regiments and of every black soldier since."[77]

From the Alaska Highway to the Aleutian Campaign

The Alaska Highway was not the only contribution made by Black troops in the territory. Some, like those in the Ninety-Seventh Army Corps of Engineers, briefly deployed to Fairbanks only to be redeployed after military commanders complained that a breach in segregation might occur if they stayed in town. As a result, most of them ended up serving in the Aleutians. Despite Lieutenant General Buckner's request that Black men not be stationed at ports or close to towns where racial mixing might occur, wartime necessity dictated that both the segregated units—including the 372nd, 373rd, and 383rd Port Battalions—and the First and Second Battalions of the Ninety-Third Engineers deployed to population centers on the Alaska Peninsula and the Aleutians during the summer of 1943. The 364th Infantry Regiment served in the Aleutians after experiencing racial violence and attacks in Phoenix, Arizona, and then at Camp Van Dorn, Mississippi. In Alaska, however, a level of what one might call incidental integration occurred, and race relations could be described as comparatively cordial.[78]

The first battalion of the Ninety-Third traveled from the newly built highway to Cold Bay, a small settlement on the Alaska Peninsula. The second battalion of the Ninety-Third included six hundred men who were stationed at Fort Glenn on Umnak, part of the Fox Islands in the Aleutian chain. By that time the Japanese had sustained their invasion of the Aleutians and attacked Dutch Harbor; Cold Bay and Umnak thus served as staging areas for a counteroffensive. At Cold Bay the Black engineers with the Ninety-Third built warehouses, expanded the water and sewage systems, improved the airstrips and road system, and assisted on the construction of a hospital and medical facilities. Nine of the men with the Ninety-Third were sent to Adak, farther down the Aleutian chain, where their knowledge and skills could be used. After having spent eight months in the brutal cold and harsh conditions along the Alaska Highway, one member of the battalion referred to his new station as "the balmy Aleutians."[79]

Still, service in a theater of war was hardly fun and games, as service members learned quickly. On Umnak Island at Fort Glenn, the engineers with the Ninety-Third worked alongside the white 802nd Engineer Aviation Battalion to surface runways, build airplane hangars, and put up huts for men to take up residence. Yet Black men remained housed in a segregated encampment labeled "N" on maps of the military installation, presumably for "Negro." According to archaeologist Chris Roe, up to six hundred Black men on Fort Glenn ate in a segregated mess hall in barracks apart from their white counterparts. The isolated encampment was set along a marsh and stream at a distance from the white troops, likely a response to Buckner's desire to maintain rigid segregation. However, the troops labored together to complete Cape Field, the westernmost airfield established on the North American continent by the army.[80]

Black troops gather on May 20, 1943, near Massacre Bay, nine days after the American invasion to retake Attu Island from the Japanese. Photographs of American Military Activities, 1918–81, National Archives and Records Administration, Record Group 111: Records of the Office of the Chief Signal Officer, 1860–1985.

Military historian Charles Hendricks has written that members of the 383rd Port Battalion arrived in Adak and Attu and immediately worked eighteen-hour shifts unloading cargo in preparation to retake the islands. A hundred Black soldiers served as litter bearers during combat on Attu, and others came under sniper fire. In a notable but tragic instance, Black soldiers in the 364th Army Infantry Regiment went into combat on Kiska Island, after having gone through training in Louisiana. Matthew Little, an infantryman with the 364th, recalled how he and others charged Kiska from the south as "Alaskan scouts were to attack it from the north side . . . and when we met we thought each other were the enemy." He continued, "Some of the people were killed actually . . . the Japanese had done, escaped, left everything intact, hospitals, ships, and everything else." Little noted that if the war had persisted beyond the spring of 1945, men in the 364th were prepared to invade Japan from the North Pacific.[81] Though the outcome was obviously not desirable, the very fact that the Black troops were sent in to combat roles represented something of a turning point.

Brig. Gen. Harry Thompson believed the Black troops who served in the Aleutians carried out their orders "nearly as efficiently" as the white troops but had proven to be more diligent. Even as white commanders openly disparaged or only tepidly approved of their performance, African American soldiers stationed in Alaska never openly rebelled as they had elsewhere, despite the dehumanizing segregation and racism. One reason may be that the color line at times collapsed as Black and white troops worked together on challenging projects. At other moments, as the deployment of 364th demonstrates, white commanding officers, if begrudgingly, permitted Black soldiers to play a more direct role in combat operations, issuing an implicit recognition that the men could fight equally as well as their white counterparts. Accordingly, morale in the Aleutians among African American servicemen seemed to have exceeded that of other spots in the United States and even overseas.[82]

This was particularly true in Adak, where a small number of Black soldiers deployed. As a far-flung location in the remote—albeit vitally strategic—North Pacific, a deployment to Adak was not viewed as prestigious or desirable. Historian Reese Palley served in the Aleutians and recalled that those who ended up in the Aleutians typically fell into one of three categories: "troublemakers, homosexuals, and P.A.F.s." *PAF* stood for "premature anti-fascist," a moniker given to outspoken leftists who were sympathetic to the Russian Revolution, civil rights, organized labor, and the Republican faction in the Spanish Civil War that raged through the late 1930s. Unsurprisingly, given the army's treatment of the theater as a dumping ground for the undesired, a relatively large contingent of Black troops were also deployed to the Aleutians.[83]

One of the troops sent to the Aleutians, a Black man named Harvey Schmidt, developed a reputation for his activism that did not sit well with his commanding officers. Schmidt's son-in-law, George Campbell Jr., recounted that his father-in-law "was court martialed during the war [World War II] for protesting segregated barber shops. He did one of the original sit-ins in 1942." Campbell continued: "He sat-in, he went to a barber shop . . . He said I'm an enlisted man, I want a haircut. They said no we don't cut Black, you know, colored's hair here. He said well I'm an enlisted man and I'm going to sit here until you cut my hair. He wouldn't cut his hair." The incident caused a stir, and his commanding officer soon put in a request to cut Schmidt loose from his company. He first received a court-martial, but "they [the army] sent him to Alaska." Schmidt went on to spearhead a legal services agency in Philadelphia.[84]

Other African American soldiers deployed to the most remote reaches of Alaska's Aleutian Islands under less than auspicious circumstances. Lucky Cordell arrived just after the war. Clearly disappointed, he "would talk to guys who had been in all these glamorous places, interesting, to Hawaii. To the Virgin Islands. To all of these places, right? And I thought, well I get a chance to see some of the world." But Cordell received his orders to report elsewhere: "When I left where we did the basic training, they put us on a ship and started us to a place called Amchitka, Alaska." He referred to it as a "God forsaken island in the middle of nowhere where trees don't grow!" He conceded: "The accommodations were fine. We had Quonset huts. And that's where I spent my time." But it was difficult for Cordell not to look back at the experience with some sense of embitterment. "The whole eighteen months on that island," he reported, "never got a chance to go to France or Japan or any of these interesting places. I really thought that I was going to Hawaii."[85] So it was that the Aleutians may have presented a milder climate than the interior of Alaska or Canada's Yukon on the construction site of the Alaska Highway. But despite its unquestionably strategic location, the Aleutians—and Alaska more generally—was a hardship post where the army's least desirable men would be sent.

Author Dashiell Hammett was the most famous figure to enlist and serve in the Aleutians. Though white, Hammett could have been categorized as a premature anti-fascist. In addition, he was a fierce advocate for civil rights and racial justice. Hammett served in the Aleutians for nearly two years, from 1943 to 1945. Already a celebrated novelist known for his noir and crime fiction, he enlisted in the army as a corporal at the age of forty-nine. His left-wing political views often clashed with the values of the army, and his age and lifestyle rendered him less than optimal for the rigors of life in the service. In addition to his open sympathies with the Communist Party, Hammett drank heavily and viewed the hierarchy of the US military as being at odds with the freewheeling life of a writer; his advocacy for civil rights put him at odds with top military brass from the start. Nonetheless, his skills as a writer, publisher, and editor led the army to accept him into the US Army Signal Corps. By the summer of 1943, over fifty thousand troops deployed across the islands, mobilizing to expel the Japanese. There Hammett assembled a group of men to write training manuals, organize variety shows and lectures for the radio, and print a newsletter, entitled the *Adakian*, for the troops to read about the war's progress. They eventually published *The Battle of the Aleutians*.[86]

Dashiell Hammett with the soldiers in the US Army Signal Corps who printed the *Adakian*, ca. 1942–43. Diane Johnson Collection, Harry Ransom Center, University of Texas at Austin.

Despite the US Army's policy of segregation, Hammett recruited two Black men into the operation, Don Miller, a Jamaican-born illustrator, and Alva Morris, a printer. Hammett leveraged his outsized personality and flouted the army's rules. He never received permission to include the Black soldiers, but together they formed a relationship that lasted through the conflict. Though it may be viewed as a minor detail in the scope of such an enormous conflict, the inclusion of Miller and Morris in Hammett's signal corps made it an integrated division in the Jim Crow military. Just as soldiers challenged the color line during the final phase of construction on the Alaska Highway, so, too, did it come under duress in the Aleutians.

One must, however, resist the conclusion that these events represented unqualified racial advancement. Reluctant moments of desegregation were necessitated by the complications of the Alaska Highway construction followed by the reoccupation and defense of the Aleutian Islands. These campaigns placed tremendous stress on Indigenous people throughout Alaska (to say nothing of the Japanese population based along the West Coast). As one example, the United States military dispossessed Alaska Natives of their ancestral homelands during the Aleutian campaign. Here racist assumptions overrode any logistical justification to force the Unangan people from their villages. The military viewed these Indigenous men and women as untrustworthy and even as potential collaborators with the Japanese, a shallow and baseless supposition based upon the phenotypical appearance of Alaska Natives in the Aleutian and Pribiloff Islands.[87]

The armed forces thus forcefully relocated entire Unangan villages across the Gulf of Alaska, hundreds of miles away from their homes in the Aleutian and Pribiloff Islands, to the territory's southeastern panhandle. The navy razed homes and destroyed property; those removed were then interned and experienced violations of their civil rights and liberties. The military forced young Unangan men to harvest seals. They endured decrepit conditions and lived in renovated structures originally built for canning salmon. Over a hundred Native men, women, and children died in what has come to be known as the "Aleut evacuation." Yet the Unangan people persisted and eventually settled land claims with the federal government. In 1988 the United States acknowledged wrongdoing and paid twelve thousand dollars to each of the survivors even as most of these families were barred from ever again returning to the place they had lived for generations.[88]

In sum, the military's record on race relations during the war should at best be viewed as a bundle of contradictions. Lt. Gen. Simon Bolivar Buckner remained an unrepentant white supremacist committed to segregation at nearly any cost. Most of the senior officers who operated under Buckner shared his beliefs. Yet troops at times worked together in common cause along the construction sites and on the islands. Life during wartime took a heavy toll on the nation's men and women in uniform, but African Americans—as well as other soldiers of color—dealt with the additional burden of discrimination as they labored in conditions inferior to their white counterparts and countenanced the everyday indignities of the Jim Crow military.

Some in Congress and other prominent public figures lauded the performance of the Black soldiers and demanded an end to segregation in the military. A. Philip Randolph, the legendary labor leader and activist, founded the League of Nonviolent Civil Disobedience Against Military Segregation and urged Black men to resist any additional service until the president or Congress acted to desegregate the military.[89] With Randolph's lobbying campaign and an increasing recognition of the contribution of Black soldiers during wartime, President Truman soon convened a committee on civil rights. It explored the effects of segregation in the military and documented the valor of minority service members. The effort and achievements of African American and other minority troops created a space in which to unequivocally lay claim to equality and full citizenship. This was, of course, precisely what many racists feared would happen if Black men participated in the war as soldiers. And in fact, the civil rights committee recognized, "Since equality in military service assumes great importance as a symbol of democratic goals, minorities have regarded it not only as a duty but as a right."[90] The committee published its findings under the title *To Secure These Rights*. In response to the findings of the committee and in recognition of the invaluable service of Black soldiers, including those who served in Alaska, Harry Truman issued Executive Order 9981 in July 1948. The order desegregated the armed forces and is widely understood as one of the landmark actions of the nascent civil rights movement. The Black men who served in Alaska during wartime not only anticipated Truman's bold action, but their service perhaps even made it a fait accompli.[91]

A New Alaska Emerges

By the end of the war, Alaska's culture, economy, and demographics had forever changed. Thousands from the Lower 48 arrived in the territory to serve a nation at war. Thousands of others who already lived in Alaska moved to other parts of the territory or enlisted with the armed forces; some served abroad. The sheer size and vulnerability of Alaska ensured copious levels of federal spending to protect its borders, land, and coast. The military presence quickly turned Southcentral Alaska into a population center, and the interior city of Fairbanks grew precipitously as well. Overall, Alaska's population nearly doubled from the late 1930s through the early 1950s; it reached over a quarter-million by the 1960 census. Without the investment by the federal government in infrastructure and military installations—first in World War I, then World War II, and throughout the Cold War—Alaska's population and economy would have likely stagnated. Instead, robust growth occurred.

Of course, the war also fueled conflict—including the so-called Zoot Suit Riots of 1943 Los Angeles—as people from different backgrounds encountered each other.[92] Not surprisingly, racial tensions did not simply cease after the conflict. In ports and military towns across America, the sensibilities of conservative whites ran up against emboldened African American soldiers who more willfully asserted their rights and challenged the discrimination and racial antagonism that many had long silently endured. In Alaska one case involved a Black man, James Willis, who went out for a night on the town in the coastal settlement of Wrangell. Willis, a member of the US Coast Guard, entered the town bar one evening in October 1945. By several accounts he and a white woman hit it off and began to dance, at which point several white men in the coast guard approached Willis and demanded that he step away from the woman. One man, Leonard Supernaw, a white sailor from Oklahoma, threw Willis to the ground and commenced a brutal attack. Fearing for his life, Willis reached for a knife on a barroom table and stabbed Supernaw.[93]

The Oklahoman died minutes later; Willis was treated for his injuries, including a damaged spine and ears that never fully healed. Willis faced a manslaughter charge. Wrangell authorities detained three other African American sailors without charge for several days to prevent a larger retaliatory uprising among the white men. Though initial military records claimed otherwise, Willis never received an attorney nor a day in court. Instead, he was sentenced to five years, stripped of his rank, and given a dishonorable discharge; his veteran benefits were revoked. He maintained that the act was in self-defense, and few doubted that the incident stemmed from the racial animosity of the white men in the coast guard. Willis waited nearly fifty years until justice eventually prevailed. In 1997, after activists and family members called upon the coast guard to reexamine the case, it became clear that Wrangell authorities and officers in the guard had falsified records. In response, Alaska's governor, Tony Knowles, granted Willis a pardon.[94] By then Willis was an elderly man who had lived with the stigma of having been dishonorably discharged and as an ex-felon for over five decades. But for the purposes of this book, Willis's case further reveals that the trend lines that prevailed nationwide also prevailed in Alaska. Though the territory offered genuinely exceptional opportunities for African Americans during and immediately after the war, it was never free from the nation's most pressing social ills.

Nonetheless, African Americans played a pivotal if underappreciated role in wartime Alaska. The case of James Willis, while illustrative of some broader tensions that lurked under the surface, did not necessarily reflect the experience of most African Americans who traveled to Alaska during the

1940s. After all, the Black population never exceeded 10 percent in the territory, despite the outsize impact its members had during the world war era. From John Conna in Fairbanks to Thomas Bevers in Anchorage, African Americans assumed prominent roles in business and politics and at war. This was especially true along the Alaska Highway, where the Black labor force stood at 40 percent, and the men constructed some of the most treacherous sections. Likewise, Black troops deployed to the Aleutians, where they defended the islands and assisted the counteroffensive against the Japanese invasion. Most of these soldiers promptly left the state after the war. If they had stayed, Alaska's Black population may have exceeded 10 percent. Today the Black population statewide is between 3 and 4 percent, with higher numbers in Anchorage and Fairbanks.[95] But again, these numbers fail to capture the influence and impact African Americans have had on Alaska during and between the world wars.

Once the war concluded, African Americans around the nation mobilized and posed tough questions about the implications of the war they had just participated in. What did it mean to fight fascism and white supremacy elsewhere if the same forces persisted at home? How could one justify fighting a war to expand democracy and freedom in other nations while such ideals remained unfulfilled in the United States?

CHAPTER FOUR

Discrimination, Opportunity, and Community in Postwar Alaska

"AS A COLORED-AMERICAN LIVING IN ANCHORAGE, ALASKA, YOU would be living 'high on the totem pole'—race relations wise," reported the *Negro Digest* in late 1963. The *Negro Digest* was among several publications to have summarized and taken an interest in Black life in Alaska during the 1950s and 1960s. Most did so in positive terms. *Ebony*, the monthly magazine with the nation's largest African American readership, twice featured stories about the good fortune Black migrants might find in Alaska. On the eve of statehood in 1958, the publication declared, "Alaska is a land of opportunity for hardworking pioneers with definite skills to offer." The article included the voice of banker and philanthropist Elmer Rasmuson, who claimed Alaska's largest city, Anchorage, wanted to attract people "progressive in outlook and conscientious in endeavor" to contribute to the city's economic, political, and cultural life.[1]

Alaska's congressional delegate and soon-to-be senator Bob Bartlett told *Ebony*, "The same opportunities open to anyone in Alaska are open to Negroes."[2] Yet *Ebony* was not so naive as to suggest Alaska remained free from the racial animus that regularly made national news. The article revealed that the booming commercial fishing industry in Ketchikan excluded Black men; African Americans and Alaska Natives reported high levels of housing segregation in Anchorage, Fairbanks, and Juneau. A high-profile case of a public hanging took place in the territory's capital city, Juneau, in 1948 and once again in 1950, the last recorded instance of the death penalty in Alaska. Both men were African Americans accused and found guilty of a 1946 robbery and murder on flimsy evidence and sentenced to death.³ On balance, however, the coverage of Alaska remained mostly positive in the Black press, particularly in comparison to other states that experienced the highest levels of racial violence.

Newly arrived Blacks bolstered the claims found in *Ebony* and the *Negro Digest* and found Alaska to be a placed of relative freedom but one most certainly not without barriers and animus toward residents of color. Maryland-born Marie Johnson-Calloway, for example, moved to Fairbanks in 1952 with her husband, a surgeon in the military. The two noted that the base remained nearly all white, though there existed a modest number of Black residents; it was apparently more integrated than what Johnson-Calloway had grown accustomed to in her hometown. She reported that Fairbanks "was our first experience in living in an integrated way, because nothing was integrated in Baltimore." Johnson-Calloway first noted the presence of other African Americans in town as she walked down the street and "all of a sudden this odor hit my nose, and I said I smell Black hair burning." In an oral history, Johnson-Calloway smiled and laughed as she recounted, "There's got to be a Black beauty parlor because there's nothing else that smells like hair being straightened." Sure enough, Johnson-Calloway continued down the road and located a Black-owned beauty parlor. Like other Black-owned establishments, the institution brought members of the community together to discuss the news of the day and forge common bonds. By Johnson-Calloway's account, the limited presence of Black men and women in Fairbanks failed to ruffle the feathers of the white majority. "We became very friendly with quite a few people there," she concluded.⁴

Johnson-Calloway's brief anecdote captured a basic point about Alaska's race relations: it was not comparable to the American South, the region most associated with extreme anti-Black racial hostility. A white construction worker who prospered in the vibrant postwar Anchorage economy wrote in a later memoir: "Black people had it hard. Not that they weren't ready to fight for their rights, but most of them had come from places a lot more prejudiced than Anchorage, and, besides, they were making money." He added: "Everyone had lots of rights, but didn't expect the government to do anything about it. You had exactly as many rights as you were willing to fight for. You could, to a fair degree, do whatever you wanted to."⁵

But at the same time, the postwar years ushered in a new era of discrimination against people of color in Alaska, even as nascent forms of activism and greater levels of political involvement among Black residents occurred.

This chapter highlights the contradictions of Black life in Alaska in the late 1940s through the 1960s. African American men and women found lucrative positions seldom available elsewhere, though they also reported persistently unequal treatment. Institutional power in Alaska remained firmly in the hands of white men, despite a growing and increasingly diverse population. As such, this chapter also troubles the conclusion of the *Negro Digest* that Alaska's Black population lived "high on the totem pole." Rather, the patterns of segregation and discrimination that largely defined the nation in the years following World War II also prevailed in Alaska. We uncover these patterns and demonstrate the ways in which racism operated in public settings and influenced the real estate market and urban landscape of Alaska's largest and most rapidly growing city as well as the ways Black Alaskans responded.

A Bonanza for Blacks?

A decade after its first piece on what became the forty-ninth state, *Ebony* posed the question "Is Alaska a Bonanza for Blacks?" The publication then furnished a generally enthusiastic response. Workers could expect to find wages 25 percent higher in Anchorage and a bit higher still in Fairbanks. Unfortunately, the higher cost of living offset the wage differential, the publication conceded. Even so, according to *Ebony*, African Americans found skilled work through the many unions in town. The article also reported that oil field lease sales brought in "$900 million—as much money as the total worth of all the gold ever found in the state and an amount almost 150 times the $7,200,000 the US paid Russia for Alaska." With just 270,000 people in the state at the time the magazine hit the shelves in 1969—"a number equal to the size of the crowd in the March on Washington in 1963"—*Ebony* concluded that Alaska may be fertile ground for Black advancement.[6]

Ebony writer Steven Morris and photographer Hal Franklin arrived in Anchorage and quickly located a few people who successfully took advantage of what the forty-ninth state allegedly offered. But none achieved as much wealth and status as Zula Swanson, dubbed by *Ebony* as "Alaska's richest Black." Morris's report on Swanson showcased an enterprising woman who captured the frontier spirit of the Wild West. Born in Alabama at the height of the Jim Crow era in the early twentieth century, Swanson later recalled, "When a small girl, I just made up my mind that I wasn't going to pick anymore cotton in the dust fields."[7] She abandoned the South and moved first to

Portland, Oregon, and then to Alaska. She arrived in the territory in 1929 and invested two thousand dollars in a burned-out building on land east of downtown Anchorage. Once renovated, Swanson's Rendezvous Building became a popular gathering spot for Anchorage's eastside residents.[8]

A former prostitute, she abandoned the Lower 48 in the wake of her pimp's arrest and a narrowly escaped drunk driving charge for an incident that left another woman dead. In Alaska she promoted herself to madam and capitalized on the nascent city's appetite for nightlife and vice. Some of her properties doubled as places of prostitution and gambling. Even so, Swanson developed a solid business reputation, though rumors swirled that intimate connections with Anchorage's political elite had furthered her ambitions.[9] Regardless, she provided the establishments and services that the population demanded. During the height of the postwar boom, an estimated 90 percent of Anchorage's eateries, clubs, and bars featured strippers or other forms of ribald entertainment.[10]

As her stature and fortunes rose, Swanson began to invest in real estate. In 1944 she told Herbert Frisby of the *Baltimore Afro-American*, "I urge all my friends to buy undeveloped land and hold onto it."[11] She had accurately foreseen and taken advantage of the rapidly rising value of land in and around Anchorage as the still young town stood poised for a generation of staggering growth. Upon her death in 1973, at age eighty-one, Swanson owned over $500,000 in real estate holdings (about $3 million in 2021 dollars), including four downtown lots.[12] It would be hard if not impossible to imagine any scenario whereby Swanson achieved a similar level of wealth, property, and status in her native Alabama.

Swanson's story, though exceptional, nevertheless highlights how African Americans accessed opportunities as Anchorage grew from an isolated railroad town to a modern city. George C. Anderson arrived after World War II to work as a linotype operator for the *Anchorage Daily News*. Soon after, he started Anchorage's first Black newspaper, the *Alaska Spotlight*. Anderson also penned a feature article for the nationally distributed magazine *Color* in April 1953. The piece described Alaska's "Negro pioneers" who had found economic and political success in their adopted home territory. He referred to Anchorage as the "Chicago of Alaska" and a hub for Black migration. It was true that most Black Alaskans worked in jobs that paid more than two dollars an hour, a decent sum for the early 1950s and higher than what Black workers typically earned elsewhere.

Zula Swanson, n.d. Zula Swanson Photographs, Anchorage Museum (B1977.104.1).

Still, Anderson admonished, though "wages are considerably higher than can be earned Outside . . . they do not begin to come up to the fantastic figures which Stateside rumors give them." He also addressed the questions of whether Anchorage, and Alaska more generally, suffered from the racism and prejudice so pervasive nationally. "No sensible person would deny that there is prejudice in Anchorage," Anderson wrote. He concluded, "There's no more [racial discrimination], and certainly less, than that found in the most liberal Stateside communities."[13] Anderson's article also described several institutions that strengthened Black civic and religious life in Anchorage. As he wrote in 1953, some of the more significant gathering spots included an Elks Lodge and two churches, Shiloh Baptist Church and the Greater Friendship Baptist Church. Like many of the other reports and articles, Anderson struck an optimistic tone; he discussed Black-owned businesses and employers who had a reputation for hiring African Americans from inside as well as outside of the territory. As one example of a Black business in Anchorage, Anderson cited the Green Acres Lodge, owned and operated by Richard and Helen Burge.[14]

However, Anderson failed to note that Green Acres, the very development where the Burges established their business, was in fact one of the few places Black men and women could settle and own a home in Anchorage during the 1950s. More generally, Anderson's article for *Color*, as well as the *Ebony* pieces, glossed over deeper patterns of racial discrimination found throughout Alaska. While George Anderson and Zula Swanson successfully navigated the predominantly white spaces of business, media, and real estate, further analysis uncovers familiar patterns of discrimination and puts Anchorage more squarely in line with other postwar American cities in the North and West. As such, Anderson's interpretation of urban Alaska might be viewed as overly optimistic if one delves more thoroughly into the systemic discrimination that lurked below the surface. In fact, doing so reveals equal or greater levels of discrimination present throughout the territory and state during the same years; however, much of the strongest documentation and many of the oral histories exist for those who spent most of their time in Anchorage.

Discrimination in Urban Alaska

The extent to which racial discrimination pervaded Alaska during the postwar decades remains disputed, but anti-Native and anti-Black views were prevalent. George Anderson claimed, "Anchorage is remarkably free from racial discrimination, both in matter of employment and public accommodation . . . most cases reported are strictly of the hearsay variety."[15] Although taking into account oral histories and testimonials, city housing and court records, and an array of documented employment practices and criminal justice figures, one finds that discrimination existed on a far greater scale than simple anecdotes or "hearsay." If Anderson concluded that Alaska's Negro pioneers had encountered a territory open, accessible, and free of discrimination, others vehemently disagreed.

One woman, Madeline Holmes, arrived in Anchorage in 1941 and described a hostile climate for African Americans and Alaska Natives. After the war Holmes wrote to the NAACP Legal Defense Fund to receive assistance to address the open levels of racism she experienced. She explained: "Negroes are very prejudiced against in this city. It has become increasingly so since the late war."[16] Holmes pointed out that Black women who worked on base also experienced discrimination during and after the war. She related: "The colored women who work at Fort Richardson are not allowed to leave the base. One even worked a day or two and was never paid and her baggage removed by some M.Ps."[17] Holmes described her conversations with other Black Alaskans and reported that "never a day passes that I do not hear some of our race complain that they may as well live in the south as to live in Anchorage."[18]

Holmes also provided the strongest account of racial discrimination within the Anchorage Police Department and among city officials during the postwar years. After having been attacked by a dog while on a walk outside of her home, Holmes called the police for protection but to no avail. She reported to the NAACP Legal Defense Fund that the officer who answered her call referred to her as a "damned nigger" and then explained he could not address the situation. When Holmes reported the incident to the chief of police, he countered that the individual who had iterated the epithet was not referring to Holmes but, instead, to a Black man in the interrogation room whom officers suspected of having committed a crime. Not surprisingly, Holmes was dissatisfied with the explanation and took up the issue with Anchorage mayor, Z. J. Loussac. In response, Loussac allegedly defended the police: "Well you can't blame them. The colored people here are all no good." Holmes then recalled that the mayor "went on to give me a long list of grievances the police had about the colored people" in Anchorage. He concluded, according to Holmes, that "if [there were] any good ones they couldn't possibly be more than three or four" in the territory.[19]

In response to the interaction with Loussac, Holmes wanted to ensure that he would not win a seat in the territorial legislature and further his political career. She wrote letters to area newspapers and spread word of her encounters to her friends and sympathetic business owners in the tight-knit community. Loussac did not prevail in the race, although it is unclear what, if any, effect Holmes's campaign against him had had on his run. In any case, he retired from Alaska politics and relocated to Seattle, where he spent the rest of his days. Holmes grew increasingly embittered by the state of race relations in Alaska and continued to lobby for a greater presence of the NAACP in the territory. She directed her ire mostly toward an unresponsive police department. In one correspondence with the special counsel of the NAACP, she wrote, "I have lived here nine years and have been a taxpayer for seven and was given no protection at all by the city and then insulted when I demanded help." She continued: "The colored people here complain bitterly of the treatment we receive but do not try to get together and help themselves, and one person cannot do anything alone. The only way we can receive any help is to have it come from the continental US especially in Anchorage where the racial prejudice is becoming more prevalent." For their part the NAACP remained hesitant to get involved primarily on the grounds that Alaska remained a territory and not a state. Against this backdrop it would come as no surprise that Holmes would soon leave Alaska. Before she left for Oakland, California, in 1951, Holmes concluded, "If these conditions are not remedied we will have a state comparable to any below the Mason-Dixon Line."[20]

As she left, Holmes received a letter from the NAACP branch office in California to check in and debrief once she arrived in the Bay Area. The director, Earle Fischer, expressed his disappointment that a Black woman would find the territory so inhospitable as to simply up and leave. Fischer wrote sympathetically, "Let me say that I am very disturbed by your decision to leave Anchorage because it indicates that there exists in that city conditions of life so frightful to colored residents, that you, as a representative of the race, find it unbearable to the point of departing."[21] Others echoed her critique of local law enforcement. One man, Larue Giddens, lived in a trailer court on the edge of Anchorage. In a letter to the editor of the local Anchorage paper, Giddens acerbically noted: "We are all aware of the fact that we have a very efficient police force. It is in some respects so efficient that it neglects its respect to the general public for which it serves. This does not apply, or course, to all members of the force, however. I personally know at least one who is polite and courteous and has human understanding. But for the rest, they comb the streets with the attitude of Gestapo police. They are belligerent and discourteous."[22] Based on the brief letter from Giddens and the longer missives from Holmes, relations between Anchorage's small but growing Black population and its police department could only be described as poor. This relationship further deteriorated in the decades to follow.

Other Black leaders emerged in the early 1950s and 1960s to critique Alaska's race relations. Blanche McSmith, a woman who arrived in Alaska via Texas and then California, would go on to lead among the most influential lives of any Alaskan, regardless of race. She served as a social worker, journalist, activist, and state legislator during her long career. She first noted the depths of racial animosity in Kodiak, where she and her husband settled in the late 1940s. The couple then relocated to Anchorage in the early 1950s and experienced discrimination in several public settings, most notably the Pagoda Café on Fifth Avenue in downtown. McSmith, along with Bert B. Babero and Eura Dell Porter, all of whom were Black, reported that the café had refused to serve them and allegedly forced the three to leave the restaurant. In response, McSmith organized a lawsuit to seek justice. The case went to trial; according to the *Anchorage Daily Times*, it "was one of the first, if not the first case involving racial discrimination to be tried before a jury in Anchorage." But after the twelve-person jury deliberated, they acquitted the owners and staff of the Pagoda on the grounds that the three African American patrons were refused service not due to their race but instead because they had failed to properly reserve a table in advance. The case animated McSmith to get more involved in activism and pursue racial justice in the years to follow. She became one of the most prolific civil rights leaders in Alaska and would also serve as a strong counterpoint to George Anderson's optimistic boosterism in the pages of the *Spotlight*.[23]

A close associate of McSmith, Willard L. Bowman, a Black state employee who moved to Alaska in 1949, also took on the role of chief advocate for racial equality in the territory and the state. He, along with the likes of McSmith and others, carved out a career dedicated to ensuring justice and access for all Alaskans. In 1963 racial tension, or at least the threat of it, became ubiquitous enough that Governor William E. Egan—Alaska's first state governor—assembled a Human Rights Commission to investigate conditions in the newly admitted state and invited Bowman to participate. Bowman's assessment of Alaska stood at odds with both George Anderson's and that of the writers at *Ebony*. In one report Bowman concluded: "The Eskimo, Indian, and the Negro Alaskan is not a full member of any of these agencies, be they federal, state, local, or private. Nowhere in Alaska does he enjoy full employment opportunities. That is a cold hard fact which you must accept, and I make this statement without fear of contradictions."[24]

Bowman explored three aspects of economic life in and around Anchorage: publicly contracted construction jobs, the retail sector, and the city's fledgling financial institutions. According to Bowman, Carrs grocery store refused to hire qualified African Americans to fill management positions; construction firms that contracted with the city and the state also denied qualified Black and Alaska Native workers these jobs in favor of whites. Taking issue with the hiring policies of Alaska's largest homegrown bank, Elmer Rasmuson's National Bank of Alaska, Bowman recalled, "Only after months of talking and appealing . . . [was] the first Negro girl hired in a banking institution last fall." He continued, "Nor is it by chance that Negro or native tourists cannot find lodging in a surprisingly large number of motels and apartment buildings." "Make no mistake about it," Bowman concluded, "this is just as discriminatory as lunch rooms and hotels of the South."[25]

Bowman's research on Southcentral Alaska led him, in 1964, to advocate for the creation of a subcommittee of the Citizens Council for Community Improvement (CCCI), a research group to act under the authority of Governor Egan's Human Rights Commission. Bowman led the CCCI and developed a comprehensive survey on discrimination in Alaska, with an emphasis on the Southcentral region. The CCCI reported high levels of housing segregation and concluded that white residents deliberately excluded minorities from the housing market and relegated them to the least desirable land. To gather information, the CCCI sent out questionnaires to real estate brokers and salesmen. They asked agents and brokers "if they sold to minorities [or] if they would sell or rent to minorities in various designated districts such as Fairview, Mountain View, Spenard, Etc." Bowman received a low response rate; of the several dozen real estate brokers who were contacted, twenty returned the questionnaire. Despite the small sample size, only two stated that they "would sell or rent to [prospective minority home buyers or renters] anywhere."[26]

Bowman's survey revealed that white property owners would not accept Alaska Native and African Americans in most parts of Anchorage or the surrounding developments beyond the city limits.[27] Bowman also learned how restrictive the area housing market had been over the previous decades. Indeed, the first racially restricted housing covenants had appeared in June 1941, a year after construction began on Fort Richardson. Abutting downtown, the affluent South Addition neighborhood was expanding to its modern, southernmost edge. The Coffey Subdivision, developed and sold by Dan Coffey, included housing covenants with its properties. One stated: "No race or nationality other than those of the White or Caucasian race shall use or occupy any dwellings on any lot, except that this covenant shall not prevent occupancy by domestic servants of a different race or nationality, if such servants are employed by an owner or tenant."[28]

When the Alaska Highway opened to the public in 1947, migrants from the Lower 48 drove through Canada and into Alaska by motor vehicle. This trend corresponded with a federal commitment to defend and militarize Alaska amid an emerging Cold War. As Alaska's population increased through the late 1940s and 1950s, developers used racial covenants primarily on new housing, often to profit from the city's burgeoning military population. In 1945 not a single developer or home seller submitted to the local recorder's office a racially restrictive deed. But in 1946 twelve of these deeds were submitted. And in 1947 developers submitted twenty-nine. By 1950 racially restricted covenants were in place throughout the new neighborhoods at the expanding edge of southern Anchorage. These covenants approximated the language found from housing contracts around the country; however, the specific wording varied slightly from development to development.[29]

Each developer, or their lawyers, found a different way to effectively segregate area housing. One subdivision illustrates how covenant language evolved to achieve its desired effect. Over the course of three filings with the local recorder's office, Nicholas and Else Weiler, a couple who had arrived in the 1930s, crafted language to limit property ownership on their land to whites only. A July 29, 1947, deed in the Weiler subdivision proposed, "Said lots shall never be sold, rented to, or occupied by any person of negro descent."[30] Three months later the Weilers amended the deed's racial covenant: "That the Grantees, their heirs, administrators and assigns, are restricted and prohibited for the period of fifty (50) years from the date hereof from selling, conveying, leasing, letting or otherwise granting the said described property or any interest or use therein to any person or persons other than Caucasians."[31] By November 1947 new deeds in the Weiler subdivision struck the reference to a fifty-year moratorium to forbid the sale of the property to people of color in perpetuity. That the Weilers revised the deed three times highlights the degree to which developers, sellers, and purchasers shaped language to exclude nonwhites from otherwise new and desirable communities. Or conversely, the covenants demonstrated a belief among developers that the desirability of a neighborhood hinged upon its ability to exclude people of color. As greater Anchorage grew swiftly after the war, the Weilers thus anticipated not only prospective Black home buyers but, presumably, Alaska Natives, who increasingly relocated to Alaska's urban centers in search of jobs and professional advancement.

Rogers Park, located south of Fairview, formerly Eastchester, and across Chester Creek, were developed explicitly as a whites-only neighborhood. So, too, did the neighborhood to the northeast, Airport Heights, named for its proximity to the airstrip at Merrill Field. In Rogers Park the restrictive covenants governing housing sales required that "the property hereby conveyed shall not be sold or alienated in any manner whatsoever to anyone other than Americans of the white race."[32] Likewise, an Airport Heights covenant from 1953 stated plainly: "No race or nationality other than those of the White or Caucasian race shall use or occupy any dwelling on any lot in said Subdivision, except that this covenant shall not prevent the occupancy by domestic servants of a different race or nationality, if such servants are employed by an owner or tenant."[33]

Many newcomers looked for property beyond the city limits to points south and west of downtown Anchorage. A scenic area around Sand Lake, almost seven miles southwest of downtown, became a popular spot to purchase land and build homes. Here, too, would-be homeowners in the Sundi Lake subdivision, a development abutting Sand Lake, signed warranty deeds subject to restrictions on race. The very first such deed, filed in 1948, required of its inhabitants: "The premises herein concerned shall not be sold or alienated in any manner whatsoever to anyone except Americans of the white race."[34]

Even in Spenard, a neighborhood adjacent to downtown Anchorage long known for its share of outcasts, misfits, and troublemakers, minority homebuyers received a cold shoulder. In what would become Spenard's Kirchner Addition, Geraldine and John Kirchner, a Black couple, purchased land in 1949 from Clifford and Joan Schofield. The deed subjected the sale of the land to several conditions and restrictions. The third restriction required "the Vendee(s), their heirs and assigns, are restricted and prohibited for the period of fifty (50) years from the date hereof from selling, conveying, leasing, letting, or otherwise granting the said described property or any interest or use therein to any person or persons other than Caucasians."[35] If this deed remained in place throughout its stated duration, the plot of land would have stayed segregated until at least the turn of the twenty-first century.

As the Kirchners purchased the land to develop, the US Supreme Court ruled, in the landmark case, *Shelley v. Kraemer*, that state and territorial courts could not legally enforce restrictive covenants or discriminatory warranty deeds. However, the narrow scope of the ruling did little to prevent housing discrimination in Alaska or elsewhere. Real estate agents and loan officers, for example, continued to prevent African Americans and Alaska Natives from purchasing homes in white communities.[36] Ocea Mae Curry relocated to Alaska in 1951, three years after the *Shelley* case, but quickly discovered "opportunities for Blacks was very, very poor, very poor." Even though Curry held a job with the US Postal Service and arrived with considerable savings, a realtor "flatly denied" her request to view a home. The agent told her the home "is not for sale to you . . . Go to your people and buy property if you want property." It was, of course, clear to Curry what the man meant by "your people." Despite Curry's anger, she ultimately "drove away," acknowledging that the agent would face no recriminations for openly denying her the freedom to preview the homes of her choice.[37]

Black and other minority home buyers such as Ocea Mae Curry faced structural barriers to ownership, but sometimes a family of color circumvented the restrictions, went to court, and secured a loan, in which case, white residents often took it upon themselves to engage in violence and intimidation to keep Black families out.[38] In one extreme instance, arson seemed to be the preferred method of intimidation. Undaunted by the legacy of the restrictive covenants and racial exclusion, Alvin and Mary Lee Campbell, an African American couple, purchased land in Rogers Park in 1950. After successfully making a legal claim to the property, the Campbell family encountered a man in the neighborhood who threatened, "You might finish the house, but you will never enjoy living in it."[39] Not long after, on October 15, 1950, the house burned to the ground as the fire department responded but failed to put out the blaze. The *Anchorage Daily Times* reported the incident: "Fire of undetermined origin last night destroyed a house under construction on Snow Cap Avenue in the Rogers Park subdivision." The article noted, "The house, being built by Alvin Campbell, was the focal point in a recent court suit involving the racial issue."[40] The "racial issue" referenced by the *Times*

Alvin C. Campbell, February 1969. Alaska Railroad Collection, Anchorage Museum (B1979.002.1909).

was, of course, that a Black family had sought to move into a neighborhood on higher ground with newer, superior housing.[41]

The suspicious fire led to a flurry of activism. It culminated with the creation of the Anchorage branch of the NAACP in 1951, just a year after Madeline Holmes had tried without success to get the NAACP involved in the territory. Apparently, the racial violence associated with an arson attack convinced the association to make an exception and endorse a presence in the territory. Anchorage's NAACP soon became a hub of civil rights mobilization. Men and women such as Blanche McSmith, Clarence and Flossie Coleman, Joseph M. Jackson, John S. Parks, and Richard Watts, among others, were associated with the early days of the NAACP. John W. Thomas, also active in the labor movement as a union carpenter, assumed the role as the first president of the newly chartered branch of the NAACP and shepherded the organization through the early 1950s with strong leadership and a commitment to organizing across lines of race and class. These men and women would assume central roles at the city and state levels over the next thirty years.[42]

The Rise and Fall of Alaska's Largest Black Neighborhood: Eastchester Flats

As the Campbell family demonstrated, purchasing a home and settling in a white neighborhood in postwar Anchorage was a treacherous proposition. In fact, African Americans could reliably find housing only beyond city limits in unincorporated neighborhoods. And even these were at times restricted. In addition, unincorporated communities lacked the tax base to provide routine services such as road maintenance, fire and rescue, and sewage. These neighborhoods and subdivisions included Nunaka Valley and Green Acres at the respective eastern and southeastern edges of greater Anchorage. But the largest concentration of African Americans settled in Eastchester Flats, known simply as the Flats.

The name Eastchester Flats referred to the surrounding geography, a relatively level parcel of marginal, mosquito-infested land along the east fork of Chester Creek. "When I came back here in 1950 I went to every real estate dealer in town trying to buy a house in town," recalled one Black resident. "Not any would sell me any property. They all referred me to Eastchester Flats."[43] This resident was not alone. Madeline Holmes recalled her arrival in Southcentral Alaska in 1941. She recalled having been turned away in her effort to buy a home and noted, "It has become so bad that we can't even purchase property except at a place called Chester Creek."[44] By 1952 Anchorage's newly formed NAACP estimated three-quarters of the area's Black population lived in the Flats, likely the result of having been denied access to other neighborhoods. No other neighborhood in Alaska contained such a concentration of African American families throughout the 1950s and 1960s.[45]

Making matters more challenging, building materials were scarce and expensive, and construction in Eastchester Flats was cumbersome. One early settler recalled: "There were a lot of shacks and very poorly built houses, small houses, and there was no sewage, no water. They had one or two wells, and people secured the water there."[46] Another resident "rented a lot with twelve-foot space for $25.00 a month, and this was just ground space with the privilege of bathing once a week in this lady's house. That's how bad it was. There were four of us, and we cooked our meals in the yard out of a tent."[47] What homes existed in the area stood haphazardly, built from materials salvaged from military sites, the railroad, and junkyards.

Eastchester Flats came to be viewed as a "colored quarter organized by and for colored people," according to the journalist Herbert Frisby, who spent significant time in Alaska covering World War II, the Cold War, and Arctic issues for a largely Black readership in the Lower 48.[48] Residents received none of the sanitary services available in Anchorage proper but were also outside the jurisdiction of city laws. "It was no police" in the Flats, recalled Joe Jackson, a resident through the 1950s.[49] Without inspectors or building codes, ramshackle homes stood alongside bars, improvised entertainment venues, and piles of debris. The area also featured Black-owned businesses, including Alaska's only known Black-owned and operated grocery store. There were real estate offices, launderers, a beauty parlor, a motel, cafés, and barbershops in Eastchester Flats. Jackson noted proudly, "We were a small city within our own selves."[50]

Not surprisingly, as with many low-income communities that exist beyond the margins of middle-class acceptability, Eastchester Flats doubled as a red-light district known for its vice but also its entertainment. Bar owner Zelmer Lawrence recalled: "You could go to the Flats and find things you couldn't find any other place in the state ... At one time there were any number of cocktail bars running full blast in the Flats, you could get Schenley's [a Canadian whiskey], you could get the finest vodkas and wines and everything, no liquor licenses. There must have been twenty to thirty of them. Just a no-man's land."[51] According to Joe Jackson, "It was shacks all over the place, and it was prostitution and gambling, and everyone that was down there had some kind of a what they call a club."[52] Two such clubs, Parker's and the Backstreet Club—a known brothel and a gambling house, respectively—operated adjacent to Fifteenth Street, one of the primary thoroughfares in the area.[53] Jackson recalled a conversation with Anchorage's chief of police, who estimated the illicit businesses in Eastchester Flats brought in over three million dollars throughout the 1950s.[54]

In 1958, when Fred Johnson, a young air force navigator, arrived in Anchorage, he too received a memorable introduction to the Flats and described the scene of a bustling working-class enclave on the margins. Although Johnson found Alaska more welcoming to Black men like himself than his home state of Illinois, he nevertheless puzzled over what at first seemed to be an exceedingly low number of other African Americans in the town. Naturally, Johnson was surprised and enthusiastic when he noticed a few other Black folks at the Anchorage Park Strip playing baseball on a neighborhood team. After introducing himself and making friends, he was led to the Flats by members of the team. The community made a sufficient impression on him that he decided, after completing his service in the military, to call Alaska home. Johnson worked in the Flats first as a bartender and then as co-owner. Johnson mixed drinks at the North Star Light Lounge, established by another Black veteran, Jesse Leroy Hayden. Unlike many of the businesses in the Flats, the North Star Light Lounge possessed a territorial liquor license even as Johnson, like Joe Jackson, recalled a lack of law enforcement and a freewheeling environment—"just a United States Marshal who'd look down from 15th Street [up the hill to the north] every once in a while." According to Johnson, few families lived in the Flats; it was primarily Black and transient workers, alongside former military men who had no other place to go.[55]

Makeshift clubs and lounges served liquor and beer; some contained small dining rooms equipped with modest kitchens to prepare and serve food. The North Star Light Lounge, where Johnson tended bar and later became co-owner, kept hours similar to the other establishments. It opened around 8:00 a.m. and served liquor until five in the morning. Between 5:00 a.m. and 8:00 a.m. the lounge remained open for breakfast. Patrons ordered "basic and primal drinks" such as Jack and Coke or Hennessey on the rocks. The goal was to have a good time and leave your troubles behind, remembered Johnson. Alaskans came to the Flats to dance and take in live performances from local and national acts, including bluesmen like T-Bone Walker and Jimmy Rushing. One woman, Lawanda Page, was particularly memorable, according to Johnson. Page arrived in the Flats, taking on the persona she dubbed the "Bronze Goddess of Fire" in an act that included a striptease, fire eating, and tricks with lit cigarettes. Page later went on to have a successful career in show business that included roles alongside Redd Foxx.[56]

The most famous Black performer to have graced Anchorage during these years was none other than jazz great Billie Holiday. Holiday visited Alaska in 1954, as Eastchester Flats had reached its peak in popularity as an entertainment district. She performed several performances at the 1042 Club between September 7 and September 20, a hotspot just east of downtown and north of the Flats, one of the few rooms in the city that could presumably accommodate the crowds. Holiday headlined the shows with Stomp Gordon, sometimes playing three sets a night, one at 10:00 p.m., another at midnight, and the third at 3:00 a.m. The international performer found Alaska a remarkable, vibrant place and Anchorage a city with a bright future. She went so far

Billie Holiday, September 1954. Ward Wells Collection, Anchorage Museum (B1983.091.C1351.1).

as to claim that she planned to buy property in the territory and perhaps even live out her days as an Alaskan. No record exists that she made good on her proclamation to move north, nor is there evidence that she ever returned to the Alaska. Holiday died five years later, but her two-week stay in Alaska in the mid-1950s signaled that it had taken its place as a destination, albeit a rather far-flung one, for Black entertainers, musicians, and performers.[57]

Ben Humphries, a longtime labor and civil rights activist, remembered the scene in similar terms as Joe Jackson and Fred Johnson; he articulated why Holiday may have been drawn to the Alaskan scene. Humphries recalled: "There were a lot of clubs, where, if you wanted to find the real action, you went to an area, uh, in the early fifties, we called it Eastchester Flats, and those clubs of course they weren't legitimate in terms of being licensed and meeting all the strict codes of law, but there was more fun there than you find anywhere else. Action happened there."[58] In addition to the Backstreet Club, Lulu's, and the North Star Light Lounge, there was the Red Hut; just beyond the Flats, one could find the Mambo Club, Club Oasis, and Ruby's—

all of which were Black owned.⁵⁹ Journalist Herbert Frisby wrote that the area developed such a reputation for fun and revelry—or some would say, trouble—that by the early 1950s the officers at Fort Richardson and Elmendorf Air Force Base prohibited their soldiers from visiting.⁶⁰

Anchorage officials understood the value of augmenting the city's tax base and aggressively sought to incorporate the new population that spread out to the south beyond the city limits.⁶¹ For their part Eastchester denizens were of a mixed mind on annexation. Most wanted to connect to city sewer and water lines. "Our most serious problem is water pollution and the need for immediate action," claimed an Eastchester Flats advocate in 1951.⁶² Anchorage city manager Robert Sharp informed residents in 1952 that the only path to acquiring a sewer system was through annexation.⁶³ Moreover, without access to city firefighters, it cost significantly more to insure one's home in Eastchester; annexation would presumably alleviate this higher cost, according to a report in the *Anchorage Times*. After more than three years of divisive public hearings, a legal challenge, and an election, in 1954 Anchorage annexed Eastchester Flats. However, some Black residents claimed that Anchorage leadership had stacked the hearings with landlords who favored annexation. Though they owned property in the Flats, these landlords had little interest in the long-term well-being of the community.⁶⁴

The advocates of annexation failed to live up to most of their promises. By 1965, more than ten years after annexation, Eastchester was not connected to Anchorage's sewer system. Despite higher taxes, Eastchester had no running water, paved roads, or sidewalks. Without regular sanitation, junk piled up as it had before. The city allowed the construction of a trailer court uphill from Eastchester, but its open cesspools flowed down to the Flats. Residents repeatedly petitioned the city for services but were denied, even as higher-quality infrastructure bypassed the area for wealthier, white developments.⁶⁵ Ocea Mae Curry, the postal worker who had been denied housing elsewhere in Anchorage, settled in Eastchester Flats and reported the disparity: "[The city] continued to say to us; there wasn't any way to improve the flats. . . . They would not be able to put city water in down here." She concluded that despite much effort, Eastchester Flats "did not get improvements" the city had long promised.⁶⁶

Then again, it may be that Anchorage city officials never intended to bestow Eastchester Flats the benefits of annexation in the first place. More likely, they viewed annexation as a chance to redevelop the area for their own purposes.

The process by which a city expends tax and federal dollars to uproot entire communities, usually under the guise of improving neighborhoods or expanding transportation networks or public works, has become known as "urban renewal." One result is very often the displacement of poor people. Anchorage, hemmed in by mountains to the east, water to the west, and military installations to the north, had limited options to expand. City officials therefore looked to the northeast and south. Eastchester had developed at the fringe of downtown, southeast of the city limits. As construction stretched from Anchorage's original townsite, Eastchester Flats represented not only an eyesore to developers but also a barrier to connect downtown with new, wealthier subdivisions to the south. Mostly low income and relatively powerless, Eastchester residents were indeed vulnerable to the machinations of Anchorage's power brokers; the entire area was an obvious target for urban renewal.[67]

The speed with which Anchorage grew during the postwar decades increased the need for housing and infrastructure. The city's swelling population surpassed the available housing supply, and it exceeded the capability to construct new homes and roads. The dearth of qualified builders and a construction season limited by Alaska's climate aggravated the situation. A non-comprehensive 1960 survey reported that 17 percent of the housing stock was "substandard and dilapidated." This percentage would have been higher if it included numerous trailer parks, many of which were "similarly unfit for use as dwellings." A 1963 analysis of Eastchester Flats claimed only two dwellings satisfied the building codes; the same study classified dozens of others "unfit for continued occupancy."[68] The Fairview neighborhood, with its newer housing stock, stood adjacent to the Flats. By the 1960s some Black families migrated to Fairview, after having found few alternatives to relocate without fear of discrimination. Unfortunately, another study calculated 66 percent of Fairview's housing stock was in "fair" or "poor" condition. By contrast, more than 60 percent of Anchorage area homes were "new or in good" shape.[69]

In the summer of 1961, the Anchorage City Council passed a resolution authorizing the Alaska State Housing Authority (ASHA) to implement urban renewal in Eastchester Flats.[70] ASHA intended to convert the neighborhood, described as "blight," into higher-density developments with easy access to downtown. Plans called for the land directly abutting the creek to be expanded into a greenbelt, and large sections of Eastchester Flats would be demolished altogether to make way for a bypass road. The city eventually made way for a multiuse sports arena and constructed a series of roads and highways to connect downtown to housing a few miles south. Anchorage developers sought to complete the renewal of Eastchester Flats by the late 1960s. While not all the plans materialized, the city expanded its greenbelt and the Seward Highway, constructed the additional multilane roads, and in the early 1980s built an ice arena (known as the Sullivan Arena and named after Anchorage mayor George Sullivan). Today northbound A Street and southbound C Street, in addition to the Seward Highway, provide a functional barrier separating the more affluent west side of Anchorage's downtown from its lower-income east side. The sum of these construction efforts drove a stake through the heart of Eastchester Flats and led to the ultimate demise of the neighborhood by the end of the 1970s, but not before some unforeseen challenges arose.[71]

As Anchorage's municipal officials tapped federal funding to redevelop Eastchester Flats, the 1964 Good Friday Earthquake struck. The most powerful earthquake ever recorded in North America devastated downtown Anchorage and the neighborhood of Turnagain, southwest of downtown; it killed over 130 people statewide. But Eastchester Flats withstood the shaking. *Jet* magazine's coverage of the disaster wryly proposed, "Housing discrimination (against Negroes, not Eskimos) spared the brothers up in Anchorage, Alaska, the wrath of the city's recent violent earthquake." The article reasoned, "Negroes are systematically barred from the exclusive areas near the business center— the area hardest hit by the cataclysm."[72] George Anderson, the publisher of the *Spotlight*, the state's first Black newspaper, wrote to the *Pittsburgh Courier* and described the earthquake as a "Passover." Anderson noted, "There are no Negro sections anywhere in the disaster area," and no Blacks were killed or injured; however, the municipality failed to restore power in the neighborhood for two weeks. Eastchester Flats was "earthquake proof," according to observers.[73]

That most of Anchorage's Black residents escaped the brunt of the earthquake is easily explained. Perhaps unknown at the time to residents and city planners alike, Eastchester Flats stood upon more solid ground than the wealthier neighborhoods to the west, with their sweeping views of Cook Inlet, Turnagain Arm, and the Chugach Mountains. The experience of Black Alaskans during the 1964 earthquake complicates the conventional, and typically correct, assumption that people of color are most adversely affected by natural disasters.[74] Indeed, as scholars have readily demonstrated, natural disasters have deeply shaped the experiences of millions of African Americans.[75] Black families endured incommensurate exposure to the 1927 Mississippi River flood; the 1948 Vanport flood outside of Portland, Oregon; and more recently, in 2005, Hurricane Katrina along the Gulf Coast, to name only a few examples.[76]

Alaska's largest Black neighborhood withstood the earthquake, but it did not withstand urban renewal. In contrast to a natural disaster, dismantling a community through public policy takes years or decades, rather than minutes, hours, or weeks. But the outcome is similar: the displacement of thousands of poor and working-class residents across the municipality. In this regard, Anchorage appears like other American cities that underwent redevelopment between the 1950s and 1970s. As historian Richard Rothstein has shown, local and municipal leaders enticed, or just as often coerced, members of low-income households to accept urban renewal with promises of fresh investments such as parks, schools, safer neighborhoods, and civic improvements—but they seldom followed through. Instead, upending minority neighborhoods usually facilitated the construction of highways to serve suburbanites more efficiently. This led to the rapid decline of historically Black and ethnic urban enclaves and devastated downtown commercial centers. In Camden, Chicago, Detroit, Los Angeles, Miami, and many other cities, minority neighborhoods were demolished and cleared for interstate highways and sometimes for green spaces and sporting venues. Appealing to white homeowners and an ascendant suburban culture organized around the automobile took priority.[77]

Though not fully equivalent to what occurred in minority communities throughout the Lower 48, Eastchester Flats represented a scaled-down version of renewal in the context of urban Alaska. But again, like cities elsewhere, many people contested the process, and divisions existed within the respective communities. Compounding the confusion, proponents of renewal did not always act in good faith. In one example, the Alaska State Housing Authority printed two different guides that described what to expect as urban renewal took place. One guide targeted residents and households in Eastchester. This text was direct and minimal, describing the appraisal process, deadlines, and payment schedules for residents who agreed to take buyouts for their properties. The guide used few words and oversimplified complicated legal proceedings; it disingenuously portrayed the process as minimally disruptive and with positive results.[78]

ASHA distributed a more detailed description of renewal plans to a non-Eastchester audience, primarily would-be developers and investors. In this, its second guide, ASHA blamed Eastchester's so-called blight on the residents themselves. The housing authority claimed that the lack of "paved streets, or sidewalks, or sewers or water or any other improvements" in Eastchester was at the behest of those who lived there. "Most of the people in Eastchester then, didn't complain about this," said ASHA. "Most of all they wanted to be let alone. They were." The documents justified any impending disruption as a chance for investment that would improve Anchorage in the long term.[79]

Some Alaskans viewed the ASHA plans with well-founded suspicion. Blanche McSmith of the NAACP invoked James Baldwin's dictum of "negro removal" to explain urban renewal.[80] McSmith was generally correct in her assessment. She predicted the policy would displace Anchorage's Black residents for the convenience of area whites. McSmith pointed out the city had repeatedly denied the requests for services and that banks had denied residents loans to improve their properties. "I thought it would have been nice if they would have given us a chance to improve, you know, would give people loans and things they could have built decent homes… [here in the Flats]," said one resident.[81] Joe Jackson, a real estate agent, could not recall a single Black man or woman in Anchorage who ever received a "big bucks" loan.[82] In contrast to the guide distributed by ASHA, residents desired infrastructural improvements, and they were even willing to incur risk and debt to invest in their community. But they were never given the chance.

Despite the divisions over how to confront or blunt the impacts of urban renewal, a united front against dismantling the Eastchester Flats never materialized among those who lived there. After McSmith, then president of the local NAACP chapter, protested the project at a public hearing, several Black Eastchester residents challenged her leadership and disagreed with her opposition to redevelopment. These men and women accepted the pronouncements of the housing authority and believed that the renewal project would bring necessary changes and new investment. Most everyone, after all, wanted clean water, public safety, and passable roads; the disagreement was over how to obtain these necessities.[83] Meanwhile, the city's two newspapers, the *Anchorage Times* and the *Anchorage Daily News*, publicized stories about internal power struggles within the NAACP and inflamed divisions between activists opposed to urban renewal and those who favored it.[84]

Divisions within Eastchester Flats hindered meaningful resistance to urban renewal and provided Anchorage city leaders a relatively easy path to implement their plans. As McSmith predicted, those who were displaced could not so easily afford new homes close to where they lived; these men and women spread across the city. One former resident, Ocea Mae Curry, had to move and start over. "A city government is supposed to see after all of its people... and if you aren't going to see after me, then I see after myself. So, I just moved into a new neighborhood," she proclaimed.[85] Ben Humphries, a Black activist who opposed the project, emphasized the Black-owned and operated businesses in Eastchester Flats that were forced to close. According to Humphries: "They ruined it. Urban renewal ruined it, ruined it, yeah they ruined the Flats."[86] Fred Johnson, however, was among the few who transitioned and found themselves better off. Johnson applied for and received what might have been the sole small business loan granted to anyone in the Flats. He used the loan to construct a new North Star Light Lounge, just north of where the Flats once stood. That establishment has been rebranded over the years as the Pussy Cat Lounge, the Metropolitan Show Club, and, most recently, the Crazy Horse. It has hosted a bar and nightclub, a disco, and adult entertainment. Johnson, for his part, left the business in the late 1970s.[87]

After the destruction of the Flats, African Americans in Anchorage lost a geographic center and had less visibility in city politics, at least in the near term. Prior to the unification of the greater Anchorage area into the Municipality of Anchorage in 1975, a Black candidate could receive votes from any part of the city. The new municipality restricted voting to districts. As one resident stated: "But now with the changes, you can vote only for someone in your own district. This makes it difficult for a Black person to depend on the Black vote."[88] Former Eastchester denizen Frank Austins suggested, "We don't have the luxury of a ghetto."[89] The words may sound counterintuitive, but his point referred to how diluted the Black vote had become with the dismantling of Eastchester Flats. Anchorage's Black community, which even at its most powerful was perhaps only modest in its political influence, would never form a voting bloc or appeal as an electoral force. In fact, it would not be until 1998 that Melinda Taylor would be the first African American elected to the Anchorage Municipal Assembly, nearly twenty-five years after Anchorage assumed its current borders and political structure. Taylor was in fact the first person of color to win a seat on the Anchorage assembly. Taylor served six years until another Black woman, Elvi Gray-Jackson, won a seat on the assembly.[90] In 2019 Gray-Jackson went on to serve in the Alaska legislature as a senator.

Familiar Patterns Prevail in Urban Alaska

In 1967 the city passed a fair housing code, a year before President Lyndon B. Johnson signed the 1968 Fair Housing Act. The local NAACP seized the moment as a victory for equal rights.[91] But as Willard Bowman had previously noted, the presence of antidiscrimination laws had seldom been the primary issue. After all, in 1945 Alaska became the first American state or territory to pass an antidiscrimination act.[92] Yet the act did not prevent the proliferation of racially restrictive housing covenants or allow people of color to live wherever they chose. Alaska's Anti-Discrimination Act could not be meaningfully enforced until the territorial legislature crafted a fix to the original language. Bowman imagined the authors of such acts and laws celebrating their achievements. He supposed that lawmakers said breezily, "Let's enact this legislation and be on about our affluent way" without providing any true means of enforcement.[93]

Today Alaska's largest city bears similarities to the rest of urban America, with its share of chain restaurants, big box stores, and rush hour traffic. While it has never had a sizable Black population, people of African descent who have relocated to the forty-ninth state share some common history and experiences with their counterparts in the Lower 48. Beyond the northern lights, moose, and bears depicted in popular culture, housing and employment discrimination also framed daily life in Alaska for many African Americans. At the same time, Alaska has stood out for some notable reasons, and there have even been some rather surprising firsts. Take the Greater Friendship Baptist Church in the Fairview neighborhood, for example. Here many Black Alaskans worship in an area not too far from what used to be Eastchester Flats. Today Fairview is one of the most diverse neighborhoods in the nation. Fairview contains one of the highest percentages of Black residents in Anchorage and throughout the state, although it has increasingly come to include greater numbers of Asian Americans and Pacific Islanders, in addition to high numbers of Alaska Natives and whites. No single demographic predominates, and integration rather than segregation prevails.[94]

In 1951 Black men and women gathered in the basement of the First Baptist Church. Once the congregation grew, it separated from that church and met at nearby Pioneer Hall. Soon after, the men and women raised money and constructed their present house of worship, calling it the Greater Friendship Baptist Church.[95] They composed Alaska's first Black congregation. But more striking, the church later joined the Southern Baptist Convention (SBC), a conservative and, for generations, whites-only alliance of Baptists who differed from the National Baptist Convention, with whom most Black congregations had affiliated. In 1965 Greater Friendship pastor Leo Josey Sr. became the first Black pastor to represent the SBC at a state Baptist convention. Not long afterward, the Greater Friendship Baptist Church joined the SBC and, as a result, integrated the convention.[96] It remains a central hub in the area's religious community. There were, of course, other such moments in Alaska's Black history. Men and women fought for justice and equality, and they persisted in the face of discrimination.

CHAPTER FIVE

Civil Rights under the Northern Lights

DURING THE SECOND WORLD WAR, BEATRICE LEE CHISOLM MOVED from Idaho to Washington State in search of steady work. Soon after her arrival in Washington, she met Robert Coleman. Chisolm and Coleman worked war-related jobs at the Puget Sound Naval Shipyard in Bremerton. The two dated, fell in love, and eventually married. After the war, the Colemans relocated together, this time to Alaska. Their first stop was Juneau, where they lived for a short time before moving once again to Fairbanks. They were among the several thousand Black men and women who arrived in the Far Northwest because of Alaska's wartime and postwar military buildup. With jobs plentiful, the two decided to stay in Alaska and called Fairbanks home for the next several decades. Beatrice Coleman found the Native culture of Alaska familiar after having grown up around an Indian reservation in Idaho. She was most comfortable in the sparsely populated, wide-open spaces of the American West and took to Alaska immediately. But nearly as soon as the couple had moved to Alaska, they experienced anti-Black discrimination. And just as quickly, they fought back.[1]

Beatrice and Robert Coleman might be considered two of the earliest Black civil rights activists in Alaska. Historian Ross Coen has convincingly demonstrated that the Colemans should be viewed alongside the well-known Alaska Native activists Roy and Elizabeth Peratrovich as central figures upon which Alaska's modern civil rights law rests. Coen's extensive documentation of the case also calls into question the commitment that Alaska's political leadership had to civil rights amid the movement for statehood and locates the role that working people such as the Colemans played in building a more inclusive postwar Alaska.[2] After Black soldiers in Alaska and Canada contributed to the war effort and helped to undermine the rationale for military segregation, Beatrice and Robert Coleman led the charge toward civil rights in the territory and then the state. The couple eventually compelled the Alaska territorial legislature to amend and strengthen the 1945 Anti-Discrimination Act. Beatrice Coleman then brought to light race- and gender-based discrimination in the newly organized US Air Force. These actions constitute the beginnings of a civil rights movement under the northern lights, one that found African Americans squarely at the center of the story.[3]

The story began on an evening in October 1946, when the Colemans went on a date to view *Dakota*, a western starring John Wayne. After the movie, the couple decided to have drinks at Hill's Cocktail Lounge, a bar adjacent to the theater and owned by popular Fairbanks resident Rudy Hill. The two entered, took a seat, and waited. Several minutes passed, then Hill approached and explained that they would not receive service. Beatrice Coleman recalled the conversation between her husband and Rudy Hill. Hill reportedly claimed, "I have a license that gives me the right to refuse service to anyone I see fit to not serve . . . and my reason for not serving you is because you are colored." Hill insisted the couple exit the bar and not return.[4] The incident sparked a two-year legal battle, revealed weaknesses in Alaska's pioneering civil rights law, and laid bare a territory only tenuously, if at all, dedicated to equality. Just as in the Lower 48 at midcentury, Black Alaskans faced endemic racism, despite a territorial law that ostensibly banned discriminatory practices. Conversant with an emerging national Black freedom movement, Black Alaskans increasingly stood up for their rights and took action to end racial discrimination. The struggle for equality transcended latitude and distance, and in Alaska, as elsewhere, Blacks forged one of the nation's great social movements.

Beatrice and Robert Coleman Fight for Justice

The Alaska territorial legislature passed the Anti-Discrimination Act in 1945. The act provided for the "full and equal enjoyment of accommodations, advantages, facilities and privileges," including at inns, restaurants, skating rinks, ice parlors, bathrooms, taverns, and "all other conveyances and amusements" open to the public.[5] Roy and Elizabeth Peratrovich, well-known

Tlingit activists in Southeast Alaska, led the legislative lobbying effort to pass the act. Elizabeth Peratrovich served as president of the Alaska Native Sisterhood, and her husband, Roy, served as president of the Alaska Native Brotherhood. Elizabeth Peratrovich, however, is best known for her eloquent testimony before the legislature on behalf of the act. It was a notable moment in the history of Alaska's race relations and in the making of a broader Native coalition to challenge white dominance in government. This story usually ends optimistically, with the passage of the legislation and well-deserved recognition of Elizabeth Peratrovich as an Alaska civil rights icon. The truth, however, grows considerably murkier once we include the story of Robert and Beatrice Coleman. In fact, without activism from the Colemans, the Anti-Discrimination Act of 1945 would have remained a largely symbolic and considerably weaker measure.[6]

Like Elizabeth Peratrovich, Beatrice Coleman knew well the laws of the territory, and she knew equally well the racism she and her husband experienced daily. Unfortunately, few lawyers wanted to take on a discrimination lawsuit against Hill, a well-regarded business owner. Rudy Hill nonetheless received a fifty-dollar misdemeanor fine from a US attorney, who interpreted Hill's action as unlawful. Seizing on a loophole in the law, Hill appealed his fine.[7] Section 2 of the Anti-Discrimination Act stated: "Any person . . . who shall display any printed or written sign indicating a discrimination on racial grounds of said full and equal enjoyment, for each day for which said sign is displayed shall be deemed guilty of a misdemeanor."[8] Since Hill never posted a discriminatory policy in print or writing, he maintained his innocence. If Hill got off, Beatrice Coleman concluded, the Anti-Discrimination Act was meaningless. Determined to eliminate the loophole, Coleman approached Warren Taylor, a former territorial legislator and someone she thought might be sympathetic to the couple's case. Taylor proposed that a civil trial would be the best way to fix the law and compel Hill to pay his fine.[9]

Beatrice Coleman believed the intent of the Anti-Discrimination Act was clear. Specifically, she pointed to other verbiage—"to provide for full and equal accommodations, facilities and privileges to all citizens in places of public accommodations within the jurisdiction of the Territory of Alaska; to provide penalties for violations"—as the language to advance the case.[10] The Colemans also recruited Emma Roberts, a Black Fairbanks resident, to testify against Hill. Roberts claimed to have been barred from the tavern because of her race. With additional evidence to demonstrate Hill's violation of the law, the US attorney filed a warrant for his arrest. But in an abrupt turnaround, Rudy Hill convinced Taylor to represent him rather the Colemans. Hill changed his story and told Taylor that he threw the young couple out of his bar for unruly behavior. The US attorney did not buy Hill's new defense and ordered him once again to pay the fine.[11]

The case, however, was not yet over. Warren Taylor, now representing Rudy Hill, appealed and argued that regardless of the reason, Hill's rights as a property owner allowed him to deny service to anyone for any reason. Beatrice Coleman wrote to the territorial governor, Ernest Gruening, to request his intervention. Gruening and attorney general Ralph Rivers conceded that the law had limits as it was written; there was no guarantee the Colemans would prevail in court. Two of the most influential politicians in the territory thus expressed little confidence in the ability of the Anti-Discrimination Act to perform its stated function and acknowledged that it was primarily a ceremonial measure. Sure enough, the court sided with Hill and dismissed the case in November 1947, over a year after the ordeal began. Beatrice Coleman's daughter, Theressa Lenear, recalled her mother discussing the open racism the family experienced as the process unfolded and their belief that discrimination in Interior Alaska grew more pervasive amid the case and in its aftermath.[12] But Beatrice and Robert Coleman remained steadfast and fully documented the extent of discrimination at Fairbanks businesses. The Colemans interviewed area bar and restaurant owners and found all but two confessed to refusing service to African Americans and Alaska Natives. These owners felt little pressure to change their behavior; a misdemeanor and a modest fine would not deter them from maintaining an all-white clientele.[13]

With the law functionally unenforceable, Beatrice Coleman turned to the legislature. Alaska territorial senator Edward Anderson of Nome acknowledged the loophole in the legislation that he had coauthored in 1945. During the next session, Anderson and his colleagues introduced a bill to amend the Anti-Discrimination Act by removing the phrase "for each day for which said sign is displayed." This change clarified the language that banned discrimination in public accommodation, regardless of whether it was verbal or written. The amendment passed unanimously in the Senate; the House of Representative passed the revised Anti-Discrimination Act, eighteen to three. Taylor, who had by then gone from representing the Colemans to representing Hill to once again serving in Alaska's territorial legislature, cast one of the three no votes.[14] The 1948 legislative amendment improved the original 1945 act, but the law remained far from comprehensive. For one, the Anti-Discrimination Act dealt only with public accommodations and did not address discrimination in employment or housing. Beatrice Coleman, for her part, continued her fight for justice and soon took on that most behemoth of American institutions: the military.

In 1949 Coleman accepted a position as the first Black clerk and typist for the Motor Vehicle Squadron at Ladd Air Force Base, located just outside of Fairbanks. She was dismissed within three years for what her supervisors described as insubordinate behavior. According to her recorded statement, Coleman "got along fine, made my grades and periodical raises and advances until the middle of 1950 when I met Lt. Peter P. Kaye, who was transferred to this organization upon the rotation of the OIC [officer in charge]." She then claimed that the "since the first time he [Kaye] set eyes on me, I became acutely aware that I displeased him greatly." Coleman detailed several instances in which the lieutenant verbally abused or intimidated her. She claimed that he relieved her of her duties and forced her to sit in a room alone with no tasks to perform; he never hesitated to throw around racial epithets and target her race and intelligence. Coleman took up a claim with the Fair Employment Office (FEO), only to be told, "It would be dood [sic] sense to drop the charges because I couldn't do anything about it anyways." Coleman, however, was characteristically unsatisfied with such a response and continued her case against race- and gender-based discrimination, this time in the military.[15]

Coleman ruffled feathers enough to receive a transfer to another position. She worked as a stenographer and recorded what were known as "Unsatisfactory Reports [URs]." Coleman recalled her job of processing "all accidents and discrepancies concerning airplanes and supplies." Coleman explained that the position invited high stress: "The finished paperwork had to be sent to the different manufacturing companies all over the US and therefore they had to be not only letter perfect, but one hundred percent informationally correct." The air force could lose millions if the job was not carried out to specifications and the reports were botched or not accepted. It was a position well suited to Coleman, who considered herself a reliable and meticulous civil servant.[16]

Coleman claimed to have completed the tasks with skill and precision, earning the respect of her fellow coworkers. During the eight months that she worked as a stenographer and relayed hundreds of reports, she disclosed, "only 4 URs were returned to me for re-doing because of MY ERRORS."[17] Unfortunately, this was not enough to placate her supervisors after she complained of "filthy" and malodorous bathrooms and breakrooms where "secret love trysts" routinely took place between a few of the female stenographers and the commanding officers. After Coleman voiced her discontent over what could only be described as a hostile work environment, her immediate supervisor said "he would personally see that [she] was fired if it was the last thing he did." By her own account, Coleman endured increasing levels of mistreatment as she continued to press her case for a hospitable and hygienic office. In what she perceived as clear retaliation and intimidation, Coleman's supervisors began to time her bathroom breaks and file written reprimands that she was "taking too long." They reassigned her once again to menial tasks and openly harassed her and told "cruel jokes." Coleman attributed racism and sexism as the obvious motivations behind the behavior of her white male supervisors. She had grown convinced that they wished to intimidate her into resigning the position.[18]

Coleman wrote the Fair Employment officer and solicited assistance from the NAACP. One NAACP representative explained, "Mrs. Coleman states that Sergeants Tipton, Anest, and Christensen have used abusive language to her and have made derogatory remarks not only about her work, but also about her personally, and her moral character."[19] But the air force Fair Employment officer, James P. Goode, defended any disciplinary measures directed at Coleman: "This Department has a long-established policy that all personnel actions will be based solely upon merit and fitness without regard to race, color, religion, or national origin."[20] In another correspondence, the air force provided a more thorough list of why Coleman had been dismissed. Her alleged offenses included "writing personal letters during duty hours, for which you were verbally reprimanded." The report continued: "You spent excessive amount of time away from your duties and especially in the ladies' room ... You have expressed dissatisfaction with your supervisors."[21] The records indicate that her advocacy did lead one officer to face disciplinary action. An exchange between Clarence Mitchell and Clarence Osthagen, both of whom worked for the NAACP, acknowledged that "Lt. Mosely has been relieved, and Lt. Kay [Kaye] is once again her supervisor. The enlisted personnel have continued their abuse of her."[22] Then again, this could have been simply a ploy for Lieutenant Kaye to resume his abusive relationship with Coleman.

In any case, Beatrice Coleman's employment with the air force ended in July 1951. She was never reinstated to the position that she felt best suited her skill set, as a stenographer, and indications suggest that Lieutenant Kaye continued his intimidation and abuse of air force employees. But her decision to take on the American military and fight for a workplace free from racial and gender discrimination, verbal harassment, and sexual assault once again revealed her courage in the face of potent opposition. Beatrice Coleman mobilized the same fearless determination to protest discrimination in the air force as she had done with her husband as they took on Rudy Hill and lobbied the legislature to strengthen Alaska's Anti-Discrimination Act. She later parlayed her opposition to injustice by founding the Fairbanks Chapter of the NAACP. Coleman remained a committed civil rights activist until her death in 1982.[23] The NAACP, for its part, continued to use Harry Truman's Executive Orders 9980 and 9981, prohibiting discrimination based on race in government employment and enabling the desegregation of the military, as a legal cornerstone for their burgeoning postwar civil rights advocacy. However, figures such as Lieutenant Kaye and the airmen who served under him proved to be formidable obstacles to a more equitable military. Coleman's case thus illustrates how much work remained to be done in holding such institutions accountable. And while Beatrice Coleman may not have brought the officers in the air force to justice, her commitment to civil rights and equality set the stage for still greater levels of activism among Black Alaskans throughout the 1950s and 1960s and beyond.

A few years later Ernest Gruening penned his 1954 manifesto advocating Alaska statehood, aptly entitled *The State of Alaska*. In it he audaciously claimed that the original 1945 Anti-Discrimination Act paved the way for lasting equality and insinuated that Alaska had overcome the racial problems that plagued other states. Gruening portrayed Alaska as a place free of discrimination. "Not an untoward incident was reported subsequent to the enactment of the 'equal-treatment bill,'" the governor proudly stated, without apparent reflection on or mention of the activism carried out by the Colemans. Gruening knew better. He reportedly had met with Beatrice and Robert Coleman, and he must have recognized that racism could not be papered over by a single law. Rather it took mobilization and action to forge a movement dedicated to equality for those Alaskans whom it had long been denied. Here the work of Beatrice Coleman fits into a broader context and marks the beginning of a sustained period of civil right activism.[24]

Civil Rights Activism Heats Up in Alaska

The territorial legislature may have fixed the Anti-Discrimination Act and made some admirable gestures toward alleviating an antagonistic racial climate, but discrimination stubbornly persisted. As a young African American girl growing up on a military base in Fairbanks, journalist and civil rights activist Charlayne Hunter-Gault remembered moments in which she felt accepted and other moments when she was openly discriminated against. Her family moved to Alaska in 1954, when she was twelve, after her father, a chaplain in the military, received his orders. Hunter-Gault was the only Black girl at her school and wanted to make friends at a dance. She recalled, "I went to a teenage club one day, and I was turned away, and I went home." She then described the situation to her father, who was determined to ensure that his daughter would never again receive such treatment. He exclaimed, "Well, we're going back to change this, to deal with this," insisting, "No one is ever going to deny you or me, for that matter." Accordingly, the two traveled back to the dance, where he demanded respect for his daughter and "gave them royal hell." It was a risky move for a Black man to demand justice and inclusion for his child during this era, but the actions of the serviceman—like those of Beatrice and Robert Coleman—suggested that a new phase of the Black freedom struggle had begun. The postwar decades would see a newly assertive stripe of self-advocacy and defense fully materialize.[25]

But at the same time, housing and employment discrimination intensified in urban Alaska, and racist attitudes hardened. Neighborhoods surrounding Anchorage resembled redlined communities in the nation's North and West. In a 1965 speech that expressed his frustration with entrenched segregation in Alaska, civil rights leader Willard Bowman asked his audience: "Do you know that in another 5 to 10 years [Fairview] will be completely substandard, the houses overcrowded, the crime rate and welfare cases soaring, while officialdom wringes [sic] its hands and hurriedly plans another urban renewal project to rid the blight?" Bowman cited the extensive literature about housing segregation and direly forecasted that the rebellions and riots of seemingly far-off places like Watts and Harlem may well occur in Alaska. "We are allowing the same seeds to take root in Anchorage," Bowman proposed, "and we are just as assuredly going to reap the same crop as Los Angeles did."[26]

Blanche McSmith, an activist and soon-to-be state representative, put it in equally stark terms. According to McSmith, Anchorage's ballyhooed moniker

Willard L. Bowman, ca. 1971. Willard L. Bowman Papers, Archives and Special Collections, UAA/APU Consortium Library.

as an "All-America City" in 1956 and then again in 1965 did not reflect the well-being of the city's Black and Native residents. "Persons driving south, past 15th Avenue, on Gambell Street, cannot escape a view of vast swampy lowlands, dotted with several bar signs, small houses, and piles of junk and debris," she wrote in late 1965 in the *Alaska Spotlight*, a Black newspaper. McSmith called Eastchester Flats an "All-American City twilight zone . . . neglected by 'City Fathers.' All of the improvements benefiting a thriving, growing city: water, sewers, sidewalks, paved streets, FHA approved and mortgaged houses, are conspicuously absent." She added, "Ninety-nine percent of the people who live and own businesses here are Negroes." McSmith, like Bowman, opposed the annexation of Eastchester Flats in 1954. She facetiously declared that since annexation, residents have "had the privilege of paying higher taxes [for] an abundance of police surveillance." The water mains, McSmith added caustically, "benefited" the community when one of them routinely "overflowed and the filth flooded the yards."[27]

Blanche McSmith and Willard Bowman also advocated for a fair employment law and inclusion of an anti-segregation clause in the Alaska state constitution. Discrimination against Black and Native workers in military contracting and on the Eklutna Dam Project near Anchorage in the early 1950s highlighted the need for a codified bill that would prevent employment discrimination based on race and gender. The Anchorage-based pastor Giles Trammel, who also served as the Alaska representative for the NAACP and writer for the *Alaska Spotlight*, traveled to Juneau to lobby on behalf of the legislation. There he met with Filipinx counterparts and members of the Alaska Native Brotherhood to discuss the bill and how to advance it. All agreed that a strong law was necessary to prohibit the kinds of on-the-job discrimination that had taken place throughout the territory in the postwar years; Beatrice Coleman's experience was simply one example of many, it turned out. The effort was spearheaded by the Central Labor Council, a coalition of over twenty Alaska-based unions, and indeed composed a relatively rare joint-lobbying effort on the part of Alaska's Native, Filipinx, and Black communities.[28]

Yet the lobbying cohort soon learned that a bipartisan majority of Republican and Democratic lawmakers, led by the Democratic representative Wendell Kay, had been working with territorial governor, Ernest Gruening, to put together a separate fair employment bill. That bill, endorsed by the Alaska Territorial Federation of Labor, was soon adopted by the Central

Blanche McSmith, 1960. Alaska State Library Portrait File, Historical Collections.

Labor Council and the NAACP. As Alaskan leaders laid the groundwork for statehood, many in the territorial legislature were prepared to act on such a bill as it would more clearly separate Alaska from the egregious civil rights offenders in the Jim Crow South and presumably demonstrate to the nation that Alaska was prepared to enter the union as a state. It also squared with Gruening's more general goal of being seen as a champion for civil rights in Alaska. As such, the Twenty-First Alaska Territorial Legislature passed the Alaska Fair Employment Practices Act in the spring of 1953. The act provided for the "elimination of discrimination because of race, color, religion or national origin." The law was buttressed by the support of a multiracial coalition of workers and contained enforcement measures that could carry up to a five hundred-dollar fine for violations. Although the final bill eliminated provisions related to an advisory commission, which Representative Kay had fought for, the eventual passage of the law seemed to bode well for advocates of civil and labor rights.[29] Together with the legislation around the Anti-Discrimination Act a few years earlier, civil rights era liberalism in Alaska had seemingly notched a few key victories.[30]

However, more entrenched struggles quickly emerged as delegates for a presumptive state constitution gathered in Fairbanks to draft the document. Blanche McSmith worked with the NAACP, Western Region, to craft language and enshrine civil rights in the founding papers of what she and other Black activists hoped would be the forty-ninth state's constitution. In a letter to Zora Banks at the NAACP office in San Francisco, McSmith explained that the rise "of the negro situation is new in Alaska," and as such, the territory could encode greater protections for its minority citizens as it advocated for statehood. She reasoned that those explicit prohibitions on segregation and housing discrimination would "let us stop any problem before it begins." The moment held much potential for McSmith. "It seems to me," she told Banks, "and I feel this very deeply, that this constitution is the last to be written in our lifetime and should be demonstrated as a model for democracy." Alaskans, therefore, had the timely fortune of drafting their state constitution amid the growing fervor of the civil rights movement. Unfortunately, the clause that McSmith lobbied for never ended up in the final document. In an exchange with the chair of the Civil Rights Committee, John Hellenthal, McSmith related that the constitutional delegates feared that carving out specific clauses on racism "didn't sound dignified."[31] Still, McSmith and others could take some measure of success. The Alaska constitution included article

1, section 3, a civil rights clause. It proclaimed, "No person is to be denied the enjoyment of any civil or political right because of race, color, creed, sex, or national origin." Yet enforcing article 1, section 3—much like the enforcement of the Anti-Discrimination Act—remained a tall order.[32]

Despite documented housing and employment segregation in Alaska's largest cities and the turbulent experience of urban renewal, Anchorage remained peaceful throughout the 1960s; so, too, did Fairbanks and Juneau. Uprisings on the scale of what took place in Harlem, Watts, Detroit, and Washington, DC, never occurred. Still, rumors of an imminent civil disturbance spread across Alaska. And to be certain, activism increased. In the summer of 1967, as riots broke out across dozens of major American cities, Governor Walter J. Hickel prepared for possible local unrest. In one document tellingly labeled "Riot Memo," Hickel addressed rumors that "outside agitators" had flown into Anchorage to encourage Blacks to take up arms against whites. "If we find any outside influence involving a criminal element we will move quickly," the governor said.[33] Elsewhere, Alaska media mogul Robert Atwood called Anchorage's police chief John Flanigan to inquire about "reports of an influx of outsiders, Muslims, [Stokely] Carmichael." The chief tried to assuage Atwood and reported "no influx of colored people."[34] Nevertheless, the Anchorage Police Department apparently took the issue seriously enough to detain several city residents and even stake out area gun retailers to make sure that rumors of Black men stocking up on arms and ammo were not true.

No evidence suggests that activists ever planned a large- or small-scale uprising. Further, fanciful rumors that the Student Non-Violent Coordinating Committee (SNCC) chairman Stokely Carmichael or the Black Muslims wanted to come to Alaska to foment rebellion, organize poor people, or initiate an armed insurrection shed more light into the psyche of the state's white civic and political elite than anything else. And though the militancy and violence that gripped other American cities never materialized in Alaska, citizens took to the streets and demanded their voices be heard. Iconic civil rights leaders on the national stage did not make trips north, but Black Alaskans developed their own modes of activism and responses to racism; these were indeed informed by the national movement and its leadership, but it also reflected local conditions. One example occurred at the Carrs grocery store in Anchorage's Fairview neighborhood. As men and women demanded service at the segregated lunch counters in the Jim Crow South and others marched and boycotted discriminatory practices in the public and private sector, so, too, did Black men and women of Anchorage.

In the summer of 1962, African Americans and other area activists joined together to picket Carrs, Alaska's largest grocery store chain. Clarence Coleman, branch president of the Anchorage NAACP, wrote to executive director Roy Wilkins at the national office in New York City: "The first picket line in the history of the Anchorage NAACP began its task of protesting the hiring policies of Carrs Food Center here in Anchorage today 31 July 10 am Alaska Standard Time."[35] Coleman's statement was not quite true. Five years earlier, Joseph M. Jackson and James E. Owens organized area workers and set up a picket outside of the Local 341 Laborers and Hod Carriers Union Hall. They and others sought an inclusive union for African American and Alaska Native workers and called for greater transparency in promotion guidelines. Owens stated that direct action "was the only way we're going to get equality."[36]

The picket of Carrs in Anchorage's Fairview neighborhood was a watershed moment in the history of civil rights in Alaska. Many in the Black community took issue with the grocery store's apparent refusal to hire African Americans to work in any capacity beyond sanitation and other so-called menial, low-level jobs. In one correspondence Bernard J. Carr Sr., an owner of the grocery store chain, conceded he had "two Negro employees," a garbage collector and a janitor. But he continued, "The time is not right to hire a Negro checker." Activist Pat Berkley recalled: "They [Carrs] didn't want to hire any Blacks. And of course, Pop Carr . . . wasn't to hire any Blacks because he had hired one [who] became very friendly with a white girl that worked there, so that was the end of that."[37] Still, the NAACP suggested the grocer benefited from having a base of African American patrons and, as such, should hire and promote a few as employees. At its Fairview store, over 30 percent of the clientele was Black, yet not a single African American worked in management or any position that interfaced with the public.[38]

In response, men and women took to the picket line outside of Carrs to raise awareness. Though she was seven months pregnant, Pat Berkley helped organize the picket and led the women to march on the line during the day; the men walked in the evening. Cars and pedestrians "booed and laughed at [us]," Berkley remembered.[39] Despite some negative reaction, the picket worked; owners agreed to hire a more diverse workforce. Organizer Joseph

Kline summarized the terms of the agreement: Carrs grocery would "hire one person immediately. The second within thirty days and the third sixty days after the first." These positions were supposed to include a clerk, cashier, or grocery checker, all of which afforded a greater possibility for advancement than the menial positions that the picketers accused Carrs of reserving for Black workers.[40]

Unfortunately, Carrs failed to hire three African Americans within the agreed-upon sixty days, but the NAACP kept up its pressure, and the grocery store eventually complied. Richard Watts was the first man Carrs hired as a result of the picket. He became the first African American bagger at the store and stayed with the grocer for over forty-five years. In accordance with what the activists envisioned, Watts did not remain a bagger for long. He ascended the chain of management; by the end of a long and distinguished career, Watts had become a district manager and participated in the local business community as a member of the board of directors for the Anchorage Chamber of Commerce.[41]

The Carrs boycott anticipated more extensive changes in Fairview that would come about by the middle of the 1960s. During this decade the neighborhood emerged as a center of activism and civic engagement in Anchorage. Its reputation as one of Anchorage's most diverse communities only grew, as did the fear that city leadership might continue to neglect the needs of its residents. After the redevelopment of Eastchester Flats, roughly the southern tier of Fairview, men and women on the community council grew more determined to ensure the existing neighborhood would not be left out as Anchorage leadership plotted new recreational outlets for residents. Olivia Holland, Ben Humphries, and John Parks, all active on the neighborhood council, led an effort to set aside land for a park and later spearheaded an effort to deliver public transportation throughout Anchorage. These efforts took considerable effort but would yield tangible results for the residents of Fairview in the decades to follow.[42]

Beyond the Carrs boycott in Fairview, activists protested and organized against mistreatment and discrimination elsewhere during the early and mid-1960s. In Anchorage and Fairbanks, residents established employment workshops to organize letter writing campaigns and rallies and to reach out to area businesses to connect minority job candidates with desirable employment. The workshops in Anchorage organized pickets at Caribou-Wards and

Woolworths; one woman in Anchorage, Lillian Morris, took a lead role in the Woolworths pickets and led the area employment workshop. Fairbanks activists also organized a picket of Woolworths in their hometown. The efforts paid off, at least to some extent. Sears, Roebuck and Company agreed to interview and hire qualified African American, Native, Filipinx, and Mexican applicants. The Spenard Caribou-Wards store hired two Black salesclerks and agreed to file and retain applications for a longer period, a concession to the employment workshop. The Anchorage Woolworths hired a Black employee for the first time. These efforts did not approach the level of equity that the employment workshop ultimately desired, but they represented a small measure of progress.[43]

Blanche McSmith, then acting in her role as branch president of the NAACP, inquired into the treatment of minority civilian workers at Fort Richardson and Elmendorf Air Force Base, Anchorage's two military installations and one of the largest employers in the city. The military had a rocky relationship with Alaska's Black and Native population. Most obviously, during World War II, General Buckner refused to allow Black and Native soldiers to serve at the base for fear they would "mix" with the white population. For her part McSmith wrote to Maj. Gen. George A. Carver, a successor to Buckner, to express concern over the treatment of people of color at the quartermaster's laundry, one of the few places one could find Black service members and civilians in the 1950s and early 1960s. She detailed more than a dozen examples of discriminatory behavior, ranging from hiring and promotion infractions to specific instances of verbal and even physical abuse. Concluded McSmith, "The problems have become progressively worse and apparently directed toward an explosive situation unless preventative measures are taken."[44] Thomas Davis, a colonel in the US Air Force, disputed McSmith's claims and contended they were overblown, if not totally baseless. But tellingly, amid McSmith's other criticisms, she demanded an explanation as to why "Negroes are addressed by first names" while white men and women "are addressed by Miss or Mrs. or Sir." Confirming her accusations, Colonel Davis opened his letter curtly, "Dear Blanche."[45]

The *Midnight Sun Reporter*, another Black newspaper launched by George Anderson, the editor of the *Spotlight*, further documented the reasons civil rights organizations had long harbored an antagonistic relationship with the military bases: "Leaders of the Negro community charge that of the 1,600 civilians employed at Elmendorf only 80-odd are minority group members."

In response, a consortium that included the NAACP, New Hope Baptist Church, First Christian Methodist Church, and other civil rights and labor activists had prepared to picket the bases in October 1964. Just days before the protest was to take place, air force officials met with residents, and the action was called off. In return, the military agreed to hire additional African Americans and Alaska Natives and more thoroughly address claims of racism and abuse. President Lyndon B. Johnson had just signed federal legislation to sanction and punish contractors who engaged in discriminatory and racist practices. Here again, the demands of the Anchorage movement intersected with marquee federal legislation, its activists in tune with civil rights mobilization nationwide.[46]

In March 1965 more than a thousand men, women, and children marched from the Anchorage police headquarters to city hall (the NAACP noted that police chief John Flanigan joined them) in solidarity with those who had marched from Selma to Montgomery in what became a defining moment in the civil rights movement. Like their fellow activists in Alabama, the Anchorage marchers also urged Congress to pass the Voting Rights Act of 1965.[47] In contrast to many of their southern counterparts, the Alaska delegation of Senator Ernest Gruening (D), Senator Bob Bartlett (D), and Representative Ralph Rivers (D) voted to do so.[48]

During the next presidential election campaign, in 1968, Alaska faced many of the same divisions that the nation confronted during that tumultuous year. And while Black and Alaska Native activism took root across the state, so, too, did a nascent white backlash. Nowhere was this more revelatory than in the effort of George Wallace's campaign to view Alaska as a fertile ground to expand his appeal. Wallace, the notorious segregationist governor of Alabama, had launched a presidential campaign in 1967 and 1968; he exceeded expectations and performed well in the primary elections of several northern states, notably Wisconsin. He decided to compete in Alaska and opened an office in Anchorage. A young Black activist, Paula McClain, recalled that Wallace had unknowingly tried to set up shop on a lot owned by Zula Swanson, then one of the wealthiest landowners in the state. McClain stated: "I remember . . . when George Wallace was running and he opened up an office [for his American Independent Party] . . . His campaign opened up an office in Anchorage that was on her land [Zula Swanson's], and she told the owners of the building that they either move their building or get rid of Wallace in the building." McClain explained, "They ended up having to tell the campaign that we're gonna have to relocate someplace else." With that the Wallace campaign conceded any permanent presence in the forty-ninth state.[49]

The Carrs boycott, the employment workshops, the proposed picket of the military bases, and the overwhelmingly negative response to the establishment of George Wallace's campaign office demonstrated a few ways Black men and women organized around conditions specific to Alaska. At the same time, these actions highlight the interconnectedness of the movement culture of the 1960s more generally. Whether it was Alaska or Alabama, the cause of equality united these men and women and animated their actions. Alaska's activism may not have received the same attention as protests in the Lower 48, but the state's patterns of racism, on one hand, and activism, on the other, fit squarely within the broader national story. An observer is struck not by the allegedly exceptional qualities of Alaska but, rather, the common struggle shared by men and women who fought for justice, regardless of their location.

However, the marches, pickets, and other protests associated with the civil rights movement failed to dismantle subtle forms of racism and an entrenched legacy of discrimination in Alaska's criminal justice system and business community. For certain, a few battles of the 1950s and 1960s would be won, as the case of Beatrice Coleman and the legislative fix of the Anti-Discrimination Act demonstrated; the Carrs boycotts exemplified the enduring utility of direct action. Meanwhile, many newly arriving Black men and women reported a more desirable racial climate to that which they had left in the Lower 48. Cal Williams touched down in Anchorage in 1965 after having fled Louisiana, a state with copious levels of racial violence. The twenty-three-year-old found Alaska "very much different socially and economically [than Louisiana]. I found a more welcoming community here for people of color and a great deal of achievement . . . a lot of Black owned clubs and restaurants were here, and I was rubbing elbows with Black people who had big wads of money in their pockets." Williams took a job washing dishes and quickly got involved in activism. He soon recognized that racism could be as dogged in Alaska as anywhere, but Williams at least felt more empowered in the newly designated state than he had in his native Louisiana.[50]

Cal Williams's story, like many others, was indeed one of perseverance, self-activity, and calculated risk. He came to Alaska in large part to get as far away from the South as possible in a place he hoped would be free from the broader history of the nation. Although Williams learned that the ugly patterns of history he had fled remained at least partly present in Alaska, he found that positive change was possible, and the limits upon his horizons in Alaska seemed less daunting than in Louisiana. But as the 1960s faded into the 1970s and then the 1980s, yet another demographic and economic transformation was at hand. The North Slope oil boom would reshape Alaska's politics and culture.

CHAPTER SIX

Black Alaska during the Oil Boom

GLADYS KNIGHT THOUGHT ALASKA COULD BE THE SITE OF A LONG-desired career expansion into film. The Empress of Soul, as Gladys Knight had come to be known by the 1970s, already earned acclaim as one of the era's great vocalists and now sought recognition on the silver screen. She first traveled to Alaska in December 1975, a year after having won a Grammy for the hit single "Midnight Train to Georgia," to scout locations for her upcoming film debut, *Pipe Dreams*. The movie would be set during the construction of the Trans-Alaska Pipeline System (TAPS), an eight-hundred-mile crude oil conduit between Prudhoe Bay on Alaska's resource-rich North Slope and the small southern Alaska town of Valdez, situated along a deepwater, ice-free port on the Prince William Sound.[1]

In the film Knight and her husband, record executive Barry Hankerson, played an estranged couple, Maria and Rob Wilson. Rob, like thousands of other men, had trekked to Alaska to seek his fortune during the state's oil boom. Hankerson's character worked as a pilot in the construction effort, leaving Maria and their struggling marriage behind in the Lower 48. But after a lonely six months away from her husband, Maria followed him north under the mistaken impression that she was in line to receive a supervisory position at a pipeline construction site. Upon her arrival, Maria quickly learned that no such position existed for women. To make ends meet and hopefully reconcile with her estranged husband, Maria Wilson reluctantly accepted work as a bartender at a rowdy Valdez roadhouse.[2]

From there the plot primarily revolved around Maria and Rob's reconciliation, culminating in a rather passionate scene that took place inside a pipeline section. The film touched on such themes as gender and racial discrimination in the so-called man camps along the construction route. Knight portrayed a dynamic Black woman who confidently navigated a male-dominated world to succeed personally as well as professionally. *Pipe Dreams* was shot on location in Valdez, with additional footage taken in and around Anchorage. Sensing free publicity, the Alyeska Pipeline Company, along with oil industry leaders that invested money to build and operate TAPS, partnered with Knight and the film crew. At one point the company escorted Knight to Fairbanks to experience life at a construction camp. Knight summarized the movie to *Jet*: "It's a very simple, very basic love story. The setting is Alaska, and we want to show that black folks do live and operate outside of the 48 continental United States, and there are black people who live in Alaska and work there, trying to survive there."[3]

Unfortunately for Knight, the movie flopped and had only a brief theater run. *Time* magazine offered a scathing if representative review: "There is undoubtedly a good movie to be made about the Alaska pipeline . . . But *Pipe Dreams* is not it. The old Yukon hands would have had a word for this pallid melodrama: mush."[4] Gladys Knight did not have another acting credit until a 1983 guest appearance on the long-running CBS sitcom *The Jeffersons*.[5] Knight later conceded that she had invested much of her own money in the development and production of *Pipe Dreams*: "I lost my shirt on the movie." Although it never propelled a second career in cinema, Knight's movie remains a treasured memory for a generation of Black Alaskans as well as enthusiasts of 1970s camp. Like the earlier *Jet* and *Ebony* features on Blacks in Alaska, the movie embraced the apparent curiosity that Black men and women made a life for themselves so far from either the American South or the large urban centers of the North and West. The movie has taken its place in the rather narrow but locally celebrated genre of "Alaskana"—idiosyncratic expressions that emphasize Alaska's cultural heritage.

More central to this study, the film also shined a light on the very different economic circumstances found in Alaska compared to the rest of the nation during the 1970s. At no point since the Great Depression had the United States encountered such headwinds. The first oil shock arrived in the fall of 1973, the result of tensions in the Middle East and the nation's reliance upon oil exported from that turbulent region. The dramatic spike in oil prices, combined with other factors, soon led to double-digit inflation rates that persisted through the decade. American industry—once the envy of the world—succumbed to global competition from Germany, Japan, and South Korea. Well-paid, industrial jobs no longer catapulted millions into the middle class as they had reliably done for the previous three decades. Union membership dropped, and disparities in wealth and income widened. The Vietnam War sapped American confidence in its military prowess, and consecutive presidencies failed, one criminally. Few would dispute that the seventies sent the nation into an economic, cultural, and political tailspin. These years became notorious for Watergate and rationed gas; words like *stagflation* and *malaise* entered the popular lexicon.[6]

And yet Alaska boomed like no time in its history, except perhaps the height of the gold rush over two generations earlier. The discovery of oil on the North Slope in the 1960s, followed by the Alaska Native Claims Settlement Act (1971), paved the way for the construction of TAPS, the decade's largest infrastructure project. As the United States resolved to gain greater energy independence, Alaska's extensive oil fields would play a pivotal role. Thousands flocked to the recently admitted forty-ninth state and took advantage of some of the highest wages available in the roaring construction and energy sectors. The population increase brought with it painful adjustments and ramped up various forms of conflict, often along lines of race and gender. And while money seemingly flowed through the state just as abundantly as the oil through the newly constructed pipeline, access was never equal. In what was perhaps a late-twentieth-century iteration of the Wild West's boomtown days, Alaska's major cities and remote towns enticed young, itinerant men in droves. After just weeks on the job, most had thick wallets, and some possessed an appetite for trouble. They came from all over, but a substantial number arrived from Texas and Oklahoma—then the center of the American oil industry. That industry reshaped Alaska in ways not seen since the expansion of military into the territory during the world wars. Oil took its place alongside the military and federal spending as pillars of the state's economy.[7]

The impact of these transformational changes would be experienced throughout Alaska. Alaska Natives who had called the state's North Slope home for over a thousand years quickly recognized that the oil industry would irrevocably disrupt subsistence modes of living even as it provided a previously unimaginable accumulation of material wealth. Black Alaskans, meanwhile, located more opportunities, but many also encountered divisions and race-based hurdles. Unresolved tensions from the postwar decades simmered and at times boiled over. Theressa Lenear, the daughter of Robert and Beatrice Coleman, grew up in Fairbanks throughout the pipeline's construction and reported a "rise in overt racism" accompanied by a flood of money.[8] Endemic inequality, disparate levels of political access, and a criminal justice system plagued by racial disparities were a few issues confronting Black Alaskans and Alaskans of color more generally.

On balance, though, the 1970s was a decade in which many Black Alaskans ascended into the middle class and participated in the state's economic expansion. African Americans contributed to the boom times even as they confronted and overcame discrimination in the post–civil rights era. Black men and women struggled for access and equity not only in the streets but increasingly in the halls and boardrooms of unions, nonprofits, multinational and local businesses, and state agencies. At the same time, a shift in demographics led the state toward a deeper strain of conservatism, rooted in the culture of the oil industry and a fealty to extractive capitalism. This in turn led to increasing and strident forms of racial antagonism, much of which would only come into view once the economy cooled down in the 1980s. To build from Gladys Knight's observation in her ill-fated film debut, Blacks did far more than simply work and survive in Alaska during the 1970s. They actively shaped the state as it transformed from one of the nation's poorest places into one of its richest.

Race Relations during the Pipeline Boom

Following the discovery of oil in and around Prudhoe Bay on Alaska's North Slope in the late 1960s, it became clear that Alaska's future would be determined by the extraction of this most lucrative natural resource. The land surrounding Prudhoe Bay contained the largest oil reserves in North America. Getting it to market, however, first required the state to settle land claims with the Alaska Natives on whose land the oil would be extracted. Drilling for oil also required vast infrastructure to transport the resource to the ice-free port of Valdez. To address this concern, the state and its corporate partners constructed the Trans-Alaska Pipeline. As depicted in *Pipe Dreams*, the construction project dominated Alaska's economy throughout the mid- to late 1970s and irrevocably altered the social, cultural, and economic dynamics of the state.[9]

In a decade of persistent economic turbulence in the Lower 48, high wages and steady work enticed thousands to relocate to Alaska. Many left once the project concluded, flush with cash in hand. Rob and Maria Wilson, the lead protagonists in *Pipe Dreams*, abandoned Alaska nearly as soon as they reconciled, as the construction project slowed. But others put down roots and contributed to the state in a variety of ways for decades to follow. Florine Walker was the first known Black woman hired to work on the pipeline. She earned a living as a culinary worker and food server in the camps along the construction route. Life on the pipeline could be grueling, with long hours to accompany the high pay. Women such as Walker had the added pressure of negotiating the hypermasculine environment of the decade's largest construction project.[10] The Alaska population and workforce before, during, and after the construction of the pipeline was disproportionately male. Only since the 1990s has Alaska's demographic balance evened out.[11]

Alaska's population grew by 33.8 percent during the 1970s. This included a stunning 66.3 percent increase in single-person households, reflecting the younger, unattached individuals who journeyed north. The Black population rose only modestly, from 3 percent of Alaska's total population in 1970 to 3.4 percent in 1980.[12] Skilled and unskilled workers were in high demand as average monthly wages more than doubled during the pipeline construction years.[13] The pipeline's construction was the single largest economic event in Alaska history aside from wartime projects, such as the construction of the Alaska Railroad over a half-century earlier. Investment from the oil industry topped $9 billion (roughly $30 billion in 2021). In comparison, the total payroll in the Alaska economy in 1973, the year TAPS was approved, was only $1.3 billion. Employment in nearly every economic sector throughout the state grew in the 1970s, including fishing, retail, and most secondary service industries. Retailer locations increased their business by 46 percent during the decade. Local government jobs more than doubled, and state government jobs increased by roughly 50 percent.[14]

Gladys Knight's character, Maria, thus reflected the very real optimism and verve of someone like Florine Walker, a woman who expected to better her life in Alaska, knowing well the challenging environment in which she had arrived. So, too, did Walker very likely comprehend the racial tensions associated with the construction effort and hostility she would encounter, at least from certain quarters. Ed McGrath, a white laborer who worked on the pipeline, detailed his experience in his 1977 book, *Inside the Alaska Pipeline*. Though he did not work alongside Black men or women, he "heard rumors" about Black welders and apprentices who encountered racism, and he reported discriminatory attitudes among his white coworkers. Many of

Florine Walker, the first Black woman to work on the pipeline, ca. 1976. Pipeline Construction and Impact Photo Collection, Alaska State Library (asl.p17.8277).

these white laborers came from the South, where much of the oil industry was based, and they brought a history of exclusionary policies and a conservative brand of politics. Fairbanks resident Theressa Lenear heard that Black workers and residents in Alaska's interior feared being "accosted by white Texans" who brought with them a mentality shaped by segregation and a culture steeped in the customs of the Jim Crow South.[15]

Skilled labor positions with the TAPS project were routed through a myriad of unions contracted by the Alyeska Pipeline Services Company, the consortium of oil companies that jointly owned and operated the pipeline. In exchange for higher wages and travel compensation, the selected unions agreed not to strike and expedite the construction effort as much as possible.[16] Many of the contracted unions were based in Texas or Oklahoma, like the Pipeliners Union Local 798 out of Tulsa. The 798ers, as they called themselves, earned a notorious reputation for its members' heavy drinking and fighting and a haughty arrogance that accompanied their position as well-paid, skilled laborers. The white welders from Oklahoma had become such a nuisance that many Alaskans wanted them gone. One cheeky bumper sticker prevalently seen affixed to Alaskans' cars wryly declared, "Happiness is a Texan headed south with an Okie under each arm."[17]

For Black Alaskans the seemingly ever-increasing presence of white Texans and Oklahomans presented more than a mere nuisance. In one traumatic moment, McGrath recounted his horror at seeing a bus driver brutally attacked, beaten, and left by the side of the road by white pipeline workers. The driver, who was white, had allegedly defended the right of a Black laborer to sit wherever he chose on the bus ride to the construction site. McGrath recorded the "constant racist statements" by fellow white laborers, something that apparently made him uncomfortable. The African Americans who worked on the pipeline, he proclaimed, faced "intolerable" and "vicious" conditions and treatment from their coworkers.[18] So entrenched had racist hiring practices become among the 798ers that a group of a Black laborers led by labor activist Harvey Adams eventually filed and won a lawsuit against the union.[19]

For certain, Black pipeliners and other construction workers persevered despite the hostile climate. Ed Wesley first arrived in Alaska in 1973 with the military and served at Fort Greely, just outside of Delta Junction. After his service he and his family stayed in Alaska; he took a supervisory and security position at Pump Station 9 on the pipeline. Wesley recalled several Black workers affiliated with Laborers Local 942 based in Fairbanks who played key roles in the union and on the construction effort. One man, Willie Lewis, took a leadership role in the union and defended his men against the discrimination that came from the outside workers, mostly the white welders and pipeliners affiliated with Local 798. As the pipeline ushered in an era of growth and prosperity, the industry's conservative roots in the American South, recalled Wesley, meant that white men sometimes received priority for the most lucrative jobs and promotions.[20]

Nonetheless, for Wesley, who grew up poor in rural Mississippi and then Chicago's Southside, the steady, well-paid work along the pipeline catapulted him and his family comfortably into the middle class.[21] Other Black men and women found work on the pipeline a novel, lucrative experience that greatly deviated from the life they had previously known. Opalanga D. Pugh may have been among the most unlikely women to join the pipeline's construction effort. Pugh was born in Denver, Colorado, in 1952. After the assassination of Martin Luther King Jr. in 1968, Pugh grew more politicized and rallied in support of civil rights and Black Power. She took a job in the Outward Bound School program in Denver before going to college at the University of Colorado Boulder and then the University of Wisconsin–Milwaukee. While at school in Wisconsin, Pugh studied abroad in Lagos, Nigeria. Upon completing her degree, she stayed in the African nation to work as a journalist for the Second World Black and African Festival of Arts and Culture. Pugh returned to the United States a few years later, and at the prompting of an old college roommate, she took a job on the Alaska pipeline.[22]

Pugh's friend explained, "Girl, I'm making more money than we ever made." Pugh conceded she was "just seeing dollar signs, ching, ching!" when she arrived in Fairbanks in January 1977 and took up residence in the nearby town of North Pole. There Pugh lived in a cramped two-bedroom apartment with seven adults and three kids. They had come to cash in on the pipeline. Unfortunately, Pugh's job application and processing papers were held up for over six weeks in Juneau. Pugh recalled how she and others in the apartment did their best to avoid taking handouts at the Salvation Army but eventually had to relent to fight off hunger. She and her roommates took home an assortment of Alaska dietary staples: "Moose meat, and you know, there were other vegetables." Breaking with her vegetarian diet, Pugh's friend "worked that moose meat and barbequed it up, girl, it was chicken licken." So it was that a Denver-born woman who had previously spent a couple of years in West Africa came to learn the culinary delicacies of Alaska.[23]

Once her paperwork went through, Pugh worked at a communications center on the pipeline. It was important work that ensured open lines of contact across the vast spaces of wilderness through which the pipeline had to pass. "I had air-ground communication, you know, with the helicopters, the medics, the security. I had four-channel based CB [citizens band] radio, 'Breaker, breaker 1–9, you got that brown sugar here,'" Pugh recounted with laughter in an interview in 2008. She continued, "I talked for twelve hours a day, seven days a week, nine weeks on, two weeks off." Pugh and friends traveled into Fairbanks during their downtime. They frequented the clubs not with the best entertainment but with the "best electrical hitching posts in

Woman and man working on the pipeline, n.d. Steve McCutcheon Collection, Anchorage Museum (B1990.014.5.P.1.126)

their parking lot so that you could plug your car up and it would keep the radiator hot—warm while you went in and partied." Otherwise, Pugh reasoned, "every hour, hour and a half, you gotta put on your coat, your gloves, and everything, come back, start your car so that the block doesn't freeze . . . It was just funny, just living there." Ultimately, however, Pugh and her friends who worked on the pipeline viewed the peculiarities and challenges of life in Alaska's interior worth the trouble. She earned over $35,000 a year, a large sum in the mid- to late 1970s, over $150,000 adjusted for inflation in 2022 dollars. With her money Pugh generously provided gifts of a hundred dollars to members of her family and her friends during the holidays; she purchased a pipe organ for her musically inclined mother and treated herself to a new car.[24]

Vernellia Ruth Randall, another Black woman who traveled to Alaska in these years, secured a novel set of life experiences and reset her understanding of race and identity. Born in Texas, Randall moved to Seattle and then to Alaska with her husband in 1979. She worked in the Department of Health and Social Services after having completed degrees in nursing and law; Randall later became a professor of law at the University of Dayton in Ohio. But before trekking back to the Midwest, she spent five years in Alaska, split between Fairbanks and Juneau. As a Black woman from Texas, she did not fit the profile of a typical laborer who came to earn a living working on the pipeline from the South. According to Randall, "Alaska taught me a lot about the nature of racism... that it's about numbers and threats." She asserted that the relatively small population of African Americans ensured that most whites did not view them as a threat, at least not enough to warrant the hostility she had experienced in the American South. However, Randall revealed that she witnessed anti-Native attitudes in Juneau, which her white counterparts tried to coerce her into adopting. Randall's experience demonstrated the multivalent currents of race and discrimination coursing through Alaska during a period of economic transformation.[25]

Ensuring Access during the Oil Boom

The complexity of racism and the Black experience in Alaska during the oil boom could be found, in part, in the disparate levels of wealth and opportunity that could be accessed. Willie Ratcliff, coordinator of the Alaska Minority Business Task Force, located high levels of discrimination among Anchorage and Fairbanks businesses, particularly in the contracting sector. As oil began to flow by the end of the 1970s, plentiful work existed in the oil field service industries and their various subsidiaries. The proliferation of jobs, in turn, created still greater needs for services in the municipalities as the economy expanded in nearly every sector. But this bounty was not accessible to everyone. Ratcliff asserted, "The Anchorage minority business community suffers from economic distress in part due to receiving disproportionately low percentages of Municipal contract awards." In fiscal year 1977, Ratcliff found that Anchorage awarded $28 million in contracts; however, "fewer than $237,000 or 8/10 of 1 percent have gone to businesses known to be owned and controlled by minorities." At the time, roughly 6 percent of the city's population was Black, and people of color constituted 15 percent of the total. Fairbanks, he supposed, looked similar in its discrimination directed at Black- and Native-owned businesses. In both cities contracts went to white-owned businesses and construction firms about 99 percent of the time, Ratcliff found.[26]

In Anchorage the assembly passed an ordinance in 1979 that ensured minority-owned businesses equal consideration for construction contracts. By then Alaska's oil industry was largely based in Anchorage, and the municipality was experiencing a housing boom to accommodate the highly compensated managers and mid-level white-collar workers who arrived after the blue-collar work of constructing the pipeline was complete. But three years later, only $7.7 million of the $77.5 million of the city construction budget went to minority-owned businesses. The $7.7 million figure included female-owned businesses, which were still white. In fact, nearly $6 million of that $7.7 million went to one firm led by a white woman. Four minority-owned firms earned about $1 million in contracts, and the thirty other minority-owned firms divided what remained.[27] A similar review revealed that only five of eighty-eight major construction contracts went to minority-owned firms. One was Black owned; Alaska Native contractors secured the four others.[28] For over twenty years, the NAACP, the Alaska Black Caucus, and state representatives such as Blanche McSmith had pointed out these discrepancies and called for legislative solutions.

Ratcliff ultimately took up his case against the head of the United States Small Business Association in Anchorage (SBA), Frank Cox, and a journalistic investigation followed. *Black Enterprise*, a magazine published for aspiring and active Black entrepreneurs, published the results. Soon after, the US House of Representatives intervened and concluded that Cox had accepted bribes, kickbacks, and gifts on behalf of clients. He had also favored white-owned businesses at the expense of those owned by Blacks and Natives. In addition, Cox and the SBA had denied loans to minority clients and flouted federal regulations that prohibited discriminatory business practices. Most damning, Cox had put together a blacklist of names for local banks. He urged them to deny loan requests on the basis that they were credit risks, but the investigation revealed that those who landed on the list had no record of financial mismanagement. Many of them had a record of political advocacy, and all were African American, Asian American, or Alaska Native. Ratcliff himself learned that Cox and the SBA had denied him access to contracts for federal projects, a decision that had serious financial implications on his contracting business.[29]

Cox allegedly told two Black businessmen from Fairbanks who sought assistance from the SBA that "Blacks just don't have the know-how or the history of running a business" and discouraged them from opening a clothing boutique. The Equal Employment Opportunity offices in Anchorage released a report in 1980 that spotlighted the lack of minority participation in state government and business. Promises by the state to hire an additional 516 minority individuals in 1981 were followed by the actual hiring of only 136.[30] Eventually, the investigation forced Cox to resign, and the SBA came under new leadership, thanks in large part to the efforts of Ratcliff, among others. Cox remained unrepentant and even exclaimed to the *Anchorage Daily News* that any discrimination mattered little since Black Alaskans "only represent two and half percent of the state," an inaccurate number in any event. Ratcliff's organizing, along with reporting in the *Daily News* and *Black Enterprise*, led to some internal reforms at the SBA, and future Black businesses would no longer need to deal with Frank Cox.[31]

The efforts of Ratcliff, however, largely supported upwardly mobile Black Alaskans and did not clearly address issues related to the poor and working class. Rather, these men and women, an outsize percentage of whom were Black and Indigenous, still encountered barriers to participate in the workforce, even as opportunities expanded at the onset of the oil boom. The erstwhile Eastchester Flats had by this time been consumed by the larger Anchorage neighborhood of Fairview, which remained one of most multicultural of the municipality's distinct neighborhoods. One longtime resident noted in 1978, "One of the interesting changes I've noticed in Fairview over the last few years has been that there are now more Spanish-American, Filipino, and Oriental families than before."[32] During this time of economic plenty, Fairview was the only Anchorage neighborhood that saw its average income drop during the pipeline construction heyday. In 1975 Fairview and the Anchorage downtown, combined for the study's purposes, reported an average annual household income of $26,033. The next year that number dropped to $19,630 and continued to decline in the years ahead, though it might be noted that these figures were far higher than mean incomes elsewhere in the United States at the time, largely because of Alaska's notoriously high cost of living.[33]

One of the greatest barriers to steady work in Anchorage's poor and working-class communities was the lack of public transportation. Indeed, Alaska's largest city was subject to months of cold, snow, and ice, all of which led to wear and tear on even the most reliable vehicles. For many low-income people, personal transportation was costly and hard to come by; the oil shocks spiked the cost of gasoline, increasing the costs of car ownership ever higher. Meanwhile, Anchorage's city limits expanded with unprecedented speed, and businesses increasingly dispersed along the newly built highways and major thoroughfares. If one had had trouble navigating Anchorage without a car in the immediate postwar decades, it was virtually impossible to do so by the 1970s. Affordable public transportation was central to the advancement of low-income Alaskans. This was precisely the argument advanced by John S. Parks, the longtime Black activist and community organizer who lived in Fairview.[34]

Unlike Willie Ratcliff, who had as his primary goal the opening and expansion of Black business opportunities, Parks understood that poor Black, brown, and white people could never secure regular employment without access to transportation in the increasingly spread-out city and borough. Parks, long active on the Fairview neighborhood council, earned the informal moniker "the mayor of Fairview" for his efforts to secure funding for Anchorage's bus system and his advocacy on behalf of working-class residents. Parks labored intensively for the suddenly plush municipality of Anchorage and the State of Alaska to fund a bus transit system he called the "People Mover." He circulated petitions to lobby Anchorage mayor George Sullivan and maintained a steady drumbeat of support for the ambitious project. Parks later assumed a post on Anchorage's Municipal Transit Commission to study the bus system and lobby city officials to address the inequities in both road improvements and access to public transportation.[35] Parks also pressed Anchorage leaders to remove junked cars and litter in Fairview alleys and to improve the severely damaged and unmaintained throughways that passed for roads.[36]

Parks consistently attended community forums, townhalls, and council meetings in which public transportation was a topic of discussion. Parks and his allies eventually succeeded in making the case to two mayors, Jack Roderick, who presided over the borough, and George Sullivan, who led the city. Roderick, a liberal who supported public transit, allied naturally with Parks to secure the funding.[37] By 1974, as the People Mover neared completion, Parks emphasized the role of public transit in a run for council: "We've got to get people out of cars. We should spend quite a bit of money upgrading the bus system."[38] Parks continued to advocate for public transportation for working-class Alaskans throughout the 1970s. He never wavered in his belief that even amid boom times, vulnerable and poor people had to organize to make their interests known to the city's power brokers if they wished to access public services.[39]

The organizing activities and advocacy of Ratcliff, McSmith, Watts, Parks, and others yielded results, but work remained. Speaking to an interviewer in the early 1980s, Richard Watts proclaimed, "So far as economics is concerned, we haven't caught up." Sounding a tone of optimism, Watts concluded, "We've made tremendous progress, but we haven't caught up."[40] Once again, Anchorage echoed much of the country in its race relations. The pivotal legislation of the 1960s—the Civil Rights Act of 1964, the Voting Rights Act of 1965, and the Fair Housing Act of 1968—had a positive impact on the lives of millions of African Americans. Nonetheless, deep-seated disparities remained well after the height of the civil rights era; this was as true in Alaska as it was in most any other place in the Lower 48. Watts's remarks could conceivably stand in for the Black experience in Alaska writ large. African Americans had come north in search of more favorable circumstances. Many arrived after overcoming the depths of injustice elsewhere, and some found what they were looking for in the forty-ninth state. However, while life in the northern latitudes obviously lacked the heat and humidity of the places many of the men and women had fled, it was not immune to the maladies of racism and discrimination. The marches and pickets demonstrated this reality, but so, too, did the workaday activism of Black residents and business leaders who demanded equity.

The last quarter of the twentieth century also brought what might best be considered incremental levels of change and modest, perhaps uneven, amounts of inclusion. An observer who located a growing number of African Americans in leadership roles throughout the state may have overlooked the presence of systemic forms of racism. In 1966 Pete Aiken ran and won his race to serve on the Fairbanks North Star Borough Assembly. The twenty-four-year-old Aiken thus became the first man recognized as Black to hold elective office in Alaska (recall that Thomas Bevers, a Black man who was elected in Anchorage a generation earlier had passed as white).[41] In the 1970s, for instance, voters sent two Black men to the Alaska legislature. Willard Bowman, long a fixture in Alaska politics and an advocate of racial justice, joined Joshua Wright, an Anchorage dentist with an impressive résumé of professional success and political potential. Both men hailed from Anchorage and arrived in Juneau with an eye toward improving the lot for minority people in the state. They succeeded Blanche McSmith, the first Black woman and first African American to serve at the state level in 1960, having been appointed by Governor William Egan to fill the seat John Rader vacated upon his appointment to serve as the state's first attorney general.[42]

In 1972 Fairbanks sent its first Black representative to Juneau when voters elected Selwyn Carrol. Carrol, a junior high school teacher who also worked in the Alaska Department of Health and Welfare, ran as a Republican and served a single term in the House of Representatives. Other African American men and women served locally, mostly on school boards in Anchorage and Fairbanks. In 1974 Governor Egan appointed John Alexander to serve as Alaska's commissioner of labor—another first. A year later Col. William Campfield Jr. became the first Black man to hold rank as a commander at Elmendorf Air Force Base in Anchorage.[43] Campfield's rise in rank through the air force should be viewed as a bold counterpoint to Lt. General Buckner, head of the Alaska Defense Command and an unrepentant bigot who had exerted such influence on the territory of Alaska in the early 1940s.

As Ratcliff uncovered the biases and illegal discrimination of the Small Business Association, Black men and women earned seats in the boardrooms of businesses and assumed leadership roles around the state and beyond. For his part Ratcliff eventually left Alaska for San Francisco, in 1987, after spending time in both places for many years. Ratcliff had by then launched a second career as the publisher of the *San Francisco Bay View*, one of the West Coast's most storied Black alternative newspapers.[44] Ben Humphries, a longtime Anchorage activist and trade unionist, received an appointment to the board of directors of the National Bank of Alaska in 1978; he was the first Black man in Alaska to hold a position on a financial board. Humphries, who had already made a name for himself in Alaska's labor movement, having advocated for strong contracts with high wages and enviable benefits, now acted to ensure that Black and Native Alaskans had representation within the state's largest financial institution and could access housing in the same desirable locations as their white counterparts.[45]

Richard Watts continued to rise through the ranks at Carrs after having been hired a decade earlier; he eventually entered upper management. John Parks stayed close to those in Fairview. He parlayed his successful organizing drive to launch the People Mover into a broader effort to register voters and strengthen the electoral voice of Anchorage's poorest residents. Parks, a proud liberal Democrat, believed that an organized bloc of working-class voters was the best strategy to curb the power of a growing conservative base that had arrived with the oil boom and garnered considerable wealth and influence in local politics.[46]

Eleanor Andrews, a Black woman born and raised in Compton, California, arrived in Fairbanks in 1965 and relocated to Anchorage two years later; she held positions in state and local government before starting her own business, The Andrews Group, in 1987. The Andrews Group provided logistics, information, technology, and support services for the US government, primarily the Department of Defense, the US Army, and the US Air Force. Within five years of starting her business, Andrews was named Alaska contractor of the year for her work with the army. Over the next decades, she earned other accolades, including the Small Business Association's small business person of the year (1998), a feat unimaginable when the SBA was run by Frank Cox. Andrews also served on a variety of councils and executive boards, becoming among the most influential people in Alaska's business circles.[47]

Black women rose to prominence in other fields during these years as well. Carolyn Jones, for example, grew up in Upstate New York, along the Hudson River. Before making her way to Alaska, Jones earned a full academic scholarship to Stanford University and graduated with distinction in 1963. She then attended Yale Law School, also on a fully funded scholarship, and completed her degree in three years. While at Yale, Jones was the first woman president of the Yale Law School Student Association. Carolyn Jones began her legal work in Alaska in 1975, taking a position for the Alaska State Commission for Human Rights. She served as an assistant attorney general and a supervising attorney for the State of Alaska until her retirement in 1998. During these years Jones earned recognition for her service through the Alaska State Commission for Human Rights Award for Distinguished and Dedicated Service in 1984 and the Alaska Bar Association Distinguished Service Award in 1990.[48]

Even as she developed an impressive legal career for the state and a reputation as an advocate for children and global human rights, Jones remained active in Anchorage and beyond. Notably, the Rotary Club invited Jones to join in 1987, the first year women were allowed to do so. Jones declined, however, after determining that the invitation was half-hearted. Eventually, though, she not only joined the Rotary Club but earned a spot on the board and then became the president of the Rotary Club of Anchorage East. In

1997 Jones won the governorship of Rotary District 5010, a district that included Alaska, Yukon, and eastern Russia; this was the largest Rotary district in the world by area. Her service to the Rotary led her to Russia three times as a volunteer to teach students with developmental disabilities and twice as a visiting faculty member in Russian universities. Carolyn Jones's career in Alaska as a human rights lawyer provided a voice of compassion in the legal and nonprofit worlds. She brought an intellectual rigor to her endeavors and gained recognition as a leader and humanitarian in the various capacities she served.[49]

Jewel Jones, no relation to Carolyn Jones, also gained prominence as a public servant in Alaska. Jones arrived in Alaska from Oklahoma in 1967 and promptly found work in local government. She worked for the City of Anchorage and then the Municipality of Anchorage (after the 1975 merger) for thirty-two years, serving in executive management for the Social Services Department and the municipality's Department of Health and Human Services. In those positions Jones mentored hundreds of men and women from underrepresented backgrounds, preparing them for careers in public service. Jones also worked as a director of the Anchorage Community Land Trust on efforts to revitalize Mountain View, a low-income neighborhood in Anchorage with a large minority population that historically suffered from a lack of investment. Throughout her six years with the land trust, Jones worked to convert abandoned buildings into office space, affordable housing, and sites for artists, entrepreneurs, and activists.[50]

Jewel Jones has also taken on roles in several community groups and nonprofit boards, including Commonwealth North, the United Way of Anchorage, and the Alaska Center for the Performing Arts. As chair of the board of the Alaska Housing Finance Corporation, Jones actively lobbied for senior housing across Alaska. She has also been active in the Anchorage NAACP, Alaska Black Caucus, and Anchorage Urban League. These institutions have empowered young men and women of color and facilitated relationships in business and government. Jones has received recognition for her efforts from the YWCA and the Anchorage Chamber of Commerce. She also received an ATHENA award for her achievement in advancing female excellence. The National Association of Social Workers, Alaska Chapter, awarded her Citizen of the Year in 2001, and she was inducted into the Alaska Women's Hall of Fame in 2013.[51]

Jewel Jones was far from the only Black woman to leave the Jim Crow South for Alaska. Etheldra Davis was born in rural Arkansas but later moved first to

Los Angeles and then to Anchorage. Her story, too, reveals broader trends that played out for millions of working-class, upwardly mobile Blacks who participated in the Great Migration. Davis attended the Los Angeles City College before matriculating from the University of California, Los Angeles, among the nation's preeminent public universities at a time when tuition was free and open to all who attended. Like other women of her generation, she entered the education field and taught at Los Angeles public schools before moving to Anchorage in 1959 to become the first Black teacher in the municipality. Within ten years Davis had obtained additional degrees from the University of Alaska and Newport University and had entered the ranks of administration as a principal, another first for Black women in Alaska.[52]

Arguably, the most impressive figure to highlight the opportunities associated with Alaska's postwar development, as well as the state's tenacious obstacles, might be Mahala Ashley Dickerson. Like Etheldra Davis and Carolyn Jones, Dickerson came to Alaska after having grown up in the Deep South at the height of the Jim Crow era. She went on to launch a highly successful career in law, one that rivals the accomplishments of Alaska's most notable politicians and leaders. Born of modest means in Montgomery, Alabama, in 1912, Dickerson obtained degrees from two of the nation's most prestigious historically Black universities. She first graduated from Tennessee's Fisk University in 1935 and then earned her law degree in 1945 from the Howard University School of Law in Washington, DC. She returned to Alabama to practice law for three years after having become the first Black women to pass the bar and practice in the state.[53]

However, the intensity of discrimination and the barriers to advancement in Alabama led Dickerson to relocate to Indiana in 1951. She then became the second Black woman admitted to the bar in the Hoosier State. Yet Dickerson remained restless and in search of new adventures, professional and personal. A few years later she vacationed in Alaska and grew enamored with the natural beauty that surrounded her. Soon after, she decided to relocate again, this time permanently, to Alaska. Dickerson took to the splendor of the landscape and traveled with her young children along the still rather primitive Alaska Highway. Upon her arrival, she filed a claim for a 160-acre homestead in the Matanuska-Susitna Valley near Wasilla, to become the valley's first Black homesteader. Months later Dickerson passed the bar and became Alaska's first Black lawyer. Though she faced discrimination in Alaska as she had elsewhere, she recognized that "racism, like cancer, moves from place to place." As such, she decided to stay in Alaska and eventually opened law offices in Wasilla and Anchorage.[54]

During the 1960s Dickerson worked as the lead attorney representing a group of Fairview property owners who opposed annexation into the Municipality of Anchorage. Though Dickerson and her partners appealed the case to the US Supreme Court, the court declined to hear it. Another case, one about which she felt the most pride, revolved around disparate pay and gender discrimination in state government and at the University of Alaska. Indeed, she won the landmark case against the State of Alaska and the university after having demonstrated the endemic levels of gender-based discrimination that persisted though the 1970s. The state and university imposed oversight and ensured equal pay for female magistrates and professors, respectively. From her lawsuits on behalf of working-class Fairview residents and of female faculty at the university, Dickerson's legal career was largely defined by her desire to battle for marginalized communities.[55]

In addition to her work in the courtroom, Dickerson received many legal honors throughout her career. She served as president of the National Association of Women Lawyers from 1983 to 1984, and in 1985 she won the Zeta Phi Beta Award for distinguished service in the field of law. In 1995 Dickerson received the Margaret Brent Award from the American Bar Association, an honor recognizing the most outstanding American female lawyers. Dickerson boasted, "Ruth Bader Ginsburg got hers before me, but I got mine before Sandra Day O'Connor."[56] In 1998 Dickerson published an autobiography, *Delayed Justice for Sale*, in which she claimed: "In my life, I didn't have but two things to do. Those were to stay Black and die. I'm just not afraid to fight somebody big."[57] As Dickerson ascended the heights of the legal profession, she raised triplet sons and practiced her Quaker faith. Her accomplishments stand among the elites of not only Alaska's history but also the history of the legal profession, civil rights, and women's activism. Dickerson's career reached new heights through the 1970s, and her determination and resolve had a tangible impact on the lives of thousands of Alaskan women and people of color. It may have been possible, though hard to realistically imagine, Dickerson ascending the ranks of the legal profession in Alabama as she managed to do in Alaska.[58]

Of course, as notable as these figures and their contributions are, more prosaic stories of arrival must also be included. Willie Odom recalled traveling to Alaska in 1976 from Mississippi after hearing about well-paying jobs in the state and, as he put it, to "find myself." He planned to stay a month, but after he took a job at an Anchorage retail shop called the Alaska Kitchen, where he made "butcher blocks, table legs, cabinet doors," Odom received an offer for full-time work. He consulted with his family in the Lower 48 and ultimately decided to stay in Alaska, knowing that it was unlikely he would find a comparable job that paid as well. A few years later, on a return visit south to attend his mother's funeral, he reconnected with LaQuita Odom, the woman he would later marry and move with to Alaska. The two of them have resided in the state for over forty-five years.

Simon Brown came to Alaska in 1975 just as construction on the pipeline began. Born in South Carolina, Brown joined the military and served in Alaska, Germany, and elsewhere but found the cold weather preferable to the heat and humidity of the South. He also noted that Alaskans treated him "more as a human rather than a Black person." After his service concluded, Brown joined thousands of other Black men and women in Alaska and settled permanently.[59]

Indeed, race relations in Alaska moved apace in contradictory and uneven ways, just as they did throughout the country. Public advocates such as Bowman and lawyers such as Dickerson located racism and discrimination embedded in national, state, and local institutions even as individual Black men and women rose to esteemed positions of authority in politics, business, and law. The determination of Willie Ratcliff to expose discrimination in the business world provided openings for an entrepreneur such as Eleanor Andrews to flourish just a couple of years later. Andrews, who came from a modest background in Southern California, started a government contracting firm and became among the most successful businesspeople in Alaska. Of course, the federal legislation that cleared the way for greater minority involvement in the nation's labyrinthine contracting system initiated greater opportunities for Alaska Natives as well as Africans Americans and women from all backgrounds.[60] Other activists, including John R. Parks, remained most concerned with the plight of poor, working-class, and immigrant Alaskans as he labored tirelessly to ensure access to public transportation, clean streets, safe neighborhoods, and quality education. Still others, like the Odoms, arrived for what they thought would be a limited amount of time but found work that paid high enough wages to support a family and decided to put down roots. These men and women, though not at the forefront of a social movement, nonetheless transformed Alaska into a diverse and dynamic state.

The End of an Era

Gladys Knight's fictional foray into Alaska's working-class life during the era of building the pipeline did not receive critical accolades, but it nonetheless showcased the very real fault lines that existed at the time, notably around race and gender. *Pipe Dreams* also issued a useful corrective to the perception that Alaska's oil boom was solely a story of white arrivals who sought unfettered access to the resources found under Native land. Black workers, business owners, and political leaders participated in the decade's boom and forged a space of their own amid the prosperity. Much of this took place in a post–civil rights context whereby marches and boycotts took a back seat to actions in union halls, municipal meetings, and courtrooms. Bureaucratic and legal maneuvering had become at least as important as traditional forms of civil rights activism. Money came easily for many who worked on the pipeline, but rising social tensions accompanied the booming economy. Enticed by lucrative wages, thousands of workers traveled to Alaska, and they brought with them their politics and racial assumptions. Some of these new arrivals, the majority of whom were white, viewed Blacks with suspicion or even outright hostility, as they did the still larger Alaska Native population. This antagonism could be seen in the day-to-day interactions on the pipeline and the tensions that resulted from potent economic growth.

This reality complicates a celebratory history of civil rights in Alaska. For certain, African Americans and Alaska Natives at times made dramatic advances during the postwar decades. Alaska Natives, for example, won a monumental land settlement in advance of the pipeline's construction. The result—the Alaska Native Claims Settlement Act, or ANCSA, signed into law in 1971 by Richard Nixon—represented a landmark piece of legislation and marked a departure in how the federal government dealt with the nation's Indigenous people of the North.[61] Even as Alaska's communities of color had vastly different histories and disparate struggles, common bonds emerged. Black Alaskans stood in solidarity with other marginalized people on issues that had not yet gained widespread or popular acceptance. Leroy Williams, in a leadership role with the Alaska Black Caucus, testified before Anchorage's assembly on behalf of a gay rights ordinance in 1976. Williams connected the struggles of Black and Indigenous Alaskans to those in the gay and lesbian community: "Until all of us are free, none of us are free." The ordinance ultimately failed to pass, but the display revealed the reach and interconnectedness of civil rights advocacy as well as the conservative pushback that it garnered.[62]

In sum, Black women and men served as agents of social change in Alaska's political and economic life during the tumultuous years of the oil boom. Blanche McSmith and Willard Bowman raised awareness and organized on behalf of Black residents. Opalanga Pugh, Carolyn Jones, and Jewel Jones—to name only a few—successfully navigated Alaska's fraught racial and male-dominated social landscape. Eleanor Andrews demonstrated her keen entrepreneurialism and took advantage of new opportunities for female contractors, who had for too long been effectively frozen out of what she called a "good old boys network." Andrews was not alone; numerous other Black women assumed high-profile positions in business, government, and nonprofits.[63] Men such as Ed Wesley and Willie Odom leveraged Alaska's high wages to secure a comfortable life and attain a material well-being beyond the reach of most Americans in the late 1970s. John Parks mobilized a coalition of Blacks, Natives, and Asian Americans in Fairview to vote for progressive candidates at the local and state levels.

But for each step forward, Black Alaskans also encountered adversity and discrimination. Nowhere was this more prominently on display than in the criminal justice system and in tensions between Black Alaskans and law enforcement, a story that reverberated around the nation throughout the last decades of the twentieth century and into the twenty-first.

CHAPTER SEVEN

Criminal Justice, Law Enforcement, and Race in Urban Alaska

IN 1978, AS CONSTRUCTION ON THE TRANS-ALASKA PIPELINE CONcluded and Alaska's economy continued its impressive ascent, the state's Black Caucus released a troubling report. Among its findings, drawn largely from the 1978 meeting of the Governor's Commission on the Administration of Justice, the Black Caucus uncovered the following facts: "Blacks and Natives convicted of fraud, forgery or embezzlement received sentences 450 percent longer than whites convicted of the same crimes. Blacks and Natives convicted of burglary, larceny, or receiving stolen goods received sentences 277 percent greater than whites convicted of the same crimes." More staggeringly, the results of the study concluded: "Black drug offenders received sentences 467 percent greater than whites . . . In fraud, forgery, embezzlement, and bad check cases defendants with a public defender or court appointed counsel received a 683 percent longer sentence." The disproportionate percentage of those reliant on public defenders and court-appointed counsel were also Black and Native men.[1]

The conclusion of the report demonstrated in no uncertain terms that racial discrimination—directed at both African Americans and Alaska Natives—remained entrenched despite the rising tides of the state's buoyant oil-driven economy. As Alaska's diverse communities garnered noteworthy achievements, few were surprised by the study's conclusions. The depth and persistence of anti-Black racism in Alaska stood out even as the Black population had slowly declined over the previous decade relative to the state's overall demographics. At the same time, high-profile police shootings and incidents of racial violence sowed greater division between white and Black Alaskans. There already existed a history of mistrust between Black residents and law enforcement; as in other parts of the country, it seemed like police unfairly targeted Black citizens. Far from exceptional in its race relations, Alaska bears a resemblance with other regions even as it has deviated in at least a few notable ways. This was especially true of its largest urban area, Anchorage. As the previous chapter put a spotlight on Black achievement and advancement in the immediate post–civil rights, oil boom era of Alaska's history, this one complicates that narrative and exposes another side of the story. It explores the criminal justice system, with a particular emphasis on the relationship between law enforcement and Black lives in Alaska's largest metropolitan region.

Former NAACP executive director Roy Wilkins stated in 1971: "Police mistreatment of Negroes [was] a concern of nearly every branch in every section of the nation." He followed up with a list purposefully chosen to include examples of police misconduct from Boston to Anchorage.[2] Despite its geographical isolation, Anchorage was, for Wilkins, inseparable from national trends. And the abuse of Black individuals at the hands of local law enforcement agencies had proven to be ingrained across the American landscape. As if on cue following Wilkins's statement, the late 1970s and 1980s were years in which police violence took center stage for Blacks in urban Alaska. This was especially true in working-class communities and among the younger generation of Alaskans who came of age in a state that was at once wealthier than it had ever been but also decidedly more conservative.

This chapter explores a deeply rooted history of distrust and abuse that led many among Alaska's Black population to view the Anchorage Police Department (APD) as an antagonistic force, often lacking a spirit of protection and service. While no evidence suggests that the APD was any more or less discriminatory than other police departments or even the public, the officers of the APD at times failed to meet a standard of ethics befitting their status as protectors of the "thin blue line" between disorder and civil society. Incidents of police abuse and mistrust throughout the 1970s and 1980s revealed a fractured relationship between law enforcement and many Black and Native Alaskans. Throughout these two decades activists, church leadership, and regular citizens protested violence, mistreatment, and what they perceived as a general lack of respect from law enforcement. Ongoing activism and vigilance among Alaska's communities of color were required if they hoped to receive equitable treatment from the state's criminal justice system. These efforts had mixed results, but they illustrate a few ways in which Anchorage's Black and Indigenous residents demanded greater accountability and transparency from those who were expected to protect and serve.[3]

Anchorage Police and the Black Community

Nearly as soon as a population of Black Alaskans coalesced within Anchorage during the postwar decade, complaints mounted against the local police. Madeline Holmes, a newcomer to the state in 1941, grew so disgusted with the discriminatory tone and actions of the Anchorage Police Department (APD) that she left Alaska for Oakland, California, after one decade. In 1954 fifteen-year Alaskan resident Harold Brown forwarded a plea on behalf of Anchorage's Black population to US attorney general Herbert Brownell Jr. to investigate abuses and mistreatment toward Anchorage residents of color and Black-owned businesses at the hands of the police. Brown claimed that the APD utilized a supposed war on local vice as a cover for harassment of Anchorage Blacks and Natives. Brown also accused the APD of enforcing informal segregation in the city. "White citizens have been warned to stay out of Negro areas," said Brown. He continued, "Some Negro tavern owners were ordered to keep whites out of their business places or face loss of licenses."[4] Brown also claimed that the APD chief "would not approve of any Negro being on the force."[5]

Brown's complaint contained a blunt admonishment. "The city manager and city council must know that any group of people can be pushed just so far and then something is bound to explode," predicted Brown. "Then," he continued, "you end up with shootings and worse still perhaps a riot taking place. Is this what the city wants to see happen?"[6] Brown's written complaint arrived two months after Eastchester Flats, the center of Alaska's Black population, was annexed by the city in June 1954. Annexation made Flats residents subject to Anchorage's municipal codes and, as residents would soon find out, an aggressive ratcheting up of policing. As Anchorage rapidly expanded, the APD raided and closed many bars and other potentially illicit businesses in newly annexed areas under which it now had jurisdiction.[7] Indeed, several of the Black-owned and operated businesses in the Flats were repeatedly targeted by the APD in the years immediately after annexation. Lucky's Hot Spot, a notorious club in Eastchester Flats, popular among

Anchorage's working-class and queer community, endured several raids and arrests for narcotics, prostitution, and individuals "guilty of impersonating females" before the municipality revoked its liquor license in 1956.[8]

Eastchester Flats business owners raised money for Brown's subsequent flight to Washington, DC, where he planned to argue for assistance and raise the issue of police misconduct to federal attorneys. There is no surviving record of Brownell's response, but federal aid failed to materialize for Anchorage's Black residents, and the APD received no rebuke from federal authorities.[9] For their part Anchorage municipal and police leadership unequivocally denied Brown's complaints. Anchorage city manager George Miller acknowledged that he had heard similar complaints from the *Alaska Spotlight* editor George Anderson. Miller asked Anderson to provide the names of the complainants for an investigation. Unsurprisingly, Anderson did not supply Miller with a list of Black residents with grievances against the APD.[10]

Beyond police harassment of communities of color and businesses, the tensions at times turned violent. On the morning of May 19, 1965, Mabel Hash, an Alaska Native woman who lived in Anchorage, was working in her garden when she was approached by two APD officers seeking information about her son, who was sought as a suspect in an area burglary. During the questioning, Hash claimed that the officers issued a series of sarcastic and vitriolic remarks about her and her family's Native heritage. In response, Hash ordered the officers off her property, at which point the officers grew more aggressive and took her into custody. The two officers twisted the 130-pound Hash's arms, pulled her hair, pressed her face into the dirt, and eventually dragged her to their patrol car. Hash's subsequent conviction for disturbing the peace was later reversed on appeal. A countersuit for false arrest, false imprisonment, and arrest and battery resulted in a five hundred–dollar compensatory damages award. Her son was never charged or arrested.[11] The two major local newspapers did not cover the case and generally avoided stories that might put Anchorage's police officers in a negative light.

The actions taken against Mabel Hash would be far from the last instance of recorded violence at the hands of the Anchorage Police Department. On March 2, 1969, the APD arrested Edwin Williams at his Fairview neighborhood home. The arresting officers claimed that they had successfully intervened in a potentially violent argument between Williams and his wife by removing Williams from the scene. Williams and his advocates claimed that the officers had entered the home without a warrant or identification, placed him in a chokehold, and dragged him down a flight of stairs before beating him into submission.[12]

The Anchorage Assembly rejected the NAACP's request for an independent, citizen-led review in favor of a commission overseen by the city's internal human relations board. Williams's attorney, civil rights advocate and Black activist Mahala Ashley Dickerson, derided the commission as a public relations stunt meant to both "appease the agitators" and allow the entire matter to be "swept under the rug."[13] At the subsequent hearing, APD arresting officer Charles Audino claimed to have only used sufficient force to subdue Williams and denied ever striking or kicking him.[14] However, Williams displayed visible wounds and scars from the arrest forty-one days later.[15] The doctor who attended to Williams the day after his arrest stated that his wounds were "superficial and capable of healing by themselves" but later reversed himself and conceded that the altercation was worse than he had originally claimed.[16]

Four days of hearings resulted in a unanimous ruling in favor of the police. The commission's four-page report also recommended several APD policy revisions, primarily related to public relations, and suggested that local officers deserved higher salaries.[17] While a loss for Williams and the NAACP, the incident received significant coverage in both major local newspapers, which could be seen as progress compared to the lack of publicity Mabel Hash's arrest had received five years earlier. For many whites who called Anchorage home, "Negro resentment in this community of the police department" was the incident's greatest revelation.[18]

The incident also publicized the use of Anchorage's police auxiliaries, a few of whom arrived on the scene not long after the APD had forcefully detained Williams. These were unpaid and untrained men who assisted the police in an unofficial capacity. They would arrive at the scene of a crime or patrol neighborhoods to supplement the efforts of uniformed police. The police auxiliary force was composed of thirty men, all of whom were white. They were permitted to carry firearms but received no direct orders from the APD. Instead, according to APD chief John Flanigan, auxiliary members chose their assignments. The *Anchorage Daily News* reported that these auxiliary members refused mundane tasks such as traffic control in favor of being "where the action is," which was usually Anchorage's low-income and working-class locales. And in the case of the arrest of Edward Williams, an auxiliary officer responded and stood nearby with control of one of the APD's two police dogs.[19]

The extralegal, armed Anchorage auxiliary police force recalled the White Citizens' Councils that had terrorized and intimidated Blacks in the American South and elsewhere.[20] Unlike the Ku Klux Klan, the White Citizens' Council publicly condemned violence and cloaked itself in a mantle of respectability and legitimacy as a volunteer wing of law enforcement, one that sought to serve the public without burdening the local treasury. Likewise, the all-white Anchorage auxiliary police force touted its public benefit even as its members spent most of their time patrolling Native, Black, and poor white neighborhoods. Ben Humphries, an African American born in Georgia who later attended Tuskegee Institute in Alabama before moving to Alaska in 1947, drew a direct link between the Citizens' Councils and the auxiliary police of Anchorage.[21] Though Humphries recognized the need for law enforcement, he continued, "there's a feeling the auxiliary is an extension of the White Citizens Council . . . on the street they [Anchorage's Black residents] feel this is a vigilante group."[22]

During the commission hearings, Black residents accused the APD and the auxiliary police of using dogs to intimidate Black residents. The APD at this time owned two police dogs. One was exclusively assigned to Fairview, the racially diverse Anchorage neighborhood that included the Eastchester Flats. Humphries also noted that police dogs were routinely utilized for domestic disturbances. Said one Black resident, "A policeman comes into a guy's home with a dog and it's snarling at him and the guy is just yelling at his wife for burning the hamburgers." For Blanche McSmith, the NAACP president, the use of dogs and heavy police presence in the neighborhood recalled Bull Connor's assault on protesters in Birmingham.[23] Another Black resident viewed the uneven policing of Blacks and other minorities as what one would find in the American South: "This is Alabama, right in Alaska."[24] The commission's exoneration of the Anchorage Police Department reinforced Black residents' worst fears. Their voices would not be heard, and police harassment could continue unabated. Dickerson claimed the commission had sent a clear message regarding police misconduct: "Nothing will be done about it."[25] Dickerson attempted to bring a civil case against the police department on behalf of Williams, but he and his family instead decided that they had had enough and soon left Alaska.[26]

In the aftermath of the commission ruling, the APD released the demographics on recent arrests to an *Anchorage Daily Times* reporter. In 1968 the City of Anchorage population was approximately 88 percent white. However, 53 percent of the 4,767 arrests involved white suspects; Alaska Natives and African Americans comprised the other 47 percent, despite collectively representing just over 10 percent of the city's population.[27] Robert Atwood, publisher of the influential paper the *Anchorage Times* and conservative proponent of aggressive policing, frequently circulated rumors about the Black population as his paper covered sensational incidents of crime that bolstered racist stereotypes.[28] By the late 1970s Anchorage's Black community had nearly three decades of what could be described as a chilly relationship with Alaska's largest police department, despite the flow of oil money and the booming economy that had indeed lifted individual Black residents into positions of authority and prestige. Yet for much of the Black population that remained working class and ensconced in relatively low-income enclaves such as Fairview, Mountain View, and Russian Jack, the relationship with the police and the broader criminal justice system continued to decline. In response, a new generation of activists emerged to hold law enforcement accountable and shine a light on the inequities in the state's criminal justice system. Most activists held formal positions in institutions such as the Alaska Black Caucus, the NAACP, or one of Anchorage's Black churches, but others came straight from their respective communities and spoke independently of any organization. Although this advocacy had mixed results, it demonstrated a consistent level of activism beyond the peak of civil rights mobilization in the 1960s and early 1970s and represented the next front in the broader struggle for Black freedom in Alaska.

Police-Community Relations in the Late 1970s and early 1980s

Not even a year after the Governor's Commission released its report, relations between Anchorage's Black community and law enforcement tumbled after Alaska State Troopers shot and killed a thirty-one-year-old Black man named Phillip Moore under contested circumstances in the midnight hour on January 17, 1979. Moore had grown up working class in Fairview and had encountered Anchorage's police on more than one occasion. This time he fled an attempted traffic stop after driving over a snow berm. That much was broadly agreed upon, but additional details were quickly revealed. According to the police report, a foot pursuit followed the stop, with Moore and

Trooper Eric Frank Feichtinger separated from the trailing officers. After catching up to Moore, Feichtinger wrestled him to the ground, apparently clutching his gun in one hand and subduing the suspect with the other. The police report stated that during the struggle Moore repeatedly reached toward his ankle. Presuming a hidden weapon, Feichtinger fired at point-blank range, killing Moore on the spot.[29]

Though he was unarmed during the pursuit, Moore possessed an unlicensed firearm, which was in his abandoned vehicle. The autopsy revealed he had cocaine in his system, and he was on probation from an earlier conviction from when he had lived in Washington, DC. But what troubled many who followed the case, and what prompted a subsequent investigation, was the fact that the officers provided contradictory statements, and the coroner made contested accusations regarding Moore's personal history of drug use. After the shooting, Feichtinger claimed to have removed a bag of marijuana from Moore's left sock. However, another trooper who arrived on the scene shortly afterward recorded that the marijuana was concealed around Moore's torso; that officer later changed his story to agree with Feichtinger's. Evidence of force on Moore's shoulder did not line up with the trooper's description of the struggle. Feichtinger's account of a face-to-face struggle and its corroboration by the coroner depended upon the trooper's stated right-handedness. During Feichtinger's testimony several Black men and women in attendance claimed to see evidence that the trooper was in fact left-handed.[30] Meanwhile, the coroner's office accused Moore of having a history of drug abuse because of what it described as track marks up his arms.[31] Yet the Black pastor who performed ablutions on Moore's body prior to burial did not observe any track marks.[32]

Nevertheless, the internal investigation absolved Feichtinger of any wrongdoing. A subsequent investigation by the Department of Public Safety and the Alaska chief prosecutor found no evidence of impropriety. Still, the report concluded that the case intensified the "extent of the suspicion and lack of confidence in the minority community with regard to law enforcement generally."[33] The investigation's inconsistencies galvanized Anchorage's Black residents, but they also ushered in a new wave of antagonism from unsympathetic white Alaskans who believed that the police had acted well within their purview to protect the public from any threat, real or perceived, posed by Moore. One letter in the *Anchorage Times* referred to activists as "militant Blacks" who sought to "intimidate" investigators. Journalist and activist E. Louis Overstreet responded by noting that the men and women who gathered at the assembly meetings included members of the NAACP, the Alaska Black Caucus, local ministers, and an assortment of Black and Alaska Native residents who had grown tired of police behavior that let them "shoot to kill" or act like a "gang" without consequences.[34]

Not satisfied that justice had been served, over one hundred Black residents confronted the Anchorage Assembly in tense meetings and later petitioned US attorney Alex Bryner and Governor Jay Hammond for an additional probe into the events surrounding Moore's death.[35] Governor Hammond ordered an independent investigation overseen by the Alaska Department of Public Safety and the Alaska chief prosecutor. Their report also found no evidence of impropriety, from the original traffic stop through the coroner's inquest.[36] Yet the report's authors also noted that neither the Alaska State Troopers nor the coroner had examined the possibility of race as a contributing factor in the shooting. This oversight, claimed the report, fueled the disinclination to trust the resulting findings and contributed to the "extent of the suspicion and lack of confidence in the minority community with regard to law enforcement generally."[37] In any case, the outcry surrounding Moore's death served as the link between the formation of local Black opposition to police seen in the 1969 case of Edwin Williams and the activism that emerged in the years to follow after still other high-profile cases of police violence and killings of Black men.

On January 12, 1981, nearly two years to the day after Phillip Moore's death, a twenty-four-year-old Black man, Cassell Williams, was fired from his job as a dishwasher at the Sheraton hotel after he allegedly assaulted his supervisor.[38] He returned to his apartment in Mountain View, a working-class neighborhood northeast of downtown that Alaska's oil boom had largely bypassed. Two days later, early in the morning on January 14, Williams reportedly knocked on his landlord's door to request a ride to the hospital. He claimed to have been suffering from a mental health crisis. The landlord agreed to drive Williams to the hospital but first had to get dressed. When the landlord returned to Williams's apartment to pick him up, no one answered the door. The lights were turned off.[39]

Later that afternoon, two police officers responded to a report of gunshots from Williams's apartment. Williams again did not answer the door. As the officers walked away from the building, Williams reportedly stepped onto his balcony, shined a flashlight at the officers, and haphazardly fired a gun at an adjacent building. The officers called for backup, and during the ensuing standoff, Williams again sporadically fired at nearby buildings. After an hour the sergeant in charge ordered a sharpshooting officer to fire a single-shot rifle at Williams. The bullet struck Williams and killed him instantly.[40]

The standoff was in some ways unremarkable, if not for the broader context of race relations in Anchorage during the preceding years. The precise circumstances around the death of Cassell Williams troubled many, and as the details emerged, so, too, did more questions about the conduct of the police. Williams's mother, girlfriend, and landlord all reported that he had experienced mental health crises. He had been institutionalized the previous year after claiming to hear voices he described as witches. Given the documented nature of his mental health, those closest to Cassell Williams wondered why the police had resorted so quickly to lethal force.[41]

Though Williams had failed to communicate with the police, the officers, for their part, had failed to contact his girlfriend or mother, de-escalate the confrontation, or inquire into the status of his mental health. The police notified both women only after Williams was pronounced dead.[42] Anchorage chief of police Brian Porter, who was not at the scene, defended his officers even as he noted a breakdown in basic protocol. The officers had not attempted to cut the electricity to the apartment or provide a trained hostage negotiator, as was typical in standoffs. When asked if a Black officer could have perhaps communicated with Williams, Porter responded that "some [Blacks] might even take offense" at such a maneuver.[43] Anchorage district attorney Larry Weeks promised an inquest in addition to an internal police investigation. However, the day after the shooting, Weeks stated, "There is no question that [the killing] was justified."[44]

Not surprisingly, Weeks quickly lost credibility among those who had demanded the investigation in the first place. Activists spoke out against the high-profile shootings and what they perceived as a lack of transparency in the subsequent investigations. Less than a day after her son's death, Cynthia Williams attended a meeting of the Anchorage Equal Rights Commission (AERC) and demanded justice.[45] At a later public hearing chaired by the AERC, Black leaders openly discussed what they viewed as an endemic level of police bias against Black men. The *Anchorage Daily News* reported on one testimony: "It seems that every two years we in the Black community find ourselves reacting to some kind of police violence." Many of the attendees expressed their frustration and lack of surprise at the absence of a police representative at the hearing.[46] Activists also noted the way in which the police seemed to handle calls—even potentially violent episodes—when the suspect was white. For instance, most conceded that Cassell Williams had posed a threat to himself and those around him. There was no debate over whether he was armed or if he had fired a weapon. But what disturbed Black activists and their allies was the apparent patience the APD afforded white offenders in similar contexts compared to those who were nonwhite. The *Anchorage Daily Times* reported, "Mrs. Cynthia Williams charged that officers used their guns before it was absolutely necessary and more quickly than they would have if Williams had been white."[47]

Cynthia Williams raised a fair objection, one rooted in the recent history of the Anchorage Police Department. Less than two years before the Cassell Williams incident, a white escort service operator, Charlene Zint, had walked into traffic on the busy Spenard Road and brandished her gun at two young women, who swerved away, crashing into a pickup. Zint retreated to her business, barricaded herself inside, and pointed her gun through a window at passersby. APD major Brian Porter, later named police chief, successfully contacted Zint's probation officer and psychiatrist to talk her into a peaceful surrender. "If that doesn't work and these antics continue, we'll just have to do something else," said Porter at the time. After a six-and-a-half-hour standoff, which included an hour-long tear gas barrage and hours of diverted traffic, the APD finally took Zint into custody. At no point did officers attempt a "kill shot" as they had for Williams.[48]

Seven months after Williams's death, a twenty-four-year-old white male from Anchorage, John Lee, drunkenly fired shots outside his Spenard neighborhood home. When officers arrived, John Lee opened fire on them from an upstairs window, twice hitting Officer Pete Nolan. During the ensuing three-and-a-half-hour standoff, officers launched four tear gas canisters through upstairs windows. Police negotiators, a friend, and Lee's wife attempted to communicate with him. Finally, Lee peacefully surrendered in exchange for a promise of safety and psychiatric treatment.[49] Lt. Charles Audino, the same officer who had arrested Edwin Williams a dozen years earlier, responded to the scene at Lee's home with apparent restraint. Asked what it would have taken to give the order for the sniper, Audino said: "I don't know. I hadn't made up my mind on that."[50] In 1993 an intoxicated and rifle-bearing Melvin Dean Altom, a white male, entered a bar in Anchorage's eastside neighborhood of Muldoon, pointed his gun at Black patrons, called them racial slurs, including the N-word, and threatened to shoot them. As patrons fled, Altom followed, striking one in the face with the butt of his gun. Shortly thereafter, officers discovered Altom at his nearby apartment. After negotiations broke down and the standoff intensified, over the course of seven hours, police fired tear gas into the apartment, prompting Altom's surrender.[51]

Zint, Lee, and Altom all posed a danger to those around them. Each had a criminal record. Each survived a lengthy armed police standoff that included protracted negotiations. Zint and Lee shared with Williams evidence of a mental health crisis. Zint had been admitted to the Alaska Psychiatric Institute (API) a year before her standoff with the police, and Lee was taken to API for evaluation immediately after his standoff.[52] Zint, Lee, and Alton, all white, nonetheless survived their encounters with the police without physical harm. But in the case of Cassell Williams, officers deployed lethal force within an hour of their arrival. APD chief Brian Porter conceded that the standoff with Williams had ended tragically, saying, "You just can't allow officers and the public to remain in jeopardy that long."[53] The disparate outcomes of these volatile encounters fed the perception that a lower bar existed to engage in deadly force when the suspect was Black.

The conservative-leaning *Anchorage Times*, Alaska's most widely read newspaper, fanned the flames of racial division. The editors dismissed activists who raised issues around police violence in the Williams case as "an overaggressive attempt by some to inject a racial element into this incident."[54] The editorial team stuck to a script: officers had a job to do, and any attempt to view the tragic death of Williams through the lens of race was corrosive to Anchorage's peace and order. The *Times* both represented and cultivated public opinion. Indeed, the letters that the paper's editors chose to publish not only supported the police but at times even welcomed Williams's death. One writer concluded that the police were "intelligent, warm, and caring people."[55] Another letter to the editor viewed the police response to Williams as "a good thing and making our town a little safer."[56] A particularly vitriolic writer believed Williams "deserve[d] to be shot."[57] Still another commenter asserted, "We should thank the Lord that this criminal has been taken out."[58]

Other Alaskans who wrote to the *Anchorage Times* feared that the killing of Williams might lead to unrest. "No one wants a Watts problem up here," stated a resident in reference to the racial unrest that had occurred in Watts, a neighborhood in Los Angeles, fifteen years earlier.[59] Similar comments appeared after other incidents of alleged police brutality. After the Edwin

Williams arrest in 1969, the *Times* editorialized, "This state has so far been spread [*sic*] the riots and turbulence of these subversive pacts, but ... we are no longer free from the influence of these militant groups," an apparent allusion to the Black Power movement.[60] After the APD killed two Black suspects in 1970, a contributor to the *Anchorage Times* claimed that the mere coverage of the controversy was incendiary: "The [reporter] should be made liable in case of a race riot."[61] After Phillip Moore's death, one writer claimed that "militant blacks" had intimidated government officials into conducting an investigation.[62]

Taken together, the selective publication of letters demonstrated a bias against Black victims of police violence. Further, the editors showed little interest in engaging with those who raised legitimate concerns about the excessive use of force against men of color.[63] The letters conveyed the extent to which white fear of Black criminality and violence had pervaded Alaska's largest population center. Though no one would mistake Anchorage for Los Angeles, the *Anchorage Times* fed suspicions of a broader, more militant movement culture making its way northward. By the late 1960s, calls for law and order became hallmarks of a nascent conservative response to the nation's racial unrest.[64] And as Anchorage convulsed with thousands of new arrivals from the Lower 48, many white newcomers brought with them the suspicion of Black militancy and rebellion.

At the same time, a unified response among Black Alaskans over how best to proceed in the face of tensions with law enforcement never materialized. Although many took decisive action, others remained hesitant to speak publicly on contentious issues such as police violence. Alonzo Patterson, the reverend at the storied Shiloh Baptist Church, chided Black residents after Williams's death for what he described as a lack of cohesion and urgency in the wake of the tragedies. "That's why the policeman is not afraid," said Patterson, "because he knows you're not going to do anything." Another young activist noted, "It seems that every two years we in the Black community find ourselves reacting to some kind of police violence."[65] Then again, it may have been too much to expect a unified response. There was a range of opinion and engagement among Black Alaskans on the topic of police violence. The destruction of the Eastchester Flats a decade earlier had left Anchorage without a centralized Black neighborhood, and the oil boom at once created great wealth but also opened class-based fissures within the community.

Activism around the issue of police violence did, however, yield modest results. The AERC submitted a list of five recommendations to Anchorage mayor George Sullivan meant to ease relations between the police department and Black residents. The recommendations included the demand for a federal investigation into the Williams shooting, a police oversight panel populated by community members, psychological testing for officers, and for the police to have mental health professionals on call in the event of such a crisis. AERC executive director Vince Casey reported a "cool reception" from Mayor Sullivan and the Anchorage Assembly.[66] Yet city officials and local leaders later negotiated a schedule of meetings between police and Black and Native activists.[67]

Over several months representatives from the APD met with Black and Native leaders, exchanged perspectives, and established an agreement between the parties. Respected community elders were to receive regular briefings from the police chief and immediate communication in the event of a "racial crisis."[68] The AERC reviewed the police department's hiring and training methods. Notably, this resulted in the 1982 implementation of psychological screening of police applicants. As APD psychologist Mike Roberts noted, the essay portions of these entry exams had in the past garnered openly racist comments, such as "I hate people with Black skin."[69] This spirit of cooperation was formalized via the June 1981 creation of the Anchorage Community Police Relations Task Force (ACPRTF) to serve as a liaison between the APD and the community. The task force, composed of representatives from law enforcement as well as Black and Native leadership, arranged to meet monthly and maintain open lines of communication.[70] Under the aegis of the AERC, the ACPRTF operated with a mandate from the mayor to "provide a forum for input and constructive dialogue between the community and Anchorage law enforcement."[71]

Unfortunately, the creation of a task force did not measurably reduce the mistrust between the Black residents and the police. On November 25, 1981, APD officer Mark Headlough shot at three Black men who had fled a crime scene; a bullet grazed one of them in the ear. After a discussion with Rev. Alonzo Patterson and NAACP president Ed Wesley, APD chief Porter removed Headlough from active duty.[72] Yet the department quickly exonerated and reinstated Headlough, despite several unanswered questions from the task force.[73] Eight days later, an off-duty officer opened fire on a Black man whom she accused of attempting to steal her purse and brandishing a gun.[74] Wesley, an architect of the ACPRTF, concluded that at least a few Anchorage police officers were "scared of blacks" and lacked the training or desire to overcome their prejudices. For Wesley this attitude created the negative "community perception that people have towards police departments across the United States, not just here in Anchorage." Referencing the city's ubiquitous marketing campaign of the early 1980s, Wesley said, "They can quit hollering 'Wild About Anchorage' because you'll have people going wild in Anchorage."[75]

Working alongside Anchorage mayor Tony Knowles, the police department responded to the AERC and the pointed remarks by Wesley and others in part by hiring a Black officer at the executive level. Ed Rhodes accepted a position in the newly created position of deputy chief of the services bureau for the department. Upon assuming the leadership role in May 1982, Rhodes quickly became the highest-ranking Black officer in the department. Rhodes was not a stranger to Alaska and in fact had already broken one barrier, becoming the first Black man to earn a commission with the Alaska State Troopers in 1966. Between his tenure with the troopers and joining the Anchorage Police Department, Rhodes had attained the rank of deputy commander at his Anchorage post. He served on the APD until 1988, retiring as the deputy chief of police.[76]

For critics of the department, the hiring of Rhodes did little to mollify soured relations. Among white conservatives, the Rhodes hire was a purely political stunt and a "token effort to placate the black community."[77] The reaction among many Black activists was not starkly different, particularly after additional high-profile instances of police violence and reports of racial animosity within department ranks. Three months after Rhodes was hired, another incident occurred on the morning of August 1, 1982. That day Inman Pitts, a thirty-six-year-old Black man, accompanied a female friend to the Anchorage Police Department to drop off a car that had allegedly been used in a crime. According to reports from the APD, Pitts initiated a scuffle with three officers. One suffered a scratched eye, another claimed Pitts had bit his finger, and the third officer reported that Pitts had choked and dragged him to the ground. The police eventually subdued Pitts and charged him with assault.[78]

The case was far from over, however, as Pitts hired Mahala Ashley Dickerson to represent him. His account of events differed starkly from those of the police officers. Pitts, five foot two and 150 pounds, described seven officers—not just the three who claimed that Pitts had injured them—who ganged up on Pitts, refused to allow him to leave the station despite not having been charged with a crime, and beat him mercilessly. "We have a large percentage of policemen who are haters of Blacks," said Dickerson in a statement later published in area newspapers.[79] Her comment caught the attention of the police department. As they had in the past, the APD launched an internal investigation, which concluded that the officers had not acted in a discriminatory or excessive manner.[80] Before the internal probe concluded, the Anchorage Police Department Employees Association (APDEA) filed a $400,000, over $1 million in 2021, defamation of character lawsuit against Dickerson. "The good will and relationship of the Anchorage Police Department Police Officers with the community has been seriously impaired . . . making it more difficult for Plaintiffs to perform their duties and in addition are creating an unnecessarily hazardous safety condition for the officers in the community at large," explained the officers' affidavit.[81]

APDEA's legal response to Dickerson reflected a national trend. As police generally lost the protection of media silence regarding shootings and claims of brutality, many police unions and individual officers pursued defamation cases against civilians who took their complaints public. A 1975 defamation case in St. Louis was possibly a trendsetter, with a patrolman seeking $183,000, approximately $850,000 in 2021, in damages after he claimed to have been beaten during a routine traffic stop. A jury awarded the plaintiff officer with $45,000, approximately $185,000 in 2021, in damages.[82] Dickerson never retracted her claims and defended herself in court. She reiterated, "There's a large percentage of the people who agree with me." Dickerson noted, "I never knew how right I was until that statement appeared in the paper."[83] About two months later, a judge dismissed the defamation case against Dickerson; however, the court order forbade her from claiming that the dismissal reflected the merits of the plaintiffs' complaint.[84] Dickerson's opinion of the APD never changed. If anything, she remained haunted by the case of Edwin Williams, repeatedly referencing him in interviews and her autobiography, *Delayed Justice for Sale*, decades after he left the state.[85]

Around the same time that the Anchorage Police Department took Dickerson to court, she filed a $9 million wrongful death lawsuit on behalf of Cassell Williams's family against the Municipality of Anchorage and three APD

Mahala Ashley Dickerson, ca. 1990s. Fran Durner Collection, Anchorage Museum (B2016.4.1021).

officers. The department, the municipality, and the Williams family settled out of court. An anonymous source within the municipality claimed the city had only agreed to cover the burial costs of Cassell Williams's funeral.[86] Neither Dickerson's case against the police and municipality nor the APD's case against Dickerson resulted in decisive victories; large sums of money never changed hands. But through her work on these cases, Dickerson bolstered her reputation as a lawyer and advocate for Anchorage's Black population, and this time police violence and endemic racism within the APD stayed in the headlines. The court cases suggested that racial incidents on the street would not go unchallenged in the courts. The fight for justice in Alaska thus had multiple fronts, from the picket line to the courthouse.

As many Black Alaskans secured a measure of material comfort in the late 1970s and early 1980s, working-class communities of color remained largely absent from the oil boom and subject to police surveillance. "The mood of the [Anchorage] Black community can best be characterized as one of suspicion, anger, frustration, and determination," concluded Rev. Theodore A. Moore, president of the Anchorage Interdenominational Ministerial Alliance in 1981.[87] Police violence then reinforced the reality even among those who had become relatively affluent among Alaska's Black population that structural racism persisted. The effects of racism and violent encounters with police on the broader community are significant and linked to negative psychological and physiological outcomes, including higher morbidity and increased rates of short- and long-term depression.[88] To address disparities in policing, a cross-class and multiracial coalition emerged that included grassroots activists, lawyers, church clergy, and institutional leadership. Their goals were generally modest as they sought to establish ongoing dialogue with the Anchorage Police Department and the mayor's office and ensure that relations did not sour further. These efforts did not always have the intended impact, but they provided Blacks and Alaska Natives a literal place at the table when it came to issues related to policing and criminal justice.

Racial Strife within the Anchorage Police Department

Racial conflict also existed within the Anchorage Police Department as officers of color registered their discontent over what appeared to be a pattern of discrimination around such issues as promotion, retention, and the day-to-day behavior of white officers. Beginning in the 1960s, the APD slowly integrated its ranks. The first Black female officer on the force was Barbara Burney, who began her career in 1970 as a meter maid, issuing two hundred tickets a day for six years.[89] The need to meet federal compliance on affirmative action, starting in the early 1970s, modestly diversified the workforce of local and state governments as well as businesses. A succession of laws, including the Civil Rights Act of 1964, the Crime Control Act of 1973, the Fair Labor Standards Act of 1974, and the State and Local Government Fiscal Assistance Act of 1976, sought to mandate equal opportunity for women in local government.[90] The Equal Employment Opportunity Commission, established as part of the 1964 Civil Rights Act, also provided an enforcement mechanism against workplace discrimination. "At that point, it was a frenzy at APD to get female personnel to become officers," noted Burney, who joined APD as a warrant officer in 1975. "Otherwise the federal funding would be cut. So, naturally, every one of us there applied to become an officer, especially meter maids."[91] But while the APD and municipal and state governments more generally, as well as their respective private contractors, faced increasing scrutiny to diversify their ranks, minority candidates were not always welcomed into the workplace.

By 1983 Burney felt that becoming a warrant officer had only moved the employment barrier by one position. At that time the warrant division did not have a representative on the executive board of the officer's union, the APDEA, and she felt that her position denied her access to training, promotions, and the "equal benefits as Caucasians and males enjoy for the same or similar work." Burney filed a lawsuit against the APD and the APDEA, citing her circumstances as a violation of the federal Civil Rights Act and state laws on human rights.[92] Her decision pointedly came after the first local Black law enforcement employee association was created to address concerns that no Black officer had been promoted above the rank of senior patrol officer.[93] She settled her case out of court and retired from the APD in 2000. Despite her negative experiences, or perhaps because of other, more positive experiences, her son also joined the force.[94]

Since Burney's 1983 lawsuit, there have been two similar lawsuits against the APD. In 1995 two Black detectives jointly filed discrimination complaints against the APD, arguing that their exemplary records and seniority had not resulted in commensurate advancement. Tyron Guillory and Tommy Nelson, both nine-year veterans in the department, claimed that testing procedures were altered to undermine their bids for promotion to the rank of sergeant.[95]

At the time Guillory and Nelson were two of fourteen Black officers. Of the fourteen, Rev. William Greene, the longtime chair of the Anchorage Community Police Relations Task Force (ACPRTF), asserted half had personally complained to him about the racist atmosphere and unfair labor practices within the department. Alonzo Patterson, an influential reverend, accused the department of failing to hire and promote more Black officers in the aftermath of the 1981 death of Cassell Williams. Eight other faith leaders from Anchorage's Interdenominational Ministers Alliance called on the assembly to investigate the APD's hiring and promotion record for Black officers.[96]

The investigation revealed "substantial evidence" that the department had discriminated against Black and Native officers despite a public relations campaign that included the hiring of a Black deputy police chief, Ed Rhodes. The decision by APD leadership to alter the testing protocol was without precedent. Notably, Nelson recorded the highest test score in his applicant group. In all previous iterations of the examination, scores were posted publicly. In this instance Nelson's superior marks were kept private. An unnamed officer quoted in the investigation claimed the change was meant to prevent the applicant from assuming "he would automatically be promoted to sergeant."[97] Over the next four years, Guillory and Nelson failed to reach a settlement and faced a municipal countersuit. In 1998 the continuing AERC inquiry found additional evidence that APD actions against Guillory specifically were retaliatory, representing an established "mindset against any promotional opportunity."[98]

Later that year a US Justice Department inquiry into an expanded set of allegations against APD promotion practices concluded with no basis for the claims of discrimination.[99] However, neither finding was legally conclusive, and the Municipality of Anchorage settled the case in 2000. Each plaintiff received $75,000 for lost wages and benefits. This settlement was one of two options proposed by Guillory and Nelson. Municipal leaders rejected an offer of a reduced payout coupled with APD hiring and promotion reform. "I feel, and I believe Tyron feels, that by having brought this to light, everyone is aware of it now," stated Nelson. "We've done the best we can do; hopefully things will go forward and change."[100]

Only a decade later, two more officers filed suit, claiming a pervasive atmosphere of racism within the department. Detectives Alvin Kennedy and Eliezer Feliciano, African American and Hispanic, respectively, alleged that the APD systemically "sanctioned racial profiling, disparate treatment of minority officers and the condoning of constitutional violations by white officers against minorities." The lawsuit also claimed that minority officers received complaints about their attire and were told that they dressed "like thugs and criminals." Further, they alleged that minority officers were more likely to be disciplined, receiving punishment when participating white officers did not.[101]

By the time the case came to trial, both Kennedy and Feliciano had retired from the force, claiming that discrimination had left them no other choice. Feliciano said, "The conduct of the APD has given me the feeling that everything I have done throughout my career has been for naught." For Kennedy his tenure with the department had left him "very angry, disappointed and occasionally sad."[102] Representing the APD, attorney Linda Johnson claimed that the "plaintiffs have embellished their fear. They have blamed everyone except themselves. There was no retaliation. Everything that APD has done happened for a reason."[103]

In March 2014 jurors returned a partial verdict. They cleared the police department on two counts of alleged discrimination. However, they split on a claim of retaliation against the officers of color. The department initiated a criminal case against the plaintiffs from 2010 that never yielded an investigative file.[104] That case, reopened in 2015 and again in 2017, finally concluded with Kennedy and Feliciano receiving one million dollars each after jurors determined that the APD had discriminated and retaliated against both plaintiffs.[105] Superior court judge Frank Pfiffner subsequently increased the award by roughly a half-million dollars because of what he described as "Nixonian" attempts by the municipality's lawyers to stall the investigation and increase Kennedy and Feliciano's legal fees.[106]

Despite this checkered history and in response to Black and Native activism, the Anchorage Police Department has expanded its efforts to better represent the municipality and rid itself of discriminatory practices. The ACPRTF consistently met with state and local law enforcement to provide a platform for residents to express their views over the next twenty-five years before slowly fading from public view. APD representatives have also participated in marches organized in response to police shootings elsewhere in the nation; APD chief Chris Tolley spoke before such a unity march in July 2016.[107] Departmental leadership has now publicly recognized that efforts to recruit Black and Native officers and promote those within the force have too often foundered and more must be done. According to a 2016 report, the police department remained 82 percent white at a time when Anchorage was 62 percent white; among those eighteen years old and younger, the population is below 50 percent white.[108]

Given this context, the promotion of Kenneth McCoy, a Black man, to chief of police was significant. McCoy's family had moved to Anchorage from Virginia in the mid-1980s. McCoy graduated from Anchorage's Bartlett High School in 1988, before earning a degree in criminal justice from the University of Alaska Anchorage. Shortly afterward, he began his near-thirty-year career in the APD. In 2017 he was promoted to deputy chief of operations, the highest APD rank achieved by any officer of color.[109] In early 2021 McCoy was promoted to serve as acting chief after the highest-ranking officer on the force, Chief Justin Doll, retired. Having assumed the interim position amid a contentious mayoral campaign, however, it was not clear that reform-minded McCoy would receive the offer from Anchorage's new mayor to stay on in a full-time capacity. However, the winner of the election, Dave Bronson, an avowed conservative and opponent of systemic reforms within the APD, nonetheless retained McCoy, making him Anchorage's first Black chief of police, a post he held from July 2021 until February 2022. But after just six months on the job, McCoy accepted a position as the inaugural diversity, equity, and inclusion officer for Providence Hospital in Anchorage. McCoy's brief tenure fueled suspicions that the Bronson administration never fully supported the new chief and planned to ease pressure on the APD to make additional reforms, most notably the implementation of a voter-backed initiative to pay for body-worn cameras for officers to wear on duty.[110]

Familiar Stories and Patterns

In sum, a history of derogatory slights and violence fueled Black attitudes toward police and contributed to an overall feeling that Anchorage was not a safe place to be Black, particularly in low-income and working-class communities. The relationship between the police and Alaska Natives was also one that too often expressed itself in acrimony and distrust.[111] These tensions played out in the streets and during everyday encounters between white officers and Anchorage's Black and Indigenous men and women. That these same tensions bled into the police department and at times influenced the relationship between officers of color and their white counterparts should come as no surprise.

At the interpersonal level, Black parents have long prepared their children for encounters with the law enforcement professionals who are legally tasked with keeping them safe. "The talk," as it has long been known, is a ritual discussion that has played out in millions of Black homes throughout the country for generations. Alaska is no different. One Black Anchorage parent advised her children: "Don't be a smart mouth even though you might be in the right . . . I'd rather you come home alive than to get a phone call that you've been shot, or killed, or in the hospital."[112] In a confrontation with police, counseled another Alaskan parent to her child, "just try to get to some place where there are witnesses because anything can happen and my word against yours, who are most people going to believe?"[113] Another Black mother prepared her daughters for adolescence and dating, explaining that a young woman must be "very mindful of the police, especially if you're in the car with a minority, a male minority." "Be aware," she continued, "if you get stopped by the police, don't open your mouth. Don't say anything, have your driver's license right up here . . . You let them do all the talking."[114] Thus, the talk migrated to urban Alaska, along with the day-to-day fears among Blacks being harassed or targeted by law enforcement.

Such fears were not without cause. Oil ushered in new levels of wealth and unprecedented growth for Alaska in the late 1970s and early 1980s, but not all shared in the prosperity. Meanwhile, Alaska underwent still another rapid transformation through the final decades of the century. The vagaries of an economy dependent upon the price of oil and government spending—at the federal, state, and local levels—brought inherent instability. Alaska was a boom-and-bust economy at the beginning of the twentieth century, and it remained a boom-and-bust economy at century's end. During the mid-1980s the price of oil collapsed, and Alaska fell into recession. Over the next twenty years, the state eventually recovered and once again experienced economic growth, albeit nothing compared to the peak years of the oil boom.

If oil wealth defined Alaska in the 1970s and early 1980s, arguably the most notable development of the 1990s and 2000s was the state's steady population growth and impressive levels of racial diversity. Nowhere was this more acute than in Southcentral Alaska. "The most diverse neighborhood in the US may surprise you," led one *Smithsonian* article.[115] "Most diverse place in America? It's not where you think," teased CNN.[116] This national reaction reflected an expectation that the nation's most diverse communities were in large cities with extensive histories of global immigration.

But in fact, the three most diverse neighborhoods in America could all be found in Alaska. According to sociologist Chad Farrell, the most diverse US Census tract aligned with Mountain View, an Anchorage neighborhood in the city's northeastern corner. The second and third most diverse census tracts overlay portions of the adjacent Fairview, Russian Jack, and Airport Heights neighborhoods of the municipality.[117] Families arrived from East Asia, the South Pacific, and Sub-Saharan Africa. Alaska Natives from the state's rural villages migrated to Anchorage in greater numbers, roughly doubling their population to about twenty-four thousand individuals by 2000, or about 9 percent of the municipality's population. Anchorage's population of international immigrants grew by 20 percent from the late 1980s through the late 1990s. Between 1990 and 2000 Anchorage's Black population grew 20 percent, its Asian population 27 percent, and the Pacific Islander population grew a staggering 415 percent, to number over three thousand individuals. The white population, meanwhile, grew at a comparatively low rate, 4 percent.[118] In response to these rapid demographic changes, in tandem with an economy that had never quite recovered to its high-flying status at the peak of the oil boom, Alaska experienced a rise in hate crimes amid a more general climate of racial resentment. Yet a younger generation of Black and Native activists and artists undertook to develop vibrant new spaces of their own, ones that reshaped the state's popular culture as it entered the twenty-first century.

CHAPTER EIGHT

Resentment, Resilience, and Cultural Rejuvenation at Century's End

ON MAY 26, 1985, ALASKA STATE TROOPERS DISCOVERED THE BODY of a forty-three-year-old Black mechanic, Julius Marshall, in a tow truck at the Wasilla salvage yard he owned. Troopers quickly arrested twenty-two-year-old Michael Dunkin, though the full story did not emerge until the trial that October. Dunkin, a white man from the area, had spent the day in question drinking and off-roading with two friends around the Knik River, between Anchorage and Wasilla. After Dunkin's Jeep got stuck in the mud and stalled out, a passerby gave him a lift to a payphone. Marshall responded to the call, pulled Dunkin's Jeep from the mud, and towed the vehicle to his garage. There Marshall managed to get the Jeep running again. Soon after, an altercation between the two began, after Dunkin disputed the $150 cost of the tow and the attendant repairs.[1]

At trial one witness, a companion of Dunkin, testified that Dunkin had killed Marshall because of the dispute. Money in hand, Dunkin approached Marshall before pulling a .38 caliber revolver and firing three rounds. The companion then stated that Dunkin smirked as he pulled the trigger and predicted that no one would miss Marshall. Dunkin referred to Marshall as a racial slur and stenciled "BOOFER HUNTER" into the mud caked to his Jeep before he drove away. Troopers later matched sand and footprints from Dunkin and his companions, and oil from the Jeep, at the crime scene.[2] At the request of the district attorney, two men raised in the American South who were stationed at Fort Richardson in Anchorage testified to the racist and pejorative connotations of the term *boofer*.[3] The jury deliberated for two hours before returning with a guilty verdict.[4] Presiding judge Beverly Cutler, the first woman named to the Alaska Superior Court, declared: "These are not mere allegations of racism. It's overwhelming proof." She sentenced Dunkin to eighty-five years in prison with no chance of parole for fifty years.[5] When Judge Cutler retired, in 2009, she remained haunted by the "really overwhelming racism" of the Marshall case.[6]

Like many of the individuals spotlighted in this text, Julius Marshall had left the South for the American West in the postwar era. Born in 1941 in Springfield, Arkansas, he had moved as a teenager to Los Angeles, where he learned to be a car mechanic. In 1969 Marshall moved his wife and four children to Alaska to open a repair shop. He opened his first shop in Anchorage and then a second in Wasilla.[7] Marshall's relocation to Alaska brought him financial success even as he contended with the racism he had sought to escape in his native Arkansas. This book has so far problematized the notion of Alaskan exceptionalism, whereby Alaskans perceive themselves as having charted a history independent of the nation writ large. Rather than exceptional or beyond the defining currents of US history, white Alaskans have just as often reproduced the beliefs and culture endemic to the places where they grew up, and many Black Alaskans have endured the racism in the South or elsewhere from which they had fled. The murder of Julius Marshall is yet another painful reminder of that fact.[8]

By the time of Marshall's murder, a significant economic downturn had exacerbated racial tensions. Though the twin oil shocks in 1973 and again in 1979 damaged the nation's economy, the high price of oil led Alaska into boom times.[9] But the oil revenue that fueled a spending spree and modernized Alaska would not last. Construction decreased by the end of 1983. In July 1985 state spending declined, reversing what had been to that point over a decade of growth. Economist Gregg Erickson proposed that this was when the "bubble popped" and Alaska entered a multiyear recession. The decline of oil prices in the later months of 1985, often cited as the cause of the recession, in fact only intensified its impact and duration. In 1986 the oil market bottomed out at around ten dollars per barrel, down from nearly forty dollars per barrel just five years earlier.[10]

Between 1985 and 1987 the Alaska recession erased roughly one in ten jobs from the state's economy, a figure that did not account for losses among those who were self-employed. The loss of jobs and decline in wages resulted in business closures, underwater mortgages, and a temporary population decline.

Five of the sixteen banks present in Alaska closed between 1987 and 1988.[11] As the state's construction, logistical, and banking center, Anchorage was hit the hardest by the recession. The municipality's taxable real estate declined 41 percent in value, from $13.9 billion in January 1986 to $8.3 billion two years later.[12] Even after the state economy slowly recovered, by the second half of 1988, Anchorage lagged as the loss of property tax revenue contributed to significant shortfalls and reductions in the municipality's budget.[13] From 1985 to 1988 Anchorage lost roughly 29,000 residents, and rental vacancies rose from 3 percent in 1982 to 25 percent in 1986. Anchorage's slow economic recovery would last into the mid-1990s, followed by only moderate economic growth for several years after.[14]

Scholars have established a countercyclical relationship between the economy and racial antipathy.[15] Financial stability and rising incomes are associated with a decrease of interpopulation hostility, as between whites and Blacks, or within disparate minority groups. Recent research has strengthened that argument. Arjun Jayadev and Robert Johnson demonstrated how racial hostility rose with white unemployment.[16] Another study, published by Emily Bianchi, Erika Hall, and Sarah Lee, found that "worse economic conditions were associated with more negative attitudes towards Blacks."[17] From this perspective Marshall's racially motivated murder was one of several events that suggested a rise in tensions amid the economic decline.

In fact, Alaska experienced hate-related events in the late 1980s and early 1990s at a greater rate than other documented periods. Although the murder of Julius Marshall was perhaps exceptional in its cold-blooded brutality, it nonetheless revealed the elevated levels of explicit racism that plagued Alaska during the later decades of the twentieth century. Even at Dunkin's trial, the audience self-segregated; whites sat behind Dunkin and Blacks behind the prosecutors.[18] For the unemployed, underemployed, and others who fell behind during the recession, their disillusionment with the new economic reality exacerbated extant prejudices. But over time Alaska's economy slowly recovered. And as it did, Alaska enticed an increasingly diverse population to relocate and make the state home. Anchorage, Alaska's largest urban center, attracted the most residents by far, some of whom came from Native villages in rural parts of the state and others who arrived from around the world.

Despite a few halting expressions of white supremacy in Anchorage during the late 1980s and 1990s, years that roughly corresponded to the beginning of an accelerated demographic change, a younger, more diverse generation that had come of age in an Alaska far different than that of the oil boom of the 1970s began to make its mark. This younger generation of Alaskans, a majority of whom were Black, Native, Asian, or Pacific Islander created a vibrant culture of resistance and resilience, one clearly at odds with the murderous white supremacy of Michael Dunkin or the marginal racist organizations trying to gain a foothold. Though economic prosperity at times lagged, these younger Alaskans nonetheless issued an alternative vision for the state rooted in inclusivity and an open embrace of Alaska's newfound demographic pluralism. As some Alaskans turned on one another, others breathed new life into a state that had entered its post–oil boom years.

Resentments during a Time of Demographic Change

The controversy over the proposed naming of Anchorage's performing arts center underscored the broader trends in Alaska's race relations during the tumultuous post-boom years. Though the episode did not culminate in violence, it spotlighted the unease with which many white Alaskans experienced the state's quickly changing demographics. After a decade of spending freely to upgrade Anchorage's recreational and cultural facilities, the municipality counted many recognizable public structures, including the Anchorage Museum, Z. J. Loussac Library, William Egan Civic and Convention Center, George M. Sullivan Arena, and a newly built performing arts center. The center anchored a redesigned downtown commercial and entertainment district that was formerly known as a "skid row," once populated with bars and adult entertainment.[19] "I hope this is the centerpiece of the future growth of our city and the rejuvenation of the downtown area," said architect Jeffrey Wilson.[20]

During construction a naming committee consisting of city leaders and community members proposed that the new performing arts center bear the name of slain civil rights leader Martin Luther King Jr.[21] After nine months of debate, in September 1986 the assembly voted ten to one to affix King's name to the new venue and explicitly nod to Anchorage's growing minority population. "This is significant and meaningful. It is a good honor," said Rev. Alonzo Patterson of the Shiloh Baptist Church. Though he presciently hedged, "But I am going to be watching until I see that name up on the building."[22] The assembly's vote came on the heels of greater national recognition of King's life and accomplishments in the 1980s, including the observance of Martin Luther King Jr. Day as a federal holiday on January 20, 1986.

Many whites still resisted public approval for a man they had long considered dangerous and whose legacy they looked upon warily. As early as 1968, just four days after his murder, conservatives in Congress blocked the first proposal for a national holiday honoring King with threats of a filibuster and a rancorous floor debate.[23] In April 1969 the Alaska State Senate voted ten to nine against a resolution to formally honor King. State senator Clyde Lewis, a member of the Far Right John Birch Society's national council, led the opposition. Said Lewis, "I have a dream too—that my five children can walk the streets in safety." He claimed King had "contributed more than anyone else to the present campus rioting and street rioting."[24] Lewis's perspective on King echoed that of other white Alaskans, some of whom viewed him as an agent of civil unrest and anti-Americanism.

It was not terribly surprising then that nearly as soon as the assembly voted to name the center after King, opposition emerged. Don Smith, a fixture in Anchorage's local politics and an erstwhile conservative assemblyman, launched a petition drive to overturn the assembly's decision. He admitted, "I just don't have the feeling about Martin Luther King that some people in the community do." He described the naming committee, which included eighteen white members out of twenty-five, as "awfully oriented toward the minority community and not representative of Anchorage."[25] Smith suggested that the Fairview center would be a more appropriate facility to name after King. As Smith reasoned, African Americans had long lived in that neighborhood; accordingly, it was more proper to place the iconic civil rights leader's name on a local landmark in the Black community rather than one with high visibility in Anchorage's downtown. For Smith and his supporters, Martin Luther King Jr. did not warrant city or statewide recognition.[26]

Within a few weeks, Smith collected over five hundred signatures. A month later he convinced assemblyman Larry Baker, who had initially voted to name the performing arts center after King, to change his position and sign the petition.[27] By the end of October, Smith and his allies had collected over ten thousand signatures, more than enough to force the assembly to rescind its decision or send the issue to voters in a special election.[28] Municipal clerks accepted the petition and called for a special election, despite significant questions surrounding the legality of Smith's methods. Not only did Smith add a paragraph to the petition after collecting roughly five thousand signatures; he also mailed coupons to signatories to receive discounts at his printing business and free beverages at his downtown restaurant.[29]

As the October special election approached, public debate intensified. The racial undertones of a white man removing King's name from public view were not lost on Anchorage residents. Longtime conservative activist and Don Smith ally Tom Staudenmaier promised to eliminate the "black cloud" over Anchorage, referring to King's name on the performing arts center.[30] Alaskans who claimed membership in the Ku Klux Klan denounced in explicitly racist terms Anchorage's only mayoral candidate who opposed removing King's name from the performing arts center.[31] One assembly member claimed to have heard more anti-Black slurs "in the past three weeks than in the past 25 years."[32] The mobilization against King's name appearing on a downtown property worked. By a three-to-one margin, voters in the special election affirmed the petition and rejected naming the facility in honor of the civil rights leader. "Half of those folks do reflect racism, half ignorance," concluded Donna Estell, treasurer for the committee to retain King's name on the building.[33]

The controversy over the naming of the performing arts center revealed the persistent divisions over race and representation in Alaska. Don Smith's successful campaign relied on a growing sense of white resentment or, at a minimum, unease in Southcentral Alaska over the state's increasing ethnic diversity, despite appeals by Anchorage's Black population to gain greater public recognition. Smith, a former Anchorage assemblyman and Alaska state legislator, positioned himself as a conservative stalwart and someone invested in elevating the "pioneer" culture of Alaska—a culture that was decidedly white and colonial.[34] Smith's appeals rested on a more subtle variant of white supremacy. His career in politics had likely taught him that public use of anti-Black slurs or explicitly racist language could generate a swift response and public backlash, undermining his broader goals, in this case ensuring that Martin Luther King Jr. was not memorialized on one of Anchorage's newest and most high-profile buildings. Smith recognized that softened racial appeals to a white electorate served his aims most effectively, a process known as "dog whistle politics."[35]

Though Smith's rhetoric appealed to those of Anchorage's white residents who were discomfited by a public memorialization of King, others struck a more strident tone in their open calls for white supremacy. Organized hate groups found a foothold in Alaska in the 1980s and 1990s, after having long viewed Alaska as a fertile recruiting ground, even during times of economic prosperity. The Ku Klux Klan (KKK) sought to expand in Alaska during the 1960s and 1970s, and rumors existed of a Klan presence in the territory during the 1920s. Imperial wizard Robert Shelton promised, "As soon as we can get to Alaska and Hawaii, we're going there."[36] In 1980 David Duke, a former grand wizard of the Klan and future Louisiana politician, filed the necessary paperwork to incorporate an Alaska chapter for his new organization, the National Association for the Advancement of White People (NAAWP). "We believe white people are losing their rights everywhere, including Alaska," said Duke, adding, "You have a lot of Native interest groups up there, and a lot of whites have a growing seed of concern because of the favoritism that's being shown some of these Indian and Eskimo organizations." He planned for 2,000 Alaska members and claimed that 125 Alaskans, primarily from the Anchorage area, had already joined the NAAWP.[37] Duke's efforts floundered, however. In fact, the backlash against Duke was sufficiently swift that the *Anchorage Times* issued a story to clarify that an area man who shared the racist's name was unrelated and thus undeserving of any harassment.[38]

As the economy nosedived, white supremacists established firmer footholds in the state. In 1987 the KKK opened its first Anchorage office. An unidentified member, contacted through a private mail service, claimed fifteen hundred local KKK members, a figure that was almost certainly inflated but nevertheless portended greater interest in the hate group than seven years earlier.[39] In 1990 Mark Watson, the self-described Anchorage spokesman for the United Skinheads of America, claimed "over ten" members in Anchorage. His newsletter featured on the cover a racist caricature of a Black man with the caption "Wild animals belong in the wild, not in our cities."[40] The same year two teenagers claiming to be affiliated with Watson vandalized an Anchorage Jewish temple, drew swastikas on the walls, and stole religious objects.[41] Three years later Anchorage skinheads again made local news when eighteen-year-old neo-Nazi Patrick Russell was convicted for the attempted assault of sixteen-year-old John Boettcher, a former member of the same skinhead gang. Russell had grown angry when Boettcher told others that Russell was an Alaska Native. Said Boettcher on the stand, "When I was a skinhead, we were supposed to filter out the nonwhites."[42]

White supremacists stepped up their recruitment efforts during these years as they targeted youth in their propaganda campaign. In 1990 Ricky Cooper, a veteran hate organizer who had once tried to establish a whites-only redoubt in Washington State, turned to Alaska for his latest campaign.[43] Cooper mailed roughly a thousand newsletters to students at Anchorage's Bartlett High School and Dimond High School. Cooper proclaimed crudely, "I am White; I am proud of my heritage; I intend to preserve the existence of my Race."[44] He described himself as "someone who believes that the races are different, physically and mentally ... whites are superior."[45] At least a few white students gravitated to such hate groups, and some took to dressing in the fashions of neo-Nazis, including shaved heads, black boots with red shoelaces (to symbolize the blood shed for white supremacy), and suspenders. Before Halloween in 1991, officials at one Anchorage school noted the emergence of students who had affiliated with the white supremacist movement and forbade students from wearing neo-Nazi attire.[46]

In May 1992 officials at Anchorage's Hanshew Junior High School suspended an eighth grade student for wearing a KKK button. The student claimed he wore the button "because that's the way I feel"; he was later part of a group that vandalized public property with racist graffiti and assaulted minority students.[47] Other students at the school etched racist slurs on their hands and painted WHITE and BLACK over adjacent water fountains, imposing the infamous signage associated with Jim Crow–era segregation.[48] In Chugiak, an overwhelmingly white community twenty miles north of downtown Anchorage, white students defaced school walls with swastikas, demanded the firing of the school's Black security guard, and petitioned for the removal of African American art.[49]

These acts occurred within the context of Alaska's rapidly changing demographics. And Anchorage, by far the state's largest metropolitan region, experienced the most extensive transformation. As late as 1976, amid the pipeline construction, 86 percent of Anchorage School District (ASD) students were white. But just fourteen years later, at the beginning of the 1991–92 school year, that figure had fallen to nearly 70 percent; 27 percent of ASD students were nonwhite. Some schools had a minority population as high as 40 percent.[50] The late 1980s and early 1990s represented a turning point in Anchorage's history as students of color became a fast-growing demographic; by century's end most of Anchorage's school-aged population would be nonwhite. The *Anchorage Daily News* first reported the emerging diversity of the student body in 1988 with the headline: "Booming minority populations move city ahead in racial mix."[51]

Hanshew Junior High, a location where several racist incidents had occurred, lagged behind the rest of ASD in terms of its diversity, with an 87 percent white student body.[52] Unlike the more multicultural schools on Anchorage's east and west side, Hanshew served one of the municipality's more racially homogeneous neighborhoods, the Hillside. Perched along the foothills of the Chugach Mountains, with sweeping views of the Turnagain Arm at a distance of ten miles southeast of downtown, the Hillside has long been known as one of Anchorage's wealthier enclaves.[53] In 1992 several high school–aged skinheads trespassed into Hanshew, confronted the principal, who had cracked down on racist behavior, and threw rocks at his car.[54] Then, in October, a fight broke out between white and Black students at Anchorage's Service High School, the secondary school for Hillside residents, after a group of white students provoked Black students by refusing to allow them to pass in a hallway.[55] Students of color in other predominantly white schools reported similar intimidation. One thirteen-year-old Black girl reported to her school staff, "The bathroom walls are covered almost every day with 'white power' and white power symbols and slogans such as, 'blacks are only good at being slaves,' and 'Whites rule over Blacks.'"[56] An Alaska Native teen admitted: "[I] wouldn't tell people I was Native. I was embarrassed. I get this fear. I didn't want to be seen."[57] "They [white students] make comments about the igloos and parkas," said another Alaska Native student.[58]

In 1991 the Anchorage School District and the Anchorage Chamber of Commerce commissioned a comprehensive study to evaluate the quality of public education in the city, including ASD and the University of Alaska Anchorage, with an emphasis on the minority student experience. Released in October 1991, the Winning with Stronger Education Project (WISE) combined mailed surveys, telephone interviews, and focus groups. Its executive summary repeatedly called for expanding multicultural approaches to educating students in Anchorage schools, including recruiting more minority teachers, offering cultural competency training courses, raising awareness of the forms of discrimination, and overhauling the history curriculum to include the voices of African Americans and Alaska Natives.[59] In one of the surveys, 37 percent of all respondents reported having experienced gender-, race-, or class-based discrimination from a teacher.[60] Parents of Black students,

8.1 percent of ASD students, agreed that "Black male students are treated differently." Said one parent, "Teachers seem afraid of Black students as they get older—about fourth or fifth grade."[61]

ASD officials were often slow to acknowledge and respond to the racial tension. When a white student, part of a group that had, according to school officials, "almost killed another kid in a fight," spat in the face of a Black security guard, the student received a relatively mild punishment of an in-school suspension.[62] "A lot of this could have been stopped had teachers not condoned [such behavior]," said one Black Anchorage student.[63] Despite mounting evidence in the form of student claims, surveys, and the WISE report, ASD superintendent Thomas O'Rourke declared: "I don't think we have a race problem in our schools. I think we've got a 'dumb' problem in our schools."[64]

The highest-ranking Black employee in the Anchorage School District at the time was Everett Louis Overstreet, the district's executive director of facilities, maintenance, and operations. A trained engineer, Overstreet had followed opportunity north to Alaska in 1975; his first job in the state was a position with the Alyeska Pipeline Service Company. An accomplished author and amateur historian, Overstreet provided editorials for local newspapers and published a history of African Americans in Alaska.[65] Offended by O'Rourke's comments and inaction, Overstreet resigned effective November 30, 1992. He quickly returned to the private sector but not before he went on the record to warn: "I see a major racial incident taking place in the district soon, and it's because people aren't paying attention to what's going on."[66] His resignation letter was equally frank, citing ASD's "rudderless" leadership. According to Overstreet, "Over the past several years, I have made repeated attempts to have the district address this problem [of racial strife] in a constructive manner." He concluded, "My attempts have fallen on deaf ears."[67] After nearly twenty years in Alaska in a variety of highly respected positions, Overstreet retired in the Lower 48.

Overstreet was far from the only one to speak out against the seemingly intractable racism he witnessed in Alaska's largest city and its schools. Alaska Native leader Byron Mallot noted the racial tension in Alaska in the early 1990s and connected it to one of the era's pivotal moments: the 1992 acquittal of the Los Angeles police officers who had beaten Rodney King a year earlier. Mallot feared that the combustible circumstances that "exploded" in California's largest city might also be found in Alaska: "anger, frustration, and hopelessness" among the youth. Mallot advised: "I am not fully familiar with the circumstance of Alaska's African American citizens. But I believe it is safe to say that they, in the main, are not satisfied with their place in Alaska society."[68]

Alaskan Youth Present a New Vision

Pushback against racism also occurred in the schools and universities as Black and Native kids and young adults spoke out and formed coalitions. This younger generation of Alaska's Black, Indigenous, and people of color (BIPOC) population forged an open and inclusive culture of its own, one that rejected violent white supremacy and celebrated Anchorage's nascent multiculturalism. Students Organized Against Racism (SOAR) was one of these student groups. SOAR organized chapters at Anchorage high schools, Alaska Pacific University (APU), and the University of Alaska Anchorage. Students led a series of events throughout the 1990s, the inaugural of which was entitled "Mastering the '90s through Education." These programs facilitated a greater awareness of Black history and culture and fostered a spirit of inclusion among students of color. They brought together students to deliver poetry, perform dances, and engage in essay competitions.[69]

Students at East Anchorage High School, known as "East High," organized a multicultural review and dance theater that emphasized the rapidly changing demographics of the school. The Black Culture Club participated in the review and celebrated its collective African ancestry as its members modeled dress and performed dances from Gambia, Upper Volta (now Burkina Faso), and Mali. Polynesian, Alaska Native, and Korean students joined the review with contributions of their own. In 1988 the review began to showcase Alaska Native culture in what was then a predominantly white school.[70] Quickly, however, it became clear that the school included a far greater variety of people from an ever-growing range of backgrounds. As the 1990s progressed and Alaska entered the twenty-first century, East High became among the nation's most diverse high schools.[71]

At Service High School, in the very neighborhood where several racist incidents had occurred, a hundred students and parents gathered for a Black History Month performance put on by the school's Ebony Culture Club. The skits presented lessons on an array of topics related to Black history and current events. One presented the story of Rosa Parks and the Montgomery Bus

Boycott; another included frank discussions of sexuality, teen pregnancy, and the AIDS epidemic that then raged across much of the country. Kim Frank, mother of one of the performers, exclaimed, "These kids showed they're proud of being black, proud of being African American, and they wanted to show that to us." Matt Fox, then a fourteen-year-old freshman at Service High and a self-described aspiring playwright, recited a poem:

> Racism
> It is all around us
> Hate between difference
> Color, religion, race
> If we took away the religion
> If we took away the race
> There would be one thing left
> One thing we all have in common
> A human face.[72]

Another student, Luciana Hayes, placed in the essay contest with a poignant reflection on "what it means to be African American," a proposition that meant "having to try four times harder" than her white counterparts to prove herself and overcome adversity.[73]

Fox's poem and Hayes's essay serve as reminders that many, if not most, younger Alaskans never subscribed to the race hatred pedaled by a segment of area whites. Indeed, young Alaskans of color more often defined the terms of their culture in ways that echoed the broader trends of the Lower 48 or broke new ground entirely. Beyond the classroom, artists and musicians led a dynamic cultural scene that provided a window into life in Alaska during the years after the oil boom. Jay King arrived in Anchorage at eighteen years old with the air force, a position he held for about a year before being kicked out. Life in the military did not fit King's creative vision. But rather than return home to California, King decided to perform in the city's nascent hip-hop and rhythm and blues scene. King honed his skills as a producer and released his first record under the name *Frost*, a nod to Alaska's icy climate. He eventually relocated to Northern California, where he produced records, yielding his most commercially successful collaboration with the Timex Social Club from Berkeley. Their 1986 hit single, "Rumors," reached number one on the *Billboard* charts and sold over 3.5 million copies.[74]

Though King's career took off in California, he left a legacy in Alaska and mentored several performers there. Sean Sullivan was among those influenced by King and became perhaps the most highly acclaimed and notorious Alaska hip-hop artist. Going by the stage name Joker the Bailbondsman, Sullivan put Alaska on the map during the rise of the "gangsta rap" era of the late 1980s and 1990s. Having grown up in what he described as an "upper-middle-class home," Sullivan nonetheless gave voice to life in Anchorage's Fairview and Mountain View communities during a volatile era of economic hardship, rising crime, and disinvestment. As Joker the Bailbondsman, Sullivan released three albums in the mid- to late 1990s with his record label, Inlet City Records, itself a reference to Anchorage's location on the Cook Inlet. Joker the Bailbondsman collaborated with the famous Cleveland rapper Bizzy Bone, of Bone Thugs-N-Harmony, on his biggest hit, "Money in a Ziplock Bag." Sullivan's life took an unfortunate turn in 2008, when he was convicted of selling crack cocaine. In fact, Sullivan's career trajectory mirrors that of other Black hip-hop artists from the era: bouts of creativity and critical acclaim amid struggles with the law. Regardless, Sullivan's career as an Alaskan hip-hop artist stands alone in its popular success and productivity. Released from prison in 2016, Sullivan continues to make music and has found creative outlets as an author and businessman, partnering with the Alaska Distillery with a line of vodka, among other pursuits.[75]

Despite the evocations of Alaska and shout-outs to Anchorage neighborhoods, certainly unique among hip-hop artists, Joker the Bailbondsman broadly followed the national trends of the era's rap music. The Alaskan musical group Pamyua, however, created a genre of its own, a fusion of hip-hop, dance, and Indigenous music from the Arctic that reflected the backgrounds of the respective members. Formed in 1995 by Stephen and Phillip Blanchett, brothers of African and Alaska Native descent, Pamyua broadcasted to the world the hybridized stylings of a new generation of Alaskan performers and musicians. The Blanchett brothers took to calling their music "tribal funk" and "Inuit tribal soul" after the disparate influences of Yup'ik, Inuit, West African, African American, and even Pacific Island cultures. The band's performances have been known to include Inuit drumming and dancing, soulful lyricism, and more conventional jazz and rock instrumentation. Pamyua's 2003 album, *Caught in the Act*, garnered national attention and won the Record of the Year from the Native American Music Awards.[76]

Toward a New Century

From the multicultural music scene of Anchorage in the 1990s to the burgeoning presence of Black culture in Alaska's schools, the post–oil boom years reflected the racial tensions of an uncertain decade. But at the same time, Alaskan BIPOC youth reimagined what the state might look like as it entered the twenty-first century as a far more diverse state than it was just a generation earlier. During the mid-1980s Alaska's economy fell into its deepest postwar recession but slowly recovered by the late 1980s and 1990s. In 1989 the Exxon Valdez oil tanker ran aground after striking Bligh Reef in the Prince William Sound, spilling nearly eleven million gallons of oil. The environmental catastrophe required a cleanup effort that included thousands of workers and ultimately cost billions of dollars. Although Alaska had already begun to rebound from the depth of the recession over a year before the oil spill, the disaster nonetheless created a temporary swell of economic activity, even as the longer-term costs to the fishing and tourist industries, as well as litigation, have run into the hundreds of millions of dollars.[77] Also in 1989, Federal Express (known today as FedEx) opened an Anchorage hub for its cargo operations and would soon play a major role in the expansion of the Ted Stevens International Airport. Southcentral Alaska likewise benefited from the opening of several new box stores, expanded hotel offerings, and increased tourism. This led to a 9 percent rise in employment between 1990 and 1995.[78]

Alaska's economy gradually improved through the 1990s, but the seemingly boundless prosperity of the 1970s and early 1980s never returned. Social tensions remained, but so, too, did a keen sense of community and civic engagement among Black Alaskans. African Americans continued to move to Alaska throughout the late 1980s and 1990s, but others left the state during this decade of national economic expansion; a strong national economy has long enticed Alaskans, those who had recently arrived or those who had lived longer term in the state, back to the Lower 48. Despite its transience and economic precariousness, Alaska remained what it had been for much of the twentieth century: a place where Black men and women could ascend into the middle class, establish a home, and build a family. The military remained a central driver of social mobility; so, too, did resource development.

Yet the Black population also encountered an uptick in hate crimes during these years, as did Alaska Natives. Open displays of white supremacy occurred in a variety of forms. The murder of Julius Marshall represented the most brutal and visceral form. Another menacing variant could be viewed in the attempts of neo-Nazi extremists and white nationalists to recruit younger Alaskans to their cause. A portion of the white population believed their power and influence would wane as demographics continued to change, particularly in Anchorage. If not as insidious as the extremist groups operating at the margins, an emboldened conservative movement led by white residents, many of whom had arrived during the oil boom and had themselves done quite well financially, continued to flex its political muscle in reaction to Anchorage's ethnic diversity. At the same time, progressive activists, business leaders, people of color, and white allies came together to present an Alaska primed for the twenty-first century. These men and women believed that Alaska's demographics were in fact a strength rather than a weakness.

Perhaps most significantly, Alaska's youth of color expressed themselves through art, music, and activism in ways that signaled a different future, one in which Indigeneity and Blackness would be embraced rather than shunned. More generally, Alaskans found themselves—as they always had—engaged in national debates around such topics as race, culture, and politics. For every individual who held racist views and justified racist actions, one could find someone like Everett Louis Overstreet, George Harper, or Blanche McSmith, all of whom regularly took to the pages of local newspapers to denounce bigotry and put forth a different vision of Alaska, one rooted to a greater understanding of how the state's many peoples have influenced its history. Through their actions, members of the Ebony Culture Club at an Anchorage area high school or Pamyua in one of the group's engaging live performances showcased the dynamism that lurked just under the surface of Alaska's mainstream white culture for all who cared to look.

CONCLUSION

The Black Past Meets Contemporary Alaska

IN THE LATE 1890S AND EARLY 1900S, ALASKA EXPERIENCED TWO of North America's greatest gold rushes, first in the Klondike and, soon after, nearly eight hundred miles to the west, on the Seward Peninsula in Nome. Miners, settlers, and fortune seekers struck gold elsewhere in Alaska's interior in the years to follow. But despite the spectacular amount of wealth extracted from the vast territory, Alaska would be recognized as one of the poorest places in the United States throughout much of the first half of the twentieth century; it remained so even after statehood in 1959. It was not at all clear if Alaska would ever be able to support itself and deliver the services and standard of living that millions of Americans in the Lower 48 had come to enjoy and expect in the aftermath of World War II. In another radical swing, a generation later, Alaska had become not only the nation's forty-ninth state but also its richest, per capita, a fact few could have accurately predicted as late as the 1950s. Until the discovery of oil, there remained a serious question as to how exactly Alaska could ever prosper. The times had changed. By the 1980s well-compensated workers had completed the pipeline; residents had started collecting an annual check, known as the permanent fund dividend (PFD), drawn from the investment earnings of the state's newly acquired oil wealth; and Alaska had become the only state in the nation with neither a statewide income tax nor sales tax. Those who stayed in Alaska, especially the three primary population centers of Anchorage, Fairbanks, and Juneau, not only expected and received many of the amenities found in the Lower 48, but they also experienced a state government that operated unlike any other in the union. The days of frontier subsistence and primitive living conditions, it would seem, failed to interest much of a new generation of Alaskans who had been reared amid the oil boom.[1]

Legislators and municipal officials earmarked millions of dollars to upgrade Anchorage parks, recreation, and cultural institutions in an effort known as "Project 80s." By century's end, Alaska's largest city was home to a museum, an all-purpose sports arena, a new convention center, and community and transit centers in several neighborhoods, all of which required the sizable budgets made possible by oil revenue. Fairbanks and Juneau upgraded their civic institutions and augmented their social and cultural offerings so that they, too, might entice families from the Lower 48 to put down roots and flourish in their adopted surroundings. Still greater transformations occurred elsewhere in Alaska's rural boroughs with Indigenous majorities as subsistence economies and traditional cultures transformed nearly overnight with a cash infusion of billions of dollars.

Despite the high-profile instances of racism, institutional discrimination, and police violence, Black residents had reasons to be optimistic in the last decades of the century. Bettye J. Davis, an ardent defender of public education, won a seat on Anchorage's school board in 1982, the first Black woman to do so; it was the first of many elected positions that Davis would hold over the next thirty-five years. That year the newly elected governor, Bill Sheffield, appointed Eleanor Andrews, a Black woman, to serve in the Department of Administration. Andrews ascended the ranks and became the commissioner of the department before starting a series of highly successful business ventures. One part of the job in the Department of Administration required Andrews to review the Small Business Association and the disbursement of federal and state contracts. She advocated on behalf of minority businesses as part of the state's affirmative action policies and ensured that they could access the bidding process in ways that Frank Cox had long denied them. Indeed, it would seem to have been a new day for Alaska's minority-owned businesses and workers.[2]

In Juneau, Rosalee Taylor Walker became the first Black woman to serve on the Juneau City Council in 1984. Fairbanks residents elected James C. Hayes as mayor, the first Black man to hold the position in any of Alaska's three largest cities. He ran unopposed as a Democrat in 1992 and won with the support of the town's mostly white electorate. The national press took note, and *Ebony* sent reporters to discuss the meaning of the predominantly white and conservative Alaskan community electing a Black mayor. Hayes claimed: "In Fairbanks, people tend to accept you as you are. They just want to hear your platform and hear what you believe in, and then see you go out and work really hard."[3] He had arrived in Alaska in the 1960s with his divorced mother, who remarried a Baptist minister in Fairbanks. Hayes graduated from the University of Alaska, became a teacher, and then worked on the construction of the pipeline. He volunteered in the community, served on the school board, and even earned an appointment in Governor William Egan's administration in the 1970s, when he was in his early twenties.

Hayes boasted a career of public service and gained the respect of many in Fairbanks and beyond.[4] In an interview with the *Fairbanks News-Miner*, Hayes proclaimed: "I tell my kids, 'You're crazy to leave this state. Get a good education, put God first in your life and you can do anything in this state.'"[5] Yet statistics and nuance complicate the narrative, and we are left with reason to celebrate the achievements of men such as Hayes, even as we reconcile the underlying structural racism that has long dogged Alaska. In fact, the same *Ebony* piece that profiled Hayes in October 1993 also pointed out that the local NAACP had undertaken an investigation over reports of racial discrimination and harassment at nearby Fort Wainwright and Eielson Air Force Base.[6]

The successes that African Americans have cultivated in Alaska showcase a determination to overcome intolerance from conservative and reactionary elements within the state. While Alaskans have applauded themselves for a streak of independence and a general disdain for "how they do things Outside," the state's (and territory's) history of racism, on the one hand, and civil rights mobilization and activism, on the other, exposes more commonality with other places than it does exceptional patterns of openness. In response, this book has explored the ways that Black Alaskans have built community in the face of varying degrees of discrimination and opposition to their presence.[7]

Returning to the naming controversy of Anchorage's Center for the Performing Arts, then, serves as a fitting place to conclude. The Anchorage assembly and advocates who wanted to memorialize Martin Luther King Jr. did not abandon their pursuit because of a failure at the ballot box or Don Smith's campaign to diminish the most iconic figure of the civil rights era. Soon after the vote to remove King's name from the performing arts venue, a multiracial coalition proposed a prominent location along the western

Martin Luther King Jr. Memorial on the Anchorage Delaney Park Strip, 2020. Photo by David Reamer.

side of downtown's Delaney Park Strip as a site for a permanent marker that would bear King's name. Immediately, these men and women launched an ambitious fundraising campaign to erect an impressive public landmark dedicated to the reverend and civil rights leader. Though it took a few more years to raise the funds and decide on a spot and design for the landmark, Alaskans gathered on a clear and bright Saturday in early December 1996 to dedicate the memorial to King.[8]

The event had been more than a decade in the making and recalled some of the most acrimonious moments in Alaska's tumultuous racial history. Indeed, ten years earlier Black activists and a few city leaders had lobbied to rename a stretch of downtown's Ninth Avenue after the visionary leader; a few years later the same group had proposed naming the performing arts center after King. In both cases those who were neither interested in the achievements of the nation's Black population nor in the iconic activist won the debate in a city where racial tensions simmered just below the surface, boiling up now and again.

Although the multiracial mobilization for the King monument was among the first such efforts to acknowledge Anchorage's diversity in its public spaces, it would not be the last. To accommodate the need for more convention space, the Anchorage assembly voted to build a new convention center to take the place of the aging Egan Center (named after Alaska governor William Egan). Completed in 2008, the Dena'ina Civic and Convention Center has hosted the Alaska Federation of Natives (AFN), high school graduations, and even an international summit on climate change that brought world leaders, including President Barack Obama, to Alaska in 2015 to discuss the fate of the Arctic. The center is named in honor of Southcentral Alaska's Indigenous people, the Dena'ina, and is the highest-profile building in the region to bear an Indigenous name.[9] More recently, in late 2018, Dena'ina sculptor and artist Joel Isaak completed a statue of a Native elder known as Grandma Olga Nikolai Ezi. The bronze statue depicts the woman fishing and drying salmon just feet from the mouth of Dgheyaytnu (Ship Creek) and is a reminder that Anchorage has served as Dena'ina fish camp far longer than it has been home to a settler population.[10]

In 2020 a coalition led by the Alaska Black Caucus proposed amending the name of Alaska's largest, most diverse high school after Bettye Davis, the first Black woman elected to the Alaska House of Representatives (1991–96). Davis, who passed away in 2018, also served three terms as a state senator (2001–12) and three terms as member of the Anchorage School Board (1982–90), making her among the most distinguished public servants in Alaska's history. Like the effort to affix Martin Luther King's name to the performing arts center, renaming East Anchorage High School, commonly referred to simply as "East High," garnered immediate pushback. But unlike in the MLK controversy, the opposition in this case was not nearly as determined as the proponents of the name change. And within a year of lobbying, the school board formally renamed the seventeen hundred-plus student school the "Bettye Davis East Anchorage High School."[11]

The presence of the King memorial, the naming of the convention center after the region's Dena'ina population, the construction of the Grandma Ezi statue, and the addition of Bettye Davis's name to the state's largest high school exemplify a newfound appreciation and celebration of Alaska's distinct population. Like the rest of the nation, Alaska has benefited from an influx of people from various backgrounds, African Americans among them. As sociologist Chad Farrell has presented, Alaska, specifically its largest city, Anchorage, "has found itself on the vanguard of America's diversity trend."[12] As detailed in this book's latter chapters, the state has drawn people of African descent but also people from Southeast Asia, the South Pacific, Latin America, and elsewhere. Some settled in Dutch Harbor, Kodiak, Nome, or Sitka, but most newcomers have chosen to reside in the three primary population centers of Anchorage, Fairbanks, and Juneau. And like the rest of the nation, Alaska's immigrants are more likely to start their own businesses, become medical professionals, and boost economic growth.[13]

Newcomers and "sourdoughs" (as many longtime residents affectionately refer to themselves) have also built a vibrant faith-based community, rooted in the social justice teachings of their respective houses of worship. The Anchorage Faith and Action Congregations Together (AFACT) has bridged an array of cultures and worked to ameliorate social tensions. Filipinx and Latinx Alaskans, a majority of whom identify as Catholic, have forged impactful relationships with Black worshippers, many of whom are Protestant (Episcopalian, Lutheran, and Methodist churches are represented). Congregations that are heavily Alaska Native have worked with the white-majority Unitarian Universalist Church on issues of racial reconciliation. AFACT has put together plans of action around such issues as homelessness, police violence, access to healthcare, and climate change.[14]

Although not the sole cause of Alaska's growth, the state's economy expanded through the 1990s and early 2000s as the state's demographics became ever more global. By some measures the politics of the state and its largest cities have moderated over the last twenty years as well. Few consider Alaska a swing state, but the political shift that has occurred in Anchorage, Fairbanks, and Juneau mirrors other western cities that have at once grown more multiracial, educated, and progressive. Outlying areas, namely the Fairbanks–North Star Borough (beyond the enclave around the University of Alaska Fairbanks), the Kenai Peninsula, and the Matsu Borough all have overwhelmingly white populations and have at the same time grown considerably more conservative. At the time of this book's release, Alaska arguably faces more serious economic and political challenges than at any time since statehood. Alaskan residents reckon with rancorous partisan divisions and political paralysis that reflect a similar national dilemma. The 2015 decline in oil prices and an additional economic dip as a result of the 2020–21 COVID pandemic led to significant reductions in state spending and, with it, a severe recession that positioned Alaska among the nation's most unstable economies. It will require resiliency, patience, and collaboration to turn the state's political climate and economy around to create new opportunities for the duration of the twenty-first century.[15]

A more racially diverse Alaska, one that has also been a sight for global migration, will require tolerance and acceptance among longtime residents. This means coming to terms with Alaska's history of racism and violence, on one hand, and celebrating differences, on the other. And though many Alaskans may prefer to see themselves as free of the biases of other parts of the country, the historical record indicates otherwise. From restrictive covenants and urban renewal to legally dubious and outright discriminatory employment practices to tensions with law enforcement and a criminal justice system that has disproportionately ensnared men and women of color, primarily Alaska Natives and Blacks, Alaska has reflected, and in some cases exceeded, national patterns of discrimination and systemic racism. A full reckoning with the legacy of settler colonialism and its impact upon Alaska's Indigenous people remains profoundly necessary.

And yet despite Alaska's fraught past, thousands of Americans of color and migrants from around the world have come to this expansive land to better their station, and many have succeeded. Black men arrived as whalers before the United States and Russia agreed to the Treaty of Cession in 1867. These were the first men of African descent to view the North Pacific and Arctic Oceans. Most did not occupy Alaska for long or even walk upon its shores. Some, however, did stay and settled in far-flung regions, thousands of miles from where they were born and raised. Evidence suggests some Black whalers married Indigenous women and started families of their own. The gold rush era brought thousands of other Black men and women to Alaska; few broke even, and fewer still struck it rich. But some, like St. John Atherton, made a quick fortune and attained legendary status. Born enslaved, Atherton fled the South, traveled north, and discovered wealth beyond his wildest imagination. Though exceptional, Atherton nevertheless revealed what *could* happen. On the other end of the spectrum might be Ronald Griffin, who froze to death in a tub, alone in a cabin set back in the woods of Alaska's capacious interior. Griffin's tragic demise spoke to the lonely isolation that many others encountered in their travels north. For most, however, neither the experience of Atherton nor Griffin adequately conveyed a "typical" life for Black individuals who arrived during the late nineteenth and early twentieth centuries. In fact, their lives could hardly be described as typical for any single demographic. Instead, like other settlers, fortune seekers, and runaways who viewed Alaska as a place to start anew, a plethora of experiences prevent generalizations.

The same point would be just as true in a discussion of Black history during the hundred years following the gold rush. Thomas Bevers highlights the possibility for advancement during the 1920s and 1930s in Anchorage, but one might note the brutal public execution of two Black men in Juneau in 1948 and 1950 to emphasize the imbalances in the territory's criminal justice system. Regarding civil rights in Alaska, one may know the story of Elizabeth Peratrovich and the Anti-Discrimination Act. But to know the whole story, one must include the activism of Beatrice and Robert Coleman and their dogged insistence that the act be strengthened and the loopholes closed. Only after the couple faced humiliating discrimination in a Fairbanks bar did legislators provide a meaningful enforcement mechanism to the law, and even then, local officials and businesspeople too often looked the other way as infringements occurred. Likewise, women such as Blanche McSmith advocated for civil rights and equality on the state and local level. All the while Zula Swanson accumulated valuable property, and Richard Watts ascended the corporate leadership ladder of Carrs after young men and women picketed the grocery store and demanded that the company promote the careers of well-qualified people of color. Mahala Ashley Dickerson overcame a series of barriers before she successfully homesteaded in Alaska and established a legal career.

At the turn of the twenty-first century, Alaskans sent African Americans to the state legislature and its superior court. Larry Card served on the Alaska Judicial Council for twelve years, from 1993 to 2005. Card's tenure on the bench blazed a trail for other Black jurists to follow. Pamela Scott Washington served on the Anchorage District Court, Kari McRea served as an Anchorage magistrate judge, and more recently, in 2015, Herman Walker received an appointment to the Alaska Superior Court . At the same time, the founding in the early 1990s of the African American Business Council by Ed Wesley—an activist who sought greater advancement for young African Americans—created new pathways for Blacks to work at the First National Bank and the National Bank of Alaska. This has led to greater representation in one of the state's key economic sectors. It also shined a light on the discrimination in the state's financial institutions that had historically failed to provide equal access to credit for Black and Native families as well as Black- and Native-owned businesses.

Black men and women have indeed assumed leadership roles in communities big and small throughout the state. Black professionals have successfully developed careers in corporate management, the nonprofit sector, medicine, law, and academia. They have established social networks more common in larger cities with much larger Black populations. In Anchorage, for example, African American men and women proudly promote their affiliation with the Divine Nine, a nationally known group of fraternities and sororities long associated with the Black middle class and elite. In addition, other social welfare and uplift groups have maintained a presence in Alaska. Some of them have included the Links, Incorporated, and Jack and Jill of America. One common denominator might be that Alaska has provided more hope than the places these men and women left. And if opportunities were not at first apparent, Black Alaskans created new ones and fought for access to existing ones. All who sacrificed to travel north did so at great personal and financial risk. And for that their histories deserve to be told.

As we have seen, the history of Black lives in Alaska has followed its own course in significant ways, but there has also been a good deal of overlap with the history of the rest of the nation. Black Alaskans have participated in civil rights activism, have confronted institutional discrimination, and have had a troubled relationship with law enforcement, trend lines that obviously extend well beyond the forty-ninth state. Likewise, what has occurred in the Lower 48 has reliably ricocheted to Alaska. As when Martin Luther King Jr.'s actions in Selma prompted sympathy marches in Anchorage and Fairbanks, police shootings in the Lower 48 provoked protests in Alaska too. Alaska Natives and African Americans have borne the brunt of abusive police practices and discrimination in the state's legal system. As such, the names of Phillip Moore and Cassell Williams have received attention in this study and provide a troubling link to national patterns of police violence. The case of the Fairbanks Four, the four Indigenous men who were wrongly convicted of a murder and spent nearly twenty years incarcerated, further highlight the impact that racist policing and bias in the criminal justice system have had upon Alaska's communities of color.

In this context it should not come as a surprise that a peaceful crowd gathered in downtown Anchorage after the August 2014 shooting death of Michael Brown in Ferguson, Missouri. Those in attendance included Black men and women as well as Alaska Natives, Filipinx, Latinx, Pacific Islanders, and others who spoke out against the prevalence of what they perceived as police misconduct in their neighborhoods.[16] A week after the Michael Brown demonstration, a similar multiracial coalition of protesters in Anchorage returned to the streets to denounce the failure of a grand jury to indict the New York police officer who choked Eric Garner to death in Staten Island, New York, for the supposed crime of selling loose cigarettes outside of a transit station. Xavier Mason, the president of the NAACP Youth Council and organizer of the Anchorage march, addressed the crowd that had peacefully gathered, quoting Martin Luther King Jr.: "I called this rally because injustice anywhere is a threat to justice everywhere." Another speaker, Andrew Freed, the president of the Black Student Union at the University of Alaska Anchorage, told the crowd, "Any single one of those people could have been me."[17]

In 2016 the police shooting deaths of Philando Castile in Minnesota and Alton Sterling in Louisiana again prompted Anchorage demonstrations. Many of the signs people carried had a similar message. "I Hope I Am Not Next." "I Hope My Husband Is Not Next." "I Hope My Brothers Are Not Next."[18] Black Lives Matter, a refrain that emerged after George Zimmerman gunned down Trayvon Martin in Florida in early 2012, carried as much emotional weight in Alaska as it did elsewhere. Indeed, according to the Mapping Police Violence project, Alaska has, per capita, the second highest rate of police killings in the United States and the second highest rate of police killings of Black men and women. The cases detailed in this book, far from aberrations, reveal a troubling pattern that puts Alaska not simply in line with the rest of the nation but, in fact, makes it an exemplar of one the most troubling and intransigent issues confronting the nation.[19]

In fact, the *Anchorage Daily News* published a troubling study that located the deaths of forty-three Alaskans at the hands of the police between 2015 and the first half of 2020. Reinforcing national trends, Alaskans of color and those in mental distress were killed at disproportionate rates; over half of those killed were not white. Alaska Natives, constituting 15 percent of the state's population, represented at least 30 percent of those killed by the police. Black Alaskans, who make up just over 4 percent of the population, represented 10 percent of those killed. The paper cautiously noted that these numbers may have been higher as it could not confirm the racial identity of every individual killed in a dispute with police. Several police departments across Alaska do not keep official demographic information on those killed by officers. Alaska's largest newspaper, in its investigation of police violence in Alaska, concurred with widely published results of the Proceedings of the National Academy of

Activists protest the murder of George Floyd in Anchorage, summer of 2020. Photo by Jovell Rennie.

Sciences that "Black and American Indian and Alaska Native people are 'significantly more likely' to be killed by police than white people."[20]

Like millions of others around the country, the authors reacted with anger and dismay, at more displays of police brutality directed at African American men and women. White vigilantes hunted down a Black man, Ahmaud Arbery, on suspicion that he had committed a crime after they witnessed him jogging through a predominantly white neighborhood in Brunswick, Georgia. In the spring of 2020, amid the COVID-19 pandemic, police in Louisville, Kentucky, forced open the door and shot Breonna Taylor, a twenty-six-year-old woman with no proven connection to criminal activity who was asleep in her bed. And perhaps most galvanizing of all, on May 25, 2020, Memorial Day, a forty-six-year-old Black man, George Floyd, writhed under the knee of a Minneapolis police officer, who slowly asphyxiated him after an employee of a neighborhood convenience store alleged that he had tried to pass off a counterfeit twenty-dollar bill. A witness, seventeen-year-old Darnella Frazier, recorded a harrowing video of the killing of Floyd that lasted eight minutes and forty-six seconds. At no point since the 1960s has the nation so viscerally confronted questions of race, violence, and white supremacy.[21]

Celeste Hodge Growden speaks at a Black Lives Matter rally in Anchorage during the summer of 2020. Photo by Jovell Rennie.

The killings of Ahmaud Arbery, Breonna Taylor, and George Floyd led to protests in every state—from the largest cities of the United States to small towns—and across many nations of the world. Activists in the forty-ninth state registered their discontent with these killings of Black individuals at the hands of the police and the closer-to-home concerns of police violence in Alaska, typically directed at the Indigenous and Black communities. A rainbow coalition of Alaskans gathered in Anchorage's park strip and on the streets of the municipality's neighborhoods in solidarity with millions of others seeking to dismantle institutional racism. Old and young people, across racial and class backgrounds, gender identities, and sexual expressions, called for an end to the systemic and historic devaluation of Black life, be it on the streets of Ferguson, Minneapolis, New York, or Anchorage, Alaska.[22]

Anchorage resident Celeste Hodge Growden emerged as a leading voice during the Black Lives Matter rallies in Southcentral Alaska. Hodge Growden, the longest-serving president of the Anchorage NAACP and a veteran activist, relaunched the Alaska Black Caucus in 2019 after years of dormancy and quickly turned it into a vital anti-racist institution and hub around which to organize community dialogues. Under her stewardship, the Alaska Black

CONCLUSION

Rallying on the Delaney Park Strip in downtown Anchorage, summer of 2020. Photo by Jovell Rennie.

Caucus has once again emerged as "the premier organization that champions the lives of the BIPOC community." According to Hodge Growden, the national reckoning that ensued after the murder of George Floyd "led to a seat at the table" for many who had been formerly marginalized. She is presently at work with allies to establish the Alaska Black Caucus Equity Center, a space to address inequities in economics, education, justice, and health among Alaska's Black and Indigenous populations.[23]

Celeste Hodge Growden and countless others who have participated in and led rallies, memorials, and marches over the past several years reveal a generation of Black Alaskans committed to social justice. These individuals carry on a legacy of activism and a belief that the Alaska they live in today might still be better than the one they inherited, even amid a strident backlash against their efforts from a vocal contingent of community members and elected officials. This book has endeavored to highlight these modern-day activists as well as honor the contributions of the men and women who made their mark on Alaska decades and generations earlier through a variety of pursuits, from whaling to law, mining to the military, working-class jobs to professional ones.

Despite the diversity of lived experience that the figures in this study have had, they have all too often been left out of Alaska's history. Or at best they might be found at the margins. George Anderson, editor of Alaska's first Black newspaper, the *Alaska Spotlight*, may have overstated the case when he proclaimed that his adopted home state constituted a "frontier in every respect, with all of the opportunities and more, that were ever offered [to the] pioneers of other days." But for many, the opportunities were at least as real as the limitations. And understanding the limits and obstacles faced by Black Alaskans—but more importantly, the freedom they seized—provides a richer and more complete history of the forty-ninth state. It reminds us that Black history is American history and that Black Lives Matter in every state, city, and town. The African diaspora has had an impact on every corner of the United States, even if the stories are little known. This book has put a spotlight on a few of the more compelling stories of Black history in the northwesternmost corner of all, Alaska.[24]

NOTES

INTRODUCTION

1 For a few examples, note the recent explosion of reality of television that has garnered millions of viewers, including the Discovery Channel's *Alaska: The Last Frontier*, *Alaskan Bush People*, *Bering Sea Gold*, *Deadliest Catch*, and *Gold Rush: Alaska*, *Ice Road Truckers*; and MTV's *Slednecks*.
2 This book has adopted the capitalization of the following terms throughout the text to recognize and signify racial identity and its centrality to the American narrative: Black, Indigenous, and Native (when used in reference to the Alaska Native population). In doing so, *Black Lives in Alaska* joins a host of other publications and adheres to the updated stylistic recommendations of the *Chicago Manual of Style*, the Modern Language Association, and the Associated Press. We also maintain usage of *African American* in the text, primarily to reduce redundant phrasing and in recognition that not all who identify as Black also identify as African American and vice versa.
3 Walter Prescott Webb, "American West: Perpetual Mirage," *Harper's Magazine*, May 1957, 30.
4 See Quintard Taylor, "The Emergence of Black Communities in the Pacific Northwest," *Journal of Negro History* 64, no. 4 (1979): 342–51; Quintard Taylor, "The Great Migration: The Afro-American Communities of Seattle and Portland during the 1940s," *Arizona and the West* 23, no. 2 (1981): 109–26; and Quintard Taylor, *The Forging of a Black Community in Seattle* (Seattle: University of Washington Press, 1994). For additional studies on Black settlement in the Pacific Northwest, see Dwayne A. Mack, *Black Spokane: The Civil Rights Struggle in the Inland Northwest* (Norman: University of Oklahoma Press, 2014); Stuart

John McElderry, "The Problem of the Color Line: Civil Rights and Racial Ideology in Portland, Oregon, 1944–1965" (PhD diss., University of Oregon, 1998); and Stuart John McElderry, "Building a West Coast Ghetto: African-American Housing in Portland, 1910–1960," *Pacific Northwest Quarterly* 92, no. 3 (2001): 137–48. See also Herbert Ruffin, *Uninvited Neighbors: African Americans in Silicon Valley, 1769–1990* (Norman: University of Oklahoma Press, 2014); and Matthew C. Whitaker, *Race Work: The Rise of Civil Rights in the Urban West* (Lincoln: University of Nebraska Press, 2004).

5   See Douglas Flamming, *African Americans in the West* (Santa Barbara, CA: ABC-CLIO, 2009); and Herbert G. Ruffin II and Dwayne A. Mack, eds., *Freedom's Racial Frontier: African Americans in the Twenty-First Century West* (Norman: University of Oklahoma Press, 2018). While the editors did not include an essay on Black history in Alaska, they did include a biographical sketch on Blanche McSmith, who is discussed in this book.

6   For other foundational works on Black history in the American West that have informed this study, see Albert Broussard, *Expectations of Equality: A History of Black Westerners* (Hoboken, NJ: Wiley Blackwell, 2012); Lawrence de Graaf, Kevin Mulroy, and Quintard Taylor, eds., *Seeking Eldorado: African Americans in California* (Seattle: University of Washington Press, 2001); and Robert O. Self, *American Babylon: Race and the Struggle for Postwar Oakland* (Princeton, NJ: Princeton University Press, 2005).

7   On civil rights in Alaska, see Everett Louis Overstreet, *Black on a Background of White: A Chronicle of Afro-Americans' Involvement in America's Last Frontier, Alaska* (Fairbanks: Alaska Black Caucus, 1988); and Ian C. Hartman, "'A Bonanza for Blacks?' Limits and Opportunities for African Americans in the Urban North," in *Imagining Anchorage: The Making of America's Northernmost Metropolis*, ed. James R. Barnett and Ian C. Hartman (Fairbanks: University of Alaska Press, 2018), 357–74.

8   Claus-M Naske and Herman E. Slotkin, *Alaska: A History* (Norman: University of Oklahoma Press, 2014). The text remains among the most widely cited general academic history of Alaska in circulation.

9   These include Harry Ritter's *Alaska's History, Revised Edition: The People, Land, and Events of the North Country* (Portland, OR: Alaska Northwest Books, 2020); and Stephen Haycox, *Alaska: An American Colony* (Seattle: University of Washington Press, 2006). The essays in Stephen W. Haycox and Mary Childers Mangusso, eds. *An Alaska Anthology: Interpreting the Past* (Seattle: University of Washington Press, 1996), include a few authors, however, who do note Black participation in the Aleutian theater of World War II and on the construction of the Alaska Highway. Walter Borneman makes one mention of Black troops on the Alaska Highway in his widely distributed treatment, *Alaska: Saga of a Bold Land* (New York: HarperCollins, 2003), 339.

10 Quintard Taylor, *In Search of the Racial Frontier: African Americans in the American West, 1528–1990* (New York: W. W. Norton, 1998), 22. On additional scholarship that has informed this study, see Andrew Weise, *Places of Their*

Own: African American Suburbanization in the Twentieth Century (Chicago: University of Chicago Press, 2004); Richard Rothstein, *The Color of Law: A Forgotten History of How Our Government Segregated America* (New York: W. W. Norton, 2017); Thomas J. Sugrue, *The Origins of the Urban Crisis: Race and Inequality in Postwar Detroit* (Princeton, NJ: Princeton University Press, 2005); Joan Singler, Jean Durning, Bettylou Valentine, and Maid Adams, *Seattle in Black and White: The Congress of Racial Equality and the Fight for Equal Opportunity* (Seattle: University of Washington Press, 2011); and Laura Redford, "The Intertwined History of Class and Race Segregation in Los Angeles," *Journal of Planning History* 16, no. 4 (2017): 305–22.

11 This casts the Alaskan cities of Anchorage and Fairbanks in a similar context to many of the western cities explored in *Freedom's Racial Frontier*. One central finding of the essays in that volume, according to Ruffin and Mack, is "African American life and culture made its greatest impact on the western United States during World War II and the postwar period." See Ruffin and Mack, *Freedom's Racial Frontier*, 10.

12 On the Black radical tradition on the West Coast, see Aaron Dixon, *My People Are Rising: Memoir of a Black Panther Party Captain* (Chicago: Haymarket Books, 2012); Laura Pulido, *Black, Brown, Yellow, and Left: Radical Activism in Los Angeles* (Berkeley: University of California Press, 2006); Robyn C. Spencer, *The Revolution Has Come: Black Power, Gender, and the Black Panther Party in Oakland* (Durham, NC: Duke University Press, 2016); and Quintard Taylor, "The Civil Rights Movement in the American West: Black Protest in Seattle, 1960–1970," *Journal of Negro History* 80, no. 1 (1995): 1–14.

13 Alaska's per capita income and median household income have consistently ranked in the top ten wealthiest states for the last forty years. Alaska has been among the top five wealthiest states many of those years.

14 "Proletarianization" is a Marxist concept and term that has been deployed by a generation of labor historians to describe one's relationship to work, notably wage labor. Joe William Trotter Jr.'s magisterial work, *Black Milwaukee: The Making of an Industrial Proletariat, 1915–1945* (Urbana: University of Illinois Press, 1985), remains among the strongest treatments of the topic.

15 Eric Sandberg, with contributions from Eddie Hunsinger and Sara Whitney, "A History of Alaska Population Settlement," Alaska Department of Labor and Workforce Development, April 2013, 8. While the US Census records a white population of Alaska at just over 50 percent in 1910, it would decline slightly up to the 1940 census. Since the 1940 census, Alaska has had a white-majority population.

16 Historian Kent Blansett articulated, in broad terms, the goals of the Red Power movement and, implicitly, what separated it from the Black freedom struggle. While his assessment is not entirely applicable to this study, it is nevertheless instructive. See Kent Blansett, *A Journey to Freedom: Richard Oakes, Alcatraz, and the Red Power Movement* (New Haven: Yale University Press, 2018), 4–10.

17 Greg Williams, "Race and Ethnicity in Alaska," *Alaska Economic Trends*, Research and Demographic Unit for the Alaska Department of Labor and Workforce Development, October 2011.
18 Juliana Hu Pegues, *Space-Time Colonialism: Alaska's Indigenous and Asian Entanglements* (Chapel Hill: University of North Carolina Press, 2021), 13–14.
19 On Alaska Native activism, see Maria Sháa Tláa Williams, ed., *The Alaska Native Reader* (Durham, NC: Duke University Press, 2009), especially pt. 2, "Empire: Processing Colonization"; Peter Metcalfe, *A Dangerous Idea: The Alaska Native Brotherhood and the Struggle for Indigenous Rights* (Fairbanks: University of Alaska Press, 2014); and William L. Iggiagruk Hensley, *Fifty Miles from Tomorrow: A Memoir of Alaska and the Real People* (New York: Farrar, Straus & Giroux, 2010).
20 For scholarship on coalitional organizing and activism in the Pacific Northwest, see Chris Friday, *Organizing Asian-American Labor: The Pacific Coast Canned-Salmon Industry, 1870–1942* (Philadelphia: Temple University Press, 1995); and Michael Schulze-Oechtering, "The Alaska Cannery Workers Association and the Ebbs and Flows of Struggle: Manong Knowledge, Blues Epistemology, and Racial Cross-Fertilization," *Amerasia Journal* 42, no. 2 (2016): 23–48.
21 For recent demographic data on Alaska, see Hunter Schwarz, "In Most States, Women Outnumber Men," *Washington Post*, November 19, 2014. Of the fifty states, Alaska had the greatest percentage of male residents, at 52.4 percent. For a historical analysis on gender demographics in Alaska, see Lael Morgan, *Gold Time Girls: Of the Alaska/Yukon Gold Rush* (Kenmore, WA: Epicenter Press, 1998), 15–17. For a view of Alaska's gender demographics in the oil and gas industry, see Carla Williams, *Wildcat Women: Narratives of Women Breaking Ground in Alaska's Oil and Gas Industry* (Fairbanks: University of Alaska Press, 2018).
22 At present the United States military counts a greater number of self-identified women than at any point in its history, a figure of 16 percent. See Lori Robinson and Michael O'Hanlon, *Women Warriors: The Ongoing Story of Integrating and Diversifying the American Armed Forces*, report prepared for Brookings, May 2020, https://www.brookings.edu/essay/women-warriors-the-ongoing-story-of-integrating-and-diversifying-the-armed-forces.
23 Quintard Taylor and Shirley Ann Wilson Moore, eds., *African American Women Confront the West, 1600–2000* (Norman: University of Oklahoma Press, 2008), 17.
24 Historians have long noted the role that women have played in predominantly male spaces. For some foundational works on the topic, see Laura E. Woodworth-Ney, *Women in the American West* (Santa Barbara, CA: ABC-CLIO, 2008); Susan Armitage and Elizabeth Jameson, eds., *The Women's West* (Norman: University of Oklahoma Press, 1987); Susan Armitage and Elizabeth Jameson, eds., *Writing the Range: Race, Class, and Culture in the Women's West* (Norman: University of Oklahoma Press, 1997); and Anne M. Butler,

Daughters of Joy, Sisters of Misery: Prostitutes in the American West, 1865–90 (Urbana: University of Illinois Press, 1987). On women's history in Alaska, see Morgan, *Good Time Girls*. Notably, these books have emphasized white women and have largely ignored the contributions and presence of Black women.

25 The authors have presented much of the research from chapters 4 and 5 in two earlier publications. The reader may wish to consult Hartman, "'Bonanza for Blacks,'" 357–74; and Ian C. Hartman and David Reamer, "A 'Far North Dixie Land': Black Settlement, Discrimination, and Community in Urban Alaska," *Western Historical Quarterly* (Summer 2019): 1–20.

26 For the foundational studies on Alaska Native claims activism and the context for the Alaska Native Claims Settlement Act of 1971, see Donald Craig Mitchell, *Sold American: The Story of Alaska Natives and Their Land, 1867–1917* (Fairbanks: University of Alaska Press, 2003); and Donald Craig Mitchell, *Take My Land, Take My Life: The Story Congress's Historic Settlement of Alaska Native Land Claims, 1960–1971* (Fairbanks: University of Alaska Press, 2001).

27 Chapters 4 and 5, with their emphasis on urban Alaska and Black activism, are informed by works on the Black freedom struggle in the cities of the American West. A few of the foundational studies are Douglas Flamming, *Bound for Freedom: Black Los Angeles in Jim Crow America* (Berkeley: University of California Press, 2005); Josh Sides, *L.A. City Limits: African American Los Angeles from the Great Depression to the Present* (Berkeley: University of California, 2006); and Self, *American Babylon*.

28 Our analysis is indebted to recent work on the topic, including Elizabeth Hinton, *From the War on Poverty to the War on Crime: The Making of Mass Incarceration in America* (Cambridge: Harvard University Press, 2016); Khalil Gibran Muhammad, *The Condemnation of Blackness: Race, Crime, and the Making of Urban America* (Cambridge: Harvard University Press, 2019); and Julilly Kohler-Hausmann, *Getting Tough: Welfare and Imprisonment in the 1970s America* (Princeton, NJ: Princeton University Press, 2019).

1. BLACK EXPLORATION, LABOR, AND TRAVEL

1 A *bark* is a ship with three or more masts that was used for whaling voyages in the mid- to late eighteenth century.

2 Gordon R. Newell, ed., *The H. W. McCurdy Marine History of the Pacific Northwest* (Seattle: Superior Publishing Company, 1966), 147.

3 Comprehensive treatments of whaling include such studies as Eric Jay Dolin, *Leviathan: The History of Whaling in America* (New York: W. W. Norton, 2007); and Richard Ellis, *The Great Sperm Whale: A Natural History of the Ocean's Most Magnificent and Mysterious Creature* (Lawrence: University Press of Kansas, 2011).

4 W. Jeffrey Bolster, *Black Jacks: African American Seamen in the Age of Sail* (Cambridge: Harvard University Press, 1998).

5 For two of the most notable works to promulgate the thesis, see Rayford Whittingham Logan, *The Betrayal of the Negro: From Rutherford B. Hayes to Woodrow Wilson* (1954; repr., New York: Da Capo Press, 1997); and Eric Foner, *Reconstruction: America's Unfinished Revolution, 1863–1877* (1987; repr., New York: Perennial Classics, 2014).
6 E. Berkeley Tompkins, "Black Ahab: William T. Shorey Whaling Master," *California Historical Quarterly* 51 (Spring 1972): 75–84; "William T. Shorey, Veteran Mariner, Dies," *Oakland Tribune*, April 15, 1919, 3.
7 On Absalom Boston, see John B. Forbes, "Story of Black Whalers at Cold Spring Museum," *New York Times*, September 17, 1982, nytimes.com/1982/09/17/arts/story-of-Black-whalers-at-cold-spring-museum.html.
8 For more on African American history in New Bedford, see the Paul Cuffe collection at the New Bedford Whaling Museum. For a brief introduction to Cuffe, see Akeia Benard, "Who Was Paul Cuffe," New Bedford Whaling Museum, February 22, 2018, https://museudabaleia-newbedford.org/explore/paul-cuffe/who-was-captain-paul-cuffe. On the history of New Bedford and its relationship to whaling and the lives of escaped slaves and free people of color, see Kathryn Grover, *The Fugitive's Gibraltar: Escaping Slaves and Abolitionism in New Bedford, Massachusetts* (Boston: University of Massachusetts Press, 2001). On Black whalers and seamen in the years before the Civil War, see Martha S. Putney, *Black Sailors: Afro-American Merchant Seamen and Whalemen prior to the Civil War* (New York: Greenwood Press, 1987).
9 Earl F. Mulderink III, *New Bedford's Civil War* (New York: Fordham University Press, 2014), 39–43.
10 Bolster, *Black Jacks*, 179.
11 Grover, *Fugitive's Gibraltar*, 1.
12 Kathryn Grover, *Fugitive Slaves in Alaska: Phase One Research Report* (Washington, DC: National Park Service, September 2001), 7. For more on Black involvement in the whaling industry, see W. Jeffrey Bolster, "'To Feel Like a Man': Black Seamen in the Northern States, 1800–1860," *Journal of American History* 76, no. 4 (March 1990): 1173–99; and James Farr, "Slow Boat to Nowhere: The Multi-Racial Crews of the American Whaling Industry," *Journal of Negro History* 68, no. 2 (Spring 1983): 159–70.
13 John Bockstoce, *Whales, Ice, and Men: The History of Whaling in the Western Arctic* (Seattle: University of Washington Press, 1986), 23.
14 Bockstoce, *Whales, Ice, and Men*, 24.
15 Grover, "Fugitive Slaves in Alaska," 22.
16 New Bedford Whaling Museum, Dennis Woods Abstracts, vol. 2: 1845–53, 31; hereafter cited as "Woods Abstracts."
17 Woods Abstracts, vol. 2: 1845–53, 31.
18 For whalers in San Francisco during the gold rush, see Sucheng Chan, "A People of Exceptional Character: Ethnic Diversity, Nativism, and Racism in the California Gold Rush," in *Rooted in Barbarous Soil: People, Culture, and Community in Gold Rush California*, ed. Kevin Starr and Richard J. Orsi (Berkeley:

University of California Press, 2000), 53. On Black whalers in Hawai'i, see Eric Jay Dolin, *Leviathan: The History of Whaling in America* (New York: W. W. Norton, 2008), 229–30; and Miles M. Jackson, *They Followed the Trade Winds: African Americans in Hawai'i* (Honolulu: University of Hawai'i at Manoa, Department of Sociology, 2004), 1–23.

19 Grover, "Fugitive Slaves in Alaska," 22.
20 Julie Roy Jeffrey, *The Great Silent Army of Abolitionism: Ordinary Women in the Antislavery Movement* (Chapel Hill: University of North Carolina Press, 1998), 10, 185, 189.
21 Woods Abstracts, vol. 2: 1845–53, 31.
22 Grover, "Fugitive Slaves in Alaska," 11–13.
23 Grover, "Fugitive Slaves in Alaska," 13.
24 On the intersections between whaling and the Underground Railroad, see Eric Foner, *Gateway to Freedom: The Hidden History of the Underground Railroad* (New York: W. W. Norton, 2016), 4, 60. On the impact of slave raiding on the maritime industries, see David S. Cecelsky, *The Waterman's Song: Slavery and Freedom in Maritime North Carolina* (Chapel Hill: University of North Carolina Press, 2012).
25 Grover, "Fugitive Slaves in Alaska," 9.
26 Bolster, *Black Jacks*, 112.
27 J. H. Newton, "Our Heroes of '61: A Series of Tabloid Reviews of the Dramatic Civil War Experiences of the Last Survivors of the New Bedford, G.A.R." *New Bedford Evening Standard*, May 26, 1932, 17.
28 Livingston F. Jones, *A Study of the Thlingets of Alaska* (New York: Fleming H. Revell Company, 1914), 210.
29 Herbert M. Frisby, "Frisby Called 'No-Good White Man' in Kotzebue," *Baltimore Afro-American*, September 9, 1944, 1.
30 George Harper, "Blacks in Alaska History," *Heritage: Quarterly Newsletter of the Office of History and Archaeology* 31 (January–March 1987): 3–4; Blacks in Alaska History Project records, box 6, folder 34, Archives and Special Collections, University of Alaska Anchorage / Alaska Pacific University Consortium Library (hereafter UAA/APU Consortium Library).
31 Charles Hallock, *Our New Alaska; or, The Seward Purchase Vindicated* (New York: Forest & Stream Publishing, 1886), 33.
32 Hallock, *Our New Alaska*, 63.
33 Hallock, *Our New Alaska*, 33.
34 US Census, 1900, ccxv, 492, 257, 118.
35 Kathryn Grover, "Whalemen of Color in Point Hope and Jabbertown," *Report Prepared for Alaska Affiliated Areas, National Park Service*, Alaska Region (December 2003), 17. Grover found statistical information in the Department of the Interior, Census Office, *Report on Population and Resources of Alaska at the Eleventh Census, 1890* (1893; repr., New York: Norman Ross Publishing, 1994).
36 Grover, "Whalemen of Color in Point Hope and Jabbertown," 30–31.

37 Grover, "Whalemen of Color in Point Hope and Jabbertown," 42–45.
38 Bockstoce, *Whales, Ice, and Men*, 189.
39 Bockstoce, *Whales, Ice, and Men*, 191.
40 Walther Noble Burns, *A Year with a Whaler* (New York: Outing Publishing Company, 1913), 166.
41 Burns, *Year with a Whaler*, 167.
42 On the collapse of the whaling industry, see Everett S. Allen, *Children of Light: The Rise and Fall of New Bedford Whaling and the Death of the Arctic Fleet* (Boston: Little, Brown, 1973); Robert Webb, *On the Northwest: Commercial Whaling in the Pacific Northwest, 1790–1967* (Vancouver: University of British Columbia Press, 1988); and Eric Jay Dolin, *Leviathan: The History of Whaling in America* (New York: W. W. Norton, 2007), 309–69.
43 See Edward Ball, *Slaves in the Family* (New York: Farrar, Straus & Giroux, 1998).
44 Joseph Skerrett Jr., "Michael Healy: Mullato [sic] Sailor," *Negro History Bulletin* 41, no. 5 (1978): 884, 887, 892.
45 Dennis L. Noble and Truman R. Strobridge, *Captain "Hell Roaring" Mike Healy: From American Slave to Arctic Hero* (Gainesville: University Press of Florida), 1–15.
46 James O'Toole, "Racial Identity and the Case of Captain Michael Healy, USRCS, Parts 1–3," *Prologue Magazine: Quarterly of the National Archives* 29, no. 3 (Fall 1997): pt. 3. See also James M. O'Toole, *Passing for White: Race, Religion, and the Healy Family, 1820–1920* (Amherst: University of Massachusetts Press, 2003).
47 Noble and Strobridge, *Captain "Hell Roaring" Mike Healy*, 138–46.
48 William Edward Brown, *The History of the Central Brooks Range: Gaunt Beauty, Tenuous Life* (Fairbanks: University of Alaska Press, 2007), 40–42.
49 Noble and Strobridge, *Captain "Hell Roaring" Mike Healy*, 8–10.
50 O'Toole, "Racial Identity," pt. 3.
51 Steve Henrikson, "The 1882 Bombardments: New Developments," *Proceedings of the Alaska Historical Society Annual Meeting, October 4–6, 1999* (Anchorage: Anchorage Historical Society, 2000), 60–75.
52 Rosita Kaahani Worl, "Alaska," in *The Oxford Handbook of American Indian History*, ed. Frederick E. Hoxie (New York: Oxford University Press, 2016), 306–8.
53 On US expansion into the Pacific and the development of an empire, see Daniel Immerwaher, *How to Hide an Empire: A History of the Greater United States* (New York: Farrar, Straus & Giroux, 2019).
54 Noble and Strobridge, *Captain "Hell Roaring" Mike Healy*, 157.
55 O'Toole, "Racial Identity," pts. 2–3.
56 Noble and Strobridge, *Captain "Hell Roaring" Mike Healy*, 253–66.
57 Douglas Kroll, *A Coastguardsman's History of the US Coast Guard* (Annapolis, MD: Naval Institute Press, 2010), 52–55.
58 O'Toole, "Racial Identity," pts. 2–3.
59 "How Shipwrecked Americans Were Treated by Captain Evans," *San Francisco Examiner*, August 14, 1892.

60 Everett Jenkins Jr., *Pan-African Chronology II: A Comprehensive Reference to the Black Quest for Freedom in Africa, the Americas, Europe, and Asia, 1865–1915* (Jefferson, NC: McFarland, 1998), 200.

2. BLACK IN THE GOLD RUSH ERA

1. On Michael Dempsey, see Andrew Goldstein, "Honoring Melvin Dempsey: Part I," Alaska Historical Society Blog, February 21, 2013, https://alaskahistoricalsociety.org/honoring-melvin-dempsey-part-i; Andrew Goldstein, "Honoring Melvin Dempsey: Part II," Alaska Historical Society Blog, February 25, 2013, https://alaskahistoricalsociety.org/honoring-melvin-dempsey-part-ii.
2. The Klondike Gold Rush occurred amid the financial panic of the 1890s. Many of the men who participated were long out of work, young, and able-bodied. For an effective description of the context, see Howard Blum, *The Floor of Heaven: The True Tale of the Last Frontier and the Yukon Gold Rush* (New York: Broadway Books, 2012), 124–30.
3. For a primary source that details the creation of the Christian Endeavor Society, see Rev. F. E. Clark, DD, *Ways and Means for the Young People's Society of Christian Endeavor* (Boston: D. Lothrop Company, 1890).
4. See Jim Lethcoe and Nancy Lethcoe, *Valdez Gold Rush Trails* (Valdez, AK: Prince William Sound Books, 1996).
5. "Melvin Dempsey May Be Dead," *Valdez Daily Prospector*, September 11, 1915, 4. There is a dispute over the circumstances surrounding Dempsey's death. Members of his family later claimed that he left Alaska near the end of his life and passed away in Battle Creek, Michigan, as late as the 1920s. See Goldstein, "Honoring Melvin Dempsey: Part II."
6. For firsthand accounts on the gold rush, see Tappan Adney, *The Klondike Stampede* (Vancouver: University of British Columbia Press, 1995); and Jack London, *Klondike Tales* (New York: Modern Library Classics, 2001). Naske and Slotkin provide an overview of events in *Alaska*, 123–56. For a strong treatment of the gold rush, see Pierre Burton, *The Klondike Fever: The Life and Death of the Last Great Gold Rush* (New York: Basic Books, 2003).
7. For a treatment of the Chilkoot Trail, see Robert J. Friesen, *The Chilkoot Pass and the Great Gold Rush of 1898* (Ottawa, Canada: National Historic Parks and Sites Branch, 1981), 40–62.
8. "Buffalo Soldiers in Skagway," National Park Service, last updated September 25, 2019, https://www.nps.gov/klgo/learn/historyculture/buffalo-soldiers.htm. For a complete recounting of the military's presence in Alaska, including during the gold rush, see Lyman L. Woodman, *Duty Station North: The US Army in Alaska and Western Canada, 1867–1987*, vol. 1: *1867–1917* (Anchorage: Alaska Historical Society, 1996–97).
9. On the Fourteenth Infantry, see the National Park Service, "The 14th Infantry in Northern Lynn Canal," last updated December 20, 2016, https://www.nps.gov/klgo/learn/historyculture/14th-infantry.htm.

10 James N. Leiker, "Black Soldiers at Fort Hays, Kansas, 1867–69: A Study in Civilian and Military Violence," in *Buffalo Soldiers in the West: A Black Soldiers Anthology*, ed. Bruce A. Glasrud and Michael N. Searles (College Station: Texas A&M University Press, 2007), 163–64.

11 On the establishment of the postwar Black regiments, see Bruce A. Glasrud, "Western Black Soldiers since the Buffalo Soldiers: A Review of the Literature," in Glasrud and Searles, *Buffalo Soldiers in the West*, 5–6.

12 William T. Bowers, William M. Hammond, and George L. MacGarrigle, *Black Soldier, White Army: The 24th Infantry in Korea* (Washington, DC: Center for Military History, United States Army, 1996), 5.

13 Bowers, Hammond, and MacGarrigle, *Black Soldier, White Army*, 6.

14 Bowers, Hammond, and MacGarrigle, *Black Soldier, White Army*, 6–7.

15 Willard B. Gatewood Jr., *"Smoked Yankees" and the Struggle for Empire: Letters from Negro Soldiers, 1898–1902* (Fayetteville: University of Arkansas Press, 1987), 6.

16 For the classic treatment of the topic, see Reginald Horsman, *Race and Manifest Destiny: Origins of American Racial Anglo-Saxonism* (Cambridge: Harvard University Press, 1981).

17 "The Immune Regiments: The President Has Named Six Colonels Who Will Command the Forces," *New York Times*, May 21, 1898, 2.

18 Quoted in Gregory Paynter Shine, "Respite from War: Buffalo Soldiers at Vancouver Barracks, 1899–1900," *Oregon Historical Quarterly* 107, no. 2 (Summer 2006): 200.

19 Gatewood, *"Smoked Yankees,"* 6–16.

20 For a brief history of the Twenty-Fourth Infantry in the late-nineteenth and early-twentieth centuries, see Bowers, Hammond, and MacGarrigle, *Black Soldier, White Army*, 3–26.

21 "Speech of Frederick Douglass," *Liberator*, July 6, 1863; Charlotte Forten, "Life on the Sea Islands, Part II," *Atlantic Monthly* 13 (June 1864): 666–76.

22 See Shine, "Respite from War," 196–227; and "Buffalo Soldiers in Skagway." For a complete recounting of the military's presence in Alaska, including the during the gold rush, see Woodman, *Duty Station North*, vol. 1. For an informative study on Skagway during the gold rush years, see Catherine Holder Spude, *Saloons, Prostitutes, and Temperance in Alaska Territory* (Norman: University of Oklahoma Press, 2015). For the most definitive and recent account of Company L Twenty-Fourth Infantry in Alaska, see Brian G. Shellum, *Buffalo Soldiers in Alaska: Company L Twenty-Fourth Infantry* (Lincoln: University of Nebraska Press, 2021).

23 For firsthand accounts on the gold rush, see Tappan Adney, *The Klondike Stampede* (Vancouver: University of British Columbia Press, 1995); and Jack London, *Klondike Tales* (New York: Modern Library Classics, 2001). Naske and Slotkin provide an overview of events in *Alaska*, 123–56. For a strong treatment of the gold rush, see Pierre Burton, *The Klondike Fever: The Life and Death of the Last Great Gold Rush* (New York: Basic Books, 2003).

24 George Harper, "Photo Exhibit Honors Role of Blacks in Alaska Gold Rush History," *Anchorage Daily News*, February 3, 1997, F2.
25 For a scholarly retelling of Smith's exploits, see Catherine Holder Spude, *"That Fiend in Hell": Soapy Smith in Legend* (Norman: University of Oklahoma Press, 2012).
26 On the development of Skagway, see Robert L. S. Spude, *Skagway, District of Alaska, 1884–1912*, Occasional Paper No. 36 (Fairbanks: Anthropology and Historic Preservation, Cooperative Park Studies Unit, University of Alaska, 1983).
27 The University of Kentucky has compiled a list of Black servicemen in Alaska in their online database, Notable Kentucky African Americans (NKAA). For Skagway, see "Kentucky African American Servicemen in Skagway, Alaska," NKAA Database, University of Kentucky, last updated July 7, 2018, nkaa.uky.edu/nkaa/items/show/2074.
28 Bowers, Hammond, and MacGarrigle, *Black Soldier, White Army*, 7.
29 "Buffalo Soldiers in Skagway." See also "Costly Rock," *Daily Alaskan*, April 4, 1901.
30 C. Spude, *Saloons, Prostitutes, and Temperance*, 148–53.
31 "Objections Arise to Colored Men in Y.M.C.A," *Daily Alaskan* (Skagway), August 16, 1900, 1.
32 Karl Gurcke, "Southeast in Sepia: The Race-Based Skaguay Y.M.C.A. Controversy," *Juneau Empire*, February 23, 2017, juneauempire.com/life/southeast-in-sepia-the-race-based-skaguay-y-m-c-a-controversy.
33 George Harper, "Cpl. Benjamin Green: Black History Month," *Anchorage Daily News*, February 21, 1997, F2.
34 David B. Tewkesbury, "Saturday's Dragline," *Fairbanks Daily News-Miner*, March 7, 1942, 1; Shellum, *Buffalo Soldiers in Alaska*, 244.
35 "Alaska News Notes," *Daily Alaska Dispatch*, January 27, 1911.
36 Joan Skilbred, "William T. Ewing, 1853–1923," Alaska Mining Hall of Fame Foundation, 2017, alaskamininghalloffame.org/inductees/ewing.php. See also George Harper, "Gold Miner Shares Fortune," *Anchorage Daily News*, February 12, 1997, C2.
37 "Henry McDame—Black Prospector," *Canada West Magazine* (Fall 1975): 31–37; George H. Junne Jr., *The History of Blacks in Canada: A Selectively Annotated Bibliography* (Westport, CT: Greenwood Press, 2003), 246.
38 Tom Kizzia, *Cold Mountain Path: The Ghost Town Decades of McCarthy-Kennecott, Alaska, 1938–1983* (McCarthy, AK: Porphyry Press, 2021), 30–31.
39 Margaret Merritt, *Roshier H. Creecy: A Black Man's Search for Freedom and Prosperity in the Koyukuk Gold Fields of Alaska* (Dubai, UAE: RDS Publications, 2019).
40 Dick Tordoff, *People of the Koyukuk Regions* (Fairbanks: Project Jukebox, University of Alaska, 1999), 53.
41 "Koyukuk Miner Missing," *Anchorage Daily Times*, January 18, 1928, 4.
42 "Elsewhere in Alaska," *Anchorage Daily Times*, January 23, 1928, 3.
43 Tordoff, *People of the Koyukuk Regions*, 20.

44 "Pioneer Nome Resident Dies," *Anchorage Daily Times*, January 2, 1948, 5.
45 "Former Resident of This City Will Probably Lose Her Life as Result of Exposure," *Iditarod Pioneer*, February 19, 1910.
46 "Preston Sentenced to Serve Ten Days," *Fairbanks Daily Times*, August 21, 1906, 3; George Harper, "Preston a Mysterious Man," *Anchorage Daily News*, February 22, 1997, D2.
47 Quoted in George Harper, "Violence Took Its Toll in Frontier Alaska," *Anchorage Daily News*, February 28, 1997, F2.
48 "A Lively Law Suit," *Fort Wrangel (AK) News*, August 10, 1898, 1.
49 Cash J. Darrell, "Eagle on the Yukon," *Alaska Life*, December 1946, 9. For more on the Eagle and Fort Egbert Historic District, see Anne Shinkwin, Elizabeth Andrews, Russell Sackett, and Mary Kroul, *Fort Egbert and the Eagle Historic District: Results of Archaeological and Historic Research, Summer 1977*, Technical Report 2 (Anchorage: Bureau of Land Management, June 1978), https://archive.org/details/BLM-Alaska-TR-2.
50 M.D.K. Weimer, *M.D.K. Weimer's True Story of the Alaska Gold Fields* (N.p.p., 1903), 156; Darrell, "Eagle on the Yukon," 9.
51 Darrell, "Eagle on the Yukon," 9.
52 Weimer, *True Story of the Alaska Gold Fields*, 156.
53 "Miss Walton's Quest," *Nome Gold Digger* 1, no. 3, November 8, 1899, 4.
54 "Former Bridgeton Woman Now Richer than Hetty Green," *Philadelphia Inquirer*, April 17, 1904, 45.
55 "A Colored Lady Financier," *Seattle Republican*, April 24, 1903, 2.
56 "Personal," *Seattle Republican*, January 11, 1901, 3; William Loren Katz, *The Black West: A Documentary and Pictorial History of the African American Role in the Westward Expansion of the United States* (New York: Touchstone, 1996), 245.
57 "Negress Returns from Alaska with a Million," *Nome Pioneer Press*, March 7, 1908, 3.
58 "Lucille Hunter," Hidden History: Black History of the Yukon, Yukon Archives, 2007, accessed October 15, 2019, tc.gov.yk.ca/archives/hiddenhistory/en/women.html.
59 Weimer, *True Story of the Alaska Gold Fields*, 156.
60 George Harper, "Woman Gets Rich during Gold Rush," *Anchorage Daily News*, February 16, 1997, K2.
61 C. Spude, *Saloons, Temperance, and Prostitution*, 110. For more on Silks, see Clark Secrest, *Hell's Belles: Prostitution, Vice, and Crime in Early Denver, with a Biography of Sam Howe, Frontier Lawman*, rev. ed. (Boulder: University of Colorado Press, 2002), 231.
62 "Fistic Stars in Town," *Daily Alaskan*, September 6, 1899, 1.
63 George Harper, "Chicago Ed: Gold Rush Con," *Anchorage Daily News*, February 15, 1997, E2.
64 Rolfe G. Buzzell, ed., "John Miscovich Interview 5, August 5, 1993," in *Flat and Iditarod, 1993-1995: Oral History Interviews*, BLM-Alaska Open File Report 66

(Anchorage: US Department of the Interior, Bureau of Land Management; State of Alaska, Department of Natural Resources, 1997), 81.
65 Buzzell, "John Miscovich Interview 5, August 5, 1993," 82.
66 Buzzell, "John Miscovich Interview 4, July 6, 1993," 64.
67 "Miss Tootsie Braved the Rugged Life of the Gold," *Anchorage Daily News*, February 11, 1997, D2.
68 Buzzell, "John Miscovich Interview 5, August 5, 1993," 82.
69 Buzzell, "John Miscovich Interview 5, August 5, 1993," 81.
70 "Miss Tootsie Braved the Rugged Life of the Gold."
71 Annaliese Jacobs Bateman, *Regulated Vice: A History of Seward's Red Light District, 1914–1954*, report prepared for National Park Service (Anchorage: Alaska Support Office, July 2002, 106–7).
72 Lillian Mabel Taylor, diary, January 1–March 14, 1905, "A Life in Yukon," box 7, series 13, folder 18, accessed in George Harper, "Blacks in Alaska History," *Heritage: Quarterly Newsletter of the Office of History and Archaeology* 31 (January–March 1987).
73 Clifford C. Hancock, "Alaska: Unalaska and Other Points of Interest," *Colored American Magazine*, August 1903, 555.
74 Hancock, "Alaska," 559.
75 Hancock, "Alaska," 561.

3. WORLD WAR ERA AND A NEW ALASKA

1 "Mrs. John N. Conna," obituary, *Seattle Republican*, July 26, 1907, 7.
2 Conna's grandson wrote about him at length for HistoryLink, Washington State's online historical encyclopedia. Douglas Q. Barnett, "Conna, John N. (1836–1921)," HistoryLink, October 28, 2004, https://www.historylink.org/File/7111.
3 United States Department of Commerce, Bureau of the Census, Thirteenth Census of the United States, 1910 (Washington, DC), 576, 592.
4 "Their One Best Bet," *Alaska Citizen* (Fairbanks), November 4, 1912, 8.
5 Thomas Bevers's father, William, died in 1919. His death certificate shows Beavers as the spelling of the family's surname. William E. Beavers, Certificate of Death, No. 12341, Danville, Pittsylvania County, VA, filed April 16, 1919, Virginia Death Records, 1912–2014, Ancestry.com. For more on Bevers, see "Thos. S. Bevers Taken Suddenly in Death," *Anchorage Daily Times*, October 5, 1944, 1. Bruce Parham and John Bagoy have researched Thomas Bevers as part of the *Legends and Legacies* project for the Cook Inlet Historical Society; see "Bevers [Beavers], Thomas "Tom": *1889–1944: Fire Chief, Real Estate Investor, and Anchorage City Council Member*," accessed September 21, 2019, https://www.alaskahistory.org/biographies/bevers-beavers-thomas-tom/.
6 "Thos. S. Bevers Taken Suddenly in Death."
7 On the beginnings of Anchorage, see Charles Wohlforth, *From the Shores of Ship Creek: Stories of Anchorage's First 100 Years* (Anchorage: Todd

NOTES TO PAGES 46–50

Communications, 2015); and William H. Wilson, "The Founding of Anchorage: Federal Townbuilding on the Last Frontier," *Pacific Northwest Quarterly* 58 (July 1967): 130–41.

8 On Anchorage's Indigenous population, see Suzi Jones, James A. Fall, and Aaron Leggett, eds., *Dena'inaq' Huch'ulyeshi: The Dena'ina Way of Living* (Fairbanks: University of Alaska Press, 2013).

9 The photo is accessible through Alaska's Digital Archives at https://vilda.alaska.edu/digital/collection/cdmg2/id/353/rec/19 and is housed at the Anchorage Museum's General Photograph File, entitled "Baseball team, Anchorage, Alaska, July 4, 1915" (Photo identifier: AMRC-b82-46-14).

10 "Horrock's Team Will Compete in Big Race," *Anchorage Daily Times*, July 1, 1916, 1.

11 "Negress Arrested on Liquor Charge," *Anchorage Daily Times*, January 16, 1918, 1; "Happenings of a Decade Ago," *Anchorage Daily Times*, January 17, 1928, 6.

12 "Ed Walker Dead," *Anchorage Daily Times*, November 4, 1918, 5; David Reamer, "In 1918, a Deadly Outbreak of Influenza Reached Anchorage. Here's How Alaskans Responded," *Anchorage Daily News*, April 19, 2020, adn.com/alaska-life/2020/04/19/in-1918-a-deadly-outbreak-of-influenza-reached-anchorage-heres-how-alaskans-responded.

13 Patrician A. Nolan, ed., *Anchorage Fire Department: 75th Anniversary Yearbook, 1915–1990* (Anchorage: Anchorage Fire Auxiliary, 1990), 76.

14 "Women Crowd Men in Signing for Election," *Anchorage Daily Times*, March 25, 1941, 1. See also "History of Mayors and Assembly Members, 1925–1985"; and "Mayors and Councilman of the City of Anchorage, Alaska, 1925–1985," 2, both from Clerk's Office, Municipality of Anchorage.

15 Minutes, January 6, 1943, Anchorage City Council Minutes. See also "Thomas S. Bevers Buried in City," *Anchorage Daily Times*, October 23, 1944, 3.

16 "Thomas S. Bevers Buried in City," *Anchorage Daily Times*, October 23, 1944, 3.

17 Elizabeth Tower, *Anchorage: From Its Humble Origins as a Railroad Construction Camp* (Kenmore, WA: Epicenter Press, 1999), 32–33. On Christensen's exclusion of the Dena'ina, see Wohlforth, *From the Shores of Ship Creek*; and Wilson, "Founding of Anchorage," 130–41.

18 Memorandum, Charles H. Flory to District Forester, January 6, 1917, 4–5, L Boundaries, Chugach, Ship Creek Area, Christensen's & Ringland's Report and Correspondence [1916], Correspondence Relating to Civilian Conservation Corps (CCC) Activities, ca. 1937–ca. 1942, Record Group 95: Records of the Forest Service, 1870–2008, National Archives and Records Administration, accessed October 23, 2019, catalog.archives.gov/id/71961726.

19 Max Stern, "Article Three: Reporter Signs Up with S.F. Firm to Work in Alaska for Chinese Boss," *Daily News* (San Francisco), September 27–28, 1922. This was a multipart series that Stern wrote to investigate the Alaska salmon industry. See also Stephanie Hinnershitz, *Race, Religion, and Civil Rights: Asian Student on the West Coast* (New Brunswick, NJ: Rutgers University Press, 2015), 74–82.

20 Bruce Nelson, *Workers on the Waterfront: Seamen, Longshoremen, and Unionism in the 1930s* (Urbana: University of Illinois Press, 1988).
21 Frank Jenkins, interviewed by Richard C. Berner, June 28, 1972, Oral History Collection, University of Washington, accessed October 23, 2019, digitalcollections.lib.washington.edu/digital/collection/ohc/id/69.
22 Orlando Miller, *The Frontier in Alaska and the Matanuska Colony* (New Haven, CT: Yale University Press, 1975).
23 Claus-M. Naske, "Blacks Blocked by Bureaucracy," *Alaska Journal* 1, no. 4 (1971): 8–10.
24 David Reamer, "Without Open Arms: Alaska Response to WWII Refugee Immigration Proposals," *Alaska History* 33, no. 1 (2018): 21–23.
25 US Congress, House of Representatives, *Hearings on H.R. 13534, a Bill to Amend the Act of Congress of June 6, 1924, Entitled "An Act for the Protection of the Fisheries of Alaska, and for Other Purposes,"* before the Committee on the Merchant Marine and Fisheries, 71st Cong., 3rd sess., December 18, 1930, 141.
26 US Congress, House of Representatives, *Hearings on H.R. 5159 to Authorize the Postmaster General to Contract for Air Mail Service in Alaska*, before a Subcommittee of the Committee on the Post Office and Post Roads, 74th Cong., 1st sess., March 21, 1935, 4.
27 Alaska demographic and census information may be found in greater detail at the State of Alaska's Department of Labor and Workforce Development website, accessed September 21, 2020, live.laborstats.alaska.gov/cen/hist.cfm.
28 "Silhouettes of Alaska," *Washington [DC] Morning Times*, August 1, 1897, 7.
29 "Waddleton Pleads," *Daily Alaska Dispatch* (Juneau), February 16, 1912, 1.
30 "Negro Lawyer Is Arrested," *Daily Alaska Dispatch*, January 26, 1912, 1.
31 See Peggy Pascoe, *What Comes Naturally: Miscegenation Law and the Making of Race in America* (New York: Oxford University Press, 2009); Thomas C. Leonard, *Illiberal Reformers: Race, Eugenics, and American Economics in the Progressive Era* (Princeton, NJ: Princeton University Press, 2016).
32 "Waddleton Case Packs Courtroom," *Daily Alaska Dispatch*, February 27, 1912, 4.
33 Alyssa Lapka, "The Life of Cornelia Templeton Jewett Hatcher," Alaska Historical Society Blog, March 13, 2019, alaskahistoricalsociety.org/category/49-history/page/2.
34 Fred Beauvais, "American Indians and Alcohol," *Alcohol Health and Research World* 22, no. 4 (1998): 253; John W. Frank, Roland S. Moore, and Genevieve M. Ames, "Historical and Cultural Roots of Drinking Problems among American Indians," *American Journal of Public Health* 90, no. 3 (2000): 344–51.
35 J. Paul Seale, Sylvia Shellenberger, and John Spence, "Alcohol Problems in Alaska Natives: Lessons from the Inuit," *American Indian and Alaska Native Mental Health Research* 13, no. 1 (2006): 1–2; Sheila S. Tann, Scott T. Yabiku, Scott K. Okamoto, and Jessica Yanow, "TRIADD: The Risk for Alcohol Abuse, Depression, and Diabetes Multimorbidity in the American Indian and Alaska Native Population," *American Indian and Alaska Native Mental Health Research* 14,

no. 1 (2007): 1–23; Allison Barlow, Lauren Tingey, Mary Cwik, Novalene Goklish, Francene Larzelere-Hinton, Angelita Lee, Rosemarie Suttle, Britta Mullany, and John T. Walkup, "Understanding the Relationship between Substance Abuse and Self-Injury in American Indian Youth," *American Journal of Drug and Alcohol Abuse* 38, no. 5 (2012): 1042–1048; and Monica C. Skewes and Jordan P. Lewis, "Sobriety and Alcohol Use among Rural Alaska Native Elders," *International Journal of Circumpolar Health* 75 (2016): 30476–77.

36 Darryl S. Wood and Paul J. Gruenewald, "Local Alcohol Prohibition, Police Presence, and Serious Injury in Isolated Alaska Native Villages," *Addiction* 101, no. 3 (2006): 393–95; Greg Kim, "Bethel Just Re-Entered 'Damp' Status. Here's How That Changes the Rules for Alcohol," Alaska Public Media, January 6, 2020, alaskapublic.org/2020/01/06/bethel-just-re-entered-damp-status-this-is-how-that-changes-the-rules-for-residents-and-alcohol.

37 "Colored Man Is Sentenced," *Daily Alaska Dispatch*, March 7, 1912, 1.

38 "On Sedition Charge Man Jailed Here," *Daily Alaska Dispatch*, June 3, 1917, 1.

39 "Items of Local Interest," *Daily Alaska Dispatch*, June 6, 1917, 4.

40 "Waddleton Found Guilty by Jury," *Daily Alaska Dispatch*, June 16, 1917, 4.

41 "Fined for Circulating Seditious Literature," *Daily Alaska Dispatch*, July 6, 1917, 5.

42 For examples of reportage on alleged sedition and disloyalty in Alaska during World War I, see "Nome Editor Is Convicted of Sedition," *Anchorage Daily Times*, January 13, 1918, 1; "Local Doings and Personal Mention," *Cordova Daily Times*, January 18, 1918, 8; "Rasmussen Give Long Imprisonment and a Heavy Fine," *Alaska Daily Empire*, February 22, 1918, 7; "Deputy Mossman Arrests Alien," *Cordova Daily Times*, February 26, 1918, 1; "Must Answer Sedition Charges," *Daily Alaska Empire*, March 26, 1918, 3; "Deputy Leaves for Nenana," *Fairbanks Daily News-Miner*, April 4, 1918, 1; "Nome Editor Indicted for Seditious Act," *Seward Gateway*, April 11, 1918, 1; "Dr. Weyerhorst Having Hearing This Afternoon," *Daily Alaska Empire*, April 29, 1918, 8; "Windmuller Gets Four Months in Jail," *Valdez Daily Prospector*, April 29, 1918, 1; "Skagway Man Is Fined for Liberty Bonds," *Alaska Daily Empire*, May 10, 1918, 6; "News Items Culled from Alaska Papers," *Anchorage Daily Times*, June 8, 1918, 3; "Petersburg Man Pays for Disloyalty," *Alaska Daily Empire*, July 12, 1918, 3; "Mitcham Takes French Leave," *Fairbanks Daily News-Miner*, June 15, 1918, 1; "Alaska Notes," *Alaska Daily Empire*, July 20, 1918, 6; "Brennan Arrested and Fined," *Petersburg Weekly Report*, August 9, 1918, 1; "District Court," *Alaska Daily Empire*, September 6, 1918, 2; "District Court," *Alaska Daily Empire*, September 12, 1918, 7; "Happenings about Town," *Cordova Daily Times*, October 12, 1918, 8; "Local Cases Before Court at This Term," *Cordova Daily Times*, October 12, 1918, 8.

43 "Rasmussen Give Long Imprisonment and a Heavy Fine," *Alaska Daily Empire*, February 22, 1918, 7.

44 "Brennan Arrested and Fined," *Petersburg Weekly Report*, August 9, 1918, 1.

45 "Colored People Aroused at Film," *Daily Alaska Dispatch*, October 9, 1917, 5.

46 "Governor Suppresses 'Birth of a Nation,'" *Daily Alaska Dispatch*, October 10, 1918, 4.
47 "The Coliseum Will Show Special Features," *Daily Alaska Dispatch*, December 5, 1918, 4.
48 "That Juneau K.K.K.," *Pathfinder of Alaska*, September 1923, 12. The report contained some spurious claims, including that Juneau's "60-day nights" were ideal for Klan activity. The report also mentioned dog teams as a prevalent mode of transportation. Neither dog teams nor sixty-day nights are features of life in Juneau.
49 "Alaska: Al-ay-es-ka, Great Country," *Kourier Magazine*, April 1931, 44. The publication exclaims: "For . . . the 'doubhting [sic] Thomas' who didn't believe there are any Klans in Alaska we here list the charters. Anchorage No. 1, Juneau No. 2, Ketchikan No. 3, Cordova No. 4, Petersburg No. 5, Fairbanks No. 6, Seward No. 8, Skagway No. 9, Wrangell No. 10, Haines No. 11." There is no explanation why No. 7 was omitted; perhaps numbers and counting were never the terrorist group's strong suit.
50 "K.K.K. Minstrel Show Program," February 26, 1921, Wrangell–St. Elias National Park and Preserve Library and Archives.
51 On anti-Native discrimination in Juneau, see Terrence Cole, "Jim Crow in Alaska: The Passage of the Alaska Equal Rights Act of 1945," *Western Historical Quarterly* 23, no. 4 (November 1992): 429–49.
52 On the demographics of Tacoma and Pierce Country, Washington, see Mapping Race and Segregation in Tacoma and Pierce County, 1950–2000, accessed on the Civil Rights and Labor Consortium website, hosted by the University of Washington, https://depts.washington.edu/labhist/maps-race-tacoma.shtml.
53 See Quintard Taylor, "The Emergence of Black Communities in the Pacific Northwest"; Quintard Taylor, "The Great Migration: The Afro-American Communities of Seattle and Portland during the 1940s"; Quintard Taylor, *The Forging of a Black Community in Seattle*. For additional studies on Black settlement in the Pacific Northwest, see Dwayne A. Mack, *Black Spokane: The Civil Rights Struggle in the Inland Northwest* (Norman: University of Oklahoma Press, 2014); Stuart John McElderry, "The Problem of the Color Line: Civil Rights and Racial Ideology in Portland, Oregon, 1944–1965" (PhD diss., University of Oregon, 1998); and Stuart John McElderry, "Building a West Coast Ghetto: African American Housing in Portland, 1910–1960," *Pacific Northwest Quarterly* 92, no. 3 (2001): 137–48. See also Herbert Ruffin, *Uninvited Neighbors: African Americans in Silicon Valley, 1769–1990* (Norman: University of Oklahoma Press, 2014); and Matthew C. Whitaker, *Race Work: The Rise of Civil Rights in the Urban West* (Lincoln: University of Nebraska Press, 2004).
54 For the definitive treatment of Alaska's role in World War II, see Fern Chandonnet, ed., *Alaska at War, 1941–1945: The Forgotten War Remembered* (Fairbanks: University Alaska Press, 2007).

55 Quoted in Lael Morgan, "Writing Minorities Out of History: Black Builders of the Alcan Highway," *Alaska History* 7, no. 2 (1992): 2.
56 John Virtue, *The Black Soldiers Who Built the Alaska Highway: A History of Four US Army Regiments in the North* (Jefferson, NC: McFarland, 2013), 55. For more on Roosevelt, World War II and Black soldiers, see Nancy J. Weiss, *Farewell to the Party of Lincoln: Black Politics in the Age of FDR* (Princeton, NJ: Princeton University Press, 1983); Audrey McCluskey and Elaine M. Smith, *Mary McLeod Bethune: Building a Better World, Essays and Selected* (Bloomington: Indiana University Press, 2002); Mary Penick Motley, ed., *The Invisible Soldier: The Experiences of the Black Soldier, World War II* (Detroit: Wayne State University, 1975); and Maggi M. Morehouse, *Fighting in the Jim Crow Army: Black Men and Women Remember World War II* (Lanham, MD: Rowman & Littlefield, 2006).
57 For more on the March on Washington Movement, see David Lucander, *Winning the War for Democracy: The March on Washington Movement, 1941–1946* (Urbana: University of Illinois Press, 2014).
58 On the impact that the Army General Classification Test had on Black soldiers, see A. Russell Buchanan, *Black Americans in World War II* (New York: ABC-CLIO, 1977), 71–72; Morris J. MacGregor, *Integration of the Armed Forces, 1940–1965* (Washington, DC: General Printing Office, 2006), 183; and Beth Bailey and David Farber, "The 'Double-V' Campaign in World War II Hawaii: African Americans, Racial Ideology, and Federal Power," *Journal of Social History* 26, no. 4 (Summer 1993): 817–43.
59 Hisashi Takahashi, "The Japanese Campaign in Alaska and the Aleutians," in Chandonnet, *Alaska at War*, 33–39.
60 Takahashi, "Japanese Campaign," 39.
61 Froelich Rainey, "Alaskan Highway an Engineering Epic: Mosquitoes, Mud, Muskeg Minor Obstacles of 1,671-Mile Race to Throw Alcan Life Line through Thick Forests and Uninhabited Wilderness," *National Geographic Magazine*, February 1943, 143–68.
62 Harold W. Richardson, "Alcan—America's Glory Road: Part 1—Strategy and Location," *Engineering News-Record*, December 17, 1942, 82–96; Harold W. Richardson, "Alcan—America's Glory Road: Part 2—Supply, Equipment and Camps," *Engineering News-Record*, December 31, 1942, 35–42; Harold W. Richardson, "Alcan—America's Glory Road: Part III—Construction Tactics," *Engineering News-Record*, January 14, 1943, 131–38.
63 Jim Marshall, "Trouble on the Trail," *Collier's*, January 15, 1944, 16, 45.
64 Herbert M. Frisby, "Frisby Bumps 1600 Miles up Alcan Hi-way," *Baltimore Afro-American*, September 4, 1943, 1, 11.
65 Herbert M. Frisby, "AFRO Reporter Greets F.D.R. in Aleutians," *Baltimore Afro-American*, August 26, 1944, 16.
66 Christine McClure and Dennis McClure, *We Fought the Road* (Kenmore, WA: Epicenter Press, 2017), 18–19.

67 McClure and McClure, *We Fought the Road*, 62–63.
68 Kenneth S. Coates and William R. Morrison, *The Alaska Highway in World War II: The US Army's Occupation of Canada's Northwest* (Norman: University of Oklahoma Press, 1992), 61–65.
69 Quoted in Virtue, *Black Soldiers*, 66.
70 Virtue, *Black Soldiers*, 92–95.
71 Heath Twichell, *Northwest Epic: The Building of the Alaska Highway* (New York: St. Martin's Press, 1992).
72 Twichell, *Northwest Epic*.
73 Virtue, *Black Soldiers*, 127.
74 Herbert M. Frisby, "Alaska Calls Highway We Built 'The Negro Road,'" *Baltimore Afro-American*, September 30, 1944, 5.
75 Rainey, "Alaskan Highway," 144.
76 According to historians Coates and Morrison, the Truman committee concluded, "Canol was just another unrealized bonanza, and a boondoggle at that." See Coates and Morrison, *Alaska Highway*, 203; Virtue, *Black Soldiers*, 161–64.
77 "Black Veterans Memorial Bridge," Alaska Highway Project, n.d., alaskahighwayproject.blogspot.com/p/bridge.html.
78 US Department of the Army, *A Historical Analysis of the 364th Infantry in World War II, 1941 to 1945* (Washington, DC: Department of the Army, 2001).
79 For the strongest statement of Black contributions during the war in the Aleutian theater, see Charles Hendricks, "Race Relations and the Contributions of Minority Troops in Alaska: A Challenge to the Status Quo?" in Chandonnet, *Alaska at War*, 277–85.
80 Mike Dunham, "Student Locates Segregated Compound on World War II Map," *Anchorage Daily News*, updated September 29, 2016, dn.com/our-alaska/article/student-locates-segregated-compound-wwii-map/2009/02/22.
81 Matthew Little (HistoryMakers A2002.145), interviewed by Larry Crowe, August 11, 2002, HistoryMakers Digital Archive. In session 1, tape 3, story 5, Matthew Little talks about his experience with the 364th Infantry Regiment in the Aleutian Islands.
82 Hendricks, "Race Relations," 281.
83 Peter Porco, "Deadline Adak: Dashing Dashiell Hammett's Adak Newspaper for the Troops," *Anchorage Daily News*, January 18, 2015, last updated September 28, 2016, adn.com/we-alaskans/article/deadline-adak-dashing-dashiell-hammett-adak-newspaper-troops/2015/01/18.
84 George Campbell Jr. (HistoryMakers A2001.009), interviewed by Julieanna L. Richardson, May 17, 2001, HistoryMakers Digital Archive. In session 1, tape 3, story 2, George Campbell describes his father-in-law, Harvey Schmidt.
85 Lucky Cordell (HistoryMakers A2001.017), interviewed by Julieanna L. Richardson, January 16, 2002, HistoryMakers Digital Archive. In session 1, tape 2, story 1, Lucky Cordell details his service in the US military. Cordell went on

to have a successful career as a radio personality and disc jockey at WVON in Chicago. According to his brief biography on the HistoryMakers digital database, Cordell "was affectionately known as 'The Baron of Bounce' and serves as the program and music director in 1965 and the general manager in the late 1970s. Under his leadership, the station increased its ratings and almost doubled the income received from advertising."

86 Dashiell Hammett, *The Battle of the Aleutians: A Graphic History, 1942–43* (Aleutian Islands, AK: Intelligence Section, Field Force Headquarters, 1943).

87 Dean Kohlhoff, *When the Wind Was a River: Aleut Evacuation in World War II* (Seattle: University of Washington Press, 1995).

88 Kohlhoff, *When the Wind Was a River*; Nick Golodoff and Rachel Mason, eds., *Attu Boy: A Young Alaskans World War II Memoir* (Fairbanks: University of Alaska Press, 2015).

89 Andrew E. Kersten, *A. Philip Randolph: A Life in the Vanguard* (Lanham, MD: Rowan & Littlefield, 2007), 47–68.

90 The President's Committee on Civil Rights authored a series of recommendations after the war. The experience of Black soldiers during wartime figures prominently into the report. See *To Secure These Rights: The Report of the President's Committee on Civil Rights* (Washington, DC: General Printing Office, 1947), 41.

91 Porco, "Deadline Adak." For more on the Aleutian Campaign, particularly the battle at Attu, see John Haile Cloe, *Attu: The Forgotten Battle* (Anchorage: Department of the Interior, National Park Service, Alaska Affiliated Areas, Aleutian World War II Historic Area, 2017). For more on the claims of Black men to democracy and citizenship on the basis of having fought in the nation's wars, see Chad Williams, *Torchbearers of Democracy: African American Soldiers in the World War I Era* (Chapel Hill: University of North Carolina Press, 2013); Gerald Astor, *The Right to Fight: A History of African Americans in the Military* (Cambridge, MA: Da Capo Press, 2001); Robert F. Jefferson, *Fighting for Hope: African American Troops of the 93rd Infantry Division in World War II and Postwar America* (Baltimore: Johns Hopkins University Press, 2008).

92 On the Zoot Suit Riots, see Eduardo Obregon Pagan, *Murder at the Sleepy Lagoon: Zoot Suits, Race, and Riot in Wartime L.A.* (Chapel Hill: University of North Carolina Press, 2003); Mauricio Mazón, *The Zoot-Suit Riots: The Psychology of Symbolic Annihilation* (Austin: University of Texas Press, 1984); and Luis Alvarez, *The Power of the Zoot: Youth Culture and Resistance during World War II* (Berkeley: University of California Press, 2008).

93 Robert Kowalski, "A Long Way to Justice," *Anchorage Daily News*, April 11, 1999, H8.

94 Kowalski, "Long Way to Justice."

95 For updated census figures in Alaska and its demographics, see US Census Bureau, Quick Facts: Alaska, accessed on September 21, 2019, https://www.census.gov/quickfacts/fact/table/AK.

4. DISCRIMINATION, OPPORTUNITY, AND COMMUNITY

1. Julia Gaines Mighty, "Prices Are High, Prejudice Is Low ... So Far: Negroes in Alaska," *Negro Digest*, November 1963, 35.
2. "Negroes in the 49th State," *Ebony*, October 1958, 144.
3. Stephanie West, "Death on the Hill," *Juneau Empire*, October 30, 2014.
4. Marie Johnson-Calloway (HistoryMakers A2005.083), interviewed by Loretta Henry, March 29, 2005, HistoryMakers Digital Archive. In session 1, tape 3, story 4, Marie Johnson-Calloway describes integrated living in Fairbanks.
5. Ronald C. Johnson, *Out of the North* (Wasilla, AK: Plover Press, 1991), 4.
6. Steven Morris and Hal Franklin, "Is Alaska a Bonanza for Blacks?" *Ebony*, November 1969, 123–26.
7. Herbert M. Frisby, "'Tootsie' Forgets Her Race in Alaska," *Baltimore Afro-American*, September 15, 1951, 15.
8. Morris and Franklin, "Is Alaska a Bonanza for Blacks," 126.
9. Lael Morgan, *Gold Time Girls: Of the Alaska/Yukon Gold Rush* (Kenmore, WA: Epicenter Press, 1998), 292–94.
10. Mary Frazer, "Igloo Inflation Item: Alaska Cafes Shell Out up to $500 per Stripper," *Variety*, July 16, 1952, 2, 124.
11. Herbert M. Frisby, "Women Pioneers to Alaska Successful," *Baltimore Afro-American*, October 7, 1944, 5.
12. Death notice, *Anchorage Daily News*, January 2, 1973.
13. George C. Anderson, "Alaska Frontier ... Attracts Negro Pioneers," *Color*, April 1953, 27–28.
14. Anderson, "Alaska Frontier," 28. Shiloh Baptist Church has remained central to Anchorage into the present day. Former pastor Alonzo Patterson emerged as a leader in the Black community in the 1970s and continues to be a respected advocate of social justice.
15. Anderson, "Alaska Frontier," 27.
16. Madeline Holmes to NAACP Legal Defense Fund, May 8, 1950, UC Berkeley Bancroft Library Manuscript Collections, 78/180, NAACP, Region 1, Records, 1942–86, carton 28, folder 28.
17. Holmes to NAACP Legal Defense Fund, May 8, 1950.
18. Madeline Holmes to Earle Fisher, November 1, 1950, UC Berkeley Bancroft Library Manuscript Collections, 78/180, NAACP, Region 1, Records, 1942–86, carton 28, folder 28.
19. Holmes to NAACP Legal Defense Fund, May 8, 1950.
20. Madeline Holmes to Earle Fisher, November 1, 1950.
21. Earle Fisher to Madeline Holmes, December 5, 1950, UC Berkeley Bancroft Library Manuscript Collections, 78/180, NAACP, Region 1, Records, 1942–86, carton 28.
22. Letter to the editor, Larue Giddens, Airport Trailer Court, n.d., UC Berkeley Bancroft Library Manuscript Collections, 78/180, NAACP, Region 1, Records, 1942–86, carton 27.

23 "Jury Clears Café Staff of Count on Discrimination," *Anchorage Daily Times*, July 1, 1953, 14.
24 Willard L. Bowman, speech for the Inter-agency Council of the Human Rights Commission, Anchorage, September 24, 1964, box 1, folder 5, Willard L. Bowman Papers, Archives and Special Collections, UAA/APU Consortium Library.
25 Willard L. Bowman, "Remarks before Anchorage Lutheran Church," n.d., box 1, folder 4, Bowman Papers.
26 Willard L. Bowman, Remarks before the Citizens Council for Community Improvement, September 1, 1965, box 1, folder 6, Bowman Papers.
27 For more on housing discrimination, restrictive covenants, and segregation in northern and western cities, see Lisa McGirr, *Suburban Warriors: The Origins of the New American Right* (Princeton, NJ: Princeton University Press, 2001); Thomas Sugrue, *The Origins of the Urban Crisis: Race and Inequality in Postwar Detroit* (Princeton, NJ: Princeton University Press, 2005); Heather Ann Thompson, *Whose Detroit? Politics, Labor and Race in a Modern American City* (Ithaca, NY: Cornell University Press, 2004); and Ira Katznelson, *When Affirmative Action Was White: An Untold History of Racial Inequality in Twentieth-Century America* (New York: W. W. Norton, 2006), 15–24.
28 Deed of sale from Edward D. Coffey and Ruth Coffey to H. L. Bliss, July 21, 1941, filed July 24, 1941, Anchorage Recording District, Alaska, City Book 30, 317–18, Alaska Department of Natural Resources Recorder's Office, Anchorage.
29 Records detailing the extent of restrictive housing are available at the Recorder's Office in Anchorage and through the Alaska Department of Natural Resources, Recorder's Office, accessed December 30, 2017, dnr.alaska.gov/ssd/recoff/default.cfm.
30 Records detailing the extent of restrictive housing, Recorder's Office in Anchorage.
31 Correction deed of sale, Nicholas Weiler and Elsa Weiler to Nicholas Thomas Casey and Anna Marie Casey, October 1, 1947, filed October 2, 1947, Anchorage Recording District, Alaska, Precinct Book 31, 156–57, Alaska Department of Natural Resources Recorder's Office, Anchorage.
32 John Fournelle, *An Anchorage History: Early Years of Rogers Park and Traversie Sub-divisions*, online report, hosted by the University of Wisconsin, accessed March 28, 2022, http://www.geology.wisc.edu/~johnf/RogersPark/RogersPark-Traversie_Talk_092211.pdf.
33 For a scan of this restrictive covenant, see "Jim Crow in Alaska," Alaskool, accessed January 4, 2016, www.alaskool.org/projects/JimCrow/warrdeed.htm.
34 Warranty deed 86908, conveying property from Meredith H. Jelsma and Wilda O. Jelsma to Walter B. Allison Jr., notarized on August 7, 1948, Anchorage Recording District, vol. 157, p. 248 (Anchorage Precinct, Anchorage, AK, filed for records on March 20, 1958).
35 Historical Books Project: Anchorage, B301-00045, vol. 45. Scanned by Tracey Wells on July 14, 2005. The volume includes a record of property and land

sales and transfers in and around Anchorage during the 1940s and 1950s. The Kirchner deed is located on pp. 22–23.
36 On the legacy of *Shelley v. Kraemer* (334 US 1), see Richard Rothstein, *The Color of Law: A Forgotten History of How Our Government Segregated America* (New York: W. W. Norton, 2017), 85–91; Joe T. Darden, "Black Residential Segregation since the 1948 *Shelley v. Kraemer* Decision," *Journal of Black Studies* 25, no. 6 (1995), 680–91. Housing discrimination and its impact on the racial wealth gap is a topic explored at length in Ta-Nehisi Coates, "The Case for Reparations," *Atlantic*, June 2014, www.theatlantic.com/features/archive/2014/05/the-case-for-reparations/361631.
37 Ocea Mae Curry, interview by Bruce Melzer, ca. 1982–83, Bruce Melzer oral history interviews, Archives and Special Collections, UAA/APU Consortium Library.
38 The intimidation of prospective Black homeowners in white communities occurred nationwide. See Kevin Kruse, *White Flight: Atlanta and the Making of Modern Conservatism* (Princeton, NJ: Princeton University Press, 2007), 60–63; Keeanga-Yamahtta Taylor, *Race for Profit: How Banks and the Real Estate Industry Undermined Black Homeownership* (Chapel Hill: University of North Carolina Press, 2019), 110–12; and Rothstein, *Color of Law*, 142–48.
39 *Alaska Blacks Salute the Bicentennial* (Anchorage: Leake Temple AME Zion Church and Great Land Visuals, 1976), 32; Alaska Black Caucus Inc., Records, 1975–93, Archives and Special Collections, UAA/APU Consortium Library.
40 "Fire Razes House Involved in Suit," *Anchorage Daily Times*, October 16, 1950.
41 Fournelle, *Anchorage History*.
42 John Lindback, "Anchorage Civil Rights Leader Mourned by Friends," *Anchorage Daily News*, June 17, 1983, B1.
43 *Alaska Blacks Salute Bicentennial*.
44 Madeline Holmes to NAACP Legal Defense Fund, May 8, 1950
45 Letter, Blanche McSmith to Golster B. Current, October 24, 1952, Papers of the NAACP, pt. 26: Selected Branch Files, 1940–55, ser. D: The West, reel 1, 1.
46 *Alaska Blacks Salute Bicentennial*, 4.
47 *Alaska Blacks Salute Bicentennial*, 7.
48 Herbert Frisby, "Tootsie Forgets Her Race in Alaska," *Baltimore Afro-American*, September 15, 1951, 15.
49 Joe Jackson, interview, ca. 1984, in *Oral HX, Blacks in Alaska* (N.p.: SKB/Prod, ca. 1984), Archives and Special Collections, UAA/APU Consortium Library.
50 Joe Jackson, interview by Bruce Melzer, ca. 1982–83, Bruce Melzer oral history interviews, Archives and Special Collections, UAA/APU Consortium Library.
51 Zelmer Lawrence, interview by Bruce Melzer, ca. 1982–83, Bruce Melzer oral history interviews.
52 Jackson, interview, in *Oral HX, Blacks in Alaska*.
53 Author interview with Fred Johnson, September 3, 2020.
54 Jackson, interview, in *Oral HX, Blacks in Alaska*.
55 Author interview with Johnson.

56. Author interview with Johnson.
57. "Tonight Billie Holiday!" *Anchorage Daily Times*, September 7, 1954, 2.
58. Ben Humphries, interview, ca. 1984, in *Oral HX, Blacks in Alaska*.
59. Author interview with Johnson.
60. Frisby, "Tootsie Forgets Her Race in Alaska," 15.
61. On incorporation and city planning of Anchorage, see Vic Fischer, with Charles Wohlforth, *To Russia with Love: An Alaskan's Journey* (Fairbanks: University of Alaska Press, 2012), 138–40.
62. "Eastchester People against Incorporation," *Anchorage Daily Times*, September 30, 1951.
63. "Eastchester Water Job, Annexation Discussed," *Anchorage Daily Times*, July 24, 1952.
64. "Woman Repeats Claim of Illegal Voting in Last Election on Annexation," *Anchorage Daily News*, May 25, 1954.
65. Blanche McSmith, "The Shame of an Alaska 'All American City,'" *Alaska Spotlight*, November 28, 1965, 1–4.
66. Curry, interview by Melzer.
67. *A Community Attitude Survey* (Anchorage: Greater Anchorage Area Borough Planning Department, 1972), 8.
68. Charles Ball, *Marketability Analysis Eastchester Urban Renewal Project Alaska UR-16* (Spenard, AK: Economic Research and Planning Associates, 1963), 1.
69. City of Anchorage, "Anchorage 1965 Neighborhood Planning Program," 115, available at the UAA/APU Consortium Library.
70. *Urban Renewal Plan Eastchester Area Project Alaska R-16 Anchorage, Alaska* (Anchorage: Alaska State Housing Authority, 1965).
71. Ball, *Marketability Analysis Eastchester*, 7.
72. "People Are Talking About," *Jet*, April 29, 1964, 42.
73. George S. Schuyler, "Views and Reviews," *Pittsburgh Courier*, May 2, 1964, 10. On the loss of power, see Curry, interview by Melzer,.
74. See Alice Fothergill, Enrique G. M. Maestas, and JoAnne DeRouen Darlington, "Race, Ethnicity and Disasters in the United States: A Review of the Literature," *Disasters* 23, no. 2 (1999): 156–73; Alice Fothergill and Lori A. Peek, "Poverty and Disasters in the United States: A Review of Recent Sociological Findings," *Natural Hazards* 32, no. 1 (2004): 89–110; and Darwin Bond Graham, "The New Orleans That Race Built: Racism, Disaster, and Urban Spatial Relationships," *Souls* 9, no. 1 (2007): 4–18. For a global discussion of environmental justice, see Gordon Walker, *Environmental Justice: Concepts, Evidence and Politics* (New York: Routledge, 2012).
75. Jason David Rivera and DeMond Shondell Miller, "Continually Neglected: Situating Natural Disasters in the African American Experience," *Journal of Black Studies* 37, no. 4 (2007): 518–19.
76. Vanport is a notable comparison. Like Anchorage, increased defense spending during World War II and then the Cold War prompted a demographic explosion in Portland as workers arrived to meet construction demands. In response

to housing shortages and discrimination that prevented most newly arrived African Americans from living in Portland proper, the town of Vanport was established just outside the city limits in a former swamp. Like Eastchester, Vanport occupied low-lying, mosquito-infested territory and consisted of poorly made homes situated among squalor and debris. On May 29, 1948, the local housing authority distributed notices that the community was safe from the rapidly rising Columbia River. The next day the river broke its dike, and flooding destroyed the community. See Manly Maben, *Vanport* (Portland: Oregon Historical Society Press, 1987); Stuart McElderry, "Vanport Conspiracy Rumors and Social Relations in Portland, 1940–1950," *Oregon Historical Quarterly* 99, no. 2 (1998): 134–63; and Dale Skovgaard, "Oregon Voices: Memories of the 1948 Vanport Flood," *Oregon Historical Quarterly* 108, no. 1 (2007): 88–106.

77 Richard Rothstein, *The Color of Law: A Forgotten History of How Our Government Segregated America* (New York: Liveright, 2017), 124–31.
78 *To Eastchester Residents and the Eastchester Improvement Committee* (Anchorage: Alaska State Housing Authority, 1966).
79 *The New Day for Eastchester: Planned Redevelopment thru Urban Renewal* (Anchorage: Alaska State Housing Authority, 1965), 1.
80 McSmith, "Shame of an Alaska 'All American City,'" 3.
81 Martha Fair, interview, ca. 1984, in *Oral HX, Blacks in Alaska*.
82 Jackson, interview by Melzer.
83 "NAACP Leader Fights Renewal of Eastchester," *Anchorage Times*, July 26, 1965; "Group Challenges McSmith Views," *Anchorage Times*, July 27, 1965.
84 In 1971 the *Anchorage Daily News* published a three-part series on a divisive NAACP leadership election, beginning with Andy Williams, "The NAACP Election: Struggle Creates Division in City Black Community," *Anchorage Daily News*, January 17, 1971.
85 Curry, interview by Melzer.
86 Humphries, interview, in *Oral HX, Blacks in Alaska*.
87 Author interview with Johnson.
88 *Alaska Blacks Salute Bicentennial*, 7.
89 Frank Austins, interview by Bruce Melzer, ca. 1982–83, Bruce Melzer oral history interviews.
90 Don Hunter, "Faces Change but Assembly Tone's the Same," *Anchorage Daily Times,* April 23, 1998, A1. While Melinda Taylor may have been the first African American to win a seat on the Anchorage Municipality Assembly, Thomas Bevers was the first to service on Anchorage's city council in 1941. As noted, however, Bevers did not claim a Black identity, and Anchorage's municipal borders differed quite drastically from the early 1940s to the late 1990s.
91 Bob Miller, "City Council Approves Historic Housing Code," *Anchorage Daily Times*, September 27, 1967, 1, 2.
92 Terrence M. Cole, "Jim Crow in Alaska: The Passage of the Alaska Equal Rights Act of 1945," *Western Historical Quarterly* 23, no. 4 (1992): 429–49; Ross Coen,

"How Alaska's Equal Rights Law Was First Put to the Test," *Anchorage Daily News*, January 15, 2017.
93 Bowman, speech for the Inter-agency Council of the Human Rights Commission.
94 Chad R. Farrell, "The Anchorage Mosaic: Racial and Ethnic Diversity in the Urban North," in *Imagining Anchorage: The Making of America's Northernmost Metropolis*, ed. James K. Barnett and Ian C. Hartman (Fairbanks: University of Alaska Press, 2018), 374–91.
95 David Reamer, "How Greater Friendship Baptist Church in Anchorage Made Its Mark in Alaska and Civil Rights History," *Anchorage Daily News*, June 7, 2020, https://www.adn.com/alaska-life/2020/06/07/how-greater-friendship-baptist-church-in-anchorage-made-its-mark-in-alaska-and-civil-rights-history.
96 *Baptist Press*, August 21, 1965, 5. On the SBC and the history of Southern Baptists, see Mark Newman, *Getting Right with God: Southern Baptists and Desegregation, 1945–1995* (Tuscaloosa: University of Alabama Press, 2001); Alan Scot Willis, *All According to God's Plan: Southern Baptist Missions and Race, 1945–1970* (Lexington: University Press of Kentucky, 2005); and Luther E. Copeland, *The Southern Baptist Convention and the Judgment of History: The Taint of an Original Sin* (Lanham, MD: University Press of America, 2002).

5. CIVIL RIGHTS UNDER THE NORTHERN LIGHTS

1 Special thanks to Theressa Lenear, who recalled growing up in Alaska as the daughter of Beatrice and Robert Coleman. She shared details of her life and her parents' activism with the author on June 20, 2019.
2 Ross Coen details the Colemans' case against Rudy Hill and its larger significance in his article "How Alaska's Equal Rights Law Was First Put to the Test in Fairbanks," *Alaska Dispatch News*, updated December 2, 2017, https://www.adn.com/alaska-life/2017/01/14/how-alaskas-equal-rights-law-was-first-put-to-the-test-in-fairbanks. Coen's research and Lenear's recollections of her parents are the basis for this section.
3 Author interview with Lenear.
4 Coen, "How Alaska's Equal Rights Law."
5 Anti-Discrimination Act, House Bill 14, from Session Laws of Alaska, 1945, chap. 2, https://vilda.alaska.edu/digital/collection/cdmg41/id/543.
6 On Elizabeth Peratrovich and the Alaska Anti-Discrimination Act of 1945, see Nora Marks Dauenhauer and Richard Dauenhauer, *Haa Kusteeyí, Our Culture: Tlingit Life Stories* (Seattle: University of Washington Press, 1994); and Peter Metcalfe, *A Dangerous Idea: The Alaska Brotherhood and the Struggle for Indigenous Rights* (Fairbanks: University of Alaska Press, 2014), 116. See also Terrence Cole's influential essay "Jim Crow in Alaska: The Passage of the Alaska Equal Rights Act of 1945," in *An Alaska Anthology: Interpreting the Past*, ed. Stephen W. Haycox and Mary Childers Mangusso (Seattle: University of Washington Press, 1996), 314–35.

7   Coen, "How Alaska's Equal Rights Law."
8   Anti-Discrimination Act, House Bill 14 (1945).
9   Coen, "How Alaska's Equal Rights Law."
10 Anti-Discrimination Act, House Bill 14 (1945).
11 Coen, "How Alaska's Equal Rights Law."
12 Author interview with Lenear.
13 Coen, "How Alaska's Equal Rights Law."
14 Coen, "How Alaska's Equal Rights Law."
15 Statement from Beatrice Coleman, n.d., ca. 1951–52, University of California (UC), Berkeley, Bancroft Library Manuscript Collections, 78/180, NAACP, Region 1 Records, 1942–86, carton 2.
16 Statement from Coleman.
17 Statement from Coleman.
18 Clarence Mitchell to Clarence H. Osthagen, July 24, 1951, UC Berkeley Bancroft Library Manuscript Collections, 78/180, NAACP, Region 1 Records, 1942–86, carton 2.
19 Mitchell to Osthagen, July 24, 1951.
20 James P. Goode to Beatrice L. Coleman, n.d., ca. 1951, UC Berkeley Bancroft Library Manuscript Collections, 78/180, NAACP, Region 1 Records, 1942–86, carton 2.
21 Palmer W. Wardman (civilian personnel officer) to Beatrice L. Coleman, May 28, 1951, UC Berkeley Bancroft Library Manuscript Collections, 78/180, NAACP, Region 1 Records, 1942–86, carton 2.
22 Clarence Mitchell to Clarence H. Osthagen, July 24, 1951.
23 Author interview with Lenear.
24 Ernest Gruening, *State of Alaska* (New York: Random House, 1968), 419.
25 Charlayne Hunter-Gault (HistoryMakers A2006.092), interviewed by Larry Crowe, June 15, 2006, HistoryMakers Digital Archive. In session 1, tape 2, story 1, Charlayne Hunter-Gault recalls her father's experience as a US military chaplain.
26 Bowman, "Remarks before the Citizens Council for Community Improvement," box 1, folder 6, Bowman Papers.
27 Blanche McSmith, "The Shame of an Alaska 'All American City,'" *Alaska Spotlight*, November 28, 1965.
28 "Negroes Send Lobbyist to Juneau," *Anchorage Daily Times*, February 17, 1953, 10.
29 "Hiring Law Passes Senate," *Anchorage Daily Times*, March 6, 1953, 5; "1953 Achievement Said 'Notable' in First Annual Report," *Anchorage Daily Times*, March 27, 1954.
30 Alaska Fair Employment Act (1953). The full text is available online: https://www.blackpast.org/african-american-history/alaska-fair-employment-practices-law-1953.
31 Blanche McSmith to Zora Banks, UC Berkeley Bancroft Library Manuscript Collections, 78/180, NAACP, Region 1, Records, 1942–86, carton 2.

32 The Constitution of the State of Alaska, adopted and ratified by the Constitutional Convention, February 5, 1956, ratified by the People of Alaska, April 24, 1956.
33 Walter J. Hickel, "Riot Memo," August 11, 1967, box 7, folder 17, Robert B. Atwood Papers, Archives and Special Collections, UAA/APU Consortium Library.
34 Robert B. Atwood, "Memo re: telephone conversation with Chief John Flanigan, Anchorage Police Department, August 11, 1967," box 7, folder 17, Atwood Papers.
35 Clarence V. Coleman to Roy Wilkins via Western Union telegram, August 1, 1962, Papers of the NAACP, pt. 27: Selected Branch Files, 1956–65, series D: The West, ed. John H. Bracey Jr., Sharon Harley, and August Meier. Available on microfilm at UAA/APU Consortium Library.
36 For reference to the picket on the Local 341 Laborers and Hod Carrier Union, see Papers of the NAACP, supplement to pt. 13: The NAACP and Labor, 1956–65, ed. John H. Bracey Jr. and August Meier (folder 14), available on microfilm at the UAA/APU Consortium Library. For additional reference, see Meier Randall Keenan, *Walking on Water: Black American Lives at the Turn of the Twenty-First Century* (New York: Vintage, 2000), 284.
37 Charlie Mae "Pat" Berkley, interview by Bruce Melzer, ca. 1982–83, Bruce Melzer oral history interviews, Archives and Special Collections, UAA/APU Consortium Library.
38 *NAACP News Letter*, Papers of the NAACP, pt. 27: Selected Branch Files, 1956–65, series D: The West, available on microfilm at the UAA/APU Consortium Library.
39 Berkley, interview by Melzer.
40 Joseph H. Kline Jr. to Roy Wilkins, March 3, 1963, Papers of the NAACP, pt. 27: Selected Branch Files, available on microfilm at the UAA/APU Consortium Library.
41 For a brief report on Richard Watts's career at Carrs, see Christine Kim, "Carrs' First Black Worker Recalls His Rise through the Ranks," February 19, 2010, on KTUU. For the announcement of Watts on the board of directors for the Anchorage Chamber of Commerce, see "Anchorage Chamber's 2013–14 Board of Directors Announced," *Alaska Dispatch News*, September 12, 2013, www.adn.com/article/20130912/anchorage-chambers-2013-14-board-directors-announced.
42 "City Officials Tour Fairview Neighborhood Park," *Anchorage Times*, August 2, 1967, 1.
43 Dianne Anderson, "Protest Group Gets Results, with and without Picketing," *Anchorage Daily Times*, August 13, 1968, 3.
44 Blanche McSmith to Maj. Gen. George A. Carver, September 17, 1965, Papers of the NAACP, pt. 27: Selected Branch Files, available on microfilm at UAA/APU Consortium Library.
45 Thomas M. Davis, colonel, USAF, to Blanche McSmith, November 8, 1965, Papers of the NAACP, pt. 27: Selected Branch Files, available on microfilm at UAA/APU Consortium Library.

46 On the campaign to picket Fort Richardson and Elmendorf Air Force Base, see "Protest Group Sets Oct. 12 Demonstration Date," *Midnight Sun Reporter*, October 3, 1964.
47 This was at least the second time that activists marched in solidarity with their compatriots in the South. In May 1963 a small group took to the streets in solidarity with the Birmingham campaign. See "12 Negroes Picket Here: It's 'Sympathy' Demonstration," *Anchorage Daily News*, May 17, 1963.
48 Anchorage Branch NAACP, Annual Report, 1965, Papers of the NAACP, pt. 27: Selected Branch Files, available on microfilm at UAA/APU Consortium Library.
49 Paula McClain (HistoryMakers A2012.069), interviewed by Larry Crowe, February 22, 2012, HistoryMakers Digital Archive. In session 1, tape 2, story 6, Paula McClain describes the Black enclaves in Anchorage.
50 Cal Williams describes his reasons for coming to Alaska, and the place he found when he arrived, in the Black oral history project *Hekima (Wisdom): Their History Is Our History*, Alaska Poor People's Campaign, 2021, https://www.youtube.com/watch?v=XGtJ2TJF9B0.

6. BLACK ALASKA DURING THE OIL BOOM

1 Gladys Knight details her life in the autobiography *Between Each Line of Pain and Glory: My Life Story* (New York: Hyperion Press, 1997).
2 Stephen F. Verona, *Pipe Dreams* (Los Angeles: AVCO Embassy Pictures, 1976).
3 "Gladys Knight's Mate Becomes Her Lover in Movie Debut," *Jet*, November 25, 1976, 57–62.
4 Christopher Porterfield, "Cinema: Heavy Weather," *Time*, January 31, 1977.
5 "Knight to Guest on Jeffersons," *Anchorage Times*, January 27, 1983, F3.
6 There now exists an impressive and growing body of scholarship on the political economy of the 1970s. See Kim Phillips-Fein, *Fear City: New York's Fiscal Crisis and the Rise of Austerity Politics* (New York: Metropolitan Books, 2017); Robert O. Self, *All in the Family: The Realignment of American Democracy since the 1960s* (New York: Hill & Wang, 2013); and Judith Stein, *Pivotal Decade: How the United States Traded Factories for Finance in the Seventies* (New Haven, CT: Yale University Press, 2011).
7 For background on the Alaska Pipeline, see James Roscow, *800 Miles to Valdez: The Building of the Alaska Pipeline* (Upper Saddle River, NJ: Prentice Hall, 1977); Dermot Cole, *Amazing Pipeline Stories: How Building the Alaska Pipeline Transformed Life in America's Last Frontier* (Kenmore, WA: Kenmore Press, 1997); and Peter Coates, *Trans-Alaskan Pipeline Controversy: Technology, Conservation, and the Frontier* (Fairbanks: University of Alaska Press, 1993).
8 Author phone interview with Theressa Lenear, June 20, 2019.
9 Cole, *Amazing Pipeline Stories*, 199–202.
10 For a brief description of Walker and an accompanying photograph, see the Alaska Digital Archives, accessed August 3, 2019, https://vilda.alaska.edu/digital/collection/cdmg21/id/9747.

11 William J. Carrington, "The Alaskan Labor Market during the Pipeline Era," *Journal of Political Economy* 104, no. 1 (1996): 188.
12 For complete demographic information on the decade's population, see "General Population Characteristics of Alaska," 1980 Census of Population, US Bureau of the Census, accessed March 29, 2022, https://live.laborstats.alaska.gov/cen/histpdfs/1980char.pdf.
13 Average monthly wages did return closer to pre-pipelines levels in Alaska once TAPS was completed in 1977. Carrington, "Alaskan Labor Market," 198.
14 Rachel Baker, Joun Boucher, Neal Fried, and Brigitta Windisch-Cole, "Long-Term Retrospective: Alaska's Economy since Statehood," *Alaska Economic Trends*, December 1999, 9–13.
15 Author interview with Lenear.
16 Carrington, "Alaskan Labor Market," 191. For more on pipeline union negotiations, see Robert Douglas Mead, *Journeys Down the Line: Building the Trans-Alaskan Pipeline* (New York: Doubleday, 1978).
17 Paul Jenkins, "Hard Pressed State Seeks to Protect Its Jobs," Associated Press, February 25, 1986.
18 Ed McGrath, *Inside the Alaska Pipeline* (Berkeley, CA: Celestial Arts Publishing, 1977), 36.
19 See Harvey Adams, Appellant, v. Pipeliners Union 798, United Association, and the Alaska State Commission for Human Rights, Appellees (Case No. S-181), May 10, 1985.
20 Author interview with Ed Wesley, September 23, 2018, Anchorage.
21 Author interview with Wesley.
22 Opalanga D. Pugh (HistoryMakers A2008.120), interviewed by Denise Gines, November 3, 2008, HistoryMakers Digital Archive. In session 1, tape 5, story 6, Opalanga D. Pugh recalls working on the Trans-Alaska Pipeline System.
23 Pugh interview.
24 Pugh interview.
25 Vernellia Randall (HistoryMakers A2006.052), interviewed by Larry Crowe, March 24, 2006, HistoryMakers Digital Archive. In session 1, tape 6, story 8, Vernellia Randall talks about racial discrimination in Alaska.
26 "Statement of Willie Ratcliff, Coordinator of the Alaska Minority Business Task Force Calling for Greater Representation of Minorities on City Contracts," reprinted in *New Horizon*, October 21, 1977, 3, UAA/APU Consortium Library.
27 "City's Contracting with MBEs under Review," *North Star Reporter*, March 15, 1983, 1.
28 "State Remains in Non-Compliance," *North Star Reporter*, April 15, 1983, 1, 7.
29 "State Remains in Non-Compliance."
30 "State Hiring Questioned," *North Star Reporter*, February 28, 1983, 1.
31 See Isaiah J. Poole, "Renegade in Alaska," *Black Enterprise*, November 1980, 66.
32 Becky Norsworthy, "Fairview: The Old Bows to the New," *Anchorage Times*, January 22, 1978, C1.
33 "Fairview Turning into Multi-Family," *Anchorage Times*, January 22, 1978, C3.

34 Hartman interview with Cal Williams on the impact of John R. Parks, Anchorage, December 13, 2020.
35 "John Parks Chosen to Study Bus System," *Anchorage Daily Times*, April 23, 1977, 39.
36 "FCC Will Have City's Voice," *Anchorage Daily Times*, September 12, 1969, 7.
37 On Jack Roderick's legacy and contributions, see Michelle Theriault Boots, "Jack Roderick, Former Mayor Who Made Enduring Contributions to Anchorage, Dies at 94," *Anchorage Daily News*, October 20, 2020, https://www.adn.com/alaska-news/anchorage/2020/10/20/jack-roderick-former-mayor-who-made-enduring-contributions-to-anchorage-dies-at-93.
38 "Support for Unification Appears Strong among Top 15 Candidates for City Council," *Anchorage Daily Times*, September 25, 1974, 57.
39 Interview with Cal Williams on the impact of John R. Parks, Anchorage, December 13, 2020.
40 Richard Watts, quoted in Alaska State Library Historical Collection, *Oral HX, Blacks in Alaska*, 1984, Sheryl Bailey and Latrice McBeth.
41 "Red Boucher Chosen Mayor," *Anchorage Daily Times*, October 5, 1966, 2.
42 Elizabeth Tower, *Alaska's First Homegrown Governor: A Biography of William A. Egan* (Anchorage: Publication Consultants, 2003), 118.
43 William Campfield later retired to Sacramento, CA. For more on his career, see Mark Clodfelter, *River Rats: Red River Valley Fighter Pilots of Vietnam* (Nashville: Turner Publishing, 1990), 96.
44 For a profile on Ratcliff's life as a publisher, see Denise Sullivan, "An Ever Changing View," *San Francisco Examiner*, February 4, 2018, https://www.sfexaminer.com/news/an-ever-changing-view.
45 For a list of the Board of Directors at National Bank of Alaska, see "National Bank of Alaska: Report of Condition," *Anchorage Times*, January 29, 1982, B6.
46 "Demo Leaders Urge Harmony," *Anchorage Daily Times*, April 19, 1974, 5.
47 Author interview with Eleanor Andrews, Anchorage, June 7, 2019. See also Eleanor Andrews's induction and biography in the Alaska Women's Hall of Fame, accessed May 24, 2018, http://alaskawomenshalloffame.org/alumnae/name/eleanor-andrews.
48 Carolyn E. Jones's entry in the Alaska Women's Hall of Fame, accessed on August 18, 2019, http://alaskawomenshalloffame.org/alumnae/name/carolyn-jones.
49 Jones's entry in the Alaska Women's Hall of Fame.
50 Lori Townsend, "Alaska Women's Hall of Fame: Jewel Jones," *Alaska Public Media*, March 26, 2013, https://www.alaskapublic.org/2013/03/26/alaska-womens-hall-of-fame-jewel-jones.
51 Jewel Jones's Alaska Women's Hall of Fame biography, accessed November 22, 2019, http://alaskawomenshalloffame.org/alumnae/name/jewell-jones.
52 Mayowa Aina, "Anchorage's First Black Teacher and Principal Remembered as 'Trailblazer,'" Alaska Public Media, January 3, 2021, https://www.alaskapublic.org/2021/01/03/anchorage-school-districts-first-black-teacher-and-principal-remembered-as-trailblazer.

53 David Reamer, "She Was a Friend of Rosa Parks, a Student of Thurgood Marshall—and the First Black Attorney in Alaska," *Anchorage Daily News*, January 19, 2020, https://www.adn.com/alaska-life/2020/01/20/she-was-a-friend-of-rosa-parks-a-student-of-thurgood-marshall-and-the-first-black-attorney-in-alaska. For more on Dickerson, see "Mahala Ashley Dickerson," in *We Alaskans: Stories of People Who Helped Build the Great Land*, ed. Sharon Bushell (Homer, AK: Road Tunes Media, 2001); Mahala Ashley Dickerson, *Delayed Justice for Sale* (Anchorage: Al-Acres, 1998); and Julia O'Malley, "Pioneer Alaska Lawyer Dickerson Dies at 94," *Anchorage Daily News*, February 21, 2007, A1.
54 Dickerson, *Delayed Justice for Sale*, 88.
55 Greeta K. Brown v. William Wood et al., 575 P.2d 760 (Alaska Supreme Court 1978), accessed April 9, 2019, law.justia.com/cases/alaska/supreme-court/1978/2564.html; Jennifer Bazeley, "An Interview with M. Ashley Dickerson," *Alaska Bar Rag*, July–August–September 1982, 12.
56 Dickerson, *Delayed Justice for Sale*, 128.
57 O'Malley, "Pioneer Alaska Lawyer," A1.
58 A short biography of Dickerson is available at Alaska Women's Hall of Fame website, accessed August 3, 2019, http://alaskawomenshalloffame.org/alumnae/mahala-dickerson.
59 The oral histories for Odom and Brown are contained in the Black oral history project, *Hekima (Wisdom): Their History Is Our History*, Alaska Poor People's Campaign, 2021, accessed March 29, 2022, https://www.youtube.com/watch?v=XGtJ2TJF9Bo.
60 Author interview with Andrews.
61 For the definitive treatment of the Alaska Native Claims Settlement Act, see Mitchell, *Take My Land*.
62 Jim Babba, "Talk, No Final Action on Rights Bill," *Anchorage Daily News*, February 11, 1976, 2.
63 Author interview with Andrews.

7. CRIMINAL JUSTICE, LAW ENFORCEMENT, AND RACE

1 *Need for Assistance*, report convened before the Governor's Commission on the Administration of Justice, July 1978, box 3, folder 7, Alaska Black Caucus Inc. Records, Archives and Special Collections, UAA/APU Consortium Library.
2 "NAACP Annual Meeting: January 11, 1971," *Crisis*, March 1971, 60.
3 This chapter has benefited from recent scholarship that has explored deeply the impact of policing on poor and urban communities, mostly of color. For some of the strongest representative work, see Michelle Alexander, *The New Jim Crow: Mass Incarceration in the Age of Colorblindness* (New York: New Press, 2012); James Forman Jr., *Locking Up Our Own: Crime and Punishment in Black America* (New York: Farrar, Straus & Giroux, 2018); and Paul Butler, *Chokehold: Policing Black Men* (New York: Free Press, 2018).

4 "Alaska Negro Asks US to Probe Police Brutality," *Jet*, September 16, 1954, 8.
5 "Negroes Appeal to Capital," *Anchorage Times*, August 21, 1954, 1.
6 "Shannon, Miller Deny Discrimination Charges," *Anchorage Times*, August 23, 1954, 1, 9.
7 Paul H. Wangness, *A History of the Unification of the City of Anchorage and the Greater Anchorage Area Borough* (Anchorage: Anchorage Urban Observatory, 1977), 38.
8 "Man Found Guilty of Maintaining Prostitution House," *Anchorage Times*, November 12, 1955, 15; "Liquor Permit Transferred," *Anchorage Times*, February 10, 1956, 7.
9 Brownell donated his records on civil rights to a historian in the late 1970s. When she died, those records were destroyed by her landlord.
10 "Shannon, Miller Deny Discrimination Charges," 9.
11 An appellate judge who confirmed the compensatory award stated in his decision: "The plaintiff herself caused whatever was done. She certainly had no cause to scream all over the neighborhood." Hash v. Hogan, 453 P.2d 468 (Alaska Supreme Court 1969), accessed March 29, 2019, law.justia.com/cases/alaska/supreme-court/1969/930-1.html; C. Robert Zelnick, "State Rules on 'Police Brutality," *Anchorage Daily News*, July 6, 1968, 12.
12 "NAACP Charges Brutality," *Anchorage Daily News*, April 18, 1969, 1, 2; "Irate Citizens Lash Out at Two City Departments," *Anchorage Times*, April 23, 1969, 2; Mahala Ashley Dickerson, *Delayed Justice for Sale* (Anchorage: Al-Acres, 1998), 104–7.
13 "Irate Citizens Lash Out at Two City Departments."
14 Stephen Brent, "A Human Relations Board Probe," *Anchorage Daily News*, May 2, 1969, 1.
15 "NAACP Charges Brutality."
16 Margaret Schmidt, "Police Brutality Testimony Given," *Anchorage Times*, May 2, 1969, 2; Paul Kampf, "The Brutality Hearing Ends," *Anchorage Daily News*, May 7, 1969, 1, 6.
17 "City Commission Reports: 'No Police Brutality,'" *Anchorage Daily News*, May 10, 1969, 1.
18 "What the Police Probe Revealed," *Anchorage Daily News*, May 13, 1969, 4.
19 "What the Police Probe Revealed."
20 The definitive text on the White Citizen's Council at its peak political significance remains the revised edition of Neil R. McMillan, *The Citizens' Council: Organized Resistance in the Second Reconstruction, 1954–64* (Urbana: University of Illinois Press, 1994). See also Clive Webb, "'A Cheap Trafficking in Human Misery': The Reverse Freedom Rides of 1962," *Journal of American Studies* 38, no. 2 (2004): 249–71; and Neal R. McMillen, "The White Citizens' Council and Resistance to School Desegregation in Arkansas," *Arkansas Historical Quarterly* 66, no. 2 (2007): 125–44.
21 "Obituaries," *Anchorage Daily News*, July 8, 2001, B7.
22 Kampf, "Brutality Hearing Ends," 6.

23 Kampf, "Brutality Hearing Ends," 6.
24 "What the Police Probe Revealed."
25 "NAACP Asks for Resignations," *Anchorage Times*, May 14, 1969, 1, 2.
26 Jennifer Bazeley, "An Interview with M. Ashley Dickerson," *Alaska Bar Rag*, July–August–September 1982, 12.
27 "Tell It to . . . Bud: A Minority Report on the Police," *Anchorage Times*, June 5, 1969, 22.
28 See Robert Atwood, memo on conversation with Governor Wally Hickel, August 11, 1967, Atwood Family Papers, pt. 1, ser. 1, box 7, folder 16, Archives and Special Collections, UAA/APU Consortium Library.
29 William R. Nix and Daniel W. Hickey, "Report on the Shooting Death of Phillip J. Moore" (unknown source) June 18, 1979, box 4, folder 17, Alaska Black Caucus Inc. Records, Archives and Special Collections, UAA/APU Consortium Library.
30 Nix and Hickey, "Report on the Shooting Death of Phillip J. Moore," 21–22.
31 Barbara Rogers, "Coroner's Jury Learns of Moore's Drug Use," *Anchorage Times*, February 15, 1979, 1, 8.
32 Nix and Hickey, "Report on the Shooting Death of Phillip J. Moore," 22.
33 Nix and Hickey, "Report on the Shooting Death of Phillip J. Moore," 5.
34 E. Louis Overstreet, letter to editor, "Black Groups," *Anchorage Times*, in the Alaska Black Caucus Inc. Records, Archives and Special Collections, UAA/APU Consortium Library; "Assembly Creates Task Force to Probe Minority Sentencing," *Anchorage Daily Times*, March 7, 1979, 4.
35 "Assembly Creates Task Force to Probe Minority Sentencing," 4.
36 Nix and Hickey, "Report on the Shooting Death of Phillip J. Moore," 14–20.
37 Nix and Hickey, "Report on the Shooting Death of Phillip J. Moore," 5.
38 Ellis E. Conklin, "Cassell Williams Was a Quiet Neighbor," *Anchorage Times*, January 15, 1981, A3.
39 Pete Spivey, "Landlady Tells of Day of Strange Events before Gunman Is Killed," *Anchorage Daily News*, January 15, 1981, 1, 16.
40 Bill Kossen, "Police Shoot, Kill Sniper Barricaded in Apartment," *Anchorage Times*, January 15, 1981, 1, 9.
41 Patti Epler, "Coroner's Jury Told William 'Heard Voices,'" *Anchorage Times*, January 29, 1981, 1.
42 Julie Anne Gold, "Equal Rights Commission May Probe Police Shooting," *Anchorage Daily News*, January 17, 1981, 16.
43 Bill Kossen, "Porter Defends Police," *Anchorage Times*, January 16, 1981, A1, A3.
44 Kossen, "Police Shoot, Kill Sniper."
45 Gold, "Equal Rights Commission May Probe Police Shooting."
46 Lindback, "Blacks Demand Shooting Investigation."
47 Maureen Blewitt, "Local Police Cleared in January Shooting," *Anchorage Times*, June 19, 1981, 1.
48 Patti Epler, "Spenard Road Standoff Ends," *Anchorage Times*, November 28, 1979, 1.

49 Steve Hansen and Mary Pat Murphy, "Police Promised to Help Gunman," *Anchorage Times*, August 13, 1981, 1, 3.
50 Steve Hansen, "Police Express Satisfaction with Handling of Shooting," *Anchorage Times*, August 14, 1981, 1, 3.
51 Pamela Doto, "Racist Engages Police in 7-Hour Standoff," *Anchorage Daily News*, March 26, 1993, B1; "Racist Assault," *Anchorage Daily News*, March 29, 1993, B6.
52 Epler, "Spenard Road Standoff Ends"; Sharon Resnick, "The Blotter," *Anchorage Times*, June 29, 1984, 17; Hansen and Murphy, "Police Promised to Help Gunman."
53 Julie Anne Gold, "Equal Rights Commission May Probe Police Shooting," *Anchorage Daily News*, January 17, 1981, A16.
54 "Proper Investigation," *Anchorage Times*, January 29, 1981, A6.
55 Charlotte Small, letter to editor, "Policemen's Duty," *Anchorage Times*, January 23, 1981, A11.
56 Ada Smith, letter to editor, "Officers' Job," *Anchorage Times*, January 26, 1981, A5.
57 R. W. (Bob) Snider, letter to editor, "Cassell Williams," *Anchorage Times*, February 5, 1981, A11.
58 Mark C. Reed, letter to editor, "Under Fire," *Anchorage Times*, January 30, 1981, A7.
59 Jean Jones, letter to editor, "Shooting," *Anchorage Times*, February 2, 1981, A5.
60 "A Firm Hand," *Anchorage Times*, May 6, 1969, 4.
61 Doris Heinbeck, letter to editor, "Resents Column," *Anchorage Daily News*, December 29, 1970, 4.
62 Robert D. Olson Sr., letter to editor, "Moore Shooting," *Anchorage Times*, March 1, 1979, 6.
63 See Calvin John Smiley and David Fakunle, "From 'Brute' to 'Thug': The Demonization and Criminalization of Unarmed Black Male Victims in America," *Journal of Human Behavior in the Social Environment* 26, nos. 3–4 (2016): 350–66.
64 Jonathan Simon, *Governing through Crime: How the War on Crime Transformed American Democracy and Created a Culture of Fear* (New York: Oxford University Press, 2007), 13–16; Hinton, *From the War on Poverty to the War on Crime*, 63–95.
65 John Lindback, "Blacks Demand Shooting Investigation," *Anchorage Daily News*, January 26, 1981, C1.
66 Lyn Whitley, "Sullivan Follow-Up on Shooting Keys on 2 Recommendations," *Anchorage Times*, February 1, 1981, B1.
67 Steve Hansen, "Police, Minorities Work to Improve Relations," *Anchorage Times*, August 6, 1981, 13.
68 Anchorage Equal Rights Commission, "An Agreement," June 1981.
69 Nancy Montgomery, "Police Tests Screen Out Unstable Applicants," *Anchorage Daily News*, February 4, 1987, A1.
70 The Anchorage Community Police Relations Task Force (ACPRTF) continues to operate; however, its stature and relevance have been greatly diminished over

the years as representatives from the Department of Justice, the Alaska State Troopers, and the Anchorage Equal Rights Commission have pulled out of the taskforce. According to municipal ombudsman, Darrell Hess, "One, to two, to three people a year from the community go to the task force with complaints about the police department." See Matt Leseman, "The Current State of Anchorage's Police Relations Task Force," KTUU, June 15, 2020, https://www.alaskasnewssource.com/content/news/The-current-state-of-Anchorages-Police-Relations-Task-Force-571284141.html.

71 "The History of ACPRTF," ACPRTF handout for the Federation of Community Councils, n.d., accessed March 30, 2022, http://www.communitycouncils.org/download/16061.pdf.

72 Steve Hansen, "Tests Confirm Officer's Story," *Anchorage Times*, December 2, 1981, A1, A3.

73 John Lindback, "Officer Exonerated: Little Reaction Voiced," *Anchorage Daily News*, December 5, 1981, A1, A16.

74 Steve Hansen, "Police Officer's Shot Misses Armed Man," *Anchorage Times*, December 3, 1981, A1, A3.

75 Sean Hanlon, "Review Sought on Police Shooting," *Anchorage Times*, December 5, 1981, A14.

76 "Deputy Police Chief Retires after 26 Years of Service," *Anchorage Times*, September 1, 1988, A9.

77 Beth Barrett, "South Anchorage Development Main Issue in Assembly Race," *Anchorage Times*, August 31, 1982, A4.

78 "Man Convicted of Assault on Police Officers," *Anchorage Times*, February 3, 1983, 17.

79 Karin Davies, "Cop Shop Scuffle Leads to Arrest," *Anchorage Daily News*, August 2, 1982, B1.

80 Tom Kizzia, "Police Probe Clears Department in Black's Beating," *Anchorage Daily News*, August 11, 1982, A1, A16.

81 Anchorage Police Department Employees Association v. Dickerson, 3AN-82-6116 (Alaska Superior Court 1982).

82 Ariel Weissberg, "Police Defamation Suits against Civilians Complaining of Police Misconduct," *St. Louis University Law Journal* 22 (1979): 676–93. For more on police defamation lawsuits, see Scott M. Finical, "Defamation of a Police Officer in a Citizen Complaint: Vindicating the Rights of the Blue in Arizona," *Arizona Law Review* 24, no. 3 (1982): 611–37; and Lee S. Brenner and Hajir Ardebili, "To Protect and to Serve: Police Defamation Suits against California Citizens Who Report Officer Misconduct," *Communications Lawyer* 28, no. 1 (2011): 8–12.

83 Tom Kizzia, "Police Launch Probe of Fight, Racism Charges," *Anchorage Daily News*, August 6, 1982, A1.

84 Anchorage Police Department Employees Association v. Dickerson.

85 Bazeley, "Interview with M. Ashley Dickerson," 12; Dickerson, *Delayed Justice for Sale*, 104–7.

86 Tom Kizzia, "Municipality Settles Lawsuit over Man Killed by Police," *Anchorage Daily News*, November 18, 1983, 1. See also Tom Kizzia, "Family of Slain Man Sues City, 3 Officers," *Anchorage Daily News*, January 12, 1983, A1.
87 Letter, Theodore A. Moore to Lewis Sears, of the Anchorage Equal Rights Commission, ca. January 1981.
88 Sirry Alang, Donna McAlpine, Ellen McCreedy, and Rachel Hardeman, "Police Brutality and Black Health: Setting the Agenda for Public Health Scholars," *American Journal of Public Health* 107, no. 5 (2017): 662–65; Devin English, Lisa Bowleg, Ana Maria del Río-González, Jeanne M. Tschann, Robert P. Agans, and David J. Malebranche, "Measuring Black Men's Police-Based Discrimination Experiences: Development and Validation of the Police and Law Enforcement (PLE) Scale," *Cultural Diversity and Ethnic Minority Psychology* 23, no. 2 (2017): 185–99; Jacob Bor, Atheendar S. Venkataramani, David R. Williams, and Alexander C. Tsai, "Police Killings and Their Spillover Effects on the Mental Health of Black Americans: A Population-Based Quasi-Experimental Study," *Lancet* 392, no. 10144 (2018): 302–10.
89 Asta Corley, "APD Career Warrants Attention: Police Work Runs in the Family for the First Black Woman Officer," *Anchorage Daily News*, October 28, 2000, E2.
90 For an overview of the legislation and the context of female presence in police forces, see Lee W. Potts, "Equal Employment Opportunity and Female Employment in Police Agencies," *Journal of Criminal Justice* 11, no. 6 (1983): 505–23.
91 Corley, "APD Career Warrants Attention."
92 "Officer Sues Police Department," *North Star Reporter*, April 15, 1983, 1.
93 "Black Police Officers Organize," *North Star Reporter*, January 15, 1983, 15.
94 Corley, "APD Career Warrants Attention."
95 S. J. Komarnitsky, "Police Detectives File Discrimination Case against APD," *Anchorage Daily News*, March 7, 1995, B1.
96 Peter Blumberg, "Ministers Ask City to Review Race Relations; Discrimination Complaints by Detectives Spur Request," *Anchorage Daily News*, March 8, 1996, B1.
97 Sheila Toomey, "Rights Staff Finds Signs of Racial Bias: Report Backs Accusations by Black Police Officers," *Anchorage Daily News*, January 13, 1995, A1.
98 Natalie Phillips and Danielle Stanton, "Probe Finds Evidence of Discrimination in City Police Department," *Anchorage Daily News*, March 29, 1997, B1.
99 Two additional officers, one white and one Black, claimed that departmental practices had arbitrarily and negatively impacted their advancement. Tom Bell, "No Bias at APD, Feds Say," *Anchorage Daily News*, May 23, 1998, D1.
100 Tim Pryor, "Police Lawsuit Settled—$150,000 Deal Ends Discrimination Case," *Anchorage Daily News*, February 29, 2000, B1.
101 Megan Holland, "Officers' Lawsuit Charges Racism—Police: Two Claim There's Discrimination in the Force and Dealing with the Public," *Anchorage Daily News*, June 30, 2010, A1.

102 Alvin Kennedy and Eliezer Feliciano v. Municipality of Anchorage S-14762 (Alaska Supreme Court 2013), accessed October 28, 2019, cases.justia.com/alaska/supreme-court/s-14762.pdf?ts=1396106769.
103 Casey Grove, "Racial Discrimination Lawsuit against Anchorage Police Goes to Jury," *Anchorage Daily News*, March 27, 2014, B1.
104 Jerzy Shedlock, "Jury: No APD Racial Discrimination on 2 Counts in Lawsuit by Former Detectives," *Anchorage Daily News*, May 21, 2014, B1.
105 Laurel Andrews, "Jury Awards Former Anchorage Police Officers Nearly $1 Million Each in Racial Discrimination Suit," *Alaska Dispatch News*, March 8, 2017, https://www.adn.com/alaska-news/crime-courts/2017/03/07/jury-awards-former-anchorage-police-officers-nearly-1-million-each-in-racial-discrimination-lawsuit.
106 Casey Grove, "Judge Orders Anchorage to Pay Ex-Cops $2.7M after City Loses Racial Discrimination Case," *Alaska Public Media*, July 18, 2017, alaskapublic.org/2017/07/18/judge-orders-anchorage-to-pay-ex-cops-2-7m-after-verdict-against-city.
107 Hanlon, "Anchorage March Makes Proactive Call for Unity."
108 Jerzy Shedlock, "Anchorage Police Department, 82 Percent White, Tries to Diversify Its Force," *Alaska Dispatch News*, January 31, 2016, adn.com/crime-justice/article/anchorage-police-work-toward-diversifying-ranks-force-more-80-pecent-white/2016/02/01.
109 Devin Kelly, "With Full Leadership Team in Place, APD Pledges Focus on Violence and Drug Crimes," *Anchorage Daily News*, August 23, 2017, https://www.adn.com/alaska-news/anchorage/2017/08/23/apd-fills-out-leadership-team-amid-salary-boosts-pledges-focus-on-violence-and-drug-crimes. For a profile on Kenneth McCoy, see Matt Jardin, "At the Intersection of Community and Agency," *UAA Alumni Magazine*, April 2021, https://www.uaa.alaska.edu/news/archive/2021/05/at-the-intersection-of-community-and-agency.cshtml. On the failure to implement and enforce body-worn cameras for Anchorage police officers, see Editorial Board, "Is the Anchorage Police Department Backing Away from Body Camera Transparency?" *Anchorage Daily News*, March 12, 2022, https://www.adn.com/opinions/editorials/2022/03/12/is-the-anchorage-police-department-backing-away-from-body-camera-transparency.
110 Tess Williams, "Bronson Says Acting Anchorage Police Chief McCoy Will Remain in Position Permanently," *Anchorage Daily News*, June 8, 2021, https://www.adn.com/alaska-news/2021/06/08/bronson-says-acting-anchorage-police-chief-mccoy-will-remain-in-the-position-permanently; "Providence Alaska Names Kenneth McCoy as Diversity, Equity, and Inclusion Officer," *Alaska Business*, January 14, 2022, https://www.akbizmag.com/industry/healthcare/providence-alaska-names-kenneth-mccoy-as-diversity-equity-inclusion-officer.
111 Perhaps the highest-profile instance of police misconduct and a failure in the justice system revolved around the so-called Fairbanks Four. Four Alaska Native men were wrongfully accused and convicted of a 1997 murder in

downtown Fairbanks. After eighteen years, several appeals, and the intervention of Governor Bill Walker, the four men—George Frese, Kevin Pease, Eugene Vent, and Marvin Roberts—finally went free in 2016. See Lisa Demer and Lauren Holmes, "After 18 Years in Prison, Fairbanks Four Settle into Life as Free Men," *Anchorage Daily News*, October 20, 2016, https://www.adn.com/alaska-news/2016/10/20/after-18-years-in-prison-the-fairbanks-four-settle-into-life-as-free-men.

112 Linda Simmons, interviewed by author, Anchorage, February 15, 2018.
113 Jennifer Alexander, interviewed by author, Anchorage, January 19, 2018.
114 Sharon Harris, interviewed by author, Anchorage, November 29, 2017.
115 Kirsten Swann, "The Most Diverse Neighborhood in the US May Surprise You," *Smithsonian*, July 7, 2016, https://www.smithsonianmag.com/travel/mountain-view-alaska-diversity-immigration-smithsonian-journeys-travel-quarterly-180959441/?no-ist .
116 Moni Basu, "Most Diverse Place in America? It's Not Where You Think," CNN, January 11, 2016, cnn.com/2015/06/12/us/most-diverse-place-in-america.
117 Chad R. Farrell, "The Anchorage Mosaic: Racial and Ethnic Diversity in the Urban North," in Barnett and Hartman, *Imagining Anchorage*, 374–91.
118 *Understanding Alaska: People, Economy, and Resources*, report prepared by the Institute of Social and Economic Research, University of Alaska Anchorage, May 2006, 5. The demographic diversity is understated in these figures as a result of a particularly high percentage of Alaskans who identified as "two or more races." An additional 9 percent claimed such an identity.

8. RESENTMENT, RESILIENCE, AND CULTURAL REJUVENATION

1 "Taxi Driver, Auto Mechanic Found Murdered," *Anchorage Times*, May 28, 1985, A1.
2 Chris Geiger, "Palmer Murder Trial Centering on Racial Issue," *Anchorage Daily News*, October 22, 1985, A1; C. L. Gilbert, "Spectators Reflect Murder Trial's Racial Issues," *Anchorage Daily News*, October 25, 1985, C1.
3 Sheila Toomey, "Anchorage District Attorney Jumps into Hot Spot Today," *Anchorage Daily News*, March 23, 1987, A1.
4 Chris Geiger, "Palmer Jury Convicts Anchorage Man in Death of Black Mechanic," *Anchorage Daily News*, October 29, 1985, A1.
5 Chris Geiger, "Dunkin Gets 85 Years for Murder," *Anchorage Daily News*, March 21, 1986, C1.
6 Zaz Hollander, "Judge Cutler to Leave Courtroom behind Her," *Anchorage Daily News*, May 13, 2009, G1.
7 "Mechanic Helped Senior Citizens," *Anchorage Times*, May 30, 1985, B5.
8 Stephen Haycox, *Frigid Embrace: Politics, Economics, and Environment in Alaska* (Corvallis: Oregon State University Press, 2002), ix–x. See also Michael Jones-Correa, "The Origins and Diffusion of Racial Restrictive Covenants," *Political Science Quarterly* 115, no. 4 (2000–2001): 541–68; and Isabel Wilkerson, *The*

Warmth of Other Suns: The Epic Story of America's Great Migration (New York: Vintage, 2011), 10.

9 Judith Stein, *Pivotal Decade: How the United States Traded Factories for Finance in the Seventies* (New Haven, CT: Yale University Press, 2011); Meg Jacobs, *Panic at the Pump: The Energy Crisis and the Transformation of American Politics in the 1970s* (New York: Hill & Wang, 2016); Jad Mouawad, "Oil Prices Hit Record Set in '80s, but Then Recede," *New York Times*, March 3, 2008, https://www.nytimes.com/2008/03/03/business/worldbusiness/03cnd-oil.html?hp.

10 Gregg Erickson and Milt Barker, *The Great Alaska Recession* (Juneau: Erickson & Associates, 2015), 7.

11 John Boucher, "Economy Rebounds from Recession," *Alaska Economic Trends*, report by Alaska Department of Labor, March 1989, 1–4.

12 Gregg Erickson, *The Recession, The Real Estate Crash, and Alaska's Economic Prospects* (Juneau: Office of the Governor, Division of Policy, 1988), 1.

13 Boucher, "Economy Rebounds from Recession," 2.

14 Northern Economics Inc., *The Anchorage Economy from 1980 to the Present* (Anchorage: Anchorage Economic Development Corporation, 2004), 1–2.

15 Carl Iver Hovland and Robert R. Sears, "Minor Studies of Aggression, VI: Correlation of Lynchings with Economic Indices," *Journal of Psychology* 9 (1940): 301–10; Muzafer Sherif, *Group Conflict and Co-operation: Their Social Psychology* (London: Routledge & Kegan Paul, 1966); Henri Tajfel and John Turner, "An Integrative Theory of Intergroup Conflict," in *The Social Psychology of Intergroup Relations*, ed. William G. Austin and Stephen Worchel (Monterey: Brooks-Cole, 1979), 33–47.

16 Arjun Jayadev and Robert Johnson, "Tides and Prejudice: Racial Attitudes during Downturns in the United States, 1979–2014," *Review of Black Political Economy* 44, nos. 3–4 (2017): 379–92.

17 Emily C. Bianchi, Erika V. Hall, and Sarah Lee, "Reexamining the Link between Economic Downturns and Racial Antipathy: Evidence That Prejudice against Blacks Rises during Recessions," *Psychological Science* 20, no. 10 (2018): 1595.

18 Gilbert, "Spectators Reflect Murder Trial's Racial Issues."

19 Dennis Kelso, *A Descriptive Analysis of the Downtown Anchorage Skid Row Population* (Anchorage: Altam Associates and Center for Alcohol and Addictions Studies, University of Alaska, 1978).

20 John Knowlton, "Project 80s: Anchorage Responds," *Anchorage Times*, July 15, 1980, A1, A3.

21 David Postman, "Mayor Proposes Naming New Road, Not Ninth Avenue, in Honor of King," *Anchorage Daily News*, January 4, 1986, A1; David Postman, "A Tangle over King Tribute: Ninth Avenue Plan Stirs Up Politicians," *Anchorage Daily News*, January 7, 1986, A1.

22 David Postman, "PAC Named for Slain Civil Rights Leader," *Anchorage Daily News*, September 3, 1986, A1.

23 Lena Williams, "Holiday for Dr. King Gaining Wider Observance," *New York Times*, January 15, 1988, A10.
24 "Senate Nixes Resolution for Martin Luther King," *Anchorage Daily Times*, April 5, 1969, 10.
25 David Postman, "Smith Seeking to Overturn Arts Center Name," *Anchorage Daily News*, September 19, 1986, A1.
26 David Postman, "Assembly Ready to Tackle the King Issue," *Anchorage Daily News*, November 18, 1986, B1.
27 David Postman and Don Hunter, "Baker Signs Petition to Overturn Naming of Arts Center for King," *Anchorage Daily News*, October 9, 1986, A1.
28 David Postman, "Voters Likely to Decide King Name Issue," *Anchorage Daily News*, November 10, 1986, A1.
29 Mitch Lipka, "City Says PAC Name Petition Flawed," *Anchorage Times*, October 25, 1986, A1, A10.
30 "Alaska Ear," *Anchorage Daily News*, November 23, 1986, C3.
31 David Postman, "KKK Recruits in Anchorage," *Anchorage Daily News*, November 20, 1987, A1.
32 Postman, "Assembly Ready to Tackle the King Issue," B1.
33 Nancy Montgomery, "Voters Reject Naming Arts Center for King," *Anchorage Daily News*, October 7, 1987, A1.
34 On Don Smith and his political career and positions, see Devin Kelly, "Former Anchorage Assemblyman Running Again," *Anchorage Daily News*, February 11, 2016, https://www.adn.com/anchorage/article/former-assemblyman-don-smith-running-midtown-assembly/2016/02/12.
35 See Ian Haney Lopez, *Dog Whistle Politics: How Coded Racial Appeals Have Reinvented Racism and Wrecked the Middle Class* (New York: Oxford University Press, 2013). For an elaboration of the phrase, see pp. 1–12.
36 Lawrence C. Falk, "Klan's Imperial Wizard Eyes Expansion to Alaska," *Anchorage Daily Times*, September 19, 1968, 33.
37 Peter Spivey, "Ex-KKK Man Tries to Form Group Here," *Anchorage Daily News*, December 24, 1980; "Free Voices Takes Stand against Klan Organization," *Anchorage Times*, December 31, 1980, B1.
38 Patti Epler, "Wrong Duke Draws Wrath of Ku Klux Klan Foes Here," *Anchorage Times*, January 2, 1981, B1.
39 Postman, "KKK Recruits in Anchorage," A1.
40 Pamela Doto, "Local Skinhead Talks about What He's Trying to Do," *Anchorage Daily News*, July 29, 1990, A1.
41 Marilee Enge, "Vandals Break into Temple, Scrawl Anti-Jewish Messages on Walls," *Anchorage Daily News*, July 18, 1990, A1; Marilee Enge, "Police Arrest Teens for Trashing Temple," *Anchorage Daily News*, July 19, 1990, B1.
42 Liz Ruskin, "Skinhead Goes on Trial," *Anchorage Daily News*, April 29, 1993, E1; Liz Ruskin, "Teen-Age Neo-Nazi Convicted of Assault," *Anchorage Daily News*, April 30, 1993, D3.

43 Wayne King, "Neo-Nazis' Dream of a Racist Territory in Pacific Northwest Refuses to Die," *New York Times*, July 5, 1986, 10.
44 Larry Campbell and Kim Rich, "Supremacists Target Youths: Anchorage Teens Get Propaganda," *Anchorage Daily News*, March 6, 1991, B1.
45 Campbell and Rich, "Supremacists Target Youths."
46 Peter Blumberg, "School District Works to Bar Guns and Gangs," *Anchorage Daily News*, August 7, 1991, A1; "Racist Skinhead Glossary," Southern Poverty Law Center, n.d., accessed September 12, 2019, www.splcenter.org/fighting-hate/intelligence-report/2015/racist-skinhead-glossary.
47 Peter Blumberg, "Racism Sparks Suspension, Meeting," *Anchorage Daily News*, May 27, 1992, B1.
48 Peter Blumberg, "Graffiti Incident Sparks Schools to Deal with Race-Relation Issue," *Anchorage Daily News*, May 26, 1992, A1; Peter Blumberg, "Frustration Fuels Tension at Hanshew," *Anchorage Daily News*, May 28, 1992, B1.
49 Peter Blumberg, "Opening Minds: Chugiak High Takes Steps against Hatred," *Anchorage Daily News*, May 16, 1993, B1.
50 Kim Severson, "Racism and the Schools Administrators, Students Try to Gauge Depth of Ethnic Tension," *Anchorage Daily News*, November 8, 1991, C1.
51 Elizabeth Pulliam, "Booming Minority Populations Move City Ahead in Racial Mix," *Anchorage Daily News*, November 22, 1988, D1.
52 Peter Blumberg, "Skinheads Show Up at Hanshew, Briefly," *Anchorage Daily News*, May 30, 1992, A1.
53 Robert Meyerowitz, "Hillside Land Plan under Fire," *Anchorage Daily News*, May 2, 1994, A1.
54 Blumberg, "Skinheads Show Up at Hanshew."
55 Pamela Doto, "Service High's Skinheads, Blacks Clash," *Anchorage Daily News*, October 7, 1992, A1.
56 Blumberg, "Graffiti Incident Sparks Schools."
57 Edward Robinson, "Confronting Racism Prejudice a Lifelong Foe for Minority Children," *Anchorage Daily News*, August 31, 1990, G3.
58 Severson, "Racism."
59 Craciun & Associates, *Winning with Stronger Education Research Reports* (Anchorage: Anchorage School District and Anchorage Chamber of Commerce, 1991), 77–79.
60 Craciun & Associates, *Winning with Stronger Education Research Reports*, 16–17.
61 Craciun & Associates, *Winning with Stronger Education Research Reports*, 80.
62 Blumberg, "Racism Sparks Suspension."
63 Blumberg, "Graffiti Incident Sparks Schools."
64 Severson, "Racism."
65 Overstreet, *Black on a Background of White*.
66 Peter Blumberg, "School Official Resigns, Cites Racism, O'Rourke," *Anchorage Daily News*, November 18, 1992, A1.

67 Letter, Everett Louis Overstreet to Brent Rock, November 16, 1992, folder 6, box 1, E. Louis Overstreet Papers, Archives and Special Collections, UAA/APU Consortium Library.
68 Byron Mallot, "Don't Let Alaska Become the Site of LA Style Anger and Frustration," *Anchorage Times*, May 28, 1992, 17.
69 Pamela Stock, "Afro-American Leaders Stress Need for Education," *Anchorage Times*, February 18, 1992, 9.
70 "East Celebrates Diverse Cultures," *Anchorage Times*, March 6, 1992, 44.
71 Matt Tunseth, "Anchorage Public Schools Lead Nation in Diversity," *Anchorage Daily News*, May 23, 2015, 1.
72 Desiree Humphrey, "Black History Skits Depict Vibrant Past," *Anchorage Times*, February 29, 1992, 15.
73 Pamela Stock, "Afro-American Leaders Stress Need for Education," *Anchorage Times*, February 18, 1992, 9.
74 A brief biography of King is available at his website: https://www.theofficialjayking.com.
75 Jerzy Shedlock, "After Prison, Sean Sullivan—Once Alaska's Most Successful Rapper—Is Working Double Time to Start Over," *Anchorage Daily Times*, October 14, 2016, https://www.adn.com/arts/music/2016/10/14/jokers-comeback-after-prison-sean-sullivan-once-alaskas-most-successful-rapper-is-working-double-time-to-start-over.
76 Ben Anderson, "For Alaska's Pamyua, It's All about Relationships," *Anchorage Daily News*, February 10, 2011, https://www.adn.com/arts/article/alaskas-pamyua-its-all-about-relationships/2011/02/10.
77 Maurie J. Cohen, "Economic Impact of an Environmental Accident: A Time-Series Analysis of the Exxon Valdez Oil Spill in Southcentral Alaska," *Sociological Spectrum* 13, no. 1 (1993): 35–63; J. Steven Picou, Duane A. Gill, and Maurie J. Cohen, *The Exxon Valdez Disaster: Readings of a Modern Social Problem* (Dubuque, IA: Kendall Hunt, 1999), 259–65.
78 Northern Economics, *Anchorage Economy*, 1–2.

CONCLUSION

1 On Alaska's oil wealth, see Claus-M. Naske and Herman E. Slotkin, *Alaska: A History* (Norman: University of Oklahoma Press, 2014), 241–74.
2 Author interview with Eleanor Andrews, Anchorage, June 7, 2019.
3 Quoted in Alton Hornsby Jr., ed., *Black America: A State-by-State Historical Encyclopedia* (Santa Barbara, CA: Greenwood Publishing), 30. See also "James C. Hayes: Alaska's First Black Mayor," *Ebony*, October 1993, 64–65.
4 For certain, this trust eroded as whispers of corruption dogged his administration, and after his tenure, James Hayes's wife faced allegations of embezzlement of funds from the church where he had become a minister.
5 "James C. Hayes," 64–65.
6 "James C. Hayes," 64.

7. A common bumper sticker affixed to many vehicles in Alaska proclaims, "We don't give a damn how they do it Outside." For an expression of this attitude, see Frank Dahl, "Los Anchorage: Longing for the Good Old Days," *Anchorage Press*, October 29, 2015, www.anchoragepress.com/opinion/los-anchorage.

8. Asta Corley, "Memorial Fit for a King," *Anchorage Daily News*, December 11, 1996, E2.

9. Richard Richtmyer, "City Center Could Honor Athabascans—TRIBUTE: Dena'ina Names Are Proposed for Use at New Facility," *Anchorage Daily News*, June 27, 2006, A1.

10. Devin Kelly, "New Alaska Native Art Installation Commemorates Cultural History and Generations of Fishing at Ship Creek," *Anchorage Daily News*, December 25, 2018, https://www.adn.com/alaska-news/anchorage/2018/12/25/new-alaska-native-art-installation-commemorates-cultural-history-and-generations-of-fishing-at-ship-creek.

11. Emily Goodykoontz, "Anchorage School Board Votes to Name East Anchorage High School after the Sen. Bettye Davis," *Anchorage Daily News*, October 21, 2020, https://www.adn.com/alaska-news/education/2020/10/21/anchorage-school-board-votes-to-name-east-anchorage-high-school-after-state-sen-bettye-davis.

12. Chad Farrell, "The Anchorage Mosaic: Racial and Ethnic Diversity in the Urban North," in *Imagining Anchorage: The Making of America's Northernmost Metropolis*, ed. James K. Barnett and Ian C. Hartman (Fairbanks: University of Alaska Press, 2018).

13. "The Contributions of New Americans in Alaska," *New American Economy: A Report*, August 2016, 6–10.

14. For a series of statements and issues that AFACT has advanced in Anchorage, see Anchoragefact.org, accessed October 18, 2020, https://www.anchoragefact.org/press.

15. See Diana Furchtgott-Roth, *The Economic Benefit of Immigration*, report prepared for the Manhattan Institute, February 13, 2013, https://www.manhattan-institute.org/html/economic-benefits-immigration-5712.html. On Alaska, see the roundtable discussion hosted by Alaska Commons, "Making the Case for Anchorage's Immigrant Population," September 9, 2019, www.alaskacommons.com/2016/09/19/making-the-case-for-anchorages-immigrant-population.

16. "Demonstration in Downtown Anchorage Targets Ferguson Grand Jury Decision," *Alaska Dispatch News*, November 26, 2014, https://www.adn.com/anchorage/article/demonstration-downtown-anchorage-targets-ferguson-grand-jury-decision/2014/11/27.

17. Devin Kelly, "'Black Lives Matter' Protest in Anchorage Echoes National Concerns," *Alaska Dispatch News*, December 6, 2014, https://www.adn.com/anchorage/article/Black-lives-matter-protest-anchorage-echoes-national-concerns/2014/12/06.

18. Tegan Hanlon, "Amid Nationwide Racial Tensions, Anchorage March Makes Proactive Call for Unity," *Alaska Dispatch News*, July 16, 2016, https://www

.adn.com/alaska-news/anchorage/2016/07/16/amid-nationwide-racial-tensions-anchorage-march-makes-proactive-call-for-unity.
19 See the Mapping Police Violence website, https://mappingpoliceviolence.org—researchers have pulled the information from a collection of federal, state, and local databases to present the most comprehensive view of police violence available.
20 Michelle Theriault Boots, "43 People Have Been Killed by Alaska Law Enforcement Officers in the Last 5½ Years. Here's What We Learned by Examining Each Case," *Anchorage Daily News*, August 3, 2020, https://www.adn.com/alaska-news/2020/08/03/43-people-have-been-killed-by-alaska-law-enforcement-officers-in-the-last-five-and-a-half-years-heres-what-we-learned-by-examining-each-case. See also Frank Edwards, Hedwig Lee, and Michael Esposito, "Risk of Being Killed by Police Use of Force in the United States by Age, Race-Ethnicity, and Sex," *Proceedings of the National Academy of Sciences of the United States of America* 116, no. 34 (August 20, 2019): 16793–98.
21 Evan Hill, Ainara Tiefenthäler, Christiaan Triebert, Drew Jordan, Haley Willis, and Robin Stein, "8 Minutes and 46 Seconds: How George Floyd Was Killed in Police Custody," *New York Times*, May 31, 2020. It was later revealed during the Derek Chauvin trial that Floyd succumbed to an asphyxiation that lasted nearly nine and a half minutes.
22 Emily Goodykoontz and Marc Lester, "'Joy Mixed with Grief': Protesters March Peacefully in Anchorage to Support Black Lives Matter," *Anchorage Daily News*, June 6, 2020.
23 Author interview with Celeste Hodge Growden, August 21, 2021.
24 George C. Anderson, "Alaska Frontier . . . Attracts Negro Pioneers," *Color*, April 1953, 25.

BIBLIOGRAPHY

ARCHIVAL COLLECTIONS

Archives and Special Collections, University of Alaska Anchorage / Alaska Pacific University Consortium Library
    Alaska Black Caucus Inc. Records, 1975–93
    Atwood, Robert B., Papers
    Blacks in Alaska Project Records, 1953–2004
    Bowman, Willard L., Papers
    Melzer, Bruce, Oral History Interviews
    NAACP Papers, part 27: Selected Branch Files (available on microfilm)
    Overstreet, E. Louis, Paper
Alaska Department of Natural Resources Recorder's Office, Anchorage
National Archives and Records Administration, Washington, DC, and College Park, MD,
Correspondence Relating to Civilian Conservation Corps (CCC) Activities, ca. 1937–ca. 1942, Record Group 95: Records of the Forest Service, 1870–2008
New Bedford Whaling Museum, New Bedford, MA, Dennis Woods Abstracts
University of California, Berkeley, Bancroft Library, NAACP, Region 1, Records, 1942–86, Manuscript Collections, 78/180

PUBLISHED SOURCES

Adney, Tappan. *The Klondike Stampede*. 1900. Reprint, Vancouver: University of British Columbia Press, 1995.
Alang, Sirry, Donna McAlpine, Ellen McCreedy, and Rachel Hardeman. "Police Brutality and Black Health: Setting the Agenda for Public Health Scholars." *American Journal of Public Health* 107, no. 5 (2017): 662–65.

Alexander, Michelle. *The New Jim Crow: Mass Incarceration in the Age of Colorblindness*. New York: New Press, 2012.

Alvarez, Luis. *The Power of the Zoot: Youth Culture and Resistance during World War II*. Berkeley: University of California Press, 2008.

Anchorage Community Land Trust. *Mountain View Targeted Neighborhood Plan*. Anchorage: Mountain View Community Council, 2016.

Anchorage Police Department Employees Association v. Dickerson, 3AN-82-6116. Anchorage: Alaska Superior Court 1982.

Antonson, Joan M., and William S. Hanable. *An Administrative History of Sitka National Historical Park*. Anchorage: Alaska Region, National Park Service, 1987.

———. *Alaska's Heritage*. Anchorage: Alaska Historical Society for the Alaska Historical Commission, Department of Education, 1985.

Armitage, Susan, and Elizabeth Jameson, eds. *The Women's West*. Norman: University of Oklahoma Press, 1987.

Astor, Gerald. *The Right to Fight: A History of African Americans in the Military*. Cambridge, MA: Da Capo Press, 2001.

Austin, William G., and Stephen Worchel. *Social Psychology of Intergroup Relations*. Monterey, CA : Brooks-Cole, 1979.

Bailey, Beth, and David Farber. "The 'Double-V' Campaign in World War II Hawaii: African Americans, Racial Ideology, and Federal Power." *Journal of Social History* 26, no. 4 (Summer 1993): 817–43.

Baker, Rachel, Joun Boucher, Neal Fried, and Brigitta Windisch-Cole. "Long-Term Retrospective: Alaska's Economy since Statehood." *Alaska Economic Trends*, December 1999, 3–21.

Ball, Charles. *Marketability Analysis Eastchester Urban Renewal Project Alaska UR-16*. Anchorage: Economic Research and Planning Associates, 1963.

Ball, Edward. *Slaves in the Family*. New York: Farrar, Straus & Giroux, 1998.

Barlow, Allison, Lauren Tingey, Mary Cwik, Novalene Goklish, Francene Larzelere-Hinton, Angelita Lee, Rosemarie Suttle, Britta Mullany, and John T. Walkup. "Understanding the Relationship between Substance Abuse and Self-Injury in American Indian Youth." *American Journal of Drug and Alcohol Abuse* 38, no. 5 (2012): 1042–1048.

Barnett, James R., and Ian C. Hartman, eds. *Imagining Anchorage: The Making of America's Northernmost Metropolis*. Fairbanks: University of Alaska Press, 2018.

Bateman, Annaliese Jacobs. *Regulated Vice: A History of Seward's Red Light District, 1914–1954*." Report prepared for National Park Service. Anchorage: Anchorage: Alaska Support Office, July 2002.

Bateson, Gregory, and Jurgen Ruesch. *Communication: The Social Matrix of Psychiatry*. New Brunswick, NJ: Transaction Publishers, 2009.

Beauvais, Fred. "American Indians and Alcohol." *Alcohol Health and Research World* 22, no. 4 (1998): 253–59.

Bianchi, Emily C., Erika V. Hall, and Sarah Lee. "Reexamining the Link between Economic Downturns and Racial Antipathy: Evidence That Prejudice against Blacks Rises during Recessions." *Psychological Science* 20, no. 10 (2018): 1584–97.

Blansett, Kent. *A Journey to Freedom: Richard Oakes, Alcatraz, and the Red Power Movement.* New Haven: Yale University Press, 2018.
Blum, Howard. *The Floor of Heaven: The True Tale of the Last Frontier and the Yukon Gold Rush.* New York: Broadway Books, 2012.
Bockstoce, John. *Whales, Ice, and Men: The History of Whaling in the Western Arctic.* 1986. Reprint, Seattle: University of Washington Press, 1995.
Bolster, W. Jeffrey. *Black Jacks: African American Seamen in the Age of Sail.* Cambridge: Harvard University Press, 1998.
———. "'To Feel Like a Man': Black Seamen in the Northern States, 1800–1860." *Journal of American History* 76, no. 4 (March 1990): 1173–99.
Bor, Jacob, Atheendar S. Venkataramani, David R. Williams, and Alexander C. Tsai. "Police Killings and Their Spillover Effects on the Mental Health of Black Americans: A Population-Based Quasi-Experimental Study." *Lancet* 392, no. 10144 (2018): 302–10.
Boucher, John. "Economy Rebounds from Recession." *Alaska Economic Trends.* Anchorage: Alaska Department of Labor, March 1989.
Bowers, William T., William M. Hammond, and George L. MacGarrigle. *Black oldier, White Army: The 24th Infantry in Korea.* Washington, DC: Center for Military History, United States Army, 1996.
Brenner, Lee S., and Hajir Ardebili. "To Protect and to Serve: Police Defamation Suits against California Citizens Who Report Officer Misconduct." *Communications Lawyer* 28, no. 1 (2011): 8–12.
Broussard, Albert. *Expectations of Equality: A History of Black Westerners.* Hoboken, NJ: Wiley Blackwell, 2012.
Brown, William Edward. *The History of the Central Brooks Range: Gaunt Beauty, Tenuous Life.* Fairbanks: University of Alaska Press, 2007.
Buchanan, A. Russell. *Black Americans in World War II.* New York: ABC-CLIO, 1977.
Buehler, James W. "Racial/Ethnic Disparities in the Use of Lethal Force by US Police, 2010–2014." *American Journal of Public Health* 107, no. 2 (2017): 295–97.
Burns, Walter Noble. *A Year with a Whaler.* New York: Outing Publishing Company, 1913.
Burton, Pierre. *The Klondike Fever: The Life and Death of the Last Great Gold Rush.* New York: Basic Books, 2003.
Bushell, Sharon, ed. *We Alaskans: Stories of People Who Helped Build the Great Land.* Homer, AK: Road Tunes Media, 2001.
Butler, Anne M. *Daughters of Joy, Sisters of Misery: Prostitutes in the American West, 1865–90.* Urbana: University of Illinois Press, 1987.
Butler, Paul. *Chokehold: Policing Black Men.* New York: Free Press, 2018.
Buzzell, Rolfe G., ed. *Flat and Iditarod, 1993–1995: Oral History Interviews.* BLM-Alaska Open File Report 66. Anchorage: US Department of the Interior, Bureau of Land Management; State of Alaska, Department of Natural Resources, 1997.
Carrington, William J. "The Alaskan Labor Market during the Pipeline Era." *Journal of Political Economy* 104, no. 1 (1996): 186–218.

Cecelsky, David S. *The Waterman's Song: Slavery and Freedom in Maritime North Carolina*. Chapel Hill: University of North Carolina Press, 2012.

Center for Policing Equity. *The Science of Justice: Race, Arrests, and Police Use of Force*. New York: John Jay College of Criminal Justice, 2016.

Chandonnet, Fern, ed. *Alaska at War, 1941–1945: The Forgotten War Remembered*. Fairbanks: University Alaska Press, 2007.

City of Anchorage. "Anchorage 1965 Neighborhood Planning Program." *To Eastchester Residents and the Eastchester Improvement Committee*. Anchorage: Alaska State Housing Authority, 1966.

Clark, Reverend F. E., DD. *Ways and Means for the Young People's Society of Christian Endeavor*. Boston: D. Lothrop Company, 1890.

Clodfelter, Mark. *River Rats: Red River Valley Fighter Pilots of Vietnam*. Nashville: Turner Publishing, 1990.

Cloe, John Haile. *Attu: The Forgotten Battle*. Anchorage: Department of the Interior, National Park Service, Alaska Affiliated Areas, Aleutian World War II Historic Area, 2017.

Coates, Kenneth S., and William R. Morrison. *The Alaska Highway in World War II: The US Army's Occupation of Canada's Northwest*. Norman: University of Oklahoma Press, 1992.

Coates, Peter. *Trans-Alaskan Pipeline Controversy: Technology, Conservation, and the Frontier*. Fairbanks: University of Alaska Press, 1993.

Coen, Ross. "How Alaska's Equal Rights Law Was First Put to the Test." *Anchorage Daily News*, January 15, 2017.

Cohen, M. J. "Economic Impact of an Environmental Accident: A Time Series Analysis of the *Exxon Valdez* Oil Spill in South Central Alaska." *Sociological Spectrum* 13, no. 1 (September 1993): 35–64.

Cole, Dermot. *Amazing Pipeline Stories: How Building the Trans-Alaska Pipeline Transformed Life in America's Last Frontier*. Kenmore, WA: Epicenter Press, 1997.

Cole, Terrence. "Jim Crow in Alaska: The Passage of the Alaska Equal Rights Act of 1945." *Western Historical Quarterly* 23, no. 4 (November 1992): 429–49.

A Community Attitude Survey. Anchorage: Greater Anchorage Area Borough Planning Department, 1972.

Copeland, Luther E. *The Southern Baptist Convention and the Judgment of History: The Taint of an Original Sin*. Lanham, MD: University Press of America, 2002.

Craciun & Associates. *Winning with Stronger Education Research Reports*. Anchorage: Anchorage School District and Anchorage Chamber of Commerce, 1991.

Darden, Joe T. "Black Residential Segregation since the 1948 *Shelley v. Kraemer* Decision." *Journal of Black Studies* 25, no. 6 (1995): 680–91.

Dauenhauer, Nora Marks, and Richard Dauenhauer. *Haa Kusteeyí, Our Culture: Tlingit Life Stories*. Seattle: University of Washington Press, 1994.

De Graaf, Lawrence, Kevin Mulroy, and Quintard Taylor, eds. *Seeking Eldorado: African Americans in California*. Seattle: University of Washington Press, 2001.

Diaquoi, Raygine. "Symbols in the Strange Fruit Seeds: What 'the Talk' Black

Parents Have with Their Sons Tells Us about Racism." *Harvard Educational Review* 87, no. 4 (2017): 512–37.

Dickerson, Mahala Ashley. *Delayed Justice for Sale*. Anchorage, AK: Al-Acres, 1998.

Dixon, Aaron. *My People Are Rising: Memoir of a Black Panther Party Captain*. Chicago: Haymarket Books, 2012.

Dolin, Eric Jay. *Leviathan: The History of Whaling in America*. New York: W. W. Norton, 2007.

Doucet, Fabienne, Meeta Banerjee, and Stephanie Parade. "What Should Young Black Children Know about Race? Parents of Preschoolers, Preparation for Bias, and Promoting Egalitarianism." *Journal of Early Childhood Research* 16, no. 1 (2018): 65–79.

Edwards, Frank, Hedwig Lee, and Michael Esposito. "Risk of Being Killed by Police Use of Force in the United States by Age, Race-Ethnicity, and Sex." *Proceedings of the National Academy of Sciences of the United States of America* 116, no. 34 (August 20, 2019): 16793–98.

Ellis, Richard. *The Great Sperm Whale: A Natural History of the Ocean's Most Magnificent and Mysterious Creature*. Lawrence: University Press of Kansas, 2011.

English, Devin, Lisa Bowleg, Ana Maria del Río-González, Jeanne M. Tschann, Robert P. Agans, and David J. Malebranche. "Measuring Black Men's Police-Based Discrimination Experiences: Development and Validation of the Police and Law Enforcement (PLE) Scale." *Cultural Diversity and Ethnic Minority Psychology* 23, no. 2 (2017): 185–99.

Erickson, Gregg. *The Recession, the Real Estate Crash, and Alaska's Economic Prospects*. Juneau: Office of the Governor, Division of Policy, 1988.

Erickson, Gregg, and Milt Barker. *The Great Alaska Recession*. Juneau: Erickson & Associates, 2015.

Farrell, Chad R. "The Anchorage Mosaic: Racial and Ethnic Diversity in the Urban North." In *Imagining Anchorage: The Making of America's Northernmost Metropolis*, edited by James R. Barnett and Ian C. Hartman, 374–91. Fairbanks: University of Alaska Press, 2018.

Finical, Scott M. "Defamation of a Police Officer in a Citizen Complaint: Vindicating the Rights of the Blue in Arizona." *Arizona Law Review* 24, no. 3 (1982): 611–37.

Fischer, Vic, with Charles Wohlforth. *To Russia with Love: An Alaskan's Journey*. Fairbanks: University of Alaska Press, 2012.

Flamming, Douglas. *African Americans in the West*. Santa Barbara, CA: ABC-CLIO, 2009.

———. *Bound for Freedom: Black Los Angeles in Jim Crow America*. Berkeley: University of California Press, 2005.

Foner, Eric. *Gateway to Freedom: The Hidden History of the Underground Railroad*. New York: W. W. Norton, 2016.

———. *Reconstruction: America's Unfinished Revolution, 1863–1877*. 1987. Reprint, New York: Perennial Classics, 2014.

Forman, John, Jr. *Locking Up Our Own: Crime and Punishment in Black America.* New York: Farrar, Straus & Giroux, 2018.

Fothergill, Alice, Enrique G. M. Maestas, and JoAnne DeRouen Darlington. "Race, Ethnicity and Disasters in the United States: A Review of the Literature." *Disasters* 23, no. 2 (1999): 156–73.

Fothergill, Alice, and Lori A. Peek. "Poverty and Disasters in the United States: A Review of Recent Sociological Findings." *Natural Hazards* 32, no. 1 (2004): 89–110.

Fournelle, John. *An Anchorage History: Early Years of Rogers Park and Traversie Sub-divisions.* Online report, hosted by the University of Wisconsin. www.geology.wisc.edu/~johnf/RogersPark/RogersPark-Traversie_Talk_092211.pdf.

Frank, John W., Roland S. Moore, and Genevieve M. Ames. "Historical and Cultural Roots of Drinking Problems among American Indians." *American Journal of Public Health* 90, no. 3 (2000): 344–51.

Frankham, Emma. "Mental Illness Affects Police Fatal Shootings." *Contexts* 17, no. 2 (2018): 70–72.

Friday, Chris. *Organizing Asian-American Labor: The Pacific Coast Canned-Salmon Industry, 1870–1942.* Philadelphia: Temple University Press, 1995.

Friesen, Robert J. *The Chilkoot Pass and the Great Gold Rush of 1898.* Ottawa, Canada: National Historic Parks and Sites Branch, 1981.

Gatewood, Willard B., Jr. *"Smoked Yankees" and the Struggle for Empire: Letters from Negro Soldiers, 1898–1902.* Fayetteville: University of Arkansas Press, 1987.

Golodoff, Nick, and Rachel Mason, eds. *Attu Boy: A Young Alaskans World War II Memoir.* Fairbanks: University of Alaska Press, 2015.

Graham, Darwin Bond. "The New Orleans That Race Built: Racism, Disaster, and Urban Spatial Relationships." *Souls* 9, no. 1 (2007): 4–18.

Green, Melissa S., and Sharon Charmard. "Experience of Racism in Anchorage." *Alaska Justice Forum* 30, no. 2 (2013): 8–9.

Green, Shirley Mae. *Anchorage, Alaska: The Myth of Racial Equality. A Study of the Experiences of Anchorage's Black Workers.* PhD diss., Union Institute & University, 1987.

Grover, Kathryn. *The Fugitive's Gibraltar: Escaping Slaves and Abolitionism in New Bedford, Massachusetts.* Cambridge: University of Massachusetts Press, 2001.

———. *Fugitive Slaves in Alaska: Phase One Research Report.* Prepared for the National Park Service. Washington, DC: NPS, September 2001.

Gruening, Ernest. *State of Alaska.* New York: Random House, 1968.

Hallock, Charles. *Our New Alaska; or, The Seward Purchase Vindicated.* New York: Forest and Stream Publishing, 1886.

Hammett, Dashiell, and Robert Colodny. *The Battle of the Aleutians: A Graphic History, 1942–1943.* Aleutian Islands, AK: Intelligence Section, Field Force Headquarters, 1943.

Harper, George. "Blacks in Alaska History." *Heritage: Quarterly Newsletter of the Office of History and Archaeology* 31 (January–March 1987).

Hartman, Ian C. *Black History in the Last Frontier.* Anchorage: University of Alaska Anchorage and the National Park Service, 2020.

Hartman, Ian C., and David Reamer. "A 'Far North Dixie Land': Black Settlement, Discrimination, and Community in Urban Alaska." *Western Historical Quarterly* (Summer 2019): 1–20.

Haycox, Stephen. *Alaska: An American Colony.* Seattle: University of Washington Press, 2002.

———. *Frigid Embrace: Politics, Economics, and Environment in Alaska.* Corvallis: Oregon State University Press, 2002.

Henrikson, Steve. "The 1882 Bombardments: New Developments." *Proceedings of the Alaska Historical Society Annual Meeting, October 4–6, 1999,* 60–75. Anchorage: Anchorage Historical Society, 2000.

Hensley, William L. Iggiagruk. *Fifty Miles from Tomorrow: A Memoir of Alaska and the Real People.* New York: Picador, 2009.

Hinnershitz, Stephanie. *Race, Religion, and Civil Rights: Asian Student on the West Coast.* New Brunswick, NJ: Rutgers University Press, 2015.

Hinton, Lizabeth. *From the War on Poverty to the War on Crime: The Making of Mass Incarceration in America.* Cambridge: Harvard University Press, 2016.

Holder Spude, Catherine. *Saloons, Prostitutes, and Temperance in Alaska Territory.* Norman: University of Oklahoma Press, 2015.

———. *"That Fiend in Hell": Soapy Smith in Legend.* Norman: University of Oklahoma Press, 2012.

Hornsby, Alton, Jr., ed. *Black America: A State-by-State Historical Encyclopedia.* Santa Barbara, CA: Greenwood Publishing, 2011.

Hovland, Carl Iver, and Robert R. Sears. "Minor Studies of Aggression, VI: Correlation of Lynchings with Economic Indices." *Journal of Psychology* 9 (1940): 301–10.

Hoxie, Frederick E., ed. *The Oxford Handbook of American Indian History.* New York: Oxford University Press, 2016.

Hu Pegues, Juliana. *Space-Time Colonialism: Alaska's Indigenous and Asian Entanglements.* Chapel Hill: University of North Carolina Press, 2021.

Immerwaher, Daniel. *How to Hide an Empire: A History of the Greater United States.* New York: Farrar, Straus & Giroux, 2019.

Jackson, Miles M. *They Followed the Trade Winds: African Americans in Hawaiʻi.* Honolulu: University of Hawaiʻi at Manoa, Department of Sociology, 2004.

Jacobs, Meg. *Panic at the Pump: The Energy Crisis and the Transformation of American Politics in the 1970s.* New York: Hill & Wang, 2016.

Jayadev, Arjun, and Robert Johnson. "Tides and Prejudice: Racial Attitudes during Downturns in the United States, 1979–2014." *Review of Black Political Economy* 44, nos. 3–4 (2017): 379–92.

Jeffrey, Julia Roy. *The Great Silent Army of Abolitionism: Ordinary Women in the Antislavery Movement.* Chapel Hill: University of North Carolina Press, 1998.

Jenkins, Everett, Jr. *Pan-African Chronology II: A Comprehensive Reference to the Black Quest for Freedom in Africa, the Americas, Europe, and Asia, 1865–1915.* Jefferson, NC: McFarland, 1998.

Johnson, Ronald C. *Out of the North*. Wasilla, AK: Plover Press, 1991.
Jones, Preston. *City for Empire: An Anchorage History, 1914–1941*. Fairbanks: University of Alaska Press, 2010.
Jones-Correa, Michael. "The Origins and Diffusion of Racial Restrictive Covenants." *Political Science Quarterly* 115, no. 4 (2000–2001): 541–68.
Junne, George H., Jr. *The History of Blacks in Canada: A Selectively Annotated Bibliography*. Westport, CT: Greenwood Press, 2003.
Katz, William Loren. *The Black West: A Documentary and Pictorial History of the African American Role in the Westward Expansion of the United States*. New York: Touchstone, 1996.
Katznelson, Ira. *When Affirmative Action Was White: An Untold History of Racial Inequality in Twentieth-Century America*. New York: W. W. Norton, 2006.
Keenan, Meier Randall. *Walking on Water: Black American Lives at the Turn of the Twenty-First Century*. New York: Vintage, 2000.
Kelso, Dennis. *A Descriptive Analysis of the Downtown Anchorage Skid Row Population*. Anchorage: Altam Associates and Center for Alcohol and Addictions Studies, University of Alaska, 1978.
Kersten, Andrew E. *A. Philip Randolph: A Life in the Vanguard*. Lanham, MD: Rowman & Littlefield, 2007.
Kizzia, Tom. *Cold Mountain Path: The Ghost Town Decades of McCarthy-Kennecott, Alaska, 1938–1983*. McCarthy, AK: Porphyry Press, 2021.
Knopf, Terry Ann. "Race, Riots, and Reporting." *Journal of Black Studies* 4, no. 3 (1974): 303–27.
Kohler-Hausmann, Julilly. *Getting Tough: Welfare and Imprisonment in the 1970s America*. Princeton: Princeton University Press, 2019.
Kohlhoff, Dean. *When the Wind Was a River: Aleut Evacuation in World War II*. Seattle: University of Washington Press, 1995.
Kroll, Douglas. *A Coastguardsman's History of the US Coast Guard*. Annapolis, MD: Naval Institute Press, 2010.
Kruse, Kevin. *White Flight: Atlanta and the Making of Modern Conservatism*. Princeton, NJ: Princeton University Press, 2007.
Jardina, Ashley. *White Identity Politics*. Cambridge: Cambridge University Press, 2019.
Jefferson, Robert F. *Fighting for Hope: African American Troops of the 93rd Infantry Division in World War II and Postwar America*. Baltimore: Johns Hopkins University Press, 2008.
Jones, Livingston F. *A Study of the Thlingets of Alaska*. New York: Fleming H. Revell Company, 1914.
Jones, Preston. *City for Empire: An Anchorage History, 1941–1941*. Fairbanks: University of Alaska Press, 2010.
Jones, Suzi, James A. Fall, and Aaron Leggett, eds. *Dena'inaq' Huch'ulyeshi: The Dena'ina Way of Living*. Fairbanks: University of Alaska Press, 2013.
Leonard, Thomas C. *Illiberal Reformers: Race, Eugenics, and American Economics in the Progressive Era*. Princeton: Princeton University Press, 2016.

Lethcoe, Jim, and Nancy Lethcoe. *Valdez Gold Rush Trails*. Valdez, AK: Prince William Sound Books, 1996.

London, Jack. *Klondike Tales*. New York: Modern Library Classics, 2001.

Lucander, David. *Winning the War for Democracy: The March on Washington Movement, 1941–1946*. Urbana: University of Illinois Press, 2014.

Maben, Manly. *Vanport*. Portland: Oregon Historical Society Press, 1987.

MacGregor, Morris J. *Integration of the Armed Forces, 1940–1965*. Washington, DC: General Printing Office, 2006.

Mack, Dwayne A. *Black Spokane: The Civil Rights Struggle in the Inland Northwest*. Norman: University of Oklahoma Press, 2014.

Mack, Kenneth W. *Representing the Race: The Creation of the Civil Rights Lawyer*. Cambridge: Harvard University Press, 2012.

Matei, Sorin Adam, and Sandra Ball-Rokeach. "Watts, the 1965 Los Angeles Riots, and the Communicative Construction of the Fear Epicenter of Los Angeles." *Communication Monographs* 72, no. 3 (2005): 301–23.

Maxwell, Angie, and Todd Shields. *The Long Southern Strategy: How Chasing White Voters in the South Changed American Politics*. New York: Oxford University Press, 2019.

Mazón, Mauricio. *The Zoot-Suit Riots: The Psychology of Symbolic Annihilation*. Austin: University of Texas Press, 1984.

McClure, Christine, and Dennis McClure. *We Fought the Road*. Kenmore, WA: Epicenter Press, 2017.

McCluskey, Audrey, and Elaine M. Smith. *Mary McLeod Bethune: Building a Better World, Essays and Selected Documents*. Bloomington: Indiana University Press, 2002.

McElderry, Stuart John. "Building a West Coast Ghetto: African-American Housing in Portland, 1910–1960." *Pacific Northwest Quarterly* 92, no. 3 (2001): 137–48.

———. "The Problem of the Color Line: Civil Rights and Racial Ideology in Portland, Oregon, 1944–1965." PhD diss., University of Oregon, 1998.

———. "Vanport Conspiracy Rumors and Social Relations in Portland, 1940–1950." *Oregon Historical Quarterly* 99, no. 2 (1998): 134–63.

McGirr, Lisa. *Suburban Warriors: The Origins of the New American Right*. Princeton, NJ: Princeton University Press, 2001.

McGrath, Ed. *Inside the Alaska Pipeline*. Berkeley, CA: Celestial Arts Publishing, 1977.

McMillan, Neil R. *The Citizens' Council: Organized Resistance in the Second Reconstruction, 1954–64*. Urbana: University of Illinois Press, 1994.

———. "The White Citizens' Council and Resistance to School Desegregation in Arkansas." *Arkansas Historical Quarterly* 66, no. 2 (2007): 125–44.

Mead, Robert Douglas. *Journeys Down the Line: Building the Trans-Alaska Pipeline*. Garden City, NY: Doubleday, 1978.

Merritt, Margaret. *Roshier H. Creecy: A Black Man's Search for Freedom and Prosperity in the Koyukuk. Gold Fields of Alaska*. Dubai, UAE: RDS Publications, 2019.

Metcalfe, Peter. *A Dangerous Idea: The Alaska Brotherhood and the Struggle for Indigenous Rights.* Fairbanks: University of Alaska Press, 2014.

Metzl, Jonathan M. *Dying of Whiteness: How the Politics of Racial Resentment Is Killing America's Heartland.* New York: Basic Books, 2019.

Miller, Orlando. *The Frontier in Alaska and the Matanuska Colony.* New Haven, CT: Yale University Press, 1975.

Mitchell, Donald Craig. *Sold American: The Story of Alaska Natives and Their Land, 1867–1917.* Fairbanks: University of Alaska Press, 2003.

———. *Take My Land, Take My Life: The Story of Congress's Historic Settlement of Alaska Native Land Claims, 1960–1971.* Fairbanks: University of Alaska Press, 2001.

Morehouse, Maggi M. *Fighting in the Jim Crow Army: Black Men and Women Remember World War II.* Lanham, MD: Rowman & Littlefield, 2006.

Morgan, Lael. *Gold Time Girls: Of the Alaska/Yukon Gold Rush.* Kenmore, WA: Epicenter Press, 1998.

———. "Writing Minorities Out of History: Black Builders of the Alcan Highway." *Alaska History* 7, no. 2 (Fall 1992): 1–13.

Motley, Mary Penick, ed. *The Invisible Soldier: The Experiences of the Black Soldier, World War II.* Detroit: Wayne State University Press, 1975.

Mountain View Community Council History and Character Summary. Anchorage: Mountain View Community Council, 2018.

Muhammad, Khalil Gibran. *The Condemnation of Blackness: Race, Crime, and the Making of Urban America.* Cambridge: Harvard University Press, 2019.

Mulderink, Earl F., III. *New Bedford's Civil War.* New York: Fordham University Press, 2014.

Muller, William G. *The Twenty-Fourth Infantry, Past and Present.* Fort Collins, CO: Old Army Press, 1972.

Naske, Claus-M. "Blacks Blocked by Bureaucracy: A Study in Frustration." *Alaska Journal* 1, no. 4 (1971): 8–10.

Naske, Claus-M., and Herman E. Slotkin. *Alaska: A History.* Norman: University of Oklahoma Press, 2014.

Nelson, Bruce. *Workers on the Waterfront: Seamen, Longshoremen, and Unionism in the 1930s.* Urbana: University of Illinois Press, 1988.

The New Day for Eastchester: Planned Redevelopment thru Urban Renewal. Anchorage: Alaska State Housing Authority, 1965.

Newell, Gordon R., ed. *The H. W. McCurdy Marine History of the Pacific Northwest.* Seattle: Superior Publishing Company, 1966.

Newman, Mark. *Getting Right with God: Southern Baptists and Desegregation, 1945–1995.* Tuscaloosa: University of Alabama Press, 2001.

New York State Task Force on Police-on-Police Shootings. *Reducing Inherent Danger: Report of the Task Force on Police-on-Police Shootings.* New York: State of New York, 2010.

Nix, William R., and Daniel W. Hickey. *Report on the Shooting Death of Phillip J. Moore.* Juneau: Alaska Department of Public Safety and Alaska Department of Law, 1979.

Noble Dennis L., and Truman R. Strobridge. *Captain "Hell Roaring" Mike Healy: From American Slave to Arctic Hero.* Gainesville: University Press of Florida, 2017.

Nolan, Patricia A., ed. *Anchorage Fire Department: 75th Anniversary Yearbook, 1915–1990.* Anchorage, AK: Anchorage Fire Auxiliary, 1990.

Northern Economics Inc. *The Anchorage Economy from 1980 to the Present.* Anchorage: Anchorage Economic Development Corporation, 2004.

North Wind Inc. *Mountain View Historic Properties Survey Report.* Anchorage: Anchorage Historic Properties, 2005.

O'Toole, James M. *Passing for White: Race, Religion, and the Healy Family, 1820–1920.* Amherst: University of Massachusetts Press, 2003.

———. "Racial Identity and the Case of Captain Michael Healy, USRCS, Parts 1–3." *Prologue Magazine: Quarterly of the National Archives* 29, no. 3 (Fall 1997): 190–201.

Overstreet, Everett Louis. *Black on a Background of White: A Chronicle of Afro-Americans' Involvement in America's Last Frontier, Alaska.* Fairbanks: Alaska Black Caucus, 1988.

Pagan, Eduardo Obregon. *Murder at the Sleepy Lagoon: Zoot Suits, Race, and Riot in Wartime L.A.* Chapel Hill: University of North Carolina Press, 2003.

Pascoe, Peggy. *What Comes Naturally: Miscegenation Law and the Making of Race in America.* New York: Oxford University Press, 2009.

Payne, Troy C. *Officer-Involved Shootings in Anchorage, 1993–2013.* Anchorage: University of Alaska Anchorage Justice Center, 2013.

Paynter Shine, Gregory. "Respite from War: Buffalo Soldiers at Vancouver Barracks, 1899–1900." *Oregon Historical Quarterly* 107, no. 2 (Summer 2006): 196–227.

Phillips-Fein, Kim. *Fear City: New York's Fiscal Crisis and the Rise of Austerity Politics.* New York: Metropolitan Books, 2017.

Picou, J. Steven, Duane A. Gill, and Maurie J. Cohen. *The Exxon Valdez Disaster: Readings of a Modern Social Problem.* Dubuque, IA: Kendall Hunt, 1999.

Potts, Lee W. "Equal Employment Opportunity and Female Employment in Police Agencies." *Journal of Criminal Justice* 11, no. 6 (1983): 505–23.

President's Committee on Civil Rights. *To Secure These Rights: The Report of the President's Committee on Civil Rights.* Washington, DC: General Printing Office, 1947.

Pulido, Laura. *Black, Brown, Yellow, and Left: Radical Activism in Los Angeles.* Berkeley: University of California Press, 2006.

Putney, Martha S. *Black Sailors: Afro-American Merchant Seamen and Whalemen prior to the Civil War.* New York: Greenwood Press, 1987.

"Racist Skinhead Glossary." Southern Poverty Law Center, n.d. www.splcenter.org/fighting-hate/intelligence-report/2015/racist-skinhead-glossary.

Reamer, David. "Without Open Arms: Alaska Response to WWII Refugee Immigration Proposals." *Alaska History* 33, no. 1 (2018): 14–33.

Redford, Laura. "The Intertwined History of Class and Race Segregation in Los Angeles." *Journal of Planning History* 16, no. 4 (2017): 305–22.

Rivera, Jason David, and DeMond Shondell Miller. "Continually Neglected: Situating Natural Disasters in the African American Experience." *Journal of Black Studies* 37, no. 4 (2007): 518–19.

Roscow, James P. *800 Miles to Valdez: The Building of the Alaska Pipeline*. Upper Saddle River, NJ: Prentice Hall, 1977.

Rothstein, Richard. *The Color of Law: A Forgotten History of How Our Government Segregated America*. New York: W. W. Norton, 2017.

Ruffin, Herbert, II. *Uninvited Neighbors: African Americans in Silicon Valley, 1769–1990*. Norman: University of Oklahoma Press, 2014.

Ruffin, Herbert, II, and Dwayne A. Mack, eds. *Freedom's Racial Frontier: African Americans in the Twenty-First Century West*. Norman: University of Oklahoma Press, 2018.

Schulze-Oechtering, Michael. "The Alaska Cannery Workers Association and the Ebbs and Flows of Struggle: Manong Knowledge, Blues Epistemology, and Racial Cross-Fertilization." *Amerasia Journal* 42, no. 2 (2016): 23–48.

Seale, J. Paul, Sylvia Shellenberger, and John Spence. "Alcohol Problems in Alaska Natives: Lessons from the Inuit." *American Indian and Alaska Native Mental Health Research* 13, no. 1 (2006): 1–31.

Secrest, Clark. *Hell's Belles: Prostitution, Vice, and Crime in Early Denver, with a Biography of Sam Howe, Frontier Lawman*. Rev. ed. Boulder: University of Colorado Press, 2002.

Self, Robert O. *All in the Family: The Realignment of American Democracy since the 1960s*. New York: Hill & Wang, 2013.

———. *American Babylon: Race and the Struggle for Postwar Oakland*. Princeton, NJ: Princeton University Press, 2005.

Shellum, Brian G. *Buffalo Soldiers in Alaska: Company L Twenty-Fourth Infantry*. Lincoln: University of Nebraska Press, 2021.

Sherif, Muzafer. *Group Conflict and Co-operation: Their Social Psychology*. London: Routledge & Kegan Paul, 1966.

Shinkwin, Anne, Elizabeth Andrews, Russell Sackett, and Mary Kroul. *Fort Egbert and the Eagle Historic District: Results of Archaeological and Historic Research, Summer 1977*. Technical Report 2. Anchorage: Bureau of Land Management, June 1978.

Simon, Jonathan. *Governing through Crime: How the War on Crime Transformed American Democracy and Created a Culture of Fear*. New York: Oxford University Press, 2007.

Singler, Joan, Jean Durning, Bettylou Valentine, and Maid Adams. *Seattle in Black and White: The Congress of Racial Equality and the Fight for Equal Opportunity*. Seattle: University of Washington Press, 2011.

Skerrett, Joseph, Jr. "Michael Healy: Mullato [sic] Sailor." *Negro History Bulletin* 41, no. 5 (1978): 884, 887, 892.

Skewes, Monica C., and Jordan P. Lewis. "Sobriety and Alcohol Use among Rural Alaska Native Elders." *International Journal of Circumpolar Health* 75 (2016): 30476–78.

Skovgaard, Dale. "Oregon Voices: Memories of the 1948 Vanport Flood." *Oregon Historical Quarterly* 108, no. 1 (2007): 88–106.

Slotkin, Richard. *Gunfighter Nation: The Myth of the Frontier in Twentieth-Century America.* New York: HarperPerennial, 1992.
Smiley, Calvin John, and David Fakunle. "From 'Brute' to 'Thug': The Demonization and Criminalization of Unarmed Black Male Victims in America." *Journal of Human Behavior in the Social Environment* 26, nos. 3–4 (2016): 350–66.
Spencer, Robyn C. *The Revolution Has Come: Black Power, Gender, and the Black Panther Party in Oakland.* Durham, NC: Duke University Press, 2016.
Spude, Robert L. S. *Skagway, District of Alaska, 1884–1912.* Anthropology and Historic Preservation, Cooperative Park Studies Unit, University of Alaska Fairbanks, Occasional Paper No. 36, September 1983.
Starr, Kevin, and Richard J. Orsi, eds. *Rooted in Barbarous Soil: People, Culture, and Community in Gold Rush California.* Berkeley: University of California Press, 2000.
Stein, Judith. *Pivotal Decade: How the United States Traded Factories for Finance in the Seventies.* New Haven, CT: Yale University Press, 2011.
Sugrue, Thomas J. *The Origins of the Urban Crisis: Race and Inequality in Postwar Detroit.* Princeton: Princeton University Press, 2005.
Tann, Sheila S., Scott T. Yabiku, Scott K. Okamoto, and Jessica Yanow. "TRIADD: The Risk for Alcohol Abuse, Depression, and Diabetes Multimorbidity in the American Indian and Alaska Native Population." *American Indian and Alaska Native Mental Health Research* 14, no. 1 (2007): 1–23.
Taylor, Keeanga-Yamahtta. *Race for Profit: How Banks and the Real Estate Industry Undermined Black Homeownership.* Chapel Hill: University of North Carolina Press, 2019.
Taylor, Quintard. "The Civil Rights Movement in the American West: Black Protest in Seattle, 1960–1970." *Journal of Negro History* 80, no. 1 (1995): 1–14.
———. "The Emergence of Black Communities in the Pacific Northwest." *Journal of Negro History* 64, no. 4 (1979): 342–51.
———. *The Forging of a Black Community in Seattle.* Seattle: University of Washington Press, 1994.
———. "The Great Migration: The Afro-American Communities of Seattle and Portland during the 1940s." *Arizona and the West* 23, no. 2 (1981): 109–26.
———. *In Search of the Racial Frontier: African Americans in the American West, 1528–1990.* New York: W. W. Norton, 1998.
Taylor, Quintard, and Shirley Ann Wilson Moore, eds. *African American Women Confront the West, 1600–2000.* Norman: University of Oklahoma Press, 2008.
Thompson, Heather Ann. *Whose Detroit? Politics, Labor, and Race in a Modern American City.* Ithaca, NY: Cornell University Press, 2004.
Tidball, John C. *Report on the Territory of Alaska, 1870.* US House Executive Document No. 5, 42nd Cong., 1st sess., 1871.
Tompkins, E. Berkeley. "Black Ahab: William T. Shorey Whaling Master." *California Historical Quarterly* 51 (Spring 1972): 75–84.

Tower, Elizabeth. *Alaska's First Homegrown Governor: A Biography of William A. Egan.* Anchorage, AK: Publication Consultants, 2003.

———. *Anchorage: From Its Humble Origins as a Railroad Construction Camp.* Kenmore, WA: Epicenter Press, 1999.

Tordoff, Dick. *People of the Koyukuk Regions.* Fairbanks: Project Jukebox, University of Alaska Fairbanks, 1999.

Trachtenberg, Alan. *The Incorporation of America: Culture and Society in the Gilded Age, 25th Anniversary Edition.* New York: Hill & Wang, 2007.

Trotter, Joe William, Jr. *Black Milwaukee: The Making of an Industrial Proletariat, 1915–1945.* Urbana: University of Illinois Press, 1985.

Twichell, Heath. *Northwest Epic: The Building of the Alaska Highway.* New York: St. Martin's Press, 1992.

Understanding Alaska: People, Economy, and Resources. Report prepared by the Institute of Social and Economic Research, University of Alaska Anchorage, May 2006.

Urban Renewal Plan Eastchester Area Project Alaska R-16 Anchorage, Alaska. Anchorage: Alaska State Housing Authority, 1965.

US Congress, House of Representatives. *Hearings on H.R. 13534, a Bill to Amend the Act of Congress of June 6, 1924, Entitled "An Act for the Protection of the Fisheries of Alaska, and for Other Purposes," before the Committee on the Merchant Marine and Fisheries.* 71st Cong., 3rd sess., December 18, 1930.

———. *Hearings on H.R. 5159 to Authorize the Postmaster General to Contract for Air Mail Service in Alaska, before a Subcommittee of the Committee on the Post Office and Post Roads.* 74th Cong., 1st sess., March 21, 1935.

US Department of the Army. *A Historical Analysis of the 364th Infantry in World War II, 1941 to 1945.* Washington, DC: Department of the Army, 2001.

US Department of Commerce, Bureau of the Census. *Thirteenth Census of the United States.* Washington, DC, 1910.

Verona, Stephen F., dir. *Pipe Dreams.* AVCO Embassy Pictures, 1976.

Virtue, John. *The Black Soldiers Who Built the Alaska Highway: A History of Four US Army Regiments in the North.* Jefferson, NC: McFarland, 2013.

Walker, Gordon. *Environmental Justice: Concepts, Evidence and Politics.* New York: Routledge, 2012.

Wangness, Paul H. *A History of the Unification of the City of Anchorage and the Greater Anchorage Area Borough.* Anchorage: Anchorage Urban Observatory, 1977.

Webb, Clive. "'A Cheap Trafficking in Human Misery': The Reverse Freedom Rides of 1962." *Journal of American Studies* 38, no. 2 (2004): 249–71.

Webb, Walter Prescott. "American West: Perpetual Mirage." *Harper's Magazine*, May 1957, 25–31.

Weimer, M.D.K. *M.D.K. Weimer's True Story of the Alaska Gold Fields.* N.p.p.: 1903.

Weise, Andrew. *Places of Their Own: African American Suburbanization in the Twentieth Century.* Chicago: University of Chicago Press, 2004.

Weiss, Nancy J. *Farewell to the Party of Lincoln: Black Politics in the Age of FDR.* Princeton, NJ: Princeton University Press, 1983.

Weissberg, Ariel. "Police Defamation Suits against Civilians Complaining of Police Misconduct." *St. Louis University Law Journal* 22 (1979): 676–93.

Wheeler, Elizabeth A. "More than the Western Sky: Watts on Television, August 1965." *Journal of Film and Video* 54, nos. 2–3 (2002): 11–26.

Whitaker, Matthew C. *Race Work: The Rise of Civil Rights in the Urban West*. Lincoln: University of Nebraska Press, 2004.

Whittingham Logan, Rayford. *The Betrayal of the Negro: From Rutherford B. Hayes to Woodrow Wilson*. 1954. Reprint, New York: Da Capo Press, 1997.

Wilkerson, Isabel. *The Warmth of Other Suns: The Epic Story of America's Great Migration*. New York: Vintage, 2011.

Williams, Carla. *Wildcat Women: Narratives of Women Breaking Ground in Alaska's Oil and Gas Industry*. Fairbanks: University of Alaska Press, 2018.

Williams, Chad. *Torchbearers of Democracy: African American Soldiers in the World War I Era*. Chapel Hill: University of North Carolina Press, 2013.

Williams, Maria Sháa Tláa, ed. *The Alaska Native Reader*. Durham, NC: Duke University Press, 2009.

Willis, Alan Scott. *All According to God's Plan: Southern Baptist Missions and Race, 1945–1970*. Lexington: University Press of Kentucky, 2005.

Wilson, William H. "The Founding of Anchorage: Federal Townbuilding on the Last Frontier." *Pacific Northwest Quarterly* 58 (July 1967): 130–41.

Wohlforth, Charles. *From the Shores of Ship Creek: Stories of Anchorage's First 100 Years*. Anchorage, AK: Todd Communications, 2015.

Wood, Darryl S., and Paul J. Gruenewald. "Local Alcohol Prohibition, Police Presence, and Serious Injury in Isolated Alaska Native Villages." *Addiction* 101, no. 3 (2006): 393–403.

Woodman, Lyman L. *Duty Station North: The US Army in Alaska and Western Canada, 1867–1987*, vol. 1: *1867–1917*. Anchorage: Alaska Historical Society, 1996–97.

Woodworth-Ney, Laura E. *Women in the American West*. Santa Barbara, CA: ABC-CLIO, 2008.

INDEX

Page numbers in *italics* refer to illustrations.

ACPRTF (Anchorage Community Police Relations Task Force), 153–54, 159, 160, 227–28n70
activism. *See* civil rights activism
Adakian (newsletter), 67–68
Adak Island (Aleutian Islands), xxv, 64–66
Adams, Harvey, 124
AERC (Anchorage Equal Rights Commission), 149–50, 153–54, 159
AFACT (Anchorage Faith and Action Congregations Together), 184
Agee (Black Anchorage resident), 47
Aiken, Pete, 131
air force, 91, 100, 103–5, 114–15, 132, 181. *See also* military
Alaska: demographics (1890 census), 11; demographics (1900 census), 10–11, 29; demographics (1910 census), 195n15; demographics (1940 census), 195n15; demographics (1960 census), 70; demographics (2010 census), xxvii, 162–63; demographics during Great Depression, 51; demographics during oil boom era, 120, 122, 140–41, 146; demographics during World War era, 52, 55, 72, 216n76; demographics post–oil boom, 162–63, 171–72; demographics postwar era, 70, 83; diverse demographics of, 183–85, 231n118; exceptionalism claims, xix–xx, 71, 164–65, 185; federal defense spending, xix, 70, 120, 162, 216–17n76; gender demographics, xxii, 196n21; impacts of World Wars on, xxiv–xxv, 45, 56–58, 70–72; national comparisons, xx–xxi, 97–98, 111, 116, 195n11; popular culture stereotypes, xvii, 193n1; purchase price, 75; relocation plans, 51–52; state constitution of, 108, 110–11, 220n32; strategic significance of, 45, 55, 70; Treaty of Cession (1867), 10; wealth of, 179, 195n13
Alaska: A History (Naske and Slotkin), xviii

Alaska Black Caucus, 128, 134, 140, 146, 183, 190–91
Alaska Bone Dry Act (1918), 47, 53
Alaska Highway construction project: background of, 58, 60; Black contributions to, 58–63; completion of, 61, 63; racism faced during, 60–61; scholarship on Black participation, 194n9; working conditions, 60–61. *See also* military
Alaska Native Claims Settlement Act (ANCSA, 1971), xxvi, 120, 138
Alaska Natives: activism of, xxi, xxvi, 100–101; alcohol misuse among, 53; and Anchorage's founding, 47, 183; and Black activism, xxi–xxii; demographics, 11, 51, 163; discrimination in criminal justice system, 140, 187; diversity among, xx–xxi; early interactions with Black whalers, 9; employed by salmon canneries, 50; employment discrimination faced by, 2, 49, 82; during the gold rush era, 23, 28, 42; housing discrimination faced by, 2, 82, 84; intermarriage with Black whalers, 11; land claims settlements, xxvi, 120, 121, 138; during the oil boom era, xxvi, 120, 121, 128, 138; police misconduct targeting, 142, 146, 187, 188–89, 230–31n111; during the post–oil boom years, 170, 172, 177–78; during prohibition, 52–53; racism faced by, 55, 68–69, 79, 170, 172, 177–78; and the Revenue Cutter Service, 16–17; settler colonialism impacting, xx–xxi, 47, 183; stereotypical portrayals of, xvii; subsistence diet, 16; violence toward, 11–13, 17; and the whaling industry, 9, 11–13, 16; during World War era, 51, 55, 68–69; youth cultural rejuvenation programs, xxviii, 174–75
Alaska Railroad, 46, 49

Alaska Spotlight (Black newspaper), 76, 81, 108, 114
Alaska State Housing Authority (ASHA), 92–93, 94–95
Alaska Steamship Company, 50
Alcan Highway. *See* Alaska Highway construction project
Aleutians Islands, xxv, 57–59, 63–70
Alexander, John, 132
Allen, Jim, 11
Altom, Melvin Dean, 150–51
Alyeska Pipeline Company, 119, 123
Anchorage (AK): activism against police violence, 147–50, 187–88, 189; activism in, 111–15; annexing Eastchester Flats, 91–92, 142; Black contributions to, 46–50, 133–37, 187; Black politicians in, 96–97, 131, 134, 217n90; business discrimination in, 127–29; comparisons to Vanport, 216n76; contracting discrimination in, 127–28; cultural and economic transformations of, xvii; demographics of, xxi, xxvii, 49, 52, 55, 127, 146, 161, 162–63, 166–67, 171–72, 216n76; Dena'ina Civic and Convention Center, 183; employment discrimination in, 79, 82, 114–15, 129–31; fair housing code (1967), 97; faith-based organizations in, 78, 97–98, 146, 159, 184, 213n14; fire department, 48, 49; founding of, 46–47; hate groups in local schools, 171–73; housing discrimination in, 78, 82–86, 106–8; Martin Luther King Jr. Memorial in, 181–82; multicultural rejuvenation in, xxvii–xxviii, 174–76; national comparisons, 97–98, 195n11; during 1980s recession, 166; during the oil boom era, 127–31, 146; original inhabitants of, 47, 183; performing arts center naming controversy, 167–69, 181–82; political shifts in, 184; post–oil boom

INDEX

era, 166–67, 171–72; postwar discrimination in, 79–86; postwar opportunities in, xxv, 73–78; postwar race relations in, 73; prohibition in, 47; Project 80s, 180; public transportation, 129–31; racism in, 49; urban renewal, 92–96; during World War II, 195n11, 216n76. *See also* Eastchester Flats (Anchorage, AK); police (Anchorage Police Department)
Anchorage Community Police Relations Task Force (ACPRTF), 153–54, 159, 160, 227–28n70
Anchorage Daily News, 76, 95, 129, 144–45, 171–72, 188
Anchorage Equal Rights Commission (AERC), 149–50, 153–54, 159
Anchorage Faith and Action Congregations Together (AFACT), 184
Anchorage Police Department (APD). *See* police (Anchorage Police Department)
Anchorage Police Department Employees Association (APDEA), 155, 158
Anchorage Times, 91, 95, 146, 151–52, 170
ANCSA (Alaska Native Claims Settlement Act, 1971), xxvi, 120, 138
Anderson, Edward, 102
Anderson, George C., 76–79, 93, 114, 143, 192
Andrews, Eleanor, 133, 137, 139, 180
Andrews Group, 133
Angoon massacre (October 1882), 17
Anti-Discrimination Act (1945), 97, 100–103, 105, 186
APDEA (Anchorage Police Department Employees Association), 155, 158
Arbery, Ahmaud, 189
Arctic (whaling ship), 6
Arnold, Rose, 29–30
arson, 40, 85–86
ASHA (Alaska State Housing Authority), 92–93, 94–95

Asian Americans, xxi–xxii, xxv, 2, 49, 97, 128, 163, 167
Atherton, St. John, 31–32, 185
Attucks, Crispus, 5
Attu Island (Aleutian Islands), xxv, 57–58, 65
Atwood, Robert, 111, 146
Audino, Charles, 144, 150
Austins, Frank, 96

Babero, Bert B., 81
Baker, Larry, 168
Banks, Zora, 110
barks (whaling ships): *Arctic*, 6–7; defined, 197n1; *Hercules*, 9–10; *Herriman*, 1–2; *Industry*, 3; *John & Winthrop*, 1; *Marengo*, 7; *Superior*, 6
Bartlett, Bob, 73, 115
Bateman, Annaliese Jacobs, 41
Berkley, Pat, 112
Berry, William, 5
Bethune, Mary McLeod, 56–57
Bettye Davis East Anchorage High School, 183
Bevers, Mary Ellen, 46
Bevers, Thomas Stokes "Tom," 46–49, 131, 186, 205n5, 217n90
Bevers, William, 46, 205n5
Bianchi, Emily, 166
Birth of a Nation (film), 54
Bizzy Bone, 176
Black Alice (Black businesswoman), 40–41
Black Americans: claiming white identity, 15, 19–20, 22, 48, 217n90; primary sources regarding, 41–43; scholarship on, xviii–xix; secondary sources regarding, 41–42; terminology usage, 193n2
Black Caucus (Alaska), 128, 134, 140, 146, 183, 190–91
Black Lives Matter movement, xxviii, 188, 190–91

257

Black Prince (boxer), 39
Black Veterans Memorial Bridge, 63
Blanchett, Phillip, 176
Blanchett, Stephen, 176
Blansett, Kent, 195n16
Bockstoce, John, 6, 12
Boettcher, John, 170
Bolster, W. Jeffrey, 8
Borneman, Walter, 194n9
Boston, Absalom, 3
bowhead whales, 5, 12, 13, 16
Bowman, Willard L., 81–83, 97, 106, *107*, 108, 131–32, 139
boxing (entertainment industry), 39
Bronson, Dave, 161
Brown, Benjamin, 26
Brown, Harold, 142–43
Brown, Michael, 187
Brown, Peter, 31
Brown, Ruth, 29–30
Brown, Simon, 137
Brownell, Herbert, Jr., 142, 143, 225n9
Bryner, Alex, 148
Buckner, Simon Bolivar, Jr., xxv, 56, 57, 64, 69, 114, 132
buffalo soldiers: discrimination faced by, 29–30; during the gold rush era, 22, 27–30; recognition of, 24–25, 26. *See also* Twenty-Fourth Infantry Regiment
Burge, Helen, 78
Burge, Richard, 78
Burney, Barbara, 158
Burns, Walter Noble, 12
business sector: Black leadership in, 187; Black-owned businesses, 74, 76, 88–91, 96, 142–43; construction contracts, 82, 127–28; discrimination in, 29–30, 116, 127–31; in Eastchester Flats, 88–91, 96; during the gold rush era, 29–30, 36–41; impact of activism on, xxv, 116; impact of urban renewal on, 96; during the oil boom era, 127–33; opportunities in, 78, 132–33, 180; police harassment of, 142–43

Callagan, Tim, 35
Campbell, Alvin, 85–86
Campbell, George, Jr., 66, 211n84
Campbell, Mary Lee, 85–86
Campfield, William, Jr., 132, 223n43
Canol (Canadian Oil) pipeline, 60, 62, 211n76
Card, Larry, 186
Caribou-Wards protest, 113–14
Carmack, George, 23
Carmichael, Stokely, 111
Carr, Bernard J., Sr., 112
Carrol, Selwyn, 132
Carrs grocery store (Anchorage, AK): boycott of, 111–13, 116, 186; hiring policies of, 82, 112; Richard Watts's career at, 113, 132, 186
Carver, George A., 114
Casey, Vince, 153
Castile, Philando, 188
CCCI (Citizens Council for Community Improvement), 82
censuses: 1870 census, 10; 1890 census, 11; 1900 census, 10–11, 29; 1910 census, 195n15; 1940 census, 195n15; 1960 census, 70; 2010 census, xxvii, 162–63
Center for the Performing Arts (Anchorage, AK), 167–69, 181–82
Central Labor Council, 108–10
Chauvin, Derek, 189, 237n21
Chisolm, Beatrice Lee. *See* Coleman, Beatrice Lee Chisolm
Christensen, Andrew, 49
churches and religious communities: Greater Friendship Baptist Church, 78, 97–98; role in activism, 146, 159, 184, 213n14; Shiloh Baptist Church, 78, 152, 213n14
Citizens Council for Community Improvement (CCCI), 82

INDEX

Civil Rights Act (1964), 158
civil rights activism: addressing employment discrimination, 82, 103–5, 108–10, 111–15, 158–60; addressing housing discrimination, 82, 86, 106–8; addressing lack of public transportation, 130–31; addressing legislative loopholes, 97, 100–103, 186; addressing military discrimination, 57, 69–70, 103–5, 114–15; addressing police misconduct, 80, 141–42, 146, 157; addressing police shootings, 147–50, 152–53, 187–91; addressing service and accommodation industries, 66, 81, 82, 99–105, 186; of Alaska Natives, xxi, xxvi, 100–101; and Alaska's state constitution, 108, 110–11; Anchorage police participating in, 160; Black Lives Matter movement, xxviii, 188, 190–91; complicated picture of, xxi–xxii; early activists in Alaska, 99–105; images of, *189*, *190*; impact of war on, 69–70; interconnectedness of, xxii, 57, 111, 115–16, 187–88, 221n47; legacy of, 191; national comparisons, xx, 111, 116; during the oil boom era, xxvii, 130–31, 138–39; ongoing disparities following, 131; postwar surveys, 81–83; and the Red Power movement, 195n16; riots, 70, 106, 111; successes of, xxvi, 160–61; white backlash, 115–16, 147–48; during World War II, xxv, 66. *See also* racism and discrimination
Civil War, 9, 24, 25, 44
Coast Guard (US), 15, 19, 71. *See also* Revenue Cutter Service (US)
Coates, Kenneth S., 211n76
Coen, Ross, 99
Coffey, Dan, 83
Coffey Subdivision (Anchorage, AK), 83
Cold Bay (AK), xxv, 64
Cold War, xxv, 70, 83

Coleman, Beatrice Lee Chisolm, 99–105, 186
Coleman, Clarence, 86, 112
Coleman, Flossie, 86
Coleman, Robert, 99–102, 186
Colgate, Dave, 34
Color (Black magazine), 76, 78
Colored American Magazine, 42
Compromise of 1850, 8
Conna, John, 44–45
Connor, Bull, 145
constitution (AK), 108, 110–11, 220n32
Cooper, Mrs. M. E., 34
Cooper, Ricky, 171
Cordell, Lucky, 67, 211n85
Couture, Bessie, 36, *37*
Cox, Frank, 128–29, 133, 180
Creecy, Nathaniel, 33
Creecy, Robert H., 22, 33–34, 53, 54
criminal justice system: bias against Alaska Natives in, 140, 187; Black contributions to, 186–87; discrimination in, 73–74, 79, 186, 225n11; Fairbanks Four case, 187, 230–31n111; impact of civil rights activism on, 116; racial disparities in arrest statistics, 146; racial disparities in sentencing, 71, 140; systemic racism within, 140. *See also* police (Anchorage Police Department); police and law enforcement
Crosby, Mattie "Tootsie," 39–40
Cuba, 26–27
Cuffe, Paul, 5
cultural rejuvenation programs, xxviii, 174–76
Curry, Ocea Mae, 85, 92, 96
Cutler, Beverly, 165

Davis, Benjamin O., 56
Davis, Bettye J., 180, 183
Davis, Etheldra, 134–35
Davis, Ewin, 52
Davis, John, 7

Davis, Thomas, 114
Dawson (Yukon, Canada), 11, 23, 36, 39
Delaney Park Strip (Anchorage, AK), 182
Delayed Justice for Sale (Dickerson), 136, 155
Dempsey, Melvin, 21–22, 201n5
Dena'ina Civic and Convention Center (Anchorage), 183
Dena'ina people (Alaska Natives), 47, 49, 183
Dickerson, Mahala Ashley, 135–36, 144–45, 154–57, 186
Dimond, Anthony, 52
discrimination. *See* racism and discrimination
Doll, Justin, 161
Douglass, Frederick, 5, 27
Drucker, Philip, 17
Duke, David, 170
Dunkin, Michael, 164–65, 166
Dyea (AK), 22–24, 28

Eagle (AK), 35, 38, 44
earthquake (1964), 93–94
East Anchorage High School (Anchorage), 174, 183
Eastchester Flats (Anchorage, AK): annexed by Anchorage, 91–92, 142; Black-owned businesses in, 88–91, 96; entertainment industry in, 88–91; impact of annexation on, 95–96, 108, 152; impact of 1964 earthquake on, 93–94; lack of services in, 87–88, 91, 95, 108; naming of, 87; police misconduct in, 142–43, 145; urban renewal in, 92–96
Ebony (magazine), 73, 75, 180–81
Ebony Culture Club, 174–75
economy: during the Great Depression, 51; impact of activism on, xxv; impact of gold rush on, 22, 179, 201n2; impact of military on, 70–72; impact of oil industry on, xxvii, 122, 162; impact of railroads on, 46; impact of World Wars on, 45, 70; impact on race relations, xxvii, 166; during oil boom era, 119–22, 162, 179–80; during post–oil boom years, 177; recent shifts in, 184–85; recessions, xxvii, 119–20, 162, 165–66; role of fishing and canneries in, 50, 51
Egan, William E., 81–82, 132, 181, 183
Eielson Air Force Base (Fairbanks, AK), 56, 62, 181
Eighteenth Engineer Battalion, 61, 63
802nd Engineer Aviation Battalion, 64
election (1968 presidential), 115–16
Eliot, Robert, 7
Elmendorf Air Force Base (Anchorage, AK), 56, 91, 114–15, 132
employment: activism addressing discrimination in, 82, 103–5, 108–10, 111–15, 158–60, 181; anti-Native racism limiting, 2, 49, 82; financial industry, 82, 132, 186; fishing and canneries opportunities, 50–51; gold rush era opportunities, 13, 21–23, 31–36, 44–45, 185–86; impact of recessions on, 165–66; impact of World Wars on, 45; legislation banning workplace discrimination, 108–10, 158; migrant labor restrictions, 50; military discrimination, 24–27, 99–100, 103–5, 114–15; military opportunities, 3, 11, 13, 25, 45; oil boom-era discrimination, 122–24, 127–31, 137; oil boom-era opportunities, 122–27, 131–37; police and law enforcement discrimination, 142, 153–54, 157–60, 229n99; during post–oil boom years, 177; postwar discrimination, 73, 79, 82; postwar opportunities, 75–78; whaling industry opportunities, 2–11, 8, 13
entertainment industry: boxing, 39; in Eastchester Flats, 88–91; gambling, 28, 38, 76, 88; postwar opportunities in, 76

INDEX

Erickson, Gregg, 165
Estell, Donna, 169
Ewing, William T., 31–32
Exxon oil spill, 177
Ezi, Grandma Olga Nikolai, 183

Fairbanks (AK): activism in, 105, 113–14; Black contributions to, 45, 180–81, 195n11; Black-owned businesses in, 74; Black politicians in, 45, 132, 180–81; demographics of, 52, 55, 61; impact of World War II on, 70; military bases, 56, 62, 103–5, 181; during the oil boom era, 127–28; political shifts in, 184; during postwar era, xxv, 61, 73, 75; racial discrimination in, 100–105, 127–28, 181
Fairbanks Four, 187, 230–31n111
Fair Employment Act (1953), 108–10, 219n30
Fair Housing Act (1968), 97, 131
Fairview neighborhood (Anchorage, AK): activism in, 113, 130–31; annexation, 136; churches in, 78, 97–98; demographics of, 97, 129, 163; housing within, 92; policing of, 145; public transportation in, 129–31
faith-based communities, 78, 97–98, 146, 159, 184, 213n14
Farnsworth, Charles W., 42
Farrell, Chad, 163, 183–84
Feichtinger, Eric Frank, 147
Feliciano, Eliezer, 159–60
Fillmore, Millard, 8
financial institutions: employment discrimination, 82; employment opportunities, 132, 186; housing market discrimination, 82, 95; impact of recessions on, 166; oil boom-era discrimination, 128
Fischer, Earle, 80
fishing industry: and Asian migration, xxi; demographics of, xxi, xxii, 50–51; discrimination in, 73; economic impacts, 50–51; gender demographics, xxii; impact of oil spill on, 177; during oil boom era, 122; salmon canning industry, xxi, 50–51
Fitzgerald, Jenkins, 10
Fitzgerald, Mary, 10
Flamming, Douglas, xviii
Flanigan, John, 111, 115, 144
Flat (AK), 39–40
Flowers, George, 32–33, 34
Floyd, George, 189–90, 191, 237n21
Folsom (judge), 53
Fort Richardson (Anchorage, AK), 56, 79, 91, 114
Fort Wainwright (Fairbanks, AK), 56, 62, 181
Fort Wrangel (AK), 28
Fourteenth Infantry Regiment, 24, 28–29
Fox, Matt, 175
Foxx, Redd, 89
Frank, Kim, 175
Franklin, Hal, 75
Frazier, Darnella, 189
Freed, Andrew, 188
Freedom's Racial Frontier (Ruffin and Mack), xviii, 195n11
Frese, George, 231n111
Frisby, Herbert, 9, 59, 61, 76, 88, 91
fur trade, 48

gambling, 28, 38, 76, 88
Garner, Eric, 188
Gatewood, Willard, 26
George, Thomas C., 11–12
Giddens, Larue, 80–81
Gilley, George, 12
gold rush era: Alaska Natives during, 23, 28, 42; beginnings of, in Alaska, 23–24; Black contributions during, xxiv, 22–23, 43, 185–86; Black women during, xxii, 11, 36–41; dangers and harsh conditions during, 21–22, 23–24, 28–29, 34–35, 38–39; demographics during, xxii, 11; economic impacts

gold rush era (*continued*)
    of, 22, 179, 201n2; impact on whaling industry, 7; military during, 22, 23–24, 27–30; opportunities during, 13, 21–23, 31–36, 41, 44–45, 52, 185–86; racism and discrimination during, 29–30, 31–32; service industry during, 21–22, 29–30, 36–41
Goode, James P., 104
Good Friday Earthquake (1964), 93–94
Goodwin, Abigail, 7
Gordon, Stomp, 89
Grant, Robert, 29
Gray-Jackson, Elvi, 97
Greater Friendship Baptist Church (Anchorage, AK), 78, 97–98
Green, Benjamin, 30–31
Green, Hetty, 36
Green Acres Lodge (Anchorage, AK), 78
Greene, William, 159
Griffin, Ronald, 34, 185
Griffith, D. W., 54
Grover, Kathryn, 5, 6, 8
Groves, Martha, 10
Groves, Thomas, 10
Gruening, Ernest, 51–52, 102, 105, 108, 110, 115
Guillory, Tyron, 158–59

Hall, Erika, 166
Hallock, Charles, 10
Hammett, Dashiell, 67–68
Hammond, Jay, 148
Hancock, Clifford C., 42–43
Hankerson, Barry, 118
Hanshew Junior High School (Anchorage, AK), 171–72
Harriman Expedition, 18
Hascell, Stephen, 6
Hash, Mabel, 143, 225n11
Hastie, William O., 56
Hayden, Jesse Leroy, 89
Hayes, James C., 180–81, 235n4
Hayes, Luciana, 175

Headlough, Mark, 153
Healy, Michael A., 15–20
Hellenthal, John, 110
Hendricks, Charles, 65
Hercules (whaling ship), 9
Herriman (whaling ship), 1–2
Hess, Darrell, 228n70
Hickel, Walter J., 111
Hill, Rudy, 100, 101–3
Hillside neighborhood (Anchorage, AK), 172
hip-hop musicians, 176
Hodge Growden, Celeste, 190–91
Hoge, William M., 60
Holiday, Billie, 89–90
Holland, Olivia, 113
Holmes, Madeline, 79–81, 86, 87, 142
Hooper, Willie, 34
housing and real estate: activism addressing, 82, 86, 106–8; discrimination faced by Alaska Natives, 2, 82, 84; discrimination in, xxv, 73, 78, 79, 82–86, 106–8; discrimination in Eastchester Flats, 87–88; discrimination in Portland, 216n76; discrimination through urban renewal, 92–96; fair housing legislation, 97, 131; impact of 1980s recession on, 166; postwar opportunities in, 76; restricted housing covenants, 83–85; Supreme Court rulings on discrimination in, 85; unincorporated neighborhoods, 87
Hovey, Henry Walter, 28, 29
Human Rights Commission, 81–82
Humphries, Ben, 90, 96, 113, 132, 145
Hunter, Charles, 37
Hunter, Lucile, 37–38
Hunter, Teslin, 37
Hunter-Gault, Charlayne, 106
Hu Pegues, Juliana, xxi

Ickes, Harold, 51
Industry (whaling ship), 3

Inside the Alaska Pipeline (McGrath), 122
integration: of Anchorage police department, 158; of the military, xxv, 56–57, 61–62, 68, 69–70; of the Southern Baptist Convention, 98; during World War II, 67–68
Iñupiat (Alaska Natives), 11, 12, 16–17
Isaak, Joel, 183

Jackson, Joe, 88, 95
Jackson, Joseph M., 86, 112
Jackson, Peter, 39
Jackson, Sheldon, 16
Jalufka, Alfred, 61, 63
Jayadev, Arjun, 166
Jenkins, Frank, 50
Jenks, Isaac C., 27, 28
John & Winthrop (whaling ship), 1
Johnson, Campbell C., 56
Johnson, Fred, 88–89, 96
Johnson, Linda, 160
Johnson, Lyndon B., 97, 115
Johnson, Robert, 166
Johnson-Calloway, Marie, 74
Joker the Bailbondsman, 176
Jones, Carolyn, 133–34, 139
Jones, Elnora, 41
Jones, Jewel, 134, 139
Jones, Livingston, 9
Jones, Madame, 38
Jones, Minnie, 34–35
Josey, Leo, Sr., 98
Juneau (AK): Black women politicians, 180; demographics of, xxi, 52, 55; political shifts in, 184; prohibition in, 52–53; racism in, 54–55

Kay, Wendell, 108, 110
Kaye, Peter P., 103, 104–5
Kelly, John W., 12
Kennecott (AK), 32–33, 55
Kennedy, Alvin, 159–60
King, Isaiah, 9–10
King, Jay, 175–76

King, Martin Luther, Jr., 167–69, 181–82, 188
King, Rodney, 173
Kirchner, Geraldine, 84–85
Kirchner, John, 84–85
Kiska Island (Aleutian Islands), 57, 65
Kizzia, Tom, 32–33
Kline, Joseph, 112–13
Knight, Gladys, 118–19, 138
Knowles, Tony, 71, 154
Kraemer, Shelley v., 85
Ku Klux Klan, 54–55, 169, 170, 209nn48–49

Ladd Air Force Base (Fairbanks, AK), 56, 103–4
Lavalais, Willie, 59, 61
Lawrence, Zelmer, 88
lawsuits: for employment discrimination, 124, 136, 158–60; filed against police violence, 154–57; police defamation lawsuits, 155; over police shootings, 155–57; over service industry discrimination, 81, 101–2
Lee, John, 150
Lee, Sarah, 166
legislation: ANCSA, xxvi, 120, 138; anti-discrimination, 100–103, 115, 158; banning interracial marriages, 46; civil rights, 131, 158; Compromise of 1850, 8; enforcement issues, 97, 100–103, 186; fair employment, 108–10, 158; fair housing, 97, 131; voting rights, 131
legislature (Alaska): amending discrimination legislation, 97, 100, 102–3; anti-discrimination legislation, 100–103; Black men serving in, 131–32; Black women serving in, 97; fair employment legislation, 100–103; impacts of activism on, xxvi, 80
Lenear, Theressa, 102, 120–21, 123, 218n1
Lewis, Clyde, 168
Lewis, Willie, 124

Lincoln, Abraham, 15
Little, Matthew, 65, 211n81
London, Jack, 19
Loussac, Z. J., 79–80

Mack, Dwayne A., xviii
Mallot, Byron, 173–74
manifest destiny doctrine, 26
Marshall, George, 57
Marshall, Julius, 164–65, 166
Martin, Trayvon, 188
Martin Luther King Jr. Memorial (Anchorage, AK), 181–82
Mason, May B., 36
Mason, Skookum Jim, 23
Mason, Xavier, 188
Mays, Isaiah, 26
McClain, Paula, 115–16
McCoy, Kenneth, 161
McDame, Henry, 32
McGrath, Ed, 122–23, 124
McRea, Kari, 186
McSmith, Blanche: activism of, 81, 86, 106–8, 110, 114, 139, 186; biographical sketch on, 194n5; discrimination faced by, 81; image of, *109*; leadership of, 81, 86, 114, 186; legislative service of, 81, 132; on police misconduct, 145; on urban renewal, 95–96, 108
Melgrim, Marie, 29
Merriman, Edgar, 17
Midnight Sun Reporter (Black newspaper), 114
military: activism targeting, 57, 69–70, 103–5, 114–15; Alaska Highway construction, 58–63; Aleutian campaign, xxv, 57–59, 63–70; Black commanders in, 132; Black contributions to, xxv, 27, 71–72; civil rights activism targeting, 103–5; Coast Guard, 15, 19, 71; conflicts with Alaska Natives, 17; desertion rates, 24, 29; discrimination in, xxv, 15, 24–27, 56–57, 71, 79, 99–100, 103–5, 114–15; early presence in Alaska, 10; employment opportunities, 3, 11, 13, 25, 45; gender demographics, xxii, 196n22; during the gold rush era, 22–24, 27–30; images of, *62*, *63*; impact on Alaska, xxiv–xxv, 70–72; impact on Alaska demographics, xix–xx, 30–33, 45, 99, 216n76; integration of, xxv, 56–57, 61–62, 68, 69–70; Revenue Cutter Service, 15–20; segregation in, 24–27, 46, 56–59, 63–64, 68–69; structural racism, 57; whites leading Black units, 59, 60; during World War II, 56–58, 58–63, 63–70, 216n76
Miller, Don, 68
Miller, George, 143
Miscovich, John, 40
Mitchell, Billy, 58
Mitchell, Clarence, 104
Moore, Phillip, 146–48, 152
Moore, Shirley Ann Wilson, xxii–xxiii
Moore, Theodore A., 156
Morris, Alva, 68
Morris, Lillian, 114
Morris, Steven, 75
Morrison, William R., 211n76
Mountain View neighborhood (Anchorage, AK), 82, 134, 146, 163
Muir, John, 18
music and musicians, 175–76

NAACP: addressing contracting discrimination, 128; addressing employment discrimination, 104–5, 112–13, 114, 181; addressing police violence and misconduct, 79–80, 144, 145–46, 148, 153, 188; addressing postwar discrimination, 79–80; on Anchorage's fair housing code, 97; creation of Anchorage chapter, 86; creation of Fairbanks chapter, 105; on Eastchester Flats, 87, 95; lobbying for fair employment laws, 108–10; lobbying for voting rights, 115

INDEX

NAAWP (National Association for the Advancement of White People), 170
Nantucket (MA), 3
Naske, Claus-M., xviii
National Bank of Alaska, 82, 132, 186
Native Alaskans. *See* Alaska Natives
natural disasters, 93–94
Negro Digest, 73, 75
Nelson, Tommy, 158–59
New Bedford (MA), 3–6, 9
Ninety-Fifth Engineering Regiment, 59, 60–61
Ninety-Seventh Engineering Regiment, 60–61, 63–64
Ninety-Third Engineer Battalion, 59–61, 64
Nixon, Richard, 138
Noble, Dennis, 18
Nolan, Pete, 150
North Star Light Lounge (Anchorage, AK), 89, 96
Northwest Mounted Police, 23, 35, 39

Obama, Barack, 183
O'Connor, Robert, 29
O'Connor, Sussie, 29
Odom, LaQuita, 137
Odom, Willie, 136–37, 139
oil boom era: activism during, xxvii, 129–31, 138–39; Alaska Natives land claim settlements, xxvi, 120, 121, 138; beginnings of, 120; Black contributions during, 121, 134, 138–39; Black women during, 118–19, 122–23, 133–36; business sector during, 127–33; conservative culture, 121, 123–24; contracting system, 127–29; demographics during, xxii, 120, 122, 127, 140–41, 146; discrimination during, 118–19, 120–24, 127–31, 137; economic impacts of, xxvii, 119–21, 162, 179–80; films portraying, 118–19; gender discrimination during, xxii, 118–19, 122; opportunities during, 120–21, 122–27, 131–37; race relations during, xxvi–xxvii, 121–27, 131, 137; recessions following, 165–66; revenues, 75; unequal opportunities during, 120, 162; white southern workers, xxvi–xxvii, 123–24
O'Rourke, Thomas, 173
Osthagen, Clarence, 104
O'Toole, James M., 16
Overstreet, Everett Louis, 148, 173
Owens, James E., 112
Owngachuck (Iñupiat woman), 11

Pacific Islanders, xxi, xxii, 97, 163, 187–88
Page, Lawanda, 89
Pagoda Cafe (Anchorage, AK), 81
Palley, Reese, 66
Pamyua (music group), 176
Parks, John R., 137
Parks, John S., 86, 113, 130–31, 132–33, 139
Patterson, Alonzo, 152, 153, 159, 167, 213n14
Pease, Kevin, 231n111
People Mover (bus system), 130–31
Peratrovich, Elizabeth, 99, 100–101, 186
Peratrovich, Roy, 99, 100–101
performing arts center (Anchorage), 167–69, 181–82
permanent fund dividend (PFD), 179
Perry, Bela C., 5
Pfiffner, Frank, 160
Pipe Dreams (film), 118–19, 138
pipeline (Canadian Oil), 60, 62, 211n76
pipeline construction (Trans-Alaska Pipeline System): beginnings of, 120; Black women working on, 118–19, 122–23; completion of, 140, 222n13; demographic impacts of, 122; discrimination during, 118–19, 120–21, 124; economic impacts of, 120, 122; films portraying, 118–19; gender discrimination during, xxii, 118–19, 122; impact on wages, 120, 222n13; race relations during, 121–27; union contracts during, 123–24

Pipeliners Union Local 798 (798ers), 124
Pitts, Inman, 154–55
Plessy v. Ferguson, 26
police (Anchorage Police Department): activism protesting violence by, 147–50, 187–88, *189*; Anchorage police task force, 153–54, 159, 160, 227–28n70; auxiliary forces of, 144–45; Black officers, 154, 157–61; discrimination in responses by, 149–51; discriminatory hiring practices, 142, 153–54; incremental changes in, 153–54, 160–61; minority community mistrust of, 141–42, 153–55; multiracial coalitions working with, 157; participating in civil rights activism, 160; police dogs, 145; postwar discrimination by, 79–81; racism within toward minority officers, 157–60; relations with minority communities, 79–81, 141–46; violence by, 153–55; women in, 158
police and law enforcement: activism targeting violence of, 187–88, *189*; Fairbanks Four case, 187, 230–31n111; hiring and promotion discrimination, 142, 153–54, 157–60, 229n99; killing of George Floyd, 189, 237n21; lawsuits filed against, 154–57; lawsuits filed by, 155; minority community distrust of, 141–42, 161–62; misconduct and harassment by, 141–46, 161–62; national trends, 141; treatment of white suspects, 149–51; violence by, 143–44, 153–55, 187–91; White Citizens' Councils, 145. *See also* criminal justice system police shootings: activism targeting, 147–50, 152–53, 187–91; Alaska statistics on, 188; divisions and mistrust created by, 140–41; lawsuits over, 155–57; national trends, xxvii, 188; shooting of Phillip Moore, 146–48; shooting of Cassell Williams, 148–53

politics: Black contributions to, xxii–xxiii, 45, 96–97, 132, 180–81, 186, 217n90; Black women in, xxii–xxiii, 96–97, 134, 180, 183, 186, 217n90; dog whistle politics, 169; impact of activism on, xxv; during oil boom era, 131–32, 134; shifts in, 184–85
Porter, Brian, 149, 150, 151, 153
Porter, Eura Dell, 81
Portland (OR), 216n76
Posey, Edward "Chicago Ed," 39
poverty: and criminal justice disparities, 140, 145–46, 157; and employment barriers, 129–31; during the gold rush era, 179; during the oil boom era, xxvii, 121, 129; and urban renewal, 92, 94
Preston, Walter, 34
prohibition, 47, 52–53
Project 80s (Anchorage, AK), 180
proletarianization, xx, 195n14
prostitution, 28, 38, 39–41, 76, 88
Pugh, Opalanga D., 125–27, 139

race relations: in American South, xxvi–xxvii, 2, 74, 111, 123–24; bias against Black victims, 151–52; contradictions in, 137; and the criminal justice system, 140–42, 146–57; emerging multiculturalism, xxvii–xxviii; impact of economy on, xxvii, 166; mistrust of police, 140–42, 147–50, 153–55, 161–62; national trends, 111, 141; during the oil boom era, xxvi–xxvii, 121–27, 131, 137; during the post-oil boom years, 166–74; in postwar Alaska, 73–75, 78, 79–87. *See also* police and law enforcement
racism and discrimination: Alaska legislation banning, 97, 100–103, 115, 158; against Asian Americans, xxi, xxv, 2, 49, 128; commonalities with national patterns, 116, 141, 181, 185, 187; countering Alaskan exceptionalism, 164–65,

185; in the criminal justice system, 71, 73–74, 79, 140, 146, 187; cultural rejuvenation countering, 174–76, 178; in employment, 2, 24–27, 49–51, 73, 79, 81, 99–100, 103–5, 108–10, 114–15, 122–24, 127–31, 137, 153–54, 157–60; exceptionalism claims, 71, 165, 185; faced by Alaska Natives, 49, 52–53, 55, 68–69, 79, 102, 140, 187; during the gold rush era, 29–30, 31–32; hiding Black identity due to, 15, 22, 48, 217n90; in housing, xxv, 2, 49, 73, 78, 79, 82–86, 106–8, 216n76; interracial marriages, 46; Ku Klux Klan, 54–55; in law enforcement, 79–81, 141–46, 149–51, 153–54, 157–62; in the military, xxv, 15, 24–27, 29–30, 56–57, 71, 79, 99–100, 103–5, 114–15; national trends, 116–17; during oil boom era, xxvi–xxvii, 118–19, 120–21, 124, 137; during the post-oil boom era, 166, 168–73, 177–78; postwar surveys on, 81–82; during prohibition, 52–53; in public accommodations, 100–103; in relocation proposals, 51–52; in schools, 171–73; and settler colonialism, xxi; structural, 78, 137, 157, 181; through urban renewal, 92–96; in wages, 136; during World War era, 54–55, 60–61, 66, 68–69. *See also* civil rights activism

Rader, John, 132
railroads, 46, 49
Rainey, Froelich, 58
Randall, Vernellia Ruth, 127
Randolph, A. Philip, 69
Rasmuson, Elmer, 73, 82
Ratcliff, Willie, 127–30, 132, 137
real estate. *See* housing and real estate
reindeer herding, 16
religious communities. *See* churches and religious communities
restricted housing covenants, 83–85
Revenue Cutter Service (US), 15–20
Rhodes, Ed, 154, 159
Richter, Albert, 10
Riggs, Thomas, 54
Ringland, Arthur, 49
riots, 70, 106, 111
Rivers, Ralph, 102, 115
Roberts, Emma, 101–2
Roberts, Marvin, 231n111
Roberts, Mike, 153
Robinson, Sarah, 38
Roderick, Jack, 130
Roe, Chris, 64
Rogers Park neighborhood (Anchorage, AK), 84, 85–86
Roosevelt, Eleanor, 56
Roosevelt, Franklin D., 51, 56, 59, 62
Rotary Club of Anchorage East, 133–34
Rothstein, Richard, 94
Roys, Thomas, 6
Ruffin, Herbert G., II, xviii
Rush (cutter), 16, *19*
Rushing, Jimmy, 89
Russell, Patrick, 170
Russian American Company, 6

salmon canning industry, xxi, 50–51
SBA (Small Business Association), 128–29, 132, 133, 180
Schmidt, Harvey, 66, 211n84
Schofield, Clifford, 84
Schofield, Joan, 84
schools: Black women on boards, 180, 183; growing diversity of, 171–72; multicultural programs in, 174–75; racism in, 171–73; white supremacy groups recruiting in, 171
Seattle (WA), 23
Sea-Wolf, The (London), 19
segregation: activism addressing, 57; during Alaska Highway construction, 60–61; in the military, 24–27, 46, 56–59, 63–64, 68–69
Service High School (Anchorage, AK), 172, 174–75

settler colonialism, xx–xxi 798ers (Pipeliners Union Local 798), 124
Seward, William H., 15
Sharp, Robert, 91
Sheffield, Bill, 180
Sheldon, Robert, 51
Shelley v. Kraemer, 85
Shelton, Robert, 170
Shiloh Baptist Church (Anchorage, AK), 78, 152, 213n14
Shorey, Julia Ann Shelton, 2, *4*
Shorey, Victoria, *4*
Shorey, William T., 1–3, *4*, 12, 18–19
Shorey, Zenobia Pearl, *4*
Signal Corps (US Army), 67–68
Silks, Mattie, 38
Sims, Refines, Jr., 61, 63
Skagway (AK), 23, 24, 28, 29–30
slavery, 2–3, 5, 7–8
Slotkin, Herman E., xviii
Small Business Association (SBA), 128–29, 132, 133, 180
Smith, Don, 168–69, 181
Smith, Jefferson Randolph "Soapy," 28–29, 38
SOAR (Students Organized Against Racism), 174
South Addition neighborhood (Anchorage, AK), 83
Southern Baptist Convention (SBC), 98
Soviet Union, 58
Spanish-American War, 26–27
Spanish influenza, 47
Spenard neighborhood (Anchorage, AK), 84–85
Spencer, Fred, 59, 61
Spotlight (Black newspaper), 76, 81, 93, 108, 114
Starkie, Benjamin, 34–35
State of Alaska, The (Gruening), 105
state troopers (Alaska), 146–48, 154
Staudenmaier, Tom, 169
Sterling, Alton, 188
Stern, Max, 50, 206n19

Steward, Tom, 10
Stillwell, John, 6
Stimson, Henry, 62
Stoney, George, 16
Strobidge, Truman, 18
Students Organized Against Racism (SOAR), 174
Sullivan, George, 130, 153
Sullivan, Sean, 176
Sundi Lake subdivision (Anchorage, AK), 84
Supernaw, Leonard, 71
Supreme Court (US), 85
Swanson, Eugene, 31
Swanson, Zula, 75–76, *77*, 78, 115, 186

Tacoma (WA), 44, 55
TAPS (Trans-Alaska Pipeline System). *See* pipeline construction (Trans-Alaska Pipeline System)
Taylor, Breonna, 189
Taylor, John, 38
Taylor, Lillian Mabel, 41
Taylor, Melinda, 96–97, 217n90
Taylor, Quintard, xix, xxii–xxiii
Taylor, Warren, 101–3
Thomas, John W., 86
Thomas, Joseph "Joe," 51
Thompson, Harry, 66 388th Regiment, 59, 60–61 383rd Port Battalion, 65 364th Infantry Regiment, 65, 66
Timberlake, Tim, 59
Tlingit (Alaska Natives), 9, 10, 17, 28, 55, 101
Tolley, Chris, 160
Trammel, Giles, 108
Trans-Alaska Pipeline System (TAPS). *See* pipeline construction (Trans-Alaska Pipeline System)
Treaty of Cession (1867), xxiii–xxiv, 10, 13, 15
Trent, Lettie, 34
Trotter, Joe, xx
Truman, Harry S., 62, 70, 105, 211n76

Tuskegee Institute, 32
Twenty-Fourth Infantry Regiment: in Alaska, 27–31; during American western expansionism, 25–26; as the "buffalo soldiers," 24; desertion rates, 29; discrimination faced by, 24–25, 26, 29–30; formation of, 25; impact on Alaska demographics, 30–33; during the Indian Wars, 24; as segregated regiment, 24–27; during the Spanish-American War, 26–27
Twichell, Heath, Sr., 61

UCIA (United Congo Improvement Association), 51
Ulmer, Fran, 63
Umnak Island (Aleutian Islands), 64
Unangan people (Alaska Natives), 69
unions: for Black law enforcement employees, 158; Black leadership in, 50, 124; lawsuits filed by, 155; lobbying for fair employment, 108; maritime industry, 50; during the pipeline construction, 123–24; police unions, 155, 158; protests targeting, 112
United Congo Improvement Association (UCIA), 51
United Skinheads of America, 170
University of Alaska, 136, 172, 174
urban renewal, 92–96

Valdez (AK), 22, 118
Valentine, Emery, 54
Vanport (OR), 216n76
Vassal, James, 5
Vent, Eugene, 231n111
Verden, Mrs. G. B., 36–37
voting rights, 115, 131

Waddleton, William, 52–55
Walker, Bill, 231n111
Walker, Ed, 47
Walker, Florine, 122, *123*

Walker, Herman, 186
Walker, James, 10
Walker, Maria, 10
Walker, Rosalee Taylor, 180
Walker, T-Bone, 89
Wallace, George, 115–16
Walton, Lena, 22, 36
Washington, Booker T., 32
Washington, Pamela Scott, 186
Watson, Mark, 170
Watts, Richard, 86, 113, 131, 132–33, 186
WCTU (Woman's Christian Temperance Union), 17–18
Webb, Walter Prescott, xviii
Weeks, Larry, 149
Weiler, Else, 83–84
Weiler, Nicholas, 83–84
Weiler subdivision (Anchorage, AK), 83–84
Wesley, Ed, 124–25, 139, 153–54, 186
West, Anna, 47
whaling industry: and Alaska Natives, 9, 11–13, 16; *bark* defined, 197n1; decline of, 6, 13; demographics of, 11; gold rush impacting, 7; images of, *14*; impact on bowhead population, 12, 13; opportunities in, xxiv, 1–11, 13, 185; peak of, 6; and the Revenue Cutter Service, 15–16; shifting to Pacific Northwest, 5–10, 11–13; and slavery, 2–3, 5, 7–8
Wham, Joseph W., 26
White, Becky, 35
white Americans: changing demographics of, xx, 163; in the criminal justice system, 140; demographics during World War era, 51, 52; fear of Black criminality and violence, 151–52; founding Anchorage, 47; during the gold rush era, 11; leading Black military units, 59, 60; and minority officers, 157–60; during oil boom era, xxvi–xxvii, 123–24, 127–29; police treatment of, 149–51; on police

white Americans (*continued*)
violence, 147–48; settler colonialism, xx–xxi; tensions between Alaska Natives and, 55; unease over growing minority population, 167–69, 178; unease with civil rights movement, 168; in white supremacy groups, 170–72. *See also* race relations; racism and discrimination

White Citizens' Councils, 145

white supremacy, xxvii–xxviii, 26, 169–72, 177–78

Wickersham, James, 44, 52

Wilkins, Roy, 141

Williams, Cal, 116–17

Williams, Cassell, 148–53, 155–57

Williams, Cynthia, 149–50

Williams, Edwin, 143–45, 150, 155

Williams, Leroy, 138

Willis, James, 71

Wilson, Ella, 38

Wilson, Jeffrey, 167

Wilson, Woodrow, 46

Winslow, Reuben, 7

Woman's Christian Temperance Union (WCTU), 17–18

women: on Anchorage's school board, 180, 183; contributions and impacts of, xxii–xxiii, 133–36, 186; gender discrimination, 118–19; gender imbalances, xxii, 11, 196n21; during the gold rush era, xxii, 11, 36–41; in law enforcement, 158; in the legal system, 133–34, 135–36, 186; in the military, 196n22; during the oil boom era, 118–19, 122–23, 133–36; in politics, xxii–xxiii, 96–97, 134, 180, 183, 186, 217n90; in the service industry, 36–41; white women in temperance movement, 17–18, 53

Woolworths protest, 114

Worl, Rosita, 17

World War I, 45, 46, 47, 53–54

World War II: Alaska Highway construction during, 58–63; Aleutian Islands campaign, xxv, 57–59, 63–70; Black contributions during, xxv, 64–66, 70, 71–72; economic impacts of, 45, 70; impacts on Alaska, xxiv–xxv, 56–58, 70–72, 216n76; integration during, 67–68; racial tensions fueled by, 70–71; racism during, 54–55, 66, 68–69; scholarship on Black participation in, 194n9; segregation during, 56–57, 63–64, 68–69

Wrangell (AK), 17, 24, 28, 71

Wright, Joshua, 131–32

YMCA (Young Men's Christian Association), 30

Yup'ik people (Alaska Natives), 12, 16–17, 174

Zimmerman, George, 188

Zint, Charlene, 150